JIM FARLEY'S STORY

The Roosevelt Years

Books by JAMES A. FARLEY

BEHIND THE BALLOTS

JIM FARLEY'S STORY
The Roosevelt Years

JIM FARLEY'S STORY

The Roosevelt Years

BY JAMES A. FARLEY

WHITTLESEY HOUSE

McGRAW-HILL BOOK COMPANY, Inc.

NEW YORK · TORONTO

JIM FARLEY'S STORY
The Roosevelt Years
Copyright, 1948, by JAMES A. FARLEY

FOURTH PRINTING

PUBLISHED BY WHITTLESEY HOUSE

A DIVISION OF THE MCGRAW-HILL BOOK COMPANY, INC.

PRINTED IN THE UNITED STATES OF AMERICA

To my mother
ELLEN GOLDRICK FARLEY

and

to my wife
ELIZABETH A. FARLEY
to whom I owe everything

I gratefully acknowledge a heavy
debt for editorial help to my good
friend, Walter Trohan of the *Chicago Tribune*, who knew almost
every word of this story for years
and never broke my confidence

CONTENTS

JIM FARLEY'S STORY

The Roosevelt Years

CHAPTER ONE

EARLY DAYS

FOR MORE than a quarter of a century, I have known, personally and quite intimately, many men who have made history.

It is my belief that history should be told by those who had a hand in its shaping. I do not propose to dwell on my deeds, but rather on my conversations with history makers and on the historical events in which I had a part.

During these decisive years, I kept extensive notes on each day's happenings. These were dictated for my own use with no thought toward publication. In recent years, friends have urged me to tell my story from my papers, insisting I owed it to history.

This debt I now pay. Whatever my story may lack in wisdom, in modesty, or in literary merit, I hope to make up in sincerity and in truth, for I am relying not on memory but on a living record.

Most of my story is concerned with politics, which has occupied most of my adult life. I started in politics at the top—before I was old enough to cast my first vote—as a Democratic chairman. For thirty-five years thereafter, I continued to be a Democratic chairman—town, county, state, or nation. In these thirty-five turbulent years, I won many triumphs, made thousands of friends, collected tens of thousands of memories, and enjoyed millions of laughs. I had also a share of defeats, suffered many disappointments, nursed a few heartaches, but escaped being marked by bitterness or hate.

Politics brought me honors and prominence from the hands of my fellow countrymen. I am too full of gratitude to let malice seep into my heart.

For my story I invoke the same kindly judgment that my fellow countrymen have ever accorded me in the past. I have tried to tell the story as honestly as I know how, because I have a high regard for the truth, and I have found through the years that telling the truth offers not only the best but also the easiest way of life.

I have also tried to make my story a human report on history. I have related conversations during important events so that the reader may form his own estimate of men and motives, in the light of what has happened since the words were uttered.

My story is being unfolded as I stand at the threshold of my sixtieth year. I find that the boy I was is drawing closer to me. With each passing year I see more of what I am in what he was. Men are given to exaggerate the importance of their birthplace; yet mine had a profound influence on my life. I was born on May 30, 1888, at Grassy Point, New York, in the lower reaches of the majestic Hudson River valley. My father, James Farley, was born at Verplanck's Point in Westchester County, New York, the son of John and Margaret Farley, who migrated from Castletown, County Meath, Ireland, in 1847. He died suddenly and tragically before my tenth birthday. My mother, Ellen Goldrick Farley, was born at Haverstraw in Rockland County, the daughter of John and Rose Goldrick, who came to America from Ireland in 1847 or 1848. I was the second of five boys, the others being John, Phil, Tom, and Bill.

My schooling began at the age of five in the Grassy Point Grammar School, which I attended through the seventh grade, when I transferred to the Stony Point Grammar School. I graduated from the Stony Point High School after two and one-half years, then completed a year's course at the Packard Commercial School in New York City.

I went to work for the Merlin Keiholtz Paper Company. Two years later I secured a position with the United States Gypsum Company, where I remained for fifteen years. Early in 1926, with my brother-in-law, Harry B. Finnegan, as my partner, I organized the building material firm of James A. Farley & Company, Inc. Two years later this partnership was increased to four members, when we were joined by Harry and Samuel Schiff, brothers, who operated the East Third Street Supply Company. In 1929, the Farley company, together with five other building material companies, formed the General Builders Supply Corporation, which is now one of the largest of its kind in the country.

In 1909, I was elected Democratic town chairman of Stony Point.

Two years later I was elected town clerk in a Republican township. I was reelected three times. These eight years strengthened my political wings. After my fourth term I climbed up the ladder a step, winning election as town supervisor. I was reelected once. In 1918 I entered big time politics. I was elected Democratic county chairman of Rockland County, a selection which launched me into state politics. In the hope of making my home county a factor in New York politics, I marched into the office of Alfred E. Smith, then President of the New York City Board of Aldermen, to urge him to become a candidate for governor. From the moment I entered his office, I sensed his dynamic personality. He was my first great American. My admiration for him never died, even though we had our differences.

Lest I be misunderstood, I make no claim to having put Al in the Governor's mansion at Albany. I was only one of many booming the man who came up from "the sidewalks of New York." Once Smith was in Albany, I got my reward by appointment as one of the port wardens of New York City, a political sinecure in which I was never happy. In 1923 I was appointed a member of the New York State Athletic Commission and a year later became its chairman. I held this honorary and stormy post until I went to Washington in 1933.

In April 1920 I married Miss Elizabeth A. Finnegan of Haverstraw, whom I had known all my life. We have three children: Betty, born August 28, 1922; Ann, born July 1, 1925; and James, born May 25, 1928.

The first summer of our marriage I had my first brief meeting with Franklin D. Roosevelt. An invitation was extended to me as county chairman, along with thousands of the party faithful, to meet the party standard bearers—James M. Cox and his youthful running mate—in New York City. Although I should like to be able to say that some psychic understanding passed between the tall, vigorous vice-presidential candidate and myself, I can only report that the meeting was nothing more than a handshake and a "How d'you do." The only memorable remark came from Bess at the end of the long, tiring day, when she said, "If I had ever realized that politicians spent their time going through such nonsensical performances, I would never have married you."

In those days Roosevelt was not widely known even in his own state. He had served in the state senate, achieving some fame for successful opposition to the election of William "Blue-Eyed Billie" Sheehan to the United States Senate. In 1914 he bucked the party leadership by entering the Democratic primaries for the nomination for United States Senator against James W. Gerard. He was soundly trounced. My vote went to Gerard because I was an organization man and strongly opposed to party rebels.

The Cox–Roosevelt ticket was buried in the Harding–Coolidge landslide. In 1922 I got my first taste of behind-the-scenes politics in charge of Al Smith's headquarters at the Democratic state convention in Syracuse. In working for Smith's return to the governorship, I helped to elect myself to the New York State Assembly. I served but one term, losing my race for reelection the next year.

I came to know Roosevelt intimately and personally for the first time at the 1924 Democratic national convention in New York City. The less said about the 102-ballot deadlock the better. It had only one lesson to offer and that lesson it demonstrated for all time—that party deadlock, arising from a clash of immovable factions, can only end in destruction of the party's chances. I was a delegate to that factional marathon as was FDR.

My greatest thrill of the session came when, overcoming pain and discomfort, he rose to place the name of Alfred E. Smith in nomination with, "He is the Happy Warrior of the political battlefield." Roosevelt was grinning broadly as I swung the New York state standard into the van of a demonstration which started through the steaming hall to the tune of *The Sidewalks of New York*. Later I learned that the effort had cost him much. His legs were numb in steel braces and his fingers were cramped from his grip on the rostrum, but his face was that of a jubilant marcher in the Smith demonstration. He was fighting back from the infantile paralysis which struck him down in 1922.

In 1928 he performed the same office for Smith at the Democratic convention in Houston. This time his body was more in tune with his spirit, and he weathered the task with strength to spare. I saw a good deal of him and, although we did not become intimate, our acquaintance ripened. That summer, when the Democratic leadership was at odds on the nominee for the Governorship of New York, I was for Roosevelt, feeling that he would be the best vote getter because of his name. Smith, the Democratic presidential candidate, had favored Herbert H. Lehman, New York banker, or Judge Townsend H. Scudder of the state supreme court; but he was finally convinced Roosevelt would help the party in New York State. He persuaded FDR to make the race.

At this time Roosevelt was attempting to walk without the aid of braces or cane. In the living room of the cottage he then occupied he often demonstrated to visitors the diagonal path he traversed unaided. But it took tremendous physical concentration and discipline. His courageous conquest of a dread affliction should be an inspiration for all time. The cottage was located at the infantile paralysis resort which he had founded. Mrs. Roosevelt and his most intimate friends wanted him to continue his treatments. He, too, wanted to spend another year at Warm Springs. But he finally yielded to Smith's importuning. It was a splendid sacrifice.

In the 1928 campaign I was in charge of the Roosevelt headquarters at the Hotel Biltmore in New York City as Secretary of the Democratic State Committee under Chairman M. William Bray. Quite early on election night, it was apparent that Smith would run behind Roosevelt in New York and lose his own state. At the same time it was evident his cause was lost. As the numbing realization of national defeat mounted, Al entered our headquarters with his family. His chin was up and his indomitable heart was high. At the sight of his jauntiness in defeat, men and women workers burst into tears. Deeply touched, Smith barked out a few words of thanks to hide his own mounting emotions, clasped loyal hands, and was gone. Perhaps never in political history was there so much distress among the rank and file of the party as there was over his defeat.

After Roosevelt's election as Governor, I concentrated on building up the Democratic party in New York. I was up to my neck in politics. No one except my family and business associates will ever know how much of my own time I gave to politics from 1928 through 1943. Roosevelt won in 1928 by a margin of 25,564 votes over Albert

Ottinger, his Republican opponent. By 1930, the Democratic machine had been developed almost to perfection, as was demonstrated by Roosevelt's reelection by an unprecedented plurality of 725,001 on November 4.

The afternoon after election night in 1930 Louis McHenry Howe, devoted follower and adviser of FDR, and I put our heads together and made political history. Al Smith had announced after his defeat in 1928 that he was through with public life. This statement Howe and I took at its face value. Our victory statement, issued in New York City over my name, contained the following explosive paragraph:

"I fully expect that the call will come to Governor Roosevelt when the first presidential primary is held, which will be late next year. The Democrats in the Nation naturally want as their candidate for President the man who has shown himself capable of carrying the most important state in the country by a record-breaking majority. I do not see how Mr. Roosevelt can escape becoming the next presidential nominee of his party, even if no one should raise a finger to bring it about."

After the statement was released, I got Roosevelt on the phone at Albany and told him its contents. While I had discussed his prospects with persons close to him, including Howe, from the 1928 election, this conversation marked the first word that passed between us on the subject. He was not in the least surprised by my statement, saying, "Whatever you said, Jim, is all right with me."

With those words he set in motion a presidential boom which was to change the history of the nation and the history of the world. Just when he made up his mind to run, I don't know. He would not have been human had he not considered it after his election in 1928, because the Governorship of the Empire State has frequently brought presidential nomination. Once the die was cast, Roosevelt lightly turned over the preconvention campaign to Louie and myself.

Never did two more unlike men work so well as a team. Louie, who was approaching sixty, was five feet five inches tall and weighed just over a hundred pounds. His face was weazened and his clothes fitted badly. Louie made no effort to be friendly and seldom bothered to be polite. Yet his eyes burned openly with devotion, and his heart drove his feeble body to give his last ounce of strength and ability for his chief.

Beyond any question of doubt, Louie was the first "Roosevelt-for-President" man, preceding FDR himself by years. As far back as 1910, when he was a legislative correspondent at Albany, Howe was attracted to the Dutchess County Senator and hitched his wagon to the latter's star.

By the end of 1928, I was past my fortieth birthday. I was and still am genuinely fond of people. I have always been careful of my appearance, and I have tried at all times to be courteous. I was attracted to Roosevelt by his charm, energy, and vote-getting potentialities. Louie and I had two things in common—loyalty and inexperience in national politics. In the task we had set for ourselves we never had the slightest dispute over authority, and we never had a quarrel.

Sixteen days after the Howe–Farley statement had tossed Roosevelt's hat into the 1932 Democratic presidential ring, I received a letter from FDR, which I treasure because it constitutes the only formal thanks I got from him for managing two gubernatorial and two presidential campaigns. The letter is interesting for striking a chord of presidential prophecy in mentioning the former historical association of Governor Grover Cleveland and Daniel Scott Lamont, his political adviser. Cleveland later became President; and Lamont, a member of his Cabinet. I am sure Roosevelt had this in mind when he wrote on stationery of the Executive Chamber at Albany from Warm Springs. The letter follows:

November 21, 1930.

DEAR JIM:

This is the first chance I have had to sit down for a few minutes and write you connectedly about the campaign. You have done a wonderful piece of work and I don't need to tell you how very appreciative and grateful I am.

As I went through the State I got expressions everywhere showing that no man since the days of David B. Hill has such hearty backing and enthusiastic cooperation from the organizations as you have.

It is not merely a fine record, but a great opportunity for us to consolidate the gains. The enclosed letters are fine, but they do not tell half the story, and everywhere our people are looking for just what we propose

to give them—information, encouragement and practical help throughout
the year and not just the two or three weeks before election.

When I think of the difficulties of former State Chairmen with former
Governors and vice versa (!), I have an idea that you and I make a combination which has not existed since Cleveland and Lamont—and that is so
long ago that neither you nor I know anything about it except from history
books.

Perhaps by the beginning of December, you will have enough stuff to
warrant your running down here. In any event, it would do you a lot of
good to get a few days' holiday and I know that you would like Warm
Springs. And it would be grand to see you. Bring your Missus too!

As ever yours,
Franklin D. Roosevelt

The capturing of a presidential nomination is one of the most formidable enterprises the political animal can tackle. The race is not always
to the swift, the wise, the able, or the prominent, or—there would be
no dark horses.

In politics, you can speak too often or not often enough; you can
speak too loud or too soft; you can start too soon or too late; you can
be too polite or not polite enough; and again you can be too friendly
or not friendly enough. Any of these extremes at any given time may
be fatal. Worst of all, one is frequently called upon to make split-
second decisions. And, unfortunately, what may look good now may
turn out disastrously six months from now. Public good will at any
given moment can be as elusive as quicksilver. It is easy to offend the
public by being too cocky or too upstage, or by being neither. Public
good will can be as difficult to capture and hang onto as a greased pig.
Many a promising political career has been blasted because an aspirant
for office has, more often than not unwittingly, wounded the feelings of a party patriarch—a being who normally has a hide as im-
pervious to criticism as that of a rhinoceros—but who displays the
tender susceptibilities of a lovelorn maiden when political amenities
are to be observed.

Is it any wonder, then, that the politician who has once juggled a
"hot potato" will never reach for a hot potato again (or a cold one
either, for that matter)?

In the case of Roosevelt in the fall of 1930, there were two roads to travel. He could conduct a passive campaign, which would avoid antagonizing the various favorite son candidates by any invasion of their bailiwicks; or he could launch an aggressive campaign and begin rounding up delegates. We chose the latter course, ignoring the formidable hazard that he who announced himself first is usually waylaid by a temporary union of all opposition. Roosevelt approved the decision. While Louie and I and a few co-conspirators were given a free hand, we left final decision on major problems to Roosevelt whenever we could. Almost invariably, he followed our recommendation. Generally we were in agreement by the time any problem reached him, having threshed out our differences.

Once committed to an aggressive campaign, we had to attack every possible means of securing delegates. This required a stupendous amount of work and a meticulous capacity for detail. This mastery of detail, I am convinced, brought success at Chicago in 1932. The nomination of our candidate came from compiling all useful and necessary information, building up organizations in every state and filling the workers with enthusiasm. At the same time, we worked in every way to impress the opposition with Roosevelt's vote appeal and to increase his public stature.

Never in the history of politics, up to that time, was there anything like our letter writing and long distance telephone campaign. From my days as town clerk I have known the value of the personal touch. I made it my business to write every county chairman, asking for a report from his district, an honest report. Often we gained recruits. Roosevelt entered into the letter writing campaign, building up much good will. Men and women in key positions throughout the country received friendly, personal calls from him. Many of these were among our last-ditch supporters in the crucial balloting. Autographed photographs were employed to great effect. Births, marriages, weddings, anniversaries, and deaths brought appropriate letters.

By the spring of 1931 we had our organization completed. While our headquarters at 331 Madison Avenue, New York City, were small, they were busy and our prospects were far brighter than we had hoped. The beginnings of our campaign fund came with contributions of $5,000 each by Frank C. Walker, New York attorney, Henry Morgenthau, Sr., former ambassador to Turkey, and William H. Woodin, industrialist. William A. Julian of Ohio contributed $1,000. Others who gave liberally before the Chicago convention included Edward J. Flynn, Democratic leader of Bronx borough in New York City; Jesse I. Straus, New York merchant; Herbert H. Lehman, banker and Lieutenant Governor of New York; Joseph P. Kennedy, capitalist; Robert W. Bingham of Louisville, who later was named ambassador to Great Britain; Laurence A. Steinhardt of New York City; and Basil O'Connor, his law partner.

CHAPTER TWO

POLITICAL DRUMMER

M AN'S MEMORY concerning things he has witnessed is often tricky, and his testimony as to important political events in which he has played a part is frequently misleading. Good and true men are prone to claim that they brought about great events, which, in reality, required the combined efforts of several if not a great number of persons. This is most true of the first Roosevelt nomination for the Presidency. Various men have staked out an assortment of claims—most of them with entire honesty in their own minds —that they brought about the nomination by directing one effort or another. Actually, the majority of the claimants did little or nothing to bring about the convention selection of Roosevelt. Many were asked for advice, after the decision at hand had actually been made, either as a matter of courtesy or as a calculated bit of flattery. Some did strike out for certain objectives and were convinced they had effected them, when the accomplishing effort had already been launched on a higher level long before.

So it was with my barnstorming trip in the summer of 1931, which many have credited with selling Roosevelt to the Democratic party. Several persons, not excluding Roosevelt himself, have claimed credit for initiating the coast to coast jaunt that took me to eighteen states in nineteen days. (In the fall of 1946 in as many days, I toured by air as many countries of the world without batting an eye, except over some rough weather. My travel horizon has broadened considerably in fourteen years.)

By 1931, I had for some years been active in the Benevolent and Protective Order of Elks. I held occasional office and frequently attended the annual Grand Lodge conventions. The annual meeting in 1931 was set for early in July at Seattle, Washington. I made my plans to attend months ahead, partly to enjoy convention camaraderie and partly for the delight in the trip. Keen-minded Louie Howe grasped my suggestion that I mix fellowship with politics. Roosevelt immediately recognized the value of my suggestion. One Sunday morning I drove up the Hudson to the family home at Hyde Park, with a fistful of railroad timetables, a map of the United States, and the latest list of Democratic state chairmen and national committeemen. After luncheon, we retired to Roosevelt's tiny study and evolved a schedule, which was one of the liveliest and most demanding ever undertaken.

I started out on Monday, June 29, 1931, shortly after noon, on a succession of sleeper jumps. In the next nineteen days I was up to my ears in meetings, conferences, luncheons, dinners, and "gab fests" with Democratic leaders. Along the route, I talked to all sorts of people to learn everything I could about the public political temper. I was a sort of combination political drummer and listening post.

At the end of the trip I reported every incident of the trip in detail to the Governor and Louie. The recital found us agreeing that we had by an aggressive campaign adopted the correct strategy for putting Roosevelt out in front.

My first meeting with the man who was to get the vice-presidential nomination came in the fall of 1931. I was standing in the Democratic cloakroom of the House of Representatives talking with Congressman Joseph Gavagan of New York, when John Nance Garner came out of the House Chamber and headed for the stairway leading to the floor below. Gavagan intercepted him with, "Just a minute, Mr. Speaker. I want you to meet Jim Farley." Garner acknowledged his introduction by saying, "How do you do, Mr. Farley. I hope things are going well with you."

Then he stepped back and subjected me to a head-to-toe appraisal with his piercing blue eyes. I must confess I was a bit flustered. I thought to myself that here was a man I could never become friendly with, so stern and aloof he seemed. Never in my life was I more mistaken by a first impression. Our first meeting lasted hardly ten seconds. In the future I was to know him most intimately; and as time went on I found more and more to admire in him, not only for his conduct in public office but also for his code as a man. Recently he wrote me, "I speak the truth, Jim, when I tell you that if every official act of 46 years in public life were put on the screen, I would not be ashamed of a single one." Few men can honestly say as much.

Garner was to enter the presidential lists a little later with the support of his own state of Texas and the backing of William Randolph Hearst, the publisher. Afterwards I learned that he never asked for support in the preconvention period, even from his closest Congressional cronies, considering such solicitation improper for one of his position. The lists were to swell impressively before the convention until they held the names of Al Smith, the 1928 standard-bearer; Governor Albert C. Ritchie, who had become a national figure by virtue of his opposition to the Eighteenth Amendment in Maryland; Governor George White, favorite-son candidate of Ohio; former Senator James A. Reed of Missouri, one of the senatorial immortals; Senator James Hamilton Lewis, favorite son of Illinois; Governor William H. Murray of Oklahoma, one of the most picturesque political figures of the day; Newton D. Baker, whose supporters were working quietly and effectively; and Owen D. Young, who was regarded as a most likely dark horse.

On January 23, 1932, Governor Roosevelt formally threw his hat in the ring in a letter to Fred W. McLean, Secretary of the Democratic State Committee of North Dakota. State law required that he announce his candidacy in his own hand in order to place a slate of delegates in the preferential primary. Roosevelt grasped the opportunity to declare he would wage his candidacy as a progressive. That same day the Democratic Territorial Convention of Alaska instructed its six convention delegates to vote for Roosevelt. These were the first delegates pledged to his candidacy.

When I came to Chicago Sunday, June 19, 1932, eight days before the convention opened, I had just passed my forty-fourth birthday and had been in politics over twenty-three years. When I left two weeks later, I had been skyrocketed into national prominence. In those two weeks I learned all about the heartaches and shocks that a campaign manager is heir to. I was ground in political mills, put on the rack by inquiring newspapermen, dragged through knotholes of worry, and wrung in wringers of helplessness. At times I faced defeat with despair clutching nauseously at my stomach. I knew the physical weariness of an athlete called upon to give a last gasp of effort. I kept my head and gave all that was in me; then I knew the delicious delight of victory. At such moments, and even in defeat, if the battle has been well fought, politics is a great game.

I have been credited by many with putting Franklin D. Roosevelt in the White House. If this is so, it was largely because I had a great deal of help from men of long political experience. Whenever I was called upon to make a decision, I tried to have the related facts laid before me and then take whatever action was indicated by the weight of reason. At every turn I sought advice. Whenever I made a mistake —and I made plenty—I wasted no time in vain regrets, but set to work repairing the damage as best I could. No one was more aware than I was that I didn't know it all. And I was busy learning all I could every minute. Even to this day I often wonder how we made it.

The Republican convention had just ended in the same city a few days before in the renomination of Herbert Hoover. The Republicans had met in apprehension that defeat was just around the corner. In contrast, the Democrats met with the joyous enthusiasm of crusaders.

Although the Roosevelt forces were first on the scene, the others were not long coming. Al Smith arrived in a fighting mood, openly avowing his intention to stop Roosevelt. He was followed by the forces of Tammany, bent on holding their lines for his candidacy. Governor Ritchie of Maryland, Governor Harry F. Byrd of Virginia, Senator James A. Reed of Missouri, and Governor "Alfalfa Bill" Murray of Oklahoma trooped in at the head of their followers.

The first opposition blast came from Mayor Frank Hague of Jersey City, floor manager of the Smith forces, who issued a statement on June 24, saying that Roosevelt would not carry a single northern state east of the Mississippi and had no chance of winning in November. This obvious exaggeration was more damaging to the Smith forces than to us, but we countered it in such fashion as to bolster our cause. After telephone consultation with Roosevelt (we had a private line from strategy headquarters in Chicago to Albany) I issued the following reply:

"Governor Roosevelt's friends have not come to Chicago to criticize, cry down, or defame any Democrat from any part of the country. This, I believe, is sufficient answer to Mr. Hague's statement."

The first round was ours.

On the eve of our convention our organization was running as smoothly as could be desired. I was glad-handing every delegate and leader I could reach. With all modesty, I knew I was at my best in meeting people and happily accepted this task. Miss Mary Dewson of New York did an excellent job at similar work with women delegates and leaders. Our strategy board had been tireless in their efforts to prepare for every possible development. On the night before the convention opened we organized our field forces for the convention floor itself. It was my idea, and it proved a good one, to introduce Arthur Mullen, floor leader, and his assistants and a few trusted lieutenants like Bill Howes of South Dakota and Joe O'Mahoney of Wyoming. I had each of them stand up and called upon all to take a good look at them, so they would know them during the convention. Then I told those present to accept whatever orders these men would give on the floor.

The next day Democratic national chairman Raskob whanged a huge gavel in the vast Chicago Stadium and droned the familiar convention call, "The convention will please come to order." More thumping at the rostrum, and he followed with, "Delegates will please take their seats." There was music and singing and oratory galore. Senator Alben W. Barkley of Kentucky won the laurels in the last field with a magnificent keynote address.

At headquarters we were concentrating on the series of test votes that were to come the next day. These were vitally important because they would demonstrate whether the opposition could win control. We knew we had to win every test or the stampede of our delegates to the opposition would make the Oklahoma homestead rush look like a turtle race by comparison.

In preparation for the tests I released a Roosevelt statement calling off the two-thirds rule fight, hoping his words would shelve the issue. I did not reckon on the die-hards. Huey P. Long, who was blustering and strutting about in great style, insisted on a vote. He had to be handled with gloves because he had been brought over to our camp with considerable difficulty by Senator Burton K. Wheeler, an able persuader. Long projected himself in the center of the limelight and, when publicity came his way, reached out and grasped it. Rules committee chairman Bruce Kremer, another champion of abrogation, pushed through a recommendation that, if the first six ballots under the two-thirds rule failed to produce a nominee, a mere majority would be sufficient on the seventh. That brought the opposition battering at our door with cries of bad faith, trickery, and deceit. A hurried personal plea to Kremer induced him to accept Roosevelt's statement and forget the issue. With his grudging acquiescence to Roosevelt's wish, that problem was buried and forgotten for four years.

Our first test was on the seating of the rival Louisiana delegations. Long had a delegation which he voted as a unit. Another delegation was entered by former Governor Jared Saunders. In order to poke fun at the contesting delegation, Long threw a third delegation into the field, which exaggeratedly pretended to oppose both its rivals. The clowning of this third delegation of Long henchmen proved to be a boomerang to Long and did him more harm than good. I was not a little worried that he might easily lose this important decision for us and did not breathe easily until the vote was announced at 638 and three-fourths to 514 and one-fourth in our favor. I sat beside Judge Joseph M. Proskauer in the New York delegation during the balloting. The face of this long and faithful friend of Al Smith fell, when the result was announced. An astute political observer, he knew the Happy Warrior was in for another defeat.

We won the Minnesota contest handily. The Roosevelt delegates were seated by a vote of 658 and one-fourth to 492 and three-fourths.

The chairmanship feud, which had been going on for months, was of Hatfield–McCoy proportions. Jouett Shouse, able Chairman of the Executive Committee of the Democratic National Committee, was the opposition candidate. He was the choice of Chairman Raskob, the industrialist, who was an excellent organizer, a superb financier, but weak on practical politics. Shouse was a skilled politician and had, months before, quietly set about gathering votes for the post of convention keynoter.

The Roosevelt forces knew nothing of this until April 4, when the

Arrangements Committee met in Chicago to go over convention pre-
liminaries. Our choice was Senator Alben W. Barkley. When the
Committee, which had power to make the keynoter selection, met,
Shouse announced his candidacy and called for a vote. We stalled, not
sure of our strength and unaware of his. Anxious to avoid any clash,
Governor Byrd of Virginia suggested a compromise under which
Barkley would be recognized as keynoter and Shouse would become
permanent chairman, a post the Arrangements Committee had no
power to name. Shouse assented readily on condition Roosevelt would
agree. When the resolution was read to Roosevelt in Albany, he was
quick to point out the committee's lack of jurisdiction, but said he
had no objection to the committee's recognition of Shouse by "com-
mending" him for the permanent chairmanship. This Roosevelt wording was adopted and the clash was avoided at that time.

Following the meeting, Shouse made speeches urging Democrats
to send uninstructed delegations to Chicago. This tensed muscles in
our camp as we felt he had thrown his lot with the enemy. It was
decided to contest his bid for the permanent chairmanship because we
knew that the man who makes the parliamentary rulings can do much
to influence delegate voting on important issues and on the balloting.

On June 5, I issued a statement which threw down the gage of battle.
This read, "Mr. James A. Farley, at the head of the Roosevelt movement, lunched with the Governor today. He stated, 'The Governor's
friends have come to the conclusion that they will urge the selection
of Senator Thomas J. Walsh of Montana as Permanent Chairman of
the Convention.' "

In no time the brickbats were flying. Roosevelt was accused of having run out on a sacred pledge to Shouse. For three weeks they ham-
mered at this theme in an effective anvil chorus. We pointed to the
wording of the resolution; we charged Shouse had put himself beyond
the pale by taking sides when he should have remained aloof as a paid
member of the national organization; and we shouted that Walsh was
a man of unquestioned fairness whose service in the chair would be
above imputation of partisanship.

Winds of contention had blown up the issue far beyond its actual
importance. Nonetheless, we were most uneasy. Shouse was well-liked

and had secured many pledges. In our own camp were many men who were determined to keep their word and vote for him. The case for Shouse was effectively presented by John W. Davis, the party's 1924 nominee, and by Mrs. Bernice S. Pyke of Ohio. Senator Clarence C. Dill of Washington and Senator James F. Byrnes of South Carolina did the honors for us.

I have the yellow legal paper on which I followed the balloting in my files and its many markings and calculations show my deep concern over the outcome. When the vote was reported at 626 for Walsh and 528 for Shouse, I began to breathe easy.

The next issue, prohibition, gave us a few uneasy moments, but the vote was a foregone conclusion. The Republicans had adopted a wishy-washy plank on this question. We had a dripping wet plank and a moist plank. Our uneasiness came when two rival candidates, Al Smith and Ritchie, took to the platform to urge outright repeal. There was a danger that either might stampede the delegates by force of personal magnetism. Cordell Hull, against our advice, spoke for the milder proposal. The wets won overwhelmingly by 934 and three-fourths to 213 and three-fourths.

CHAPTER THREE

BATTLING FOR BALLOTS

ALTHOUGH I did not know it, my troubles had only begun. I was to have many bad moments before the final gavel. Our heaviest efforts were directed on Illinois, Indiana, and Ohio because there was considerable sentiment for Roosevelt within the delegations.

The name of Newton D. Baker, Secretary of War in Wilson's cabinet, kept haunting us in the next few days like Banquo's ghost at the banquet table. He was considered the most likely dark horse in the event of a deadlock. There were reports that Roy Howard, one of America's greatest newspaper executives, was reportedly using Smith as a stalking horse for his true candidate, Baker.

We were not asleep. Kremer and Roper were in constant touch with McAdoo, hoping to win California's 44 votes, which were enough to crush the opposition. I was cautiously tendering support for the vice-presidential candidacy in return for delegations. I offered to support Ritchie for the second place if he would withdraw his name for the presidency, which he refused to do through Mayor Howard W. Jackson of Baltimore. We offered the same post to Governor Byrd of Virginia through his brother Admiral Richard E. Byrd. Not until after the convention was over did I learn that Ritchie had not expected Smith to take his own candidacy seriously. He had previously been given to understand that Smith's only interest was in stopping Roosevelt and confidently expected to get Smith's strength and the nomination in the balloting. He felt that he had been doublecrossed.

Others on our strategy board and many of our well-wishers were working to break the impending log jam of votes. That is why so many persons have claimed they effected the understanding which turned the tide in our favor. As a matter of fact, the first move came jointly from Senators Key Pittman of Nevada and Harry B. Hawes of Missouri. They called Roosevelt at Albany to ask if he had any objection to Garner as a running mate. FDR pronounced a Roosevelt–Garner ticket as "fine." Hawes wired me:

GROUP BELIEVE WINNING TICKET WOULD BE ROOSEVELT AND GARNER STOP NINETY VOTES OF CALIFORNIA AND TEXAS WOULD ELIMINATE DISPUTE STOP AM ADVISED WOULD BE SATISFACTORY TO PARTY HERE STOP SEE SAM RAYBURN TOM CONNALLY AND CHECK MY OWN IMPRESSION STOP BEST WISHES.

First I found Silliman Evans of Texas, whom I had come to know in the preconvention fight, and he promised to bring Sam Rayburn to my rooms at the Congress Hotel. At this meeting Rayburn made no promise, but made it clear he did not want a repetition of Madison Square Garden Convention. He did not even indicate interest in the vice-presidential nomination for Garner. We promised to keep our conference a secret.

That was Monday, June 27, the day before the convention opened. Thursday I met Rayburn and Evans again. I told them we would positively give Garner the second place nomination. Rayburn asked me what I wanted him to do. I told him to have Texas cast its vote for Garner on the first ballot and switch to Roosevelt immediately after the roll call. Sam said he had to vote for Garner for two or three ballots at least and asked how long I could keep our forces intact. Quite frankly, I told him certainly for three ballots, very likely for four, and possibly for five. Sam's answer was, "We just must let the convention go for a while even if we are interested in the Vice Presidency, and I'm not saying that we are." During these negotiations, Arthur Mullen was working in the same direction with Senator Tom Connally of Texas.

Thursday afternoon, June 30, nine candidates for President had their names placed in nomination.

Nine nominating speeches is a lot of oratory, even if it is all good —and it wasn't. Dozens of seconding speeches dragged the show through the afternoon and into the night. I repaired to our gallery headquarters where I rested on a cot.

In a scene reminiscent of the engraving of Osawatomie John Brown receiving visitors while lying in jail awaiting trial for his raid on Harper's Ferry, I summoned leaders to my bedside. I was too weary physically to get up, but I was alert mentally. The consensus was for a ballot before adjournment. I pulled myself to the phone and told Roosevelt what our verdict was. "Go to it, Jim," were his orders.

All of the glamor and most of the enthusiasm had gone out of the hall by that hour. Galleries which had been whooping it up for Al and booing Roosevelt, were yawningly empty. Delegates were napping in their seats. Clothes were wilted, collars were askew, ties hung open, and hats sagged at the brims. Aisles were littered with the debris of demonstrations. The scene was one of general dejection. Even the bunting drooped limply.

Finally at 4:28 A.M. dauntless Tom Walsh went to work with his gavel, more for the purpose of waking the delegates up than to secure quiet.

"The clerk will call the roll," he announced.

"Alabama," the clerk called.

"Alabama," the delegation chairman echoed in a southern drawl, "twenty-four votes for Franklin D. Roosevelt."

I thrilled to the response even though I knew it was coming because the delegation was pledged to us. I marked down 24 under Roosevelt's name on my personal tally sheet. At last the balloting was under way. Weariness and exhaustion were forgotten. I was grinning broadly, confident to the last cell of my being that we would win on the first ballot. The roll call took almost two hours.

Our delegates held their lines like soldiers. The vote was announced as 666 and one-fourth for Roosevelt, which was 450 votes ahead of his nearest rival, but a good way short of the 770 needed to nominate. I leaned back and looked over the hall to see where the break for the band wagon would begin. I was so sure that the opposition lines would break that the disappointment was almost more than I could bear. Nothing happened. Not a single delegate shifted. Two years of tireless work seemed headed for political oblivion. I closed my mind to such gloomy thoughts and charged into action.

On the floor I pleaded with Mayor A. J. Cermak to switch Illinois, knowing full well Indiana would follow his lead. Cermak was sympathetic, but regretful his delegation could not switch without a caucus. I knew better, but could do nothing. He had everything in his hands at that moment—national prominence, possibly the Senate which he had his eyes on, and life itself—but he postponed the decision and political opportunity passed him by. Had he jumped to our band wagon then, he would not have been in Miami a few months later seeking political favors only to stop an assassin's wild bullet aimed at Roosevelt.

The second ballot got under way. Not being entirely off guard I had held out a few votes for a second ballot, aware that if we lost on a second roll call, our delegates might melt away like a late snow before a warm spring sun. The final vote on the second ballot was 677 and three-fourths votes for Roosevelt, a gain of 11 and one-half votes, which was not much—but a gain. Missouri gave most of the votes we picked up because Tom Pendergast, boss of Kansas City, was friendly.

After the second ballot, we were ready to recess. Arthur Mullen, our floor leader, moved for an adjournment. The opposition, sensing a possible deflection from our ranks, objected and a third roll call started. I knew I was face to face with disaster. As it got under way, I turned to Bob Jackson, Secretary of the Democratic National Committee, and, attempting a smile, said, "Bob, watch this one closely. It will show whether I can ever go back to New York or not."

We did little more than hold our own on that ballot, and we came close to setting off a landslide toward the opposition. We managed to inch ahead to 682.79 votes. There was no sign of a break. It was then 9:15 A.M. Friday morning. Everyone welcomed a motion to adjourn.

Our situation was desperate. There were indications that we could not hold our delegates through the fourth ballot. Up and down hotel corridors, the convention wise men were pronouncing Roosevelt out of the picture.

The crisis was at hand.

Ed Flynn, Frank Walker, Joe Guffey, Vincent Dailey, and a few other trusted men went to Louie Howe's suite in the Congress Hotel. He was lying on the floor in his shirt sleeves between two blowing electric fans. He had sat through the night beside the radio. Never physically strong, he was racked by strangling asthma during the Chicago stay. He had been unable to visit the convention hall. He looked as though he couldn't last through the day. But his mind was plotting the coralling of votes for "Franklin," as he always called Roosevelt. I flung myself on the floor beside him, and, while the others stood back, whispered to him, "Texas is our only chance." Louie agreed.

Pat Harrison called Rayburn at my request. The conference lasted only a few minutes. Like many another event in history, it was casual and without any heroic statements. I said we needed the Lone Star State to win; that the alternative was a victory-sapping deadlock, and that we could swing the vice-presidential nomination to Garner. Neither Sam nor Silliman Evans, who accompanied him, made any promise. Sam merely said, "We'll see what can be done." That was good enough for me, and I raced back to Howe's room.

When I poured my story into the ear of the man who had worked for years for such a moment, he blinked and said, "That's fine." Roosevelt was far more effusive when I broke the news to him over our private line.

I sat down to work. There was much to do. We had to hold our delegates. The opposition was predicting we were about to fold our delegates and steal away. Paul McNutt said the Roosevelt vote was disappointing, otherwise Indiana would have led the band wagon. Others flatly said, "We have Roosevelt stopped."

Rayburn was rounding the Texans up for a caucus. Jack Garner had called from Washington with the curt instruction, "I think it is time to break that thing up," referring to the impending deadlock. The California delegation met to caucus in an adjoining hotel room. Rayburn informed McAdoo that he was about to telephone Garner and advised McAdoo to release the California delegation. The conversation between Garner and Rayburn is a model of brevity.

"Do you authorize me to release the Texas delegation from voting for you for the presidential nomination?" Rayburn asked.

"Yes."

"Do you release the Texas delegation from voting for you for the presidential nomination?"

"Yes."

The Garner die-hards, led by Amon G. Carter, Fort Worth publisher, bucked like bronchos, but at length accepted Rayburn's mas-

tery. The California caucus was less stormy. When news of the shifts
were brought to me, I knew all was over and that the nomination lay
ahead. I wasted no time in gloating, but went around to urge various
delegations to join the band wagon procession. I was particularly interested in securing the New York delegation in the interests of party
harmony, aware that Smith had an idolizing personal following. I saw
John F. Curry, Tammany leader, and John H. McCooey, Brooklyn
leader. Curry was adamant, so I abandoned the effort, aware that politicians often believe what they want to believe.

Neither the California nor the Texas delegation could have been
released without Garner's direct authorization. The California delegation was under constant pressure from various quarters as its forty-
four votes were a great prize. Publisher William Randolph Hearst had
been largely responsible for securing the delegation for Garner. Various of his associates, who were attending the convention, were doubtful of the wisdom of opposition to Roosevelt. Hearst had long been
a political foe of Smith, and he loathed Baker, who had been an ardent
advocate of American entry into the League of Nations. Several Hearst
men were worried over the Baker threat. Joseph P. Kennedy, who was
closely associated with Hearst, called the publisher to warn him of
the blossoming Baker movement and to urge him to use his influence
to get the California delegation to switch to Roosevelt.

Damon Runyon, the noted Hearst writer, brought the publisher's
secretary, Joseph Willicombe, to see me. They suggested a phone
call to Hearst at his San Simeon, California, ranch. The publisher
listened courteously as I emphasized the menace of the Baker movement, which he deplored, but he did not commit himself. A number
of others made similar calls. I am sure Hearst threw his weight to
Roosevelt because he decided Baker must be stopped.

On my way to the convention hall in a taxi, I was sandwiched in
between two Tammany Braves, who sought to persuade me to desert
Roosevelt and switch to Smith.

I have never held a card in the Disloyal Brotherhood of Political
Switchmen. I have known men to weave in and out of political factions
as a switch engine shuttles through a freight yard. Somehow they never
pick up anything in their search for political preferment. Like chronic

liars and men who habitually break their word, they seldom reach their goal.

The fourth ballot got under way in an attitude of hushed expectancy. The break came sooner than most of them expected. William Gibbs McAdoo, who held a majority in 1924, but suffered disappointment, was on his feet. Few heard him. There were shouts of "Louder!"

"I'll make it loud enough," he cried into the battery of microphones. "California came here to nominate a President of the United States. She did not come to deadlock the Convention or to engage in another devastating contest like that of 1924."

A hush spread from the platform and engulfed the hall. A few more sentences and McAdoo shouted, "California casts 44 votes for Franklin D. Roosevelt."

The vote on the fourth ballot was 945 for Roosevelt, 190 and one-fourth for Smith and 13 scattered. The convention hall was in a turmoil of excitement. Everyone knew we had just nominated the next President of the United States.

The next order of business was the nomination of a candidate for Vice President. A number of men in our ranks were potential candidates, up to the conclusion of the California–Texas deal, which carried its pledge to Garner. Senator Hull and Senator Dill were among the first prominent men to join the Roosevelt movement. I know Dill was disappointed that his invaluable early organizational work went unrecognized by the vice-presidential nomination. I have suspected Hull, our preconvention choice for second place, was also a bit discontented, although I am sure he was more than satisfied later by his selection as Secretary of State. Senator Wheeler and Governor George Henry Dern of Utah were among the steadfast who were in the running for the fourth ballot. Strangely enough, the Vice Presidency was not mentioned to Garner until just before the actual balloting for it got under way. Rayburn called him to inform him that he was about to be nominated and suggest he speak to the delegates briefly by wire after Roosevelt delivered his acceptance speech in person. Garner had no desire for the office. His sole purpose in breaking the deadlock was to advance the welfare of the Democratic party.

The next day I was on hand at Municipal Airport to greet our candidate on his arrival by plane, which had been planned at Hyde Park. I managed to make my way through the press to his side. He clasped my hand and exclaimed, "Good work, Jim."

On the ride to the convention hall, Louis Howe pushed a speech into Roosevelt's hand. The faithful old gnome had stayed up most of a second night to prepare what he thought was a proper acceptance speech. Roosevelt had with him a speech, prepared largely by Raymond Moley, brilliant professor of public law at Columbia University, who was to become the outstanding member of the "Brain Trust," the early group of White House advisers under the New Deal. In the automobile, FDR looked over Louie's effort and discarded all but the first page, which he substituted for the first page of the Moley speech. Louie was elated as his words came over the air and crushed when those of Moley were used for the rest of the speech.

It was a great speech and magnificently delivered. Few who witnessed the scene will ever forget it. The Roosevelt charm was on full blast and captured the convention hall. Over the air his vibrant tones fired the enthusiasm of the nation with:

"I pledge you, I pledge myself, to a new deal for the American people. Let us all here assembled constitute ourselves prophets of a new order of competence and courage. This is more than a political campaign; it is a call to arms. Give me your help, not to win votes alone, but to win in this crusade to restore America to its own people."

The New Deal was born.

The day was not without a note of tragedy, almost Shakespearean. That morning, as I was leaving the hotel for a brisk walk, I saw a familiar figure ahead of me. It was Al Smith. The idol of millions would not stay in Chicago to congratulate his successful rival. He had observed the amenities by sending a congratulatory wire. Now he was making his way to the railroad station alone. All eyes were turned to the new standard-bearer. Before I could catch up to Al, he had turned the corner, symbolically enough, and was gone. Perhaps there is no more grievous burden of disappointment to bear than a lost chance at the Presidency. I will say this for Al, he walked with his shoulders back and his head erect, although he walked alone.

The Democrats had one more choice to make before leaving Chicago. The Democratic National Committee gathered to select a new chairman. The party's new candidate made a dramatic entrance to nominate, in a few gracious words, his blushing campaign manager. This was thanks for James Aloysius Farley, who had reached the estate of political maturity.

CHAPTER FOUR

FIRST CAMPAIGN

AFTER THE epic struggle of the convention, the campaign itself was a breeze. In no time our machine was functioning smoothly. The Republicans were making blunders right and left. Our confidence was high. Everyone in the organization from Roosevelt to the youngest Young Democrat considered the election a foregone conclusion. Yet, we never were drugged into inactivity by overconfidence.

On a hot August afternoon in 1932, I went to Hyde Park to ask Roosevelt whether he would stay in his family home or take to the road. I gave him a summary of the opinions of party leaders. He rubbed his chin thoughtfully and asked, "Jim, what do you think yourself?"

"I think you ought to go," I laughed, "and I know you are going anyway."

"That's right," he grinned. "I have a streak of Dutch stubbornness in me, and the Dutch is up this time. I'm going campaigning to the Pacific Coast and discuss every important issue of the campaign in a series of speeches."

No trip was more carefully planned. Men like Senators Walsh of Montana, Pittman of Nevada, and Wheeler of Montana went along to make sure that responsible party leaders were let aboard. Janarius Arthur Mullen, powerful and mentally alert son of the Nebraska Democratic leader, went along to see that gate crashers were kept off. Flynn, Kennedy, and Moley went along too. Stephen T. Early and Marvin H. McIntyre, newspaper friends of the candidate's days as Assistant Secretary of the Navy, who later became White House Secretaries, had charge of the press. I was the official glad hander and stimulator of the party faithful.

The western trip and other tours were a tremendous success. The candidate found enthusiastic crowds everywhere. He drove through miles of streets packed with cheering voters. His speeches were flashes of political lightning, followed by thunderous applause.

Our troubles were vexatious but not damaging. One of our worries was the removal proceedings brought against Mayor James J. Walker of New York. In the midst of his campaign Roosevelt was compelled to sit in trial of Tammany's darling, the popular, dapper, witty chief magistrate of the nation's largest city. After a few weeks of hearings, Walker resigned.

Some years later I brought them together in the White House. I asked Roosevelt if he would see Walker. He replied that he would be happy to do so. He had Walker down for tea and a chat on old times. Walker and I were friends to the day of his death. No friend could be truer or more companionable.

Tammany bobbed up to trouble us again. Roosevelt wanted his Lieutenant Governor, Herbert H. Lehman, to succeed him at Albany. The Wigwam backed Mayor John Boyd Thatcher of Albany. After a bit of maneuvering Tammany capitulated and Lehman was nominated without a contest. At this period in its history Tammany was, unfortunately for itself and the Democratic cause in New York, guided by a kindly and honorable gentleman, who was far beyond his political depth, John F. Curry. His political blunders and those of successors contributed to the downfall of the organization.

Perhaps our biggest problem was Alfred Emanuel Smith. The question on every Democratic tongue was, "What will Al do?" On all sides reports were cropping up that Al considered Roosevelt unfit, untrustworthy, and unreliable. These whisperings were doing us no good. There was no open break, nor was there any show of friendliness.

The handshake heard and seen around the country came at a convention session in the vast armory at Albany. The building was jammed. Roosevelt came on the platform to the blaring of bands. Smith was in his seat as a delegate. When he rose to nominate Lehman and came forward with outstretched hand, pandemonium broke loose.

"Hello, Frank, I'm glad to see you," Smith said enthusiastically.

"Hello, Al, I'm glad to see you too—and that's from the heart."

I was the only one who heard the conversation. I was standing beside them and had difficulty in hearing their words, because the tumult and the shouting were so great. The reconciliation was a great help to us. While it was theatrical in its own right, it was helped no end by a line written for the occasion by amiable and alert Fred Storm of the United Press. Big Fred was in the press section below the platform, where he could hear nothing. His wire was open before him and sputtering a dot and dash request for text of the greeting. Reaching into his Albany correspondent background, Storm had an inspiration. He banged out a familiar Smith greeting, "Hello, you old potato." This line intrigued popular fancy and dramatized the reconciliation.

In the late days of the campaign, when a Roosevelt victory was as certain as one could be, the candidate and I were chatting about the situation and discussing individuals who were handling the campaign around the country. Suddenly he cocked his head at me, as though a thought had just popped into it, and said, "I've thought a lot about the problem that's going to be mine after I get to Washington. Jackson and Lincoln and the others had their troubles with job seekers. Right now, Jim, I have determined definitely on only three appointments—Louis for my secretary, George Dern for Secretary of the Interior, and you for Postmaster General."

I thanked him. I would be less than honest if I did not say I felt I had deserved it, since it was the common reward for successful campaign managers. The other appointments were made, except that Dern was switched to the post of Secretary of War.

Out of the million and one scenes of the campaign—the tears and the laughs—one is etched vividly in my mind. We were having lunch at Hyde Park. I can see everyone in the group and the meeting at the table. Huey Long was down at the end of the table near Roosevelt and I was seated beside the President's mother. Huey was tossing "I's" about the dining room and sounding ideas at a great rate. He was gesticulating and blustering as was his fashion. At one point when he paused for breath, Mrs. Roosevelt leaned toward me and in a voice which carried around the table asked, "Who is that terrible person?" If Huey heard it, and I'm sure he did, he gave no sign but went on where he left off, albeit a bit less enthusiastically, I thought.

Election night came at last with every promise of being a gala affair. The President-elect and Mrs. Roosevelt came to headquarters with a few friends and members of their family. Louis Howe refused to leave his own headquarters across the street where he was a well of pessimism, overflowing now and then with dire predictions, to the amusement of the rest of us.

The first returns put us into the lead which we never lost. About eleven o'clock, when even Louie conceded that things "looked good," Mrs. Eleanor Roosevelt and I went over to pay him a visit. We found him hoarding favorable election returns and almost unable to wait until President Hoover's wire conceding defeat and offering congratulations should come in.

This did not come until 2 A.M. With the wire in his hands, the President-elect suggested we open the door of his room and admit the hundreds of workers and other faithful to congratulate him. The handshaking went on and on and on. Among those who came were Al Smith, ever magnanimous; Kermit Roosevelt, the son of President Theodore Roosevelt; John J. Raskob; Senators Wagner and Copeland; and Governor-elect Lehman.

When Mrs. Farley reached his side, Roosevelt leaned over and whispered in her ear, "Get ready to move to Washington."

"I'm not going to Washington," Bess replied.

"Well, get ready anyway," he laughed, "because Jim is coming down there after the fourth of March."

In the ballroom of the Biltmore Hotel, Roosevelt thanked the more than five hundred workers in the National Committee headquarters. In his brief remarks he said the major credit belonged to Louie and myself. I like to think he was right.

Only one thing remains to be told of this campaign. Even then I had something of a reputation as a political prophet. On November 4, 1932, I made a public prediction of the outcome of the election. I give it with the results as follows:

PREDICTION		RESULT	
Oregon	100,000	Oregon	77,852
Washington	150,000	Washington	144,605
California	750,000	California	476,255
Mountain States	300,000	Mountain States	295,430
(Montana, Idaho, Wyoming, Colorado, Utah, Nevada, New Mexico and Arizona)			
Farm Belt	1,235,000	Farm Belt	1,203,594
(Kansas, Wisconsin, Minnesota, Iowa, North Dakota, South Dakota and Nebraska)			
Border States	1,000,000	Border States	1,312,188
Illinois	850,000	Illinois	449,548
Michigan	150,000	Michigan	131,806
Ohio	250,000	Ohio	74,016
Indiana	150,000	Indiana	184,870
New Jersey	150,000	New Jersey	30,988
New York	750,000 up	New York	596,966

CHAPTER FIVE

ON TO WASHINGTON

THE GLOW of complete satisfaction I had on election night faded into cold irritation against the droves of office seekers who descended on us within a few days. Where I thought the worst was over, I found that my troubles had just begun. From election day I was swamped by job hunters. They thronged in my outer office; they stopped me on the streets; they came to my table in restaurants; they did a Swiss bell ringer act on my phones, and they snowed me under a mountain of letters and telegrams.

Of course, as President-elect, Franklin Roosevelt had his serious problems, and the job of Cabinet making was one of his most delicate tasks. Into ten chairs he must fit the party's deserving and able, giving thought to geographical, religious, and general qualifications. At Warm Springs shortly after his election, FDR talked to me again about his Cabinet, saying he wanted Senator Walsh of Montana for Attorney General, Senator Hull for Secretary of State, Senator Glass of Virginia for Secretary of the Treasury, and Governor Dern for Secretary of Agriculture. He seemed to have difficulty in fitting Dern into the Cabinet, having previously mentioned him for the Interior post.

At the conference he made it clear he was giving no consideration to Smith, Baker, Ritchie, Byrd, or Traylor, his rivals for the Democratic nomination, whom he had mentioned as possibilities in 1931, or to James M. Cox, the head of the ticket on which he ran in 1920. Presidential appointment of rivals to the Cabinet is not unprecedented, but it invites dissension and difficulty. Abraham Lincoln had four rivals in his official family—Seward, Cameron, Chase, and Bates—but he was not one to hesitate about naming men as strong or stronger than himself or to be influenced by personal dislikes.

Senator Glass turned down the Treasury post as too great a strain for one of his years; and William H. Woodin, New York industrialist, was selected. Senator Claude A. Swanson of Virginia was given the Navy Department in recognition of his services and because of his long experience on House and Senate naval affairs committees. Henry Wallace was selected for Secretary of Agriculture because of his experience with farm problems and because his ideas for relief of industry paralleled those of Roosevelt. The Commerce seat went to Daniel Roper of South Carolina. Early in the Cabinet framing it was decided that the Interior Department should go to a progressive Republican, because of the substantial support the group had given the New Deal ticket. Senator Bronson Cutting of New Mexico refused the chair, as did Senator Hiram Johnson of California. At the request of Senator Johnson, supported by Arthur Mullen of Nebraska, it was given to Harold L. Ickes, who would have been content to serve as Commissioner of Indian Affairs. The position of Secretary of Labor went, in a precedent-breaking personal choice of the President, to Frances Perkins, who had served as Industrial Commissioner of New York State.

During the cabinet making I gave a dinner at my home at 3 East 84th Street on the night of January 11, 1933. Our guests were Patrick Cardinal Hayes, the guest of honor, the President-elect, Mrs. Roosevelt, Mr. and Mrs. Edward J. Flynn, and Monsignor Robert F. Keegan. The dinner was remarkable for a note of prophecy struck by Roosevelt during a discussion of the problems of the Church in Mexico and the independence of the Philippines.

"Most of the people in the Philippines are anxious for independence," Roosevelt said, addressing the Cardinal. "But before they can be given full freedom, some guarantee of protection must be given them. The Philippines must have security from Japan.

"After extending herself in China, Japan will be casting her eyes about for new fields of conquest. It is likely she will move southward and try to extend her possessions along a chain of islands even as far as Australia. Japan will give a lot of concern to the world generally within the next ten years."

I do not have the time or space to go into the various appointments. It is sufficient to say that choices were made for a wide variety of reasons—personal, political, geographical, and experience. Many appointees were personal friends of FDR; others won their jobs for services rendered the party; still others were named because Roosevelt was indebted to their sponsors, and not a few were selected because of ability.

While many criticize the spoils system, I have always felt that it is just as easy to find a good Democrat as a good Republican or vice versa and that the party in power should reward its own. With few exceptions appointments passed through my hands during most of my seven and a half years in the Cabinet. Members of Congress made their recommendations to me and I passed them on to the President. In turn he took up with me at our frequent meetings those which came directly to him.

From Warm Springs Roosevelt went to Jacksonville, where he boarded Vincent Astor's yacht *Nourmahal* for a ten-day cruise. The rest of the party went on to Miami. There I conferred with Democratic leaders who had helped us—and also with some who were telling how they had fought and bled for us when in reality they had done their best to stop Roosevelt in Chicago. I gave all a respectful ear, as behooves a national chairman interested in building a united party. I did have to suppress a laugh now and then as some leaders recounted what they had done, when I had in my files confidential reports on each delegation which disclosed that they had been doing just exactly the opposite. In this period I had several conferences with Mayor Cermak of Chicago on the situation in Illinois.

I headed back for New York headquarters, arriving February 14, 1933. The next night came the terrifying report that the President-elect had been fired upon by an assassin whose bullets struck down Cermak. The incident brought beads of cold sweat to the brows of Roosevelt's intimates. Being confident of his destiny, he was less concerned than any of us. Quietly the rest of us went about increasing his protection and dodging unnecessary risks. I don't think we fooled him much.

As Inauguration Day neared, the banking system of the nation, undermined by the depression, began to sag ominously. From Washington President Hoover sent frantic appeals for endorsement of his measures and for formation of a bipartisan program. Roosevelt was silent. The banking collapse began in Michigan on February 14, 1933, where the pressure of unemployment forced an eight-day bank holiday. At the end of the eight days, the banks were still insolvent and remained closed. Fear surged from Michigan and panic seized the nation; depositors rushed to withdraw their savings. Banks began to collapse everywhere.

Plans were made to leave New York for Washington on March 2, aboard a special train carrying members of Roosevelt's private and official families and friends. The day dawned tragically with news of the death of Attorney-General-Designate Thomas Walsh, Montana's beloved and respected Senator. Given to superstition, FDR was concerned over this omen. After a hurried consultation, it was decided to give the post to Homer Cummings. The train was carrying the President-elect to meet a crisis comparable to that which faced Abraham Lincoln seventy-two years before, when the Union was crumbling under waves of sectional strife.

One person aboard the train was as lively as a cricket—Mrs. Sara Delano Roosevelt, the President-elect's mother. When I mentioned the serious situation ahead, she said quite confidently, "I am not the least worried about Franklin. His disposition is such that he can accept responsibilities and not let them wear him down."

Roosevelt was by no means gloomy, although he was fully aware of the problem before him. He would not have been human had he not been happy over the fact that he was on his way to take the helm of the nation, particularly since he was confident he would find means of dealing with the crisis. I dropped into a chair beside him.

"On Inauguration Day, before the actual ceremony," he confided, "I am going to have all members of the Cabinet and their families accompany me to St. John's Episcopal Church, the 'Church of Presidents,' as it is known. I attended the church during my days as Assistant Secretary of the Navy in Wilson's time.

"You know, I think a thought to God is the right way to start off my administration. A proper attitude toward religion, and belief in God, will in the end be the salvation of all peoples. For ourselves it will be the means of bringing us out of the depths of despair into which so many have apparently fallen."

Roosevelt took a suite at the Mayflower Hotel. I was in another across the hall with my family. Flynn and Walker also had suites near by. I talked many times with Roosevelt during the hours preceding his inauguration. The press of business was terrific. Everyone wanted to see the incoming President. By contrast, the White House, where President Hoover was spending his final hours, was practically deserted. I pondered the contrast during a walk around the Executive Mansion the night before March 4, 1933.

The next morning Mrs. Farley accompanied me to the special church services conducted by Dr. Endicott Peabody, head master of Roosevelt's school, Groton. From the church the President drove to the White House. President Hoover came out, shook hands, and took a seat for the ride to the Capitol. Chief Justice Hughes, whose striking appearance made him the very personification of Justice, administered the oath of office, which the new President repeated after him in a firm voice. The First Inaugural Address, possibly his greatest speech, was magnificently delivered.

After the inaugural parade down Pennsylvania Avenue past the White House, members of the new Cabinet and White House secretariat were instructed to gather in the Oval Room with their families. This marked the first time I crossed the threshold of the nation's most famous dwelling. I was deeply stirred by thoughts of its famous occupants and of the historic events enacted therein. The President sat at a desk, smiling broadly. He called out the names of those to be sworn and each took the oath from Justice Benjamin N. Cardozo of the United States Supreme Court. Roosevelt then bade us welcome to the new administration and expressed the hope that we would work as a team for our common good and the best interests of the nation.

"No Cabinet has ever been sworn in before in this way," he concluded. "I am happy to do it in just this way because it gives the families of the new Cabinet an opportunity to see the ceremony. It is my intention to inaugurate precedents like this from time to time."

The last remark was something of an understatement. No President so shattered tradition and no President set so many precedents. Roosevelt had an instinctive flair for the dramatic which was to serve him well. In the hundred days following his inauguration, beginning with his summoning Congress into special session and his proclamation closing all banks, the new President initiated a historic succession of relief and recovery measures.

I have always felt that Roosevelt's Banking Day Address will go down in history as one of the greatest utterances of an American President. It has always been my belief that the hundred days' session of the Congress in the spring of 1933 passed more legislation which was beneficial to the American people than any other session of a like nature in the history of the Republic.

It is not my purpose to discuss the steps one by one because this is a personal story and I must, in all honesty, acknowledge that I had very little to do with his daring program. I was not in on its formation, although I was acquainted with measures as they developed; and my contribution was largely in helping to guide the program through Congress. From the outset he exhibited courage and daring, which was to characterize his administration. Perhaps the greatest manifestation of this side of his character was his assumption of personal responsibility for the spending of more than two billion dollars for the development of the atomic bomb in the war years.

As President in the prewar years, Roosevelt was stamped by administrative daring and essential reform. Few, if any, can dispute the value of such organizations as the Securities and Exchange Commission, the Federal Deposit Insurance Corporation, and the Home Owners Loan Corporation. All must concede the magnificence of such projects as Grand Coulee, Fort Peck, and the Tennessee Valley Authority. While these originated in other minds, he had the audacity to adopt them and follow them through. It is also true that he was the head of a party with a long tradition of advancing the status of the common man. Perhaps no President since Jackson did more for the common people or showed greater administrative courage. Roosevelt made mistakes. So have we all. Perhaps his greatest mistake was in remaining too long in office. He won himself a place in history in his first two terms. That position would have been enhanced had he withdrawn to the role of elder statesman in 1941, lending his aid to his successor. As it is, I am convinced that a large share of the world's ills today, and in this I have the support of many leading statesmen, may be traced to the fact that he was a very ill man in the final year of the war. I will return to this subject later.

The first Cabinet meeting was held on Sunday, March 5, 1933. Naturally, I was considerably impressed on taking my seat at the board of directors of the nation. The first meeting was largely a get-together, with Vice President Garner in attendance by special inclusion in the official family. There was a general outline of the banking situation.

The second Cabinet meeting the following Tuesday was more interesting, because the new President again turned to the possibility of war with Japan. The Japs were swarming in Jehol Province toward the Great Wall of China. There was much discussion of Japan's attitude in the Orient, Japan's clashes with China, and other possible avenues of Japanese activity. The consensus was that, as neighbors, we should exert every effort to keep from getting involved and should make no diplomatic moves which might be so misconstrued as to plunge us into war. There was general agreement that we could defeat Japan by starvation, but that it would take from three to five years to do so.

The President discussed possible plans of action in the event of war. Others made contributions. He said that our army would not be of material help; that we should abandon the Philippines and other islands in the far Pacific. Roosevelt said the Navy should be operated from Hawaii and air bases should be established in the Aleutians. He said we would have to depend largely on air bases in the Aleutians against Japan, because the fleet could not operate efficiently over great distances. For every thousand miles the fleet moved away from its base, he explained, it would lose 10 per cent of its efficiency; so that if we started out with 100 ships from the West Coast, the fleet would only be 70 per cent efficient by the time it got 3,000 miles into the Pacific. Thirty per cent of the fleet would have to be diverted to furnish supplies and maintain communications, he said.

During the early months of the administration, I had my hands more than full of patronage problems and repeal of the Eighteenth Amendment. I was on the road during the summer, particularly in the dry South, urging repeal as an expression of confidence in the

Roosevelt recovery program. I know I helped in one quarter at least, because a life-long dry from Pennsylvania wrote me that he was going to support repeal just to get me off the air. He said that every time he flicked on his radio, I was cluttering up the airways. I took a lot of good-natured joshing and some severe scolding for my support of the wet cause because I did not drink then, nor have I since. However, I had never favored prohibition and am convinced that the Volstead Act did much to tear down respect for law and order.

In the same period, Roosevelt bobbed up with the suggestion that it might be advisable to have checking accounts with Postal Savings. After consultation with experienced postal men, I objected because it would put my department into the banking business. It was then suggested that the Treasury issue certificates of $5 and $10 which could be cashed only at post offices. Both suggestions were, fortunately for me, tabled as the recovery program got under way.

Through the summer and into the fall, universal attention was focused on the World Economic Conference at London, which began badly and ended worse. Roosevelt torpedoed the conference from aboard the U.S.S. *Indianapolis*. The American delegation was rendered ineffective by a break between Secretary of State Hull and Assistant Secretary of State Moley brought on by Roosevelt's radio message stating he would regard it as a "catastrophe" if the conference ceased the major effort "to bring about a more real and permanent financial stability and a greater prosperity to the masses of nations" than by minor attempts at temporary stabilization involving a few nations.

I am not qualified to say whether the conference offered a chance to save the world from the war which came six years later. I leave that verdict to history. I do know that the collapse of the conference offered comfort to the opposition, who had been silenced by the accomplishments of the administration up to that time. It was a reversal, though it did not seem to be a major one. It is my conviction that the President wrecked the conference because he thought bankers, whom he had castigated in his inaugural address, were engaged in a great international plot against him. I say this, because he told me Thomas Lamont of J. P. Morgan and Company was responsible for Herbert Bayard Swope's being on the American delegation. Lamont thought that Swope might have some influence on Moley in connection with the stabilization scheme. FDR said Lamont had placed someone on the boat to contact Swope and Moley. He was quite incensed about this, saying Lamont was a personal friend and should not have acted so.

Actually Swope was prevailed to go along to render public service. Swope was and is my valued friend, one who, while as courteous as any eighteenth century gentleman, never hesitates to tell the truth in a world where it has become the fashion, in giving advice, to offer flattery rather than facts.

Moley was one of the ablest of the men around Roosevelt in the early days. He had a brilliant, analytical mind and a gift for marshalling ideas on paper. Unfortunately for him, he lacked schooling in the rough and tumble academy of practical politics. He was the core of the "Brain Trust," when it included Rexford Guy Tugwell, also of Columbia; Judge Samuel I. Rosenman, an adept word doctor; Adolph A. Berle, master mind on banking and corporations; and Hugh S. Johnson, army officer and industrialist. Moley's departure was an immeasurable loss to Roosevelt. Hugh, a phrase coiner and driving worker, stepped out of the advisory class into an executive role as administrator of the contentious National Recovery Administration, where he demonstrated he could take criticism as well as dish it out. Like Moley, he left in a blaze of indignation, high-lighted by not a few purple passages, to become the author of a provoking and successful newspaper column until his untimely death. As is often the case with advisers, the Brain Trust did not exercise as much influence as the opposition endeavored to make the public believe. It is even doubtful whether they did as much in molding policy as they themselves believed.

In August of 1933, I was wrestling with ship subsidies, a subject about which I knew less than nothing. I spent nights poring over reports and studies, and days in gathering opinions from men of various interests. When I felt I knew what I was talking about, I trooped over to the White House with two of my assistants, Joe O'Mahoney and Bill Howes, to have FDR determine the policy for ship subsidies. The President indicated he was against subsidies generally, but appreciated that American ships must be kept on the high seas. He was against a ten year contract with the shipping companies, favoring a five year term, which the companies held was not long enough to compensate them for any vessels they might have to build under the existing shipping contract.

The President asked me to look into the situation and try to effect a compromise. Senator Hugo Black of Alabama, who was investigating ship subsidies, came to my office. Black was startlingly frank, telling me he had looked into the activities of the Post Office Department officials and found our record clear in every respect. Then he said his investigations had uncovered some facts which might prove embarrassing when they were brought to light. One of the President's fishing companions had received 25,000 shares in a ship company for securing a favorable contract. Another, (he told me) also interested in shipping, had contributed $50,000 to the Roosevelt campaign. I went from my office to the White House to unfold the story to Roosevelt, knowing that he was about to take a second fishing trip in a few weeks. He was not in the least disturbed.

"Jim, so long as it doesn't happen until after my boat trip, it's all right."

He then switched to a report of his talk with Charles M. Schwab, chairman of the board of the Bethlehem Steel Company, and Myron C. Taylor, president of the United States Steel Corporation. In high glee, he told how he had discomfited the gentlemen when they said they were giving their employees a fair wage.

"I told them quite bluntly they were not paying a living wage," he said. "Furthermore, I said that the miners had to live in 'coke ovens' under very unsatisfactory conditions. And then I told Schwab that it would be unwise for him to appear in some mining sections because the miners were much incensed against such things as paying million dollar bonuses as had been done in the past. I looked him in the eye and went on to say hereafter the employees would receive a living wage and there would be no more million dollar bonuses paid to the top out of stockholders' money. They didn't like it, but they had to listen."

That fall I was plagued with the New York City campaign. Tammany leaders persisted in their shortsighted policy and nominated Surrogate John P. O'Brien, a scholarly jurist, but no executive, to run for Mayor. On September 21, 1933, I had dinner at the White House with the President, Ed Flynn, Vincent Dailey, and Missy Le Hand at which it was decided that Joseph V. McKee, young, able acting Mayor, should make the race. The President suggested we have committees of various sorts—businessmen, lawyers, doctors, and others—demand that he run. Flynn was to support him with the Bronx organization, of which McKee was a member. The President was not to take any part in the campaign, but said he would invite McKee to the White House "just to show the way the wind was blowing." He also said Secretary of Treasury Woodin, Secretary of Labor Perkins, and other prominent persons, affiliated with the national administration, would endorse the candidate of the Recovery party.

McKee was never invited to the White House. The promised administration help did not materialize. I went through with my promise that I would publicly state I would vote for McKee. When I did I was roundly attacked by Tammany Hall, which was another chapter of my political education.

Earlier in the year I had made a trip, which was of great personal satisfaction. I was awarded an honorary degree, my first college degree, from the University of the South. It was pleasing to me to become a college man. Since then I have acquired over ten other honorary degrees. While these are flattering to my vanity, I would trade them all for an earned A.B.

In the period between his election and his inauguration, Roosevelt had indicated he would seek to reestablish relations with Russia. On October 10, 1933, he addressed a letter to Mikhail Kalinin, President of the Soviet Union, asserting it was time two great nations resumed speaking to one another. In November, Maxim Litvinov, who impressed me as a sharp trader, arrived to conclude the recognition agreement. During the negotiations I had dinner with the President in the White House.

"Everything is coming along splendidly and I am confident everything will work out all right," he told me when I mentioned the Russian negotiations. "Of course, Litvinov wanted me to recognize Russia and then work out the conditions. He's a great trader, but I wasn't going to let him get away with that. I made it clear that everything must be cleared up first."

I asked about the problem of religious freedom, saying that many clergymen, of all faiths, were hoping the negotiations would be an opening wedge. I had hopes this might be so, but I was not without doubts, which history has shown, to my regret, were justified.

"Oh, I was very definite on that," he said. "I told Litvinov the situation must be cleared up, because the people of this country give everyone the right to freedom of religious belief, and there is no reason why Russia should impose her ideas on Americans who might be in that country. I said guarantee of religious freedom must be given Americans before anything could be done.

"And then, Jim, I threw one straight from the shoulder at him. You'll enjoy this. I told Litvinov that I knew he had his opinion of me, and that, in turn, I had my own ideas of him. Then I followed that up by saying I was willing to wager that five minutes before his time would come to die, and he was conscious of it, that he would be thinking of his parents and wanting to make his peace with God. Jim, he looked at me closely, but didn't say a word."

Roosevelt threw back his head and laughed.

A few days later at a Cabinet meeting, he produced the final agreement and said he would announce recognition of Russia at once. He said he felt the agreement would be very pleasing to the people of this country, and that those who had opposed recognition on religious grounds would no longer do so. He acknowledged that the safeguards to religion involved Americans alone, but expressed himself confident he had opened the door to similar bargaining by other countries. The weak point of this bargain was that there were only a handful of Americans in Russia, and that religious freedom in the Soviet Union was not advanced an iota. He said that because of the agreement we could collect 150 million dollars worth of debts which had accrued. In this, too, he was over optimistic.

"Generally speaking," he concluded, "I feel I have driven a good bargain, not only for this country, but for the world, and that it will go a long way toward preserving the future peace of the world."

As the year, which had been a most busy one for me, drew near an end, I planned a rest cruise to Europe with Mrs. Farley. We sailed on the *Conte di Savoia* in November and had Litvinov for a fellow traveler. He spoke frequently of his appreciation for what Roosevelt had done, adding he would do everything in his power to fulfill the terms of the agreement. He impressed me as more slippery than sincere.

In Italy we had an audience with Pope Pius XI, who was as unassuming as a parish priest, and dinner with Cardinal Pacelli, who was to succeed to the papacy in 1939. I also had an audience with Il Duce, who reminded me of Huey Long. It was a hurried trip. We returned to New York the day before Christmas.

CHAPTER SIX

TAKING IT ON THE CHIN

THE YEAR 1934 brought me one of my saddest experiences in public life. I cannot think of it now without being stirred by regrets, although it has generally been forgotten. I refer to the cancellation of the air mail contracts. This was one of the most controversial decisions of the Roosevelt administration up to the third term and the war.

On February 9, 1934, I issued an order, to be effective ten days later, canceling all domestic air mail contracts. Although the order was mine, the decision was approved by Attorney General Cummings and by President Roosevelt. It had general approval because a Senate investigating committee had found that the contracts were let without competitive bidding, as provided by law, and at figures wholly unjustified by the services rendered.

In considering cancellation, I wanted to allow the domestic lines to continue to carry mail until new contracts could be negotiated. Cummings was behind me in this. The alternative was to have the Army, which had carried the first air mail fifteen years before, resume its flying until the contract situation was adjusted. General Benjamin F. Foulois of the Army Air Corps said the Army was ready to take over and the President favored giving the service an opportunity to distinguish itself.

The result was disaster after disaster. Ten brave young fliers lost their lives, as the country was swept by storms and gales. The army pilots took off in sleet, snow, fog, rain, and high winds with the bravery that comes of youth and *esprit de corps*.

The unhappy series of accidents took all minds off any consideration of the ethics surrounding the negotiation of the private contracts. The wrath of an aroused public descended on my head as the author of the order canceling the contracts. I had learned in the past to take abuse and criticism, but when I was called a murderer, I began to look around frantically for help. I looked to the White House. No help came. I was hurt that the President had not seen fit to divert the wrath. Later I realized it was part of my job to take as many blows for him as I could. Nonetheless, a kind word would have been a great help when the lashes were falling.

On March 10, the President issued an order instructing the Air Corps to curtail service. All service was suspended for a week, then resumed in better weather. Two months later the flying of air mail was turned back to private lines.

During this period and throughout the year, I saw the President every few days either at his bedside, in his executive offices, at his Hyde Park home, or in the evening at the White House. We had many patronage problems. Members of Congress were seeking a greater voice in patronage, claiming their reelections depended upon getting jobs.

The President was fully cognizant that 1934 was an election year, which would have an important bearing on his reelection in 1936. This was, naturally enough, his chief political goal. He felt, and I thoroughly agree, that it was most important that the Democratic party make gains in the Senate and House, because such advances would constitute a confirmation of his administration and its program.

On June 28, just before leaving for a month's cruise, Roosevelt delivered his first "fireside" chat of 1934. It was a review of the achievements of the Seventy-third Congress and gave a recapitulation of his administration. It also previewed the program he intended to carry on in the future. I was invited to listen. When he had finished, I went over to congratulate him. With a wink, he asked, "Jim, didn't you think it was a good campaign document?" I agreed wholeheartedly, and we made much use of it.

On my return in the fall from a series of political tours, I dictated the following letter to the President on November 3, 1934, the Saturday before election:

I am going right out on a limb now and make some very radical predictions about what is going to happen next Tuesday. I am quite willing to do this, so you can have a lot of fun kidding me Wednesday or Thursday, whenever you see me, if the results do not turn out as I predict.

I am certain we will elect Senators in the following states: Missouri, Ohio, Indiana, West Virginia, Maryland, and New Jersey. (This proved to be one hundred per cent correct.) These are definite. I also feel we will elect Peter Gerry in Rhode Island and Francis Maloney in Connecticut; also Frank Picard in Michigan. (Error, Vandenberg was reelected.) I am not entirely sold on Michigan as far as Governor is concerned. (Partial redemption of error.)

If we had a real candidate in Delaware, we might win there. . . . (We did not.)

I reserved Pennsylvania for the last so that you can be all set for it. I honestly believe Guffey is going to win. . . . (Correct.)

When we look ahead following this election, this year's group of Republican Senators should not contain more than nine names. (Right on the button, including Senators La Follette, Wisconsin Progressive, and Shipstead, Minnesota Farmer-Laborite as republicans.)

So far as the Congressional race is concerned, I believe whatever losses we have, if any, west of the Mississippi River, will be made up by the gains we will make in that territory, so that in the final analysis, we will stand about even.

Three days after the election the President was grinning broadly as he came into the Cabinet room. We were all in our places when he was wheeled in.

"I want to read a letter, written a day or so before the election, by a fellow who has been in politics some time," he began in mock seriousness. "When I opened it I got mad, because I couldn't understand how anyone could be so foolish. I didn't think that anyone who had been around as long as this fellow would lose his head."

Then he began reading the letter, noting that he had considered this or that prediction impossible or foolish. Then, speaking seriously, he said it was the most remarkable prediction he had ever heard of during his entire political career. (I still had a better one to come.)

Saturday before election he phoned me at headquarters to ask how things looked. He was in high spirits and said, "Hello, Jim." As usual I addressed him as "Governor," a habit that clung from his service in Albany and that I was a long time in breaking. I told him that things looked great.

After he had hung up, I found a note from him in my mail. It was written in ink in his own hand and read:

DEAR JIM:

As soon as Election Day is past—in fact on Saturday Nov. 3rd—three days *before* election, please see to it that the *cost* of National Headquarters is from that date on cut to not to exceed $1,000 per week pay roll and not to exceed $500 a week for all other expenses.

F.D.R.

This was a bit of a shock. We had a loyal and faithful staff. It was true that we Democrats always had more difficulty raising money than our Republican brethren. 1936 was a presidential year when we would need every cent. And the note seemed to be ordering us to cut things pretty fine. This was especially so since many of the workers had been put on the staff by the President and on recommendation by Mrs. Eleanor Roosevelt. I threw the note in my files and stretched the pay rolls a bit.

After voting on election day, Mrs. Farley and I went to Stony Point to talk and visit with old friends and neighbors. I have made it a practice to return to my old home every election day and to say a prayer at my parents' graves. In the late afternoon I returned to headquarters to catch returns as they came in. The scene was a repetition of the presidential election night on a smaller scale. The President did not come, receiving returns in his family home. I talked to him a number of times. He was elated and so was I. We had quite a celebration around headquarters and entertained a number of distinguished visitors.

Three nights before Christmas I received a phone call from the President in my Mayflower Hotel apartment.

"Jim, it has just been brought to my attention that the Democratic organization in Chicago is to have a meeting and plans to endorse Ed Kelly as the Democratic mayoralty candidate for the April election." There was a disturbed note in his voice.

"What do you want me to do?" I asked, puzzled.

"I want you to take the necessary steps to stop Kelly's nomination." He was emphatic.

"Why, I don't know if I could do it or whether it would be advisable," I said. "I'll see what the situation is."

I called various friends in Chicago, including persons not in politics, and was told that it would be a mistake for the administration to oppose Kelly. There was agreement that Kelly could win regardless of anything the administration might attempt.

I saw the President the next morning and told him the story. I added my nickel's worth of advice and said I believed it would be a serious mistake to inject ourselves into the Chicago situation. Reluctantly FDR agreed, but he showed me a long letter from Secretary Ickes which had evidently spurred his original request. A White House copy is still in my files.

My education as a politician continued to be in the School of Hard Knocks. At the turn of the year the New Deal's No. 1 problem child, Huey P. Long, tossed his mane and pawed the carpets of the Senate aisles, as he snorted and whinnied in demanding an investigation of me. As I look back on it now, the whole affair was just another one of the tempests under Capitol Dome, which seem highly important as they rage, but soon fade into forgetfulness. I learned that the best way to ride out a storm of vicious, unfair attacks is to put your trust in a clear conscience and show that your hands are clean.

Day after day, Huey was threatening to "blow the roof off the Capitol." Skillfully he wove together a varied assortment of unrelated truths, half-truths, innuendoes, insinuations, and downright lies. He intimated that he was prepared to expose the Roosevelt administration. I was unworried, because I knew I was completely innocent. I was, however, annoyed. I knew that Long was not concerned with me, but was sighting his oratorical guns on the Roosevelt administration, having third-party ambitions in 1936.

Roosevelt was aware that he was the real target of Long's attack and was most anxious that I clear myself. I was disappointed that, knowing the charges to be without foundation, he did not issue a statement on my behalf.

The answers to Long's charges were placed before the Senate in my behalf by Senator Josiah W. Bailey of North Carolina. No member of the United States Senate did more for me in that fight than Senator Kenneth McKellar of Tennessee. I will always feel grateful to him. In the vote, largely on party lines, the Senate decided Long had failed to establish the shadow of a case. I was pleased when such outstanding members of the opposition as Johnson of California, Borah of Idaho, and Shipstead of Minnesota voted against Long.

After the shooting was all over, Long told an acquaintance of mine that he had brought the charges against me because "Jim was the biggest rooster in the yard, and I thought if I could break his legs, the rest would be easy."

That summer he was felled by an assassin's bullets. It is to be regretted he was removed from the national scene by bullets rather than ballots.

The ifs of politics are always interesting. One frequently considered is what would have happened had Huey lived. As I said before, I did not underestimate the man, although personally I regarded him as a cowardly braggart. The Democratic National Committee conducted a secret poll on Long's bid for national power which disclosed, to our surprise, that he might poll between 3,000,000 to 4,000,000 votes at the head of a third party. His support was not confined to Louisiana and near-by states, but his "share the wealth" program was attracting strength in industrial and farm areas of the north.

Long was the most formidable of the then current array of demagogues of the "Damaged Souls" school, our poll showed. It was conceivable that his third party movement might constitute a balance of power in the 1936 election, although indications were that he would cost us no more than the electoral votes of a few states. He was high in our political thoughts, however, because the poll indicated that he could control at least 100,000 in New York State, which could have been a critical bloc, particularly since he was recruiting Democrats rather than Republicans.

I am firmly convinced Long would have been a source of annoyance rather than a threat in 1936. What he might have done in 1940 is difficult to conjecture. It is possible that the Senate might have refused to seat him. This might have been food and drink to dictator ambitions, however, and made him so formidable that FDR would have passed up his try for the third term, as some observers believe. I have great confidence that sooner or later he would have disgusted the public by his clowning and arrogant blustering.

In the summer of 1935 Roosevelt and I discussed the President's position before the country. Quite frankly I told him that he had lost ground, but that I saw no cause for alarm. I expressed myself certain he would pick up as the campaign came around, since it was only natural there should be a falling off in a noncampaign year. He told me to forget about resigning from my Cabinet seat, as I had offered to do after the vote on the Long imbroglio, and asked me to have a long talk with him about conditions on his return from a Warm Springs vacation.

On May 1, 1935, at my request, the President summoned Vice President Garner, Speaker Byrnes, Senate Majority Leader Robinson, Attorney General Cummings, Secretary of State Hull, former Congressman Charles West, Frank Walker, and myself to the White House for a night meeting. When we had seated ourselves in his oval study, he began:

"I've called this meeting in order to have a heart to heart talk about conditions in general, and I want everyone to be free to express himself frankly. I'm going to start off by saying that Henry Wallace has made a number of speeches, particularly in Massachusetts, which have been tactless and probably will have a bad effect politically. I'm going to speak to him about it on his return.

"And Harold Ickes has done harm, particularly in the speech he made at Philadelphia in which he talked about Townsend, Long, and Coughlin. I had no objections to what he said about Long or Townsend, but his reference to Father Coughlin was very unwise. Right now Frank Murphy is doing a splendid job in handling Coughlin. I'm going to make him High Commissioner of the Philippines and bring him back after a month or two so that he may devote his entire time to the Coughlin situation."

I urged that we become politically minded and do everything possible to satisfy the Senators, Congressmen, and state leaders, who would have to carry the load in the 1936 campaign.

"And I want to say, without flattery, I think you have done a splendid job, considering the obstacles placed in your way by ambitions and jealousies," I said.

"I shall endeavor to carry on in such a way that my successor will

THE WHITE HOUSE

PRIVATE & CONFIDENTIAL

The Honorable

The Postmaster General,

3 East 84th Street,

New York City, N. Y.

Dear Jim –

As soon as Election Day is past – in fact on Saturday Nov. 3rd – three days *before* Election please see to it that the *cost* of Nat Headquarters is from that date on, cut to not to exceed $1,000 per week payroll and not to exceed $500 a week for all other expenses

F.D.R.

"Private & Confidential" memos from FDR to me were not unusual. But this one, dated November 3, 1934, came as a shock (see page 49).

THE WHITE HOUSE
WASHINGTON

November 4, 1936

Dear Jim:

You were right — so right that I thought you were more of an optimist than a prophet. I find I am the one who needs to have his long-range spectacles adjusted. But in this instance, Jim, I don't mind being wrong at all.

Very sincerely yours,

Franklin D Roosevelt

Honorable James A. Farley,
Chairman,
Democratic National Campaign Committee,
Hotel Biltmore,
New York, N. Y.

Here is FDR's special testimonial letter for me, intentionally predated, which Charley Michelson requested late in January of 1937. I hadn't received any previous letter, thanking me for my services, since 1930 (see page 70).

be able to carry out the policies of the Democratic party," Roosevelt said. "You all know that when Taft succeeded Theodore Roosevelt, Taft brought back the old crowd much to TR's disappointment.

"I am going to do all in my power to prevent a continuance of conditions which would permit Wall Street to dominate not only the policies but the politics of the nation. Of course, everything can't be accomplished in a year or two. It took Jefferson twenty years to have his policies approved by the people of the country."

On the week end of May 11, 1935, the President was at the Woodmont Gun and Rod Club, Maryland, with a party. Vice President Garner and I rode back to Washington with him. During the trip he discussed the bonus and other legislation. Garner told him that the right thing for him to do would be to veto the bonus, in temperate language, so as not to incur the ill-feeling of veterans, explaining that he had to maintain the credit of the nation.

Garner and I said it would be best for the party if the bonus were passed over the President's veto. The President agreed that if the bill were passed over his veto, it would not affect the credit of the country and would not have the inflationary effect which many feared. We felt that the money, if made available in the next three months, would move into trade and commerce and would do much toward bringing about recovery.

Eight days later I was in Monticello, New York, dedicating a post office, when I was ordered to report to the White House the next day for a conference on the bonus situation. I thought the matter had been thrashed out pretty well and couldn't imagine what was up. I found Roosevelt fuming.

"Jack Garner has been talking too much," he said. "He's got me in a spot where I can be accused of bad faith if the bonus is passed over my veto."

"Is our conversation on the return trip from Woodmont overboard?" I asked.

"Yes."

"I can't believe Jack let it out," I said. "Did you talk to anyone else?"

"It's out," he said curtly. "I want you to contact Robinson and work with him to get enough Senators to uphold my veto."

This I did. The President was a bit jumpy because he was aware, from our reports, that in recent weeks his popularity had dropped. The National Committee's secret poll found him weaker than at any time since Inauguration. I was certain the picture would improve and that he would win by more than 5,000,000 votes.

That month the Supreme Court took to overhauling the New Deal. In the process, the nine old men began throwing vital parts of the machinery out the window. The Railroad Retirement Act was invalidated by a 5 to 4 decision. Two weeks later the Coal Conservation Act followed by a vote of 6 to 3. A week later in *Louisville Joint Stock Land Bank v. Radford*, the Court limited Congressional power to limit distress of the huge number of bankrupts. And in a unanimous decision in a case involving the marketing of allegedly ill poultry, the Court ended the NRA. The Blue Eagle was literally replaced by a sick chicken.

The President was bitterly disappointed and angry over the decision. At a Cabinet meeting he talked disparagingly of the Court and of its members. He did not criticize the decision of the Court at the meeting, but he had already done so in his press conference statement, "We have been relegated to the horse-and-buggy definition of interstate commerce." This hurt him, I thought, but he was convinced that he had popular support on the NRA.

Roosevelt was never down in the dumps for any length of time. At the next Cabinet meeting he indulged in a bit of needling that I shall always remember. Miss Perkins was discussing the Social Security Board. The thoughts of the rest of us were wandering, because she did considerable talking at official family sessions.

"When you get around to it," the President began in a tone that let us all know something was coming. When he knew he had our attention he repeated with studied innocence, "When you get around to it, I want to talk to you about an old flame of Jack Garner's."

The Vice President blushed to the roots of his picturesque white eyebrows. The President roared with laughter. We all joined in. Then Garner made a plea for the appointment of Miss Margy Neal to the board, riding out the laughter by detailing her qualifications. It was, of course, merely a presidential jest.

Election night, 1935, I was in headquarters. We were disappointed over losing the control of the New York State Assembly. However, when I talked to Roosevelt he was jubilant because in his home district, which he had failed to carry in 1932, a Democratic supervisor was elected for the first time in forty years.

"And Jim," he chortled, "the issue was the New Deal."

Analysis of the New York vote showed the federal administration was sustained by more than 500,000 majority. This was a sufficient answer to any question of Roosevelt's popularity. We were happy over the election of A. B. Chandler as governor of Kentucky by the largest majority for a state office in Kentucky's history, but we were unhappy over our failure to capture the city administration in Philadelphia.

On November 14, 1935, during a luncheon at the President's desk, I said I had been advised that Secretary of War Dern was surprised by the appointment of General Malin Craig as Chief of Staff of the United States Army. Dern was then visiting Hawaii. I was also surprised since I had supported Major General Hugh Drum.

"Your information is absolutely correct, Jim," Roosevelt laughed. "He didn't know about it. You see General Douglas MacArthur, during his service as Chief of Staff, had been trying to have all his favorites placed in responsible positions. He was arranging it so that he would be succeeded by Major General George S. Simonds.

"Last spring Simonds had four years left to go before retirement and could have served out the term of a Chief of Staff. I had to think fast, so I asked MacArthur to stay until October on the representation that I needed him to assist in the formulation of legislation relative to the War Department.

"MacArthur stayed. When October rolled around Simonds only had three and a half years to serve and that eliminated MacArthur's man. If I had told Dern about it, he might have mentioned it, innocently, to someone in the War Department clique and pressure might have been brought to bear to force the appointment of Simonds while he still had four years to go. Consequently, I waited; then when Dern and MacArthur left the country, I made the appointment."

Roosevelt talked at length about the war Mussolini had forced on

Ethiopia. This, along with Hitler's formal announcement of German rearmament were the major international developments of the year. He predicted that the League of Nations meeting, which was to open within a week, would be the start of a sanctions movement that would seriously cripple Italy. At all times Roosevelt was much more interested in foreign affairs than he indicated in public utterances and press conferences.

"I know I'm walking a tight rope and I'm thoroughly aware of the gravity of the situation," he said. "All I have tried to do is prevent the shipment of implements of war to Italy. I do not consider oil, cotton, automobiles, trucks, and the like implements of war, although some nations do. Later it may be necessary for me to publish a list of the American firms making shipments of materials to Italy, which are being used in prosecution of the war. I realize the seriousness of this from an international as well as a domestic point of view."

In this connection he mentioned the fact that Ambassador Breckinridge Long did not want to return to Italy. I took the opportunity to press for the appointment of James W. Gerard, wartime ambassador to Germany and faithful servant of the Democratic party. Roosevelt was evasive, saying he did not want to make any commitment for a long period until after the 1936 election. I had proposed Gerard for Paris; Roosevelt promised favorable action, but William C. Bullitt was named. I had suggested Gerard for Rome; Roosevelt was sympathetic, but William Phillips was nominated. Gerard told me to cease my efforts, holding that Roosevelt would never forget the defeat he suffered at Gerard's hands in the Democratic senatorial primary of 1914. Nonetheless, I persisted and succeeded in having Gerard named as the President's representative at the coronation of King George VI in 1938.

After his fall vacation at Warm Springs, the President went to Chicago and spoke at the International Live Stock Exposition, pointing with pride to New Deal agricultural accomplishments. That afternoon en route to South Bend, Indiana, where he received an honorary degree at the University of Notre Dame, we spent more than an hour discussing the coming presidential campaign. Frank Walker joined this conference.

"I think we ought to conduct a very aggressive campaign, Jim," he said. "Every effort should be made to get public sentiment in our favor before the Republican convention meets. I'm going to send Ickes out on a week's tour. Then I'll send out Wallace and Cummings, and maybe Roper. The trouble is most of the fellows get into matters they have no business touching on, like Ickes discussing oil and Roper interpreting the neutrality agreement."

"If I can offer some advice," I said, "I would use Ickes where his department has been active and where PWA has rendered service. Harold deserves every credit for a splendid job there. I'd use Wallace in the farm areas and keep him away from industrial sections. I don't think Harry Hopkins should make any speeches, since he has been the target of much unfavorable criticism. People are being led to believe his sole purpose is to create jobs and spend money, regardless of necessity. I don't think Rex Tugwell should be used either."

"I agree thoroughly," Roosevelt said. "I'm going to take steps to eliminate criticism in the future.

"By the way," he continued, "I have been thinking of the two-thirds rule. I think now that the party is in power and there is no question about my renomination, we should clear up the situation for all time and submit the matter to the convention."

I replied I would prepare a resolution for submission to the meeting of the Democratic National Committee early in the coming year.

At the Cabinet meeting of December 27, 1935, the President looked bad. He was suffering from a cold, his face was drawn, and his reactions were slow. It was the first time I thought the strain of office was telling on him. However, I was summoned to his bedside three days later and found him much better, looking like his former self.

CHAPTER SEVEN

SECOND CAMPAIGN— PROPHET WITH HONOR

T HE 1936 ELECTION was one of the high-water marks of American politics. Some have been kind enough to call it "the campaign without a mistake." I wouldn't go so far, nor do I consider it the peak of my career. Personally, I prefer the campaign of four years later, when I suffered defeat, but went down fighting for a principle.

Not since the days of Washington and Monroe had a candidate received such a popular plurality or such an overwhelming electoral vote, actually or proportionately. This result was due in a large measure to the personal popularity of Franklin Delano Roosevelt and to his keen insight into political advantage. It was also due to magnificent teamwork in the Democratic National Committee and Democratic state, county, and city organizations throughout the country. We began at the first of the year and never let up until the polls closed ten months later. We tried not to miss a single trick. We didn't miss many.

In the call for the convention, the National Committee voted to include the question of abrogation of the two-thirds rule. There was sufficient strength in the committee to block inclusion of the controversial question in the call, but I induced the objectors to fall into step. When the third term issue arose four years later, many of these reminded me that I had made the nomination possible because of this change. I don't think the responsibility for the change is entirely mine and, if it is, I still believe the change should have been made years before.

On January 19, 1936, I rode from New York City to Washington with Roosevelt after his dedication of the Theodore Roosevelt Memorial. I put in a few licks for veto of the bonus bill. When I finished my argument, he leaned over, grasped my hand, and said, "Thanks very much for your statement; most of the people I have talked to have urged me to sign it." Then he added he felt the bill would be passed over his veto anyway, so that the party would not suffer and he could preserve his record.

Three days later I told the President the campaign proper would largely be a one man show, that he would have to carry the load. I said that while the public would listen to our speakers, they wanted to hear him and that it would be necessary for us to buy time for him on the radio. He was very anxious that we start organizing different committees at once, such as Friends of Roosevelt, Good Neighbor League, Roosevelt Republican League, and the Committee of One. He was captivated by the last-named group, the theory of which was that everyone friendly to the administration constitute himself a "Committee of One" to sell the New Deal to others.

"In the Committee of Twelve," he continued, "I would like to have five clergymen. I think we should have a Catholic priest, a Baptist minister, a Presbyterian minister, an Episcopalian minister, and a rabbi."

"What about the Methodists?" I asked.

"Well, we could leave out the Jews," he laughed. "No, there are more of them than there are Episcopalians. Take the Jews and leave out the Episcopalians."

In late January, Smith made his "I'm going to take a walk" Liberty League speech. Our strategy board debated about finding someone to answer him and finally chose his 1928 running mate, Senator Joseph T. Robinson of Arkansas. Roosevelt did not consider the Smith speech too damaging. In fact, he thought we got the better of the break because the Senator effectively contrasted Al's statements in the past with his desertion of party.

On February 7, 1936, in discussing the defections of Smith and John J. Raskob, my predecessor as chairman, the President told me a most interesting story.

"At the time Smith and Raskob were trying to get me to run for Governor, I told Raskob I had some obligations at Warm Springs," he said. "I had thought I was out of politics and intended to operate the resort. Raskob wanted to know what they were. I told him it would take a couple of hundred thousand dollars. Raskob assured me he would assist in getting the money and promised $50,000 himself.

"Well, to make a long story short, he made a payment of $12,500 in 1928 and a like amount in 1929. He made another payment in 1930 or 1931, but he still owes $12,500 on the promise he made to me at the time I agreed to run for Governor to help him and Smith."

Raskob made the final payment as pledged.

In the next month a curious parallel involving Roosevelt cropped up in the campaign. There was a whispering campaign that Roosevelt was not a man of his word because he had gone back on a pledge to the Cathedral of St. John the Divine in New York. I wrote to the White House asking for information and got the following reply from Marguerite Le Hand, the President's personal secretary:

> You can tell . . . that while the President is not in the habit of telling the world all about his contributions to charity, there is no reason why . . . you should not know in confidence, that several years ago the President was the Chairman of the drive to raise money for the Cathedral of St. John the Divine in New York, that the drive was extremely successful and $10,000,000 was given or pledged. At that time the President pledged a gift of $5,000, to be paid in installments as fast as he was in a position to do so. $1,000 was paid in 1934 and $1,000 a month or two ago. Naturally the additional $3,000 will be paid in accordance with the original pledge.
>
> In addition to this the President gave, at the time of the drive $100 in the name of each of his children, or a total of $500. The total of these sums is, of course, very large in view of the President's somewhat limited financial means.
>
> Will you find out confidentially where the story came from?

Late in February Roosevelt called me to the White House for a general review of the political situation. In its course he expressed his annoyance with the courts, particularly the Supreme Court. McIntyre, Early and the President's brother-in-law, Hall Roosevelt, were at this conference. Former Congressman Charles West of Ohio was also there.

"I've been thinking that it would be a good idea if we could appoint fifty Federal judges to hold office for about five years," he said. "They could hold roving commissions which would permit them to operate in sections of the country where they could be helpful. What do you think?"

McIntyre and I didn't like it. Early, West and Hall Roosevelt thought it might be good. McIntyre said that if we could get the Chief Justice to recommend the legislation, it would be all right, which prompted a presidential suggestion that Homer Cummings get Chief Justice Hughes to make the suggestion. I have often thought this was the germ of the Supreme Court packing plan, which he was to give Congress a year later.

Late in March the President went on a Florida vacation. Although he was tired, he was in excellent humor and exceedingly happy over the evident turn in his favor in recent months.

On April 18, 1936, Louis Howe died in his sleep. I was genuinely distressed at his death, because he had helped my political education more than any one man. He was as loyal as any man I ever knew. I shall never forget his rapt expression when, in urging me to postpone my vacation for a week to help "Franklin," he said, "I have done these things for Franklin for years, Jim—postponed vacations, canceled engagements, and the like too many times to mention."

I never went to the White House while he was well that I did not call on him. I visited him frequently when he was ill and tried to call him by phone at least once a day.

On April 20, 1936, the President expressed to me how badly he felt about the passing of his faithful friend. Then he said to me, "But in view of the circumstances, it must be considered a blessing in disguise, because Louis had been getting to the point where he gave a lot of orders that were annoying and likely to cause a lot of trouble. He indicated that he was going to go to headquarters in the Biltmore Hotel to run the campaign and if he did that, of course, he would cause a lot of confusion."

On May 19, 1936, the President and I went over the entire political situation. He said he thought he would take another boat trip off the coast of Maine as he had done in 1932, following the convention. Then he could inspect PWA projects and flood damage in New England. He thought he might follow the inspection pattern in other states, although he proposed to spend most of the summer between Hyde Park and Washington.

"And, of course, there won't be anything political about the inspection trips." He gave me a broad wink and threw back his head and laughed.

One of my western trips got me into hot water. At Grand Rapids, Michigan, on May 22, 1936, I referred to Alf Landon as Governor of "a typical prairie state." The newspapers picked it up and made what political capital they could out of it. On May 22, Roosevelt dispatched an admonitory memorandum to me, which read:

MEMORANDUM FOR J.A.F.

I thought we had decided that any reference to Landon or any other Republican candidate was inadvisable.

Now that the water is over the dam, I told Michelson that possibly a somewhat facetious reference to Frank Knox between now and June ninth, by you might soften the effect of the Landon reference.

Another good rule which should be passed down the line to all who are concerned with speech material is that no section of the country should be spoken of as "typical" but only with some laudatory adjective. If the sentence had read "one of those splendid prairie states," no one could have picked us up on it, but the word "typical" coming from any New Yorker is meat for the opposition.

F.D.R.

I deserved it. It was a blunder I should have caught. After all, I was aware that a phrase can lose a campaign. I knew Grover Cleveland owed his election in 1884 to the remark, "Rum, Romanism and Rebellion," made by the Rev. Dr. Samuel D. Burchard, a supporter of James G. Blaine, at the Fifth Avenue Hotel. Happily for me, my remark cost us few, if any, votes although it was a nine day wonder in its own time.

The Democratic convention at Philadelphia was more of a family reunion than anything else. We could have completed our work in one day and gone home. The convention's crescendo of Democratic enthusiasm came the night of Saturday, June 27, when Roosevelt stood in the glare of massed spotlights to address more than 100,000 persons seated in the dark horseshoe of Franklin Field. Millions throughout the country heard his fighting denunciation of "economic royalist."

Within the week I was back at my desk in headquarters organizing for the campaign. The process was largely one of swinging from preconvention to postconvention campaigning. We were smoothly under way before the Republicans were getting started. The Republican machine had been smashed by two election defeats, so I was quite confident it could not be in running order by Election Day.

On July 7, 1936, the President, McIntyre, Early, Michelson, "Chip" Robert, and myself had a strategy meeting at the White House. We considered at what moment Harold Ickes should take out after Alf Landon, deciding the attacks should come after Landon had made his acceptance speech.

"I also think it would be a good idea to have speeches made by the Ministers and Ambassadors who are or will be in the country," Roosevelt said. "They could speak effectively in cities where there are a goodly number of inhabitants from the countries they represent abroad. They could bring out forcefully the fact that this country is a peaceful nation and that all the others in North and South America are living together in a peaceful manner, while the governments in Europe are crumbling. They could go on to say these governments are looking to this country as the savior of the world. They could say that the people in this country have confidence in Roosevelt as do the people abroad. This could be most effective."

This employment of envoys to unite various groups of nationals behind the New Deal, although most effective in both the 1940 and 1944 campaigns, was a mistake. For men charged with representing this nation in foreign lands should not run political errands. I said so at the time.

Everything was moving along nicely in July and August, except for me. I was collecting an assortment of punches, many of them below the belt. I was accused of bribing voters with relief and other public funds. I was portrayed as the worst type of spoils politician. What I caught was nothing to what the President took. Lest anyone have an impression to the contrary, unfair criticism and unwarranted attacks do not roll off me like water off a duck's back. They do hurt—the more unjust, the deeper the hurt—but I do not let them rob me of my peace of mind or warp my outlook.

In this period I called Harry Hopkins to complain about his making speeches on relief during his western trip. I told him that 75 per cent of the complaints we were receiving were about WPA and that most of the dissatisfaction within the party had been caused by WPA. Evidently he found my frankness disturbing, because he phoned me August 24 to say we were real friends and that he did not want anything to come between our friendship. I told him that I might be wrong, but believed that the people had the impression he was a spendthrift and that he was extravagant in his use of government funds.

On September 17, 1936, Garner visited me at New York headquarters. He told me that in two recent talks with the President he had mentioned my contribution to the campaign, adding that I should be entitled to every consideration for the effort I was putting forth.

"The Boss told me he appreciated what I had to say and my frankness," Garner said, "but he said no more. Could it be he's a little jealous of your popularity in the party?"

I said I didn't know. Roosevelt hadn't said anything to me one way or the other since the "prairie state" episode.

Roosevelt opened his avowed political campaign at the Democratic state convention in Syracuse, New York, September 29. He received a marvelous ovation and his speech was great. From that moment on, the campaign was a triumph. Everywhere he went, crowds jammed to see and hear him. This bore out my contention through the months that the campaign was a one man show and that he was more popular than the New Deal itself. This insistence displeased some members of the circle around him. Perhaps the height of the campaign was reached at Chicago on October 14 when 500,000 persons turned out to greet him in the most enthusiastic demonstration I have ever seen. Some 150,000 men and women marched from the station to the Chicago Stadium, singing and chanting, to hear him make possibly the greatest speech of the campaign. In ringing tones he struck at those aligned against him, particularly industrialists. In his address he said that it was his administration that "saved the system of private profit and free enterprise after it had been dragged to the brink of ruin by these same leaders who now try to scare you."

His trip through Connecticut and Massachusetts at the end of October was another triumphal procession. He wound up the campaign, as he had that of 1932, with a speech in Madison Square Garden, October 31, the Saturday before election. The speech was received with the greatest enthusiasm. Early in the day he had visited headquarters and, in the course of an expression of thanks to the workers, took the occasion to answer those who had vilified me. He said:

"I am proud of the fact that our information has been kept at a pretty high level. One reason for that is the fact that we have at the head of this campaign a man who has always been square.

"I have known Jim Farley for a great many years and I have never known him yet to do or think a mean thing.

"For a long time now—for a good many years, he has been taking it on the chin—taking it with a smile and not batting an eyelid, because, I think, in the back of his head he has had the idea that in spite of all kinds of unfair attacks, the American people, just like you and me, will read him for what he is, absolutely on the level.

"And incidentally, of course, I get reports not only from Jim but from lots of people—about what has been going on here in New York, and I have come to the very definite conclusion that the national headquarters this year has been what we call in the Navy 'a happy ship'! No crossed wires, everything clicking; and the result is going to bear that out next Tuesday.

"And I am very grateful, grateful to you all from Jim down to the office boy. And maybe the office boy will be National Chairman or President about thirty years from now."

On November 1, 1936 I sat down and wrote my election prediction in a headquarters pool. It read:

11/1/36

LANDON WILL ONLY CARRY MAINE AND VERMONT. 7 ELECTORAL VOTES.

J. A. FARLEY

On election eve I sent a messenger from headquarters to the President at Hyde Park with a book containing copies of letters from Democratic leaders, giving their picture of the situation. I summarized each state and included my prediction:

"After looking them all over carefully and discounting everything that has been given in these reports, I am still definitely of the opinion that you will carry every state but two—Maine and Vermont."

I went into details on a number of states and various contests within states and concluded:

"I am risking all the reputation I have, if any, as a prophet, but I am very sincere about it because as you know we have discussed this situation many times."

I talked to the President a dozen times on election night. He was overjoyed, as well he might have been, as the landslide grew. I was talking to him when Landon conceded defeat at 1:45 A.M. I gave him the latest reports as they came into headquarters. Once I called him to demand, "Who are the fourteen persons who voted against you in Warm Springs? You ought to raise hell with them."

When, at 3:36 A.M. I got the information from John L. Sullivan of Manchester, New Hampshire, that Roosevelt had pulled ahead in that city, I knew that my prediction would stand up. I left headquarters tired but elated. It was a wonderful victory.

The next morning the President was on the phone.

"Jim," he said, "nothing would give me greater pleasure than to be a newspaperman to read the record of your prediction and the outcome. It was the most uncanny prediction in the history of the country. I thought it was too optimistic, but I am pleased on your account that you called the result so accurately."

"Why don't you speak for yourself, Boss?" I could not help but cut in.

His laugh rang over the phone.

"I'm going to go to South America on the 16th or 17th," he said. "I want you to come down to Washington as soon as you can."

"Well, I'll come down for a day or so and clean up some loose ends and get away on a vacation by the 11th. I am taking Ambrose O'Connell and Eddie Roddan with me to Ireland."

At the Cabinet meeting, November 6, the President mentioned his prediction which was 360 electoral votes for himself and 171 for Landon. He then mentioned my prediction and expressed his thanks to me for what I had done and said he was pleased with the way the campaign was handled. He said everything had worked out fine. Members of the Cabinet congratulated me.

The White House announced that the President had already received about 12,000 congratulatory telegrams. I received nearly as many. One of them is still among my treasured possessions. It reads:

Uvalde, Texas.

Hon. James A. Farley, Biltmore Hotel.

HEARTY CONGRATULATIONS AS THE MOST EFFICIENT CHAIRMAN OF ANY NATIONAL COMMITTEE IN THE HISTORY OF THE REPUBLIC.

Jno N Garner

CHAPTER EIGHT

DRIFTING APART

MUCH HAS been written, some of it true, and much more has been spoken, most of it untrue, about my break with Franklin D. Roosevelt. Actually there was no sharp, clean fracture of friendship, but rather a slow, almost imperceptible drifting apart on political principles. I am certain neither of us knew how far we had drifted apart until the gap yawned unbridgeable between us.

Looking back through the years, I find it hard to put the finger of memory on the beginning of the drift, so gradual was the process. Almost before I knew it, I was no longer called to the White House for morning bedside conferences. My phone no longer brought the familiar voice in mellifluous tones. Months dragged between White House luncheon conferences. Soon I found I was no longer being consulted on appointments, even in my own state. Then, too, I found I was as much in the dark about the President's political plans as the Chairman of the Republican National Committee. White House confidence on politics and policies went to a small band of zealots, who mocked at party loyalty and knew no devotion except unswerving obedience to their leader.

At first this did not disturb me. What few people realize is that relationship between Roosevelt and me had been basically political and seldom social. Strange as it may seem, the President never took me into the bosom of the family, although everyone agreed I was more responsible than any other single man for his being in the White House. Never was I invited to spend the night in the historic mansion. Only twice did I ever make a cruise on the presidential yacht. Both cruises were political. Never was I invited to join informal White House gatherings. My appearances there were for official social functions or for informal dinners followed by exploration of political and patronage problems. Mrs. Eleanor Roosevelt once said, "Franklin finds it hard to relax with people who aren't his social equals." I took this remark to explain my being out of the infield.

In my probing of the past, it must be remembered that I came to Washington almost unknown outside of New York State. I entered the Cabinet a little bewildered by the pace of events about me. Woodrow Wilson said, "Every man who takes office in Washington either grows or swells." There have been those who said I was one who grew. I sincerely hope I was one of that number. Deep within me I know I learned much about men and events.

The first ripple across the placid pond of our relations came and went, almost unnoticed, in the 1936 campaign. On October 14, I met the President when he arrived in Chicago, where he was given a tremendous reception from throngs in the street and at the Stadium where he delivered a militant campaign address. I came in for a share of the ovation, as campaign leader. On occasions when I joined the President on rear platform appearances, taking care to be deep in the background, I was invariably greeted by shouts of "Hello, Jim," or "Hi, Jim." I was singled out because even the most enthusiastic in the crowds hesitated at crying, "Hello, Frank," or "Hi, Frank."

The day after the Chicago speech Marvin H. McIntyre came to see me in my room aboard the Presidential Special, somewhat ill at ease, to tell me that "they thought it best" that thereafter I should not appear on the platform with the President because of the Tammany situation. I was indignant, knowing my presence could not have been resented by anyone except those disturbed by the widespread friendship I had gained. At that time there was no situation in Tammany. If there had been one, I could not have been involved in it. I knew the President did not want me on the platform, but I could only guess why. I was certain that my temporary banishment was the result of presidential direction, because I ate with him several times on the trip and he never remarked on my absence.

The taste of ashes was not long in my mouth, however, because when the President came to the Biltmore Hotel in New York City, on October 31, to address committee workers, his reference to me was most generous.

A few weeks later I learned the pendulum of presidential favor again swung against me when Basil O'Connor, Roosevelt's former law partner, reported the President thought that I was nursing presidential aspirations for 1940. This simply was not true. The campaign was then almost four years away, and there were more deserving men in the party than myself. Yet, I have often wondered whether this uneasy suspicion colored my subsequent relations with Roosevelt.

Jealousy may be too strong a word to describe reluctance to praise those who rendered him invaluable services or to elevate the deserving. He was fond of confuting critics by saying they could not see the forest for the trees; which, in turn, gave rise to the observation that he did not like to see the trees grow too tall around him. Many, many times Vice President Garner told me that whenever he praised me to the President, Roosevelt would look at the ceiling, at the floor, or out of the window, or he would busy himself with papers on his desk. Garner said that the President, on such occasions, never returned the Vice President's gaze or never echoed the latter's friendly reference. I also have remarked on this curious hesitancy of FDR's, which made it appear that praise of others embarrassed him.

An instance of his reluctance to praise is in my files. Late in January of 1937, Charley Michelson came to me saying I might as well know, since I would probably find it out anyway, that I was going to be given a testimonial dinner by the Democratic National Committee in the Mayflower Hotel on February 15. He said he would like to have a letter from the President thanking me for my services to reproduce for the program. "Dead in the room," I said, to emphasize the secrecy I wished him to observe, "I haven't received such a letter since 1930." Charley growled that knowing Roosevelt, he wasn't surprised to hear it; but he promised to correct this oversight by going to the White House to demand a predated letter of gratitude. This turned up a few days later, and Charley brought it in with a wry smile. It read:

November 4, 1936.

DEAR JIM:

You were right—so right that I thought you were more of an optimist than a prophet. I find I am the one who needs to have his long-range spectacles adjusted. But in this instance, Jim, I don't mind being wrong at all.

Very sincerely yours,

FRANKLIN D. ROOSEVELT

There was no mention of my services even after a special request. However, as Charley acidly observed, FDR had admitted he was wrong for the first time since he entered the White House. Yet in his remarks at the dinner a few nights later, the President was most generous in saying:

"History has recorded, and will continue to record, a great many interesting facts about Jim. In due time history will talk, talk out loud about his younger days of public service to his town on the Hudson River, and his county, and his state. History will talk about his organizing of campaigns in state and nation. It will speak of his fine service as a member of the Cabinet of the United States—as administrator of an important department of the Federal government.

"It may even add his name to the distinguished list of the 'Major Prophets.' Some of us old people remember 1896. Even as the name of William Jennings Bryan stood for, even as the name of the great Commoner sometimes suggests, the arithmetic of 16 to 1, even so perhaps the name of Jim Farley will suggest the more modern arithmetic of 46 to 2.

"But when history is written, after all of us have passed from the scene, there will be something more important than the mere chronicle of success in Public Office. In the book of history there are going to be other things written. *Loyalty* will be written there—that *loyalty* to friends that results in *loyalty* from friends.

"Honor and decency will be written there—the honor and decency that have done much to raise the standards of public service in the American nation. Good temper will be writ there—the kind of good temper that is based on a sense of perspective, a sense of humor, and a sense of forgiveness."

During the dinner, the President, Vice President Garner, and I chatted between courses. One exchange involved Paul V. McNutt, former Governor of Indiana, and his impending appointment as United States High Commissioner to the Philippines.

"I'm not so sure," the President mused, "because McNutt is inclined to be dictatorial in his attitude and he might not be the right fellow to send out there. Maybe he ought to go on the Maritime Commission."

"I don't know him very well," Garner put in, "but I know he is a candidate for the Presidency in 1940 and it might not be a bad idea to send him out there."

The President smiled thoughtfully.

"Do you think the Philippines will be far enough?" I asked.

"Yes, yes," he laughed.

Somewhere around the salad course, I asked him how his legislative program was shaping up. "Famously," he answered, adding that he hoped to send Congress away in June with everything cleaned up.

"And next year," he went on with the air of imparting a great secret, "why, they'll have nothing to do up on the Hill but campaign for reelection." He became suddenly solemn. "You know, Jim, it's a great comfort to me to know that there is no campaign lying in wait for me at the end of this four years. Yes sir, nothing but a nice, long rest at Hyde Park."

Yet, in the months to come, he was to find fault with a long list of suspected and actual aspirants to his succession. They were either too old or too young; too ambitious or too unknown; too conservative or too radical, or in too poor health or too lacking in personality. Basil O'Connor had revealed the President as cataloguing me in the ambitious class. In many cases, displeasure was rooted in the Supreme Court reorganization plan; I am not sure it was not so in my case. Although I supported him to the hilt in his drive for Court reform, I could not and did not go along with him on the no less disastrous and ill-fated attempt to purge the Democratic party of those who had opposed his will. While he approved my course, even to certifying my statement that as party chairman I would not participate in the purge, I believe that deep down inside, he never forgave me for putting party welfare above the personal allegiance he considered his due.

On February 4, 1937, the day before he sent what came to be known as the "Court Packing Plan" to the Senate, I saw the President in his bedroom at 9:15 A.M. Not a word did he drop about the program during the conference devoted to consideration of a number of appointments. I was aware that something was in the making, but was not in on the framing conferences with Attorney General Cummings, Judge Sam Rosenman of New York, and others. Tuesday night, February 2, he had given his annual dinner to the Supreme Court. All but two of the "Nine Old Men"—eighty-year-old Louis D. Brandeis and sixty-four-year-old Harlan Stone—broke bread with him. No doubt Roosevelt hugely enjoyed every minute of the dinner, knowing the surprise he had in store for his guests.

I, like the members of the Court, first learned the details of the plan from the newspapers. I was in New York City and did not attend the Cabinet meeting at which he outlined his plan. I did not return to Washington until February 11. Before my return, I had heard of the Capitol Hill mutterings against the plan and the manner of its submission. In the morning I discussed the program with Homer Cummings, with reference to the attitude of Democratic Senators. I twitted Homer about Senator Glass's sizzler: "The country is infinitely in greater need of an Attorney General than of additional judges of the Supreme Court, or judicial wet-nurses for six of the present members of the Court." He took it good-naturedly. At noon I lunched with the President, who was in the best of humor.

"Boss," I asked him, "why didn't you advise the Senators in advance that you were sending the Court bill to them?"

"Jim, I just couldn't," he answered earnestly. "I didn't want to have it get out prematurely to the press. More than once when I've had groups of Senators and Congressmen down here, reporters have gathered a detailed account of what went on within 48 hours. I didn't want it to happen again."

"Well," I yielded, "I suppose it's all right, but I wouldn't let it happen again. You ought to be more careful, because you know how they like to be consulted, and justly so."

"True, true," he nodded, "I'll watch out for it in the future. This is very important to me; it's something that affects the heart of my program. I'll keep them here all year to pass it, if necessary."

"If you don't get it through this session, I think it will be far more difficult to pass it in an election year."

"You're right, Jim, I must pass it at this session. I'll need help. I want you to help. I'm going to have Senators and Congressmen down in groups and explain what this means. We must bring the Court in step with the New Deal."

"Are you entirely satisfied with the wisdom of your course?" I asked

pointedly. "Certainly," was his unhesitating answer. "Certainly."
"You can count on me then, Boss. I will keep in contact with those
who are supporting you on the Hill, and do my best to bring the
others around."

"First off," continued the President, "we must hold up judicial appointments in states where the delegation is not going along. We must
make them promptly where they are with us. Where there is a division, we must give posts to those supporting us. Second, this must apply to other appointments as well as judicial appointments. I'll keep in
close contact with the leaders."

During the next few weeks I was busy seeing Senators and Congressmen, urging support of the program. I found no serious opposition to
three proposals advanced in the message. These would have granted
the Chief Justice power to make assignments of lower judges, on a
temporary basis, from one court to another when dockets became con-
gested; would have created a new officer, a proctor, who would watch
for congestion and recommend relieving transfers; and would have
granted challenges of constitutionality direct access to the Supreme
Court. The issue was drawn in the following words in his message: "I
therefore earnestly recommend the appointment of additional judges
in all Federal courts, without exception, where there are incumbent
judges of retirement age who do not choose to retire or resign." This
would have empowered him to appoint not more than fifty new judges
to duplicate men of seventy years who had had at least ten years on
the bench. The crucial point in the appointments was that it would
have permitted him to increase the Supreme Court, in the event those
of retirement age would not leave, by six justices. As the opposition put
it: he would pack the Court with six New Dealers to give him a majority of two over the confirmed conservative Court bloc which had
consistently opposed him.

The battle lines developed slowly. On the Democratic side Senators
Wheeler of Montana, Clark of Missouri, and Burke of Nebraska came
out against the plan early. Senator Johnson, California's veteran Republican, who had enjoyed Roosevelt support, was among the first to
protest on the spare Republican side of the Senate chamber. Majority
Leader Robinson of Arkansas, Venerable Senator Harrison of Mis-

sissippi, and suave Senator Byrnes of South Carolina, a skillful cloak-room operator, took up cudgels for the program. Early in the game it was apparent that some thirty Senators, holding the balance of power, were lying low to see how the wind would blow from home.

The Republican strategy, which was perfected by the wily, leonine Borah, was masterful: the only way to beat the program was to let the Democrats fight the issue out among themselves. He was aware that opposition to the plan in the Democratic ranks was strong and that even the party's leadership had grave doubts of its wisdom. Borah knew that if the Republicans, reduced to a corporal's guard in Congress by the 1936 landslide, were to make a party issue of the Court plan, the Democrats would unite and steam-roller the program through the Senate and House. He had difficulty in persuading less astute colleagues from trying to steal the issue from the Democratic opposition. In this event Roosevelt would have been triumphant on what would certainly have become a party-line vote. As it was, the battle lines were almost evenly drawn on issue rather than by party. The Roosevelt forces strove mightily to make the plan a matter of party loyalty.

At the Washington Democratic Victory Dinner, Roosevelt publicly avowed his intention to retire at the end of his second term, which he had confided to me not long before. In one of his best orations, delivered to the nation, more than to the 1,500 diners who had paid $100 a plate to attend the function, he said:

"A few days ago a distinguished member of Congress came to see me. . . . I said to him, 'John, I want to tell you something that is very personal to me—something that you have a right to hear from my own lips. I have a great ambition in life. . . . John, my ambition relates to January 20, 1941!' "

He paused dramatically. There was not a sound in the room. Everyone leaned forward to listen. He was speaking in studied earnestness; but he later acknowledged to me he knew he had his audience in the palm of his hand and was enjoying himself immensely.

"I could just feel what horrid thoughts my friend was thinking. So in order to relieve his anxiety, I went on to say, 'My great ambition on January 20, 1941, is to turn over this desk to my successor, whoever he may be, with the assurance that I am at the same time turning over to him as President, a nation intact. I want to get the nation as far along the road of progress as I can. I do not want to leave it to my successor in the condition in which Buchanan left it to Lincoln."

I was never able to identify "John." It was not John Nance Garner or John Bankhead. The President referred to "John" on other occasions, when he wanted to emphasize his position on some measure pending in Congress. Evidently "John" was a convenient character he created as a composite of various Congressional leaders.

Roosevelt's words had a familiar ring. Later I found their substance was contained in an interview secured by Arthur Krock of the *New York Times*. Roosevelt added "John" in making the interview his speech.

Roosevelt did not directly mention the Court plan. But he did say "you know who" vetoed the Agricultural Adjustment Act and "you know who" vetoed the Democratic administration's efforts to raise wages, reduce hours, abolish child labor, and eliminate unfair trade practices. The address won wide approval and heartened his supporters in the Court battle.

His oratorical guns were directly trained on the Supreme Court in his tenth "fireside" chat the next week. He pulled no punches in a direct denunciation of the Court's personnel, saying:

"Our difficulty with the Court today rises not from the Court as an institution but from the human beings within it. But we cannot yield our Constitutional destiny to the personal judgment of a few men who, being fearful of the future, would deny us the necessary means of dealing with the present."

He sought to dignify the "Court packing" taunt of the opposition by asserting that the charge he wished to place "spineless puppets" on the bench was ridiculous. He continued:

"But if by that phrase the charge is made that I would appoint and the Senate would confirm justices worthy to sit beside present members of the Court who understand . . . modern conditions—that I will appoint justices who will not undertake to override the judgment of Congress on legislative policy; . . . then I say that I and with me the vast majority of the American people favor doing just that thing—now."

CHAPTER NINE

THE COURT FIGHT

L
ONG BEFORE the Court bill reached the Senate floor and even before any committee hearings were held in either branch of Congress, the issue touched off oratorical fireworks in the Senate and House. The cry of dictatorship was raised. The tumult and uproar in Congress was nothing to the sound and fury in the press. Up and down the land the issue was being debated. Before he left for a Warm Springs, Georgia, vacation the President said he was surprised that the opposition was far less thunderous than he anticipated. I do not know how much of this was whistling in the dark, because I found the opposition was making more than enough noise for me, especially the vocal Democratic opposition.

As party chairman I recognized at once that the introduction of the judicial program gave the President's scattered opponents a common ground to mobilize on. The Republicans had been routed by his overwhelming defeat of Landon. Other opposition had been scattered. Now they had an opportunity to reorganize and they were making the most of it, which was certainly good politics. However, the President was undismayed, although he knew that the issue marked a turning point in his administration. He was confident of victory, while I was tormented with doubts. Reform of the Court had crossed his path with bad luck for four years like an ill-omened black cat, but it was close to his heart. He was fully aware of the bearing this legislation would have on the course of his administration.

The President entered the fight in an excellent frame of mind. He indicated that he would seek to woo the opposition with flattery and soft words; that he had no intention of blustering or browbeating. Before he left for Warm Springs, he told me he felt all right, except that he was a bit tired. He expected to come back "rarin' to go." Of course, he was always happier when he was in a fight.

By phone from Warm Springs a few days later, he told me he was feeling great; that he was ready and eager for the fray. I reported the Senate was divided into almost equal thirds—one group in favor of the bill, another opposed, and a crop of fence sitters. He said we would have to get the fence sitters back into the barnyard. He said he was sending Tommy Corcoran, RFC counsel, and Joseph Keenan, of the Department of Justice, around to "turn the heat on" the opposition. He expressed himself certain that he had the situation under control, refusing to discuss the various alternative and compromise proposals floating around the Hill. Keenan and Corcoran set to work scolding and beating Senators in amazing fashion.

While he was still in Warm Springs, I went to Texas to dedicate a number of post offices. I was satisfied that things were coming along all right. By the end of the month almost everything that could be said for and against the program had been said in Congress. Both sides settled down to working on the undecided, undetermined, and unsettled one-third. The old game of jockeying for position, tempting with favor, and appealing to principle began.

The political tug of war was going on behind the scenes, while the public show was going on before the Senate Judiciary Committee. The administration marshalled an impressive parade of deans of law schools, who were in turn heckled by the opposition. Homer Cummings and Assistant Attorney General Robert H. Jackson ably presented the administration's case. For the opposition, Senator Wheeler exploded a bombshell by producing a letter from venerable Chief Justice Hughes which assailed the argument that the Court was overburdened. This was a staggering blow. From a sickbed came that doughty old gamecock, Senator Glass, to scream such epithets as "frightful . . . iniquitous . . . hateful . . . repugnant . . . utterly destitute of moral sensibility" against the plan.

As usual, there was never a dull moment along the Potomac.

On his return to Washington, the President closeted himself with Vice President Garner, Speaker Bankhead, Majority Leader Robinson, and House Leader Rayburn to be brought up to date on the Court fight. On April 1, I had lunch at the White House with the President and Senator Hugo Black of Alabama. Our conference was largely devoted to the progress of the Court fight.

"All we have to do," the President said happily, "is to let the flood of mail settle on Congress. You just see. All I have to do is deliver a better speech, and the opposition will be beating a path to the White House door."

The President said that the proponents of the plan unquestionably were having the better of the argument; that the program would soon be brought to the Senate floor where it would be passed. In general, I agreed, but noted that it might take longer than he expected. Black cautioned that the opposition was most determined and would exercise every means of delay, knowing that their only hope lay in avoiding a vote.

"We'll smoke 'em out," the President said. "If delay helps them, we must press for an early vote."

Black had expressed displeasure over the appointments of Rear Admiral Emory S. Land and Rear Admiral H. A. Wiley to the Maritime Commission. Black was irked because the appointments were announced without his having been advised, when he had understood that he was to be consulted. The President soothed him and soon had him smiling and promising to go along with the appointees, whose capacities he had questioned.

On April 12, 1937, I talked with Roosevelt by phone from New York City after the Supreme Court validated the Wagner Act by a five to four decision. He was jubilant.

"We did it," he chortled. "I am very, very pleased. You ought to see Homer Cummings, who's sitting with me now. He looks like the Cheshire cat that swallowed the canary. It's wonderful.

"I am convinced more than ever that the proposals for reform of the Court are warranted. It's the same four justices who have dissented all along that are against me this time—McReynolds, Butler, Sutherland, and Van Devanter."

I called up Senator Wagner to congratulate him and found him also riding the clouds. He addressed me as "Mr. President" by way of recognizing the fact that my name was high on a Gallup poll list of possibilities for the 1940 Democratic presidential nomination the day before. He, like the President, was surprised by the Court's decision as it had been expected to go the other way. I quoted Finley Peter Dunne,

"No matter whether th' constitution follows th' flag or not, th' Supreme Court follows th' iliction returns." I suggested maybe the Court was doing a little electioneering against the packing plan in the decision.

The decision did serve to support arguments for the need of a change. None of us had any doubt of passage of the program. Thomas G. Corcoran, who was shuttling through the halls of Congress on behalf of the program, dropped by a few times to discuss his lobbying. I was polite, but hardly warm because I was never certain whether the chubby White House confidant was working for the President or for himself; I was quite certain he was not too concerned about the Democratic party. Also, I had reports that he and Keenan were doing more harm than good among Democrats by their tactics.

So swimmingly were things moving along that when I went to the White House for a bedside conference on April 19, the Court program was barely mentioned.

"Jim, we've got an unpleasant job ahead of us," he began. "I've told you that I would keep my Cabinet as it stands except Harry Woodring. At the time I appointed him, after George Dern's death, it was understood that the appointment would be temporary. I am going to send for Harry Woodring. You send for Louis Johnson. Maybe it would be a good idea for you to talk to Harry, too. Be sure to tell them both it will not be a permanent appointment."

"General Malin Craig was in to see me about Harry; the Army thinks very highly of him," I said. "Louis was in, too, to ask me about getting into the Cabinet. I think Harry is doing a good job and deserves an appointment to prove his fitness for the job. Incidentally, I may be wanting to get out, if I make a satisfactory business connection, which will bring up consideration of William Howes, my first assistant, as my successor."

"I'd hate to see you go, Jim, but if you must, you must; and as long as you remain as party Chairman, it will be all right," Roosevelt said. "I suppose I'd have to give some consideration to Frank Walker and Ed Flynn."

"Walker would make a splendid Cabinet officer, so would Flynn; I'll talk further with you when the time comes—when and if, that is."

"Fine. You know I'd like to get rid of Dan Roper; he talks too much and doesn't get anywhere. I'd like to send him to the Philippines, but I guess it would be better to send Woodring. You know there might be some objection to Dan because he has been accused of being a Klansman. While I don't believe it for a minute, the feeling exists that he has such leanings; probably he was so labeled because he didn't come out for Al Smith in 1928. Maybe we could find him a diplomatic post."

Late that April, I went on one of my stamp selling tours, as I called them, into New England and the Middle West. Before I left I saw Woodring and Johnson as I promised. On reporting to the White House, I found the President had put off tackling Woodring. I was not surprised, as he invariably avoided a showdown, if he could. Subsequently he reappointed Harry. Whether rightly or wrongly, Woodring and General Craig attributed the decision to my support.

It was in May that the handwriting on the wall, which had been regarded as favorable to the Court plan, was translated into the bitter truth of opposition by Senate leaders. Defeat was certain unless enough Democratic Senators could be persuaded to support the President. There was still hope that a compromise might be effected. Senator Burke seized upon the argument for young blood on the bench to propose a Constitutional amendment which would allow Justices to retire on full pay at the age of seventy and require them to do so at the age of seventy-five. This was originally suggested by Representative Hatton Summers of Texas. Senator Norris of Nebraska would have limited the Court's power to declare laws unconstitutional. Senator Ashurst of Arizona would have amended the Constitution to give the Federal government power to achieve New Deal aims. Senator Wheeler would have been satisfied with an amendment permitting Congress to override a Court "veto" after the next general election following an adverse Court decision. Senator Borah proposed to rewrite the Fourteenth Amendment so as to redefine its "due process" clause to make it apply only to the Federal government, leaving the states unlimited power to conduct social and economic experiments.

Congressional leaders said the situation was bad. Tommy Corcoran came by with the corners of his mouth turned down. I told him that as soon as the President returned from his fishing cruise in the Gulf of Mexico, we should sit down with him to find out just what course to pursue; if we had enough votes, we should go through with the contest to the finish; if not, we should determine what we might gain in a compromise. Congressional leaders agreed that the President should be advised before his return. James Roosevelt, son and secretary, went to meet his father at Fort Worth. I went to meet him at Indianapolis.

I found Roosevelt undaunted. Thoroughly rested by his vacation, he was thrilling to the scent of battle in the air. He would not consider compromise. When I told him polls were showing the Senate so evenly divided that Garner might have to cast the deciding vote, he snapped, "Let him do it." I counseled him to consider the possibility that the party would be split beyond repair, which provoked the surprising declaration "and good riddance, too." At one point he looked out of the window of his special car and said, almost to himself, "This comes from telling them I would not be a candidate again." He said with all the finality at his command that he would not withdraw as much as an inch and he would not compromise.

In Washington, the President was greeted at Union Station by a few members of his official and private families. Three years before, he returned from a southern fishing trip to throw down the gauntlet to another Congress in revolt, to find thirty Senators and two hundred Congressmen on hand with a band to meet him. That revolt vanished in the warmth of that welcome, but not a member of the second rebelling Congress was on hand that May morning.

The Court packing plan was defeated by a one-two punch. The paralyzing blow was delivered in the resignation of Justice Van Devanter, staunch member of the "Old Guard" bloc. The knockout blow was the death a few weeks later of Joe Robinson, who kept the plan afloat in troubled Congressional currents by the sheer force of a remarkable personality. Robinson had unflinching support from Byrnes and Harrison.

It was on May 18, 1937, that Van Devanter sent his resignation to the White House. Despite denials, the move was widely interpreted as an adroit conservative maneuver calculated to weaken the President's wavering Senate ranks, by a voluntary breaking up of the bloc which had long troubled the President.

If other "Old Guard" resignations would follow, I felt the President would accept a compromise, since he would be able to make several liberal appointments. I felt hopeful the Senate and the President might be able to save face. If he could appoint a number of liberal justices, he might be willing to hold the packing down to two new justices as proposed by Senator Hatch. The Senate, I thought, would be inclined to go along, particularly if one of the new Court posts would go to Robinson in recognition of his services. I was encouraged in these thoughts by the friendly tone of the President's letter accepting the resignation. He wrote:

May 18, 1937.

DEAR MR. JUSTICE VAN DEVANTER:

I received your letter of this morning telling me that you are retiring from regular active service on the bench June 2, 1937.

May I as one who has had the privilege of knowing you for many years, extend to you every good wish.

Before you leave Washington for the summer, it would give me great personal pleasure if you would come in to see me.

Very sincerely yours,
FRANKLIN D. ROOSEVELT

When I saw the letter on the office news ticker, I called the President. I found him unperturbed about the future.

"I wanted you to know I thought you wrote a most interesting and amusing letter," I said, "particularly in the line extending the invitation to him to pay a call before he leaves."

"If I receive the resignation of a certain other judge on the bench, you can be sure he won't get a similar invitation," he said meaningly.

"It wouldn't happen to be a certain southern gentleman answering to the name of McReynolds?" I asked.

"Still the prophet, Jim. That's exactly the one I had in mind. I'd love to write him a letter, even though he wouldn't go where I'd like to invite him to go—not yet."

He laughed uproariously.

In the midst of the Court struggle, Vice President Garner packed up and went home to Uvalde, Texas. He had told me he was going to take a vacation, so I thought nothing of it until newspaper stories attributed Garner's absence to a rift with the President, precipitated by the Court fight. At a White House luncheon on June 18, 1937, I found the President smoldering over the absence of the presiding officer of the Senate.

"Why in hell did Jack have to leave at this time for?" he fumed through a cloud of cigarette smoke. "I'm going to write and tell him about all these stories and suggest he come back. This is a fine time to jump ship. What's eating him?"

"Well, Boss, I'm sure Jack isn't peeved at all. I do know he was peeved over a friend in the HOLC, a fellow named Dick Tullis, who had not been reinstated because of activity against Congressman Maverick in the last campaign."

"Send for Maverick and try to work it out. He's got to come back."

"O.K., but I think you'll find Jack just went on a vacation and dropped off to see his son, Tulley."

"He ought to be back. I'll have Mac call him." He called McIntyre in from the outer office and gave him orders.

"Let him spend a couple of weeks in Uvalde," I suggested.

"All right, if you insist; a couple of weeks more won't make any difference," he grumbled.

I don't think the President ever forgave Garner. I believe this marked the beginning of coolness on his part. In the past he had accepted criticism from Garner good-naturedly, evidently aware Jack would finally support him even against his own judgment. Thereafter things were never the same between them; so I judged from my seat at the Cabinet table. I wrote Garner, enclosing several pertinent news clippings and suggesting he return. On July 1, 1937, he wrote the following interesting reply from Uvalde:

Dear Jim:

Your favor of the 28th, with enclosures, is just received.

When I see articles such as Mr. Stokes's story, especially those saying that there is a break between the "Boss" and myself, it peeves me, and yet I know that you and the "Boss" and the others who are acquainted with the facts know that there isn't any truth in it.

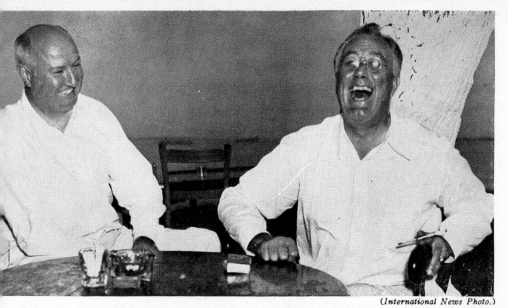

June 27, 1937—Although the Supreme Court fight defeat rankled in the President's breast, he and I had a hearty laugh at the Jefferson Island Club only a few days after the bill was lost (see pages 94–96).

This is one of those rare pictures in which the President and I are not smiling. It presents an interesting contrast to the one above, especially in view of events as they developed.

September 5, 1938—Purge prescribed. FDR went to Crisfield, Maryland, in an attempt to purge Senator Millard Tydings, a candidate for renomination. This picture shows, left to right, President Roosevelt, Representative David Lewis (Tydings's opponent), and Representative T. Alan Goldsborough of Maryland (see page 144).

I have never said a word touching the Administration that the "Boss," you and the others could not have been present and heard. Frankly, Jim, I have almost gotten to love Roosevelt from a personal standpoint.

I think he has been over-reached in some things or else he has arrived at conclusions which to my mind can't be sustained from a standpoint of statesmanship or patriotism. I refer particularly to the sit-down strikes and mass lawlessness, which, to me, is intolerable and will lead to great difficulty, if not destruction.

I am not only unalterably opposed to mass violation of the law, but any kind of tolerance of violation of the law, regardless of class. That is why I have for twenty-odd years cried out against the combined Wall Street violation of the spirit of the law as well as a large percentage of actual violation without receiving punishment. Moreover, as you well know, I have believed for the last two years that we should have been materially reducing our expenditures; that we could not go on indefinitely borrowing money to run the Government.

The "Boss" apparently makes up his mind that he is going to follow a certain line of economy, but within three to six months somebody has talked him into a different policy or, by asking so many exceptions to the policy, the exceptions become the rule.

I know you have heard me say in the Cabinet that I thought Henry Wallace's agricultural policy was fundamentally unsound, but I realize that he and the President's advisers, who have had actual experience in the premises, have observed the practical difficulties more than I have, and I have gone along with that policy whole-heartedly; and, I am egotistical enough to say that I have been helpful in it.

Now, my feelings about the above propositions have been freely expressed to you and the "Boss." I have not expressed them as freely to others since it would appear that I was too much of a critic. Jim, I have got to be honest, honest with myself, with you, with the "Boss," and others with whom I have to deal, therefore I can only speak frankly.

Along about last March you will recall that I announced that I was going to take my vacation all at once, beginning about the first of June. Everyone thought we would be thru about then for the program was short. Later on the "Chief" decided he would enlarge the program very materially. I didn't see any reason why I should change my vacation plans, in view of Mrs. Garner and the grandchild's arrangements, because of the enlarged program.

I have taken the time to encumber you with this long letter so that you may have the whole picture and know how I feel. I know the "Boss" knows it, and it made me unhappy when Marvin McIntyre told me that he was annoyed by me leaving. If he had told me, at any cost I would have made other arrangements. I plead for his unlimited confidence since he has mine to the fullest extent. I am subject to his call at any moment.

Mrs. Garner joins me in love and best wishes for you and the family.

Sincerely your friend,

Jno. N. Garner

I wrote him the President thought it would be best for him to return as soon as possible. Garner replied July 8, saying if the President needed him he would head for the capital, "as soon as I conveniently can, if I have the strength to travel, and I surely have it now, as I am feeling fine and getting hard as a brick and black as a Yaqui Indian." I sent the "Boss" copies of the letters.

Returning to the White House conference, the President and I talked of the Court fight. He still refused to regard the situation as desperate, which it was. He could have had a two-justice compromise easily in April, but this concession was most doubtful in early June. He would not talk of yielding ground. I urged again the appointment of Robinson to the Van Devanter vacancy, holding that the nomination would be an excellent thing with which to end the session, as it would leave a good taste in everyone's mouth. Homer Cummings came in and added his voice to mine. The President said he would make the appointment. I asked him to keep the name of Owen D. Young in the back of his mind for other vacancies which might occur. The next morning I called Robinson and relayed the President's promise after greeting him as "Mr. Justice." I told him to sit steady in the boat and not to rock it, and all would be well. He was most grateful for the news.

It was Robinson who finally persuaded the President to take a realistic view of the Court battle. In a two hour night conference, he convinced the President that compromise was the only course. Unfortunately the grains of sand in his hourglass were running low and he was not to have time to direct the final phase of the lost cause. He might have saved much.

I left to attend the annual Elks' convention in Denver, arriving in that city Tuesday morning, June 13, 1937. Wednesday morning at 6:30 A.M. I was awakened by the Associated Press reporting that Robinson was dead. I had known of Robinson's heart ailment for a long, long time. In the midst of the Court fight, he took a two weeks' rest; he had been observing a strict diet. There is no question that the strain of the Court battle, together with the heat of a Washington summer, was responsible for his sudden collapse. I had great admiration for the hot-tempered statesman, because he was a man of courage and loyalty. While he did not agree with some of the policies advanced by the President, he fought ably for their passage, giving freely of his time and efforts. At the time of the news of his passing, I recognized that the opposition would seek for early adjournment in the hope that the Court plan would be abandoned. I expected the President would elect to carry on the battle.

Friday morning I attended the services for Senator Robinson in the Senate chamber. As we gathered in the President's room, there was muttering about the "Dear Alben" letter Roosevelt had addressed to Senator Barkley denouncing rumors that the Court bill was to be abandoned. Friends of Senator Harrison felt the Chief Executive had employed the letter to indicate he favored Barkley for the leadership. When the President entered he asked me to drop by the White House for a chat at 4:15 P.M. This I did. I was on time but had to wait for fifteen or twenty minutes while the President talked with Senator Byrnes, who was managing Harrison's campaign for the leadership as Guffey was managing Barkley's.

The "Dear Alben" letter said, "Since the untimely death of our majority leader I had hoped, with you, that at least until his funeral services had been held, a decent respect for his memory would have deferred discussion of political and legislative matters." It wound up with a demand for a fight to the finish. Many Congressional faces flushed with anger when the letter was made public because it was felt that the President had taken up politics before the Robinson funeral, while accusing others of not observing a decent mourning period. The President decided against attending the funeral. I considered this decision a grave mistake.

The finish fight which the President called Barkley to wage was on the Robinson measure which specified one new Justice for every Court member over the age of seventy-five but limited the President to one appointment a year. When debate opened, I came in for a heavy verbal barrage for an off-the-record remark I made on leaving the President. A reporter put me on the spot by asking how the Court fight stood. I dodged by countering with an off-the-record question as to how such Senators as McCarran of Nevada and O'Mahoney of Wyoming could afford not to vote for the bill if they ever wanted anything from the administration. My remark lost no news value in the reporting. This was one of only two times in seven and one-half years in Washington when a statement I put off the record was published.

McCarran rose from a sickbed to make a dramatic appearance before the Senate. He announced that he was speaking against his doctor's orders and sealing his own political death.

"I think this cause is worthy of any man's life," he cried, most effectively. He added, "When Farley said that if I asked for something for my humble state there would be a different viewpoint, he wrote my death warrant and he knew it, and I may today be delivering my valedictory by reason of a mandate of Mr. Farley."

It wasn't that bad, as time has proved; but it was bad enough for me. Worse for me, in fact, than for either McCarran or O'Mahoney, because I knew I had made it impossible for either of them to vote for the President. It taught me a powerful lesson in holding my tongue.

"Boss, I want to be very direct," I said after exchanging greetings, when I was ushered to Roosevelt's desk that afternoon by McIntyre.

"Well, shoot, Jim," he invited.

"Why did you write that letter to Barkley?"

"A letter was the easiest way to get over what I wanted."

"But criticism has come from the fact that it was addressed to Barkley."

"Simple enough, Jim. I couldn't have sent it to Garner who's away, or to Key Pittman who was in the Chair; so, inasmuch as Barkley is acting leader, I properly sent it to him."

"But the impression has got around . . ."

"Yes, I know," he interrupted, "that I'm supporting Barkley against Harrison. Well, it just isn't so."

"I'm glad to hear it," I said. "I'm going to keep my hands off. It's a matter for the Senate—the Democratic members of the Senate. I'm going to tell Barkley and Harrison that."

"Good," he approved, "I'm going to see Pat Harrison at five o'clock and tell him I'm not against him. Of course, if he's elected, Pat will have to spend all his time at the job, because it will be necessary that he familiarize himself with all legislation. He will have to be on the floor all the time and, if he does that, it will be difficult for him to carry on his work as Chairman of the Finance Committee. It might mean he will have to resign that post and, if he does, it would go to Senator King of Utah, who, as you know, is a bitter foe of the administration. King is just impossible to deal with."

"Let's leave that until we have to face it," I said.

"Joe's death was a heavy loss," the President said. "I appreciated his splendid services. He was wonderful in the Court fight. I was going to put him on the Supreme Court for it. By the way, are you going to Little Rock for the funeral?"

"Yes."

"Jim, I wish you'd be my eyes and ears on the trip. Visit around among the Senators and Congressmen on the train to and from Arkansas and try to get a line on what they're thinking. Report to me as soon as you return."

"Of course. I'll see Garner at the funeral."

"Oh, yes. Ask him about his return here. I am satisfied that Jack is coming back because I've talked with him, but be sure and visit with him as soon as you can in Little Rock."

The funeral train arrived at Little Rock at 7:30 A.M. I went to Mass with Senator Henry F. Ashurst and Congressman John O'Connor of New York. Funeral services were held at the First Methodist Church, where I was pleased to see the Most Reverend John B. Morris, Catholic Bishop of Little Rock, give a splendid lesson in tolerance by entering a pew to pay homage to the dead.

During the ride down and back I had conferences with all the Senators and Congressmen of both parties. I was amazed at the amount of bitterness which had been engendered by the long struggle over the Court issue. I found men of stature growing quite petty in their remarks about one another. It was evident that it would be difficult to heal the split made by the fight, since the salt of unkind words had been rubbed into the party's wound. I was satisfied that only the soothing passage of time and the most delicate nursing would bring the factions into a united Democratic front again. Both sides were claiming victory in the contest. There was no doubt, however, that the best the President could hope for was a compromise.

CHAPTER TEN

COURT AFTERMATH

O N THE RETURN trip Garner boarded the funeral train. He told
me he was all set to clear up any erroneous impressions caused
by his absence. I had visits with Harrison and Barkley, the contenders for the leadership, and their respective campaign managers,
Byrnes and Guffey. I told them, without equivocation, each in the
presence of the other, that I would not turn a hand in their contest,
and that the President had assured me he also would not. Harrison
said the President had so advised him Friday afternoon. I said they
were both friends of mine and that the selection of either would be
entirely satisfactory to me. I added I intended to keep my friendship
with the winner and the loser in the race; and both declared, as far
as they were concerned, that would be so.

Byrnes told me I had probably done more to make Robinson's last
days happy than anyone else. He said he and Harrison were with Robinson the Saturday morning I made the call advising him of the impending Court appointment. Robinson repeated my conversation, saying he could not keep the wonderful news from such good friends.
The news buoyed Robinson up in the fight, Byrnes added, because
the Majority Leader was confident that when I told him it would work
out satisfactorily, he could go to sleep on it.

Robinson was vexed, according to Byrnes, over the President's silence on the appointment. I explained that the President probably felt
that it was desirable for him to be in a position to say he had never
discussed the appointment with Robinson when the time came to
make it. I said I was sure the President wanted to be able to say Robinson had not fought the good fight on account of any commitment
made him about judicial hopes, even though he was aware Robinson expected elevation to the Court; so did Mrs. Robinson and so did their
friends.

We returned to Washington at 11:45 P.M. Monday. I went directly

91

to my apartment in the Mayflower. Late the next night the special
line from the White House jangled.

"Hello," I answered.

"Hello," said the voice at the other end.

"Who is it?" I asked somewhat impatiently.

"It's me," the voice responded, none too clearly.

"Who in the hell is 'me'?" I shouted.

"The President."

"Oh," said I. "What's keeping you up?"

"Jim, I want you to call Ed Kelly of Chicago right now. It's necessary to get him to put the pressure on Senator Dieterich to get him to
vote for Barkley."

"I can't do it," I said. "I said I wouldn't turn a hand either way,
for Barkley or Harrison."

"Dieterich's weakening; all we need is a phone call."

"I can't help it, I can't call Kelly."

"You mean you won't," the President said in hurt accents.

"Boss, I just can't," I protested. "I gave my word—my word to
Harrison, Barkley, Byrnes, and Guffey on the train. You yourself said
it was right for me to take no sides."

"Very well," he said curtly. "I'll get Harry Hopkins to do it."

He hung up before I could say, "Good night." I tossed restlessly
for a time afterward in distress at the thought he was going back on
his promise to Harrison, and in annoyance that he should seek to
have me go back on mine. It was the only time he ever called me at
night on the White House wire. Jesse Jones used to use it occasionally
and now and then other Cabinet officers would reach me through
the White House switchboard. Several days later Senator Dieterich
confided that Kelly had called and persuaded him to switch to Barkley.

The next morning the President called me over to his office around
eleven o'clock. He was in excellent spirits as I reported on my observations on the trip.

"Jim, I've made up my mind that after the leadership fight, I'll let
the situation ride along, if possible, to see what happens. If nothing
happens on the part of the leaders, I'll get on the radio. I'll appeal to

the people. I want the Court bill, slum clearance, wage and hour legislation, and a farm bill passed at this session."

"I believe, generally speaking, the man in the street is for your program," I said, "but those who opposed you in the last election and the party conservatives have grabbed this opportunity of the Court fight to oppose the entire legislative schedule."

He thanked me for my report on what he called my "look-see" and told me to come in tomorrow to go over the whole situation. He did not mention the phone call of the night before.

I saw the President almost immediately after Barkley was elected leader by a vote of 38 to 37. He was pleased although he acknowledged surprise at the closeness of the vote.

"I'll invite Barkley and Harrison in to lunch," he exclaimed. "It's a splendid idea. You stay, too, Jim. Then we can all get together and work everything out."

"If you don't mind," I put in, "I'd rather not. I think it would be better if I were not with you. They should eat alone with you."

"Maybe so," he let me off. "Jim, what I have in mind is this. Senator Pope was in the other day and indicated it might be well to try to pass some of the important legislation now pending, and let the Court program ride along a while. Then, in October, Congress would come back to take it up. What do you think of it?"

"Sounds all right, except I think it might be a terrible mistake on your part to abandon the fight."

"But it wouldn't be abandoning the fight; it would be just a postponement."

This was the first indication I had from him of surrender.

"I want to get wage and hour, reorganization, slum clearance, farm and judicial legislation through at this session. Then there won't be very much to do at the next session and we can take things easier."

"I think you ought to carry on the fight," I said. "I think it's just a question of getting the story before the voters."

"Yes, I know," he agreed. "I'll have to make a radio address. I know full well slum clearance is necessary, that crop control is vital to keep farm prices from getting out of hand, that wage and hour legislation

is keenly desired by all labor, and that the government needs reorganization to increase efficiency. I must tell the people that.

"And I want to tell them that some Senators and Congressmen and
the Vice President, too, are more or less antiquated in their thinking.
We can't proceed, as they would have us, on the theory that we
should let well enough alone."

I pointed out that little had been done by Congress, due to the Court
fight, except passage of the Neutrality Bill and the Farm Repeal Act.
We briefly discussed the anti-Supreme Court packing statement of
Governor Lehman of New York. The President screwed up his face
to show as expressively as he could by words his annoyance at Lehman's butting into a situation which was of deep concern to the President. I said I thought the Lehman letter was out of order and he agreed
most emphatically.

In forty-eight hours the Court bill was dead. The Senate referred it
back to the Judiciary Committee. In the final hours, it was widely recognized that Presidential defeat was inevitable. On July 23, I had lunch
with the President and found him fuming against Garner.

"He didn't even attempt to bargain with Wheeler," he said in ex-
asperation. "He just accepted Wheeler's terms. If Garner had put up
any kind of a fight, the thing could have been worked out differently."

"Weren't you a party to the agreement?" I asked.

"I most certainly was not," he snapped. "I told Garner to make
the best compromise he could. It's apparent Garner made no effort
to do so. He just capitulated to the opposition."

"Boss," I said, "I must take issue with you on Jack, who is my friend
and yours. Without knowing what happened, I'm sure that Jack did
all he could, and more than anyone else might have done. I'm certain
you'll find he tried to salvage what he could of the program, but it just
wasn't in the cards for him to win. He didn't have a winning hand."

Later the same day I talked to Garner and learned that he had most
carefully canvassed the Senate and found that the opposition had sufficient strength, for the first time in the long battle, to kill the program.
Several Senators, who were prepared to go along in order to help Robinson win a seat on the Supreme Court bench, said they were now
throwing their lot with the opposition. Aware that the President was

beaten, Garner went to Senator Wheeler and found the latter fully cognizant of the fact that he held the winning hand. Garner asked what Wheeler would settle for and was forced to capitulate when the Senator called for unconditional surrender.

"What about the rest of your program?" I asked Roosevelt at our conference.

"I'll put it up to the leaders whether they want to clean it up in a few weeks or adjourn and come back the first of October or thereabouts. Then they could clean it up before Christmas."

The President expressed himself pleased at the way he had handled his press conference that morning. He said he had showed the newspapermen he could take defeat, that he had preserved good humor throughout.

By the time luncheon ended he was in a happy frame of mind. As a matter of fact, after he had shut the Court fight surrender out of his mind, he became quite gay. I did not gather, however, that he was prepared to let bygones be bygones. I knew he was disappointed, and even incensed at some Democrats. His attitude was that he had been doublecrossed and let down by men who should have rallied loyally to his support. I was certain he would not dismiss it all as part of the game, but would carry the scars of his defeat for some time.

For this reason I was hopeful that he could get the rest of his program through, and without further clashes with a Congress that had tasted executive blood. I hoped that next year would bring a short and uneventful session of Congress. A campaign year, I felt, would be an excellent time to bury party grudges. Nothing erases past differences so much as working for a common cause. Not being one to harbor illwill, I was confident time would heal the wounds of the violent judiciary fray.

The Supreme Court fight, when the harsh accents of heated debate died away, lived on in the President's memory. Seared into his political soul was defeat, the worst he had suffered since election night in 1920 when James M. Cox and he were soundly trounced by Warren G. Harding and Calvin Coolidge. Presidential pride was sorely scorched. For weeks and months afterward I found him fuming against the members of his own party he blamed for his bucket of bitterness.

Outwardly he was as gay and debonair as ever; inwardly he was seething, I knew, because to me he made no secret of his annoyance with those who had crossed the party line.

Immediately after the defeat he began summoning Senators and Congressmen down to the White House to discuss various matters. Almost invariably he would drop some suggestion that those who had opposed him had better be on guard. It was not so much what he said as what he left unsaid. What he left unsaid lost nothing in being relayed to Capitol Hill. There they were searched for hidden meanings. Various members of Congress came to me seeking enlightenment which I was unable to give.

The President enjoyed his little game thoroughly. On August 3, 1937, I found him chortling over the uneasiness he was creating. During luncheon he recounted in detail conversations he had had with various members of Congress, acting out his own part and the puzzlement of those he had called to his office. He was an excellent actor and at his best when he was taking off himself. He had me laughing throughout the meal.

"I've got them on the run, Jim," he cried. "They go out of here talking to themselves, memorizing my lines to repeat up on the Hill. I'd like to see the faces sag over my mumbo-jumbo. They have no idea what's going to happen and are beginning to worry. They'll be sorry, yet."

"Boss, you're a hard man," I said half in jest and half in earnest. "I hope you never get angry at me."

The Democratic opponents of the Court plan were not the only ones who didn't know what was going to happen. I did not know myself. The thought of a serious purge never crossed my mind. Shadows of concern flitted across my consciousness in the first months after the defeat, but these were quickly forgotten in the problem of the depression of 1937 and the controversy over the appointment of Senator Hugo Lafayette Black to the Supreme Court.

The straw in the wind was presidential treatment of opposing Senators on his trip to the Northwest that fall. He went through Nebraska without inviting Senator Burke to join his party. In Wyoming, Joe O'Mahoney was not invited, but came anyway as a member of a citizens' welcoming committee. When Roosevelt spied Joe, he stuck out his hand and cheerily greeted, "Hello, Joe! Glad to see you." That was at Cheyenne. At Caspar, where O'Mahoney left the train, the President, who had not mentioned O'Mahoney in rear platform appearances in the state, made a pointed reference to politicians who paid lip service to the New Deal while frustrating its objectives. In Montana, Wheeler, arch-foe of the President, was uninvited, while New Deal Senator Murray smiled welcome at the Gardiner stop. To illuminate the lesson for recalcitrant Democrats, the President was all cordiality to Senator Borah, Idaho Republican stalwart, at Boise.

Before he left on the western trip, which was to give him a "look-see" across the continent, a visit to his grandchildren at Seattle, and an excuse to be out of Washington when Justice Black returned from Europe, I called the President at his Hyde Park home on September 22, 1937. I said I had nothing in particular on my mind except to wish him a good trip. I kidded him about taking my regards to the Senators who had been out of step with his program.

"They'll know I was there, Jim," he laughed. "Let 'em begin eating their votes now."

At the time there was more public interest in the disclosure that Black had been a member of the Ku Klux Klan than there was in the Court fight. This startling revelation in the *Pittsburgh Post Gazette* came a few weeks after the Chief Executive had tossed the Alabama Senator's name into the Senate hopper for the Van Devanter vacancy on the high Court. The appointment was as much of a surprise to me as it was to all. I was not consulted nor was I advised before the appointment was read in the Senate chamber. I had a conference with the President the day before and discussed the Court appointment, but he gave no hint that he had made his decision. I was plugging for Judge Sam G. Bratton of New Mexico or Owen D. Young.

"I am aware that many of the Senators would like to see me appoint Bratton," he told me dryly. I gathered that this killed the chances of Bratton, a former Senator. It was also evident he was still feuding with the Senate.

Since the appointment of his old boss, former Secretary of the Navy Josephus Daniels, as Ambassador to Mexico in 1933, he had never failed to notify me of an appointment. Black was the first exception. Others came later. White House executive clerk Rudolph Forster had instructions to call me on every appointment that crossed his desk on its way to the Hill. The Black appointment was given special routing, going without Forster's knowledge.

Later the President told me he had wanted to make the appointment a surprise. He said he had started with a list of more than fifty names and one by one cut his list down to three defenders of his New Deal: Solicitor General Stanley F. Reed, Senator Sherman Minton of Indiana, and Black. Finally, he said, he chose Black because the latter had served the New Deal longer and more zealously; so he scrawled out the nomination with his pen: "I nominate Hugo L. Black of Alabama to be an Associate Justice of the Supreme Court." He concluded the recital with the gleeful statement, "And they'll have to take him, too." I gathered his reference was to the anti-Court Democrats, who would be under pressure of Senatorial courtesy.

During Senate debate on Black's nomination, there was mention of the Klan connection. The issue was not treated seriously until the press disclosure that Black had donned white robes to take the Klan oath in Birmingham in 1923, a year before he succeeded anti-Klan Senator Oscar W. Underwood. At the time of the disclosure, Klan spokesmen said Black's name was no longer on the rolls.

Black was in London when the scandal broke. The Republican press made much of the disclosure. Black preserved a silence until his return, when he made a radio speech from the home of a friend in which he acknowledged former membership in the Klan but denied the unsolicited life membership. The radio speech was without precedent. For an Associate Justice to broadcast on any controversial subject was unusual enough, but for a Justice to defend himself, as Black did, was sensational. He was on a tough spot, as tough a spot as any man in public life has ever faced, perhaps.

Tommy Corcoran called me after the radio admission and disclaimer to ask me what I thought of it. I replied quite honestly that I felt that Black had done the best he could under trying circumstances; however, I felt that Black should have denounced the Klan in the speech, an organization of that character having no place in American life.

Corcoran said the Black speech was prepared by Claude E. Hamilton, Jr., an RFC attorney, who owed his post to the Justice when the latter was in the Senate.

Corcoran said he saw the first draft of the speech and thought it was terrible. He called Black, who said he had not wanted to join the Klan in the first place but did so because he felt under obligation to friends. Corcoran said he made every effort to get Black to denounce the Klan but the Justice would not do so because he felt he would be throwing down friends in Alabama who had helped him through the years. The original draft, according to Corcoran, stated that Black had joined the nightshirt organization, as had many others, for political purposes.

Corcoran and I agreed that Black was—I still think he is—a fine fellow and would make a good member of the Court. We were sorry that he had made so poor an explanation of his klan connection. I told Corcoran I had taken the position at a Cabinet meeting that the Klan issue was not dead, as the President suggested, but was a live one and would arise from time to time as cases involving the issue of tolerance came before the Court. This has been so, but I am glad to say that Black's position in such cases has been above suspicion.

CHAPTER ELEVEN

DEPRESSION AGAIN

I CALLED THE President at Hyde Park on October 7, 1937, to welcome him back from his western trip and to tell him I was heading out west and would not see him until I returned at the end of the month. He insisted I come down for the Cabinet meeting on the eighth. I said I would so arrange my plans.

"What d'you think of Hugo's speech of the other night?" he asked.

"He did the best he could under the circumstances, but I think he should have hit the Klan."

"It was a grand job," he countered. "It did the trick; you just wait and see." He switched the subject. "I want to talk about conditions in this country at the Cabinet meeting. That's why I want you to be sure to come down."

I went to Washington on the night train and secured an appointment with Roosevelt for a few minutes before lunch.

"I am more convinced than ever I was right about the Court," he told me. "Everywhere crowds were bigger than they were in the last campaign. I'm sure the people are for my program. Maybe they don't understand all the program, although I think they know more about it than some people seem to think. Anyhow, I know they're for the Court program because I'm for it, if for no other reason."

He thrust out his chin challengingly. I acknowledged there was much in what he said.

"I've talked to all kinds of people—businessmen, farmers, workers, and others. I think I know what they want and they want my program. Jim, I'm going to call a special session."

"If you do, you ought to make it as late as you can and still allow enough time for putting through the legislation you want," I suggested.

"I think I'll make it November 10 or maybe November 15. I don't want the program going over to the next session where it will get all tangled up with the controversial items like the Court, the Black appointment, and the antilynching bill. At the special session I can hold them to the program."

At the Cabinet meeting that afternoon, October 8, 1937, Roosevelt leaped down the throat of Secretary of Commerce Roper during a discussion of the business recession which was disturbing the Administration, making no effort to disguise his irritability.

"Dan," he said sharply at one point, "you have just got to stop issuing these Hooverish statements all the time."

Roper, unabashed by the rebuke, tried to argue to justify his statements. I am sure Dan failed to understand that the President wanted him to keep silent in the critical period.

"I know that the present situation is the result of a concerted effort by big business and concentrated wealth to drive the market down just to create a situation unfavorable to me," the President said. "I have been around the country and know conditions are good. Crops are good. Farmers are getting good prices. Industry is busy and is bound to keep busy if crops and prices are good. I am sure the situation is just temporary. Everything will work out all right if we just sit tight and keep quiet." He looked meaningly at Roper, who was blissfully unaware of the point. "The whole situation is being manufactured in Wall Street."

The next day I talked to the President by phone. I remarked that his suggestion for silence appeared to have been lost on Dan.

"Jim," he said, "there's entirely too much talking going on. There's entirely too many press conferences and too many statements being issued."

"I haven't had a press conference since last June," I put in.

"I'm going to put the lid on," he continued. "When I was in the Navy, Daniels had two press conferences a day and they got pretty awful. There's too much talking and it's causing a lot of unfavorable comment. There's just too much being said all around."

On my return from the West I went to New York City for the final days of the mayoralty campaign in which Fiorello La Guardia was pitted for reelection against Judge Jeremiah Mahoney. On October 27, the President called to talk about the campaign.

"If La Guardia really gets tough," I said jokingly, "I'll pin his ears back."

"Watch out," he cautioned, "he might bite you."

"He's too short to reach above my ankles," I retorted.

Three days before the election Roosevelt let it be known that he had telephoned his best wishes to La Guardia. This was a heavy blow to a campaign which had only a slight chance to begin with. Election night we were snowed under by the American Labor Party vote of 672,823 votes which brought La Guardia's total to 1,344,016 as against 889,591 for Mahoney. Around headquarters there were no post-mortems; we were licked—soundly licked. There was a laugh, however, when someone around headquarters remarked, "Well, time is a great healer."

Two days later the President asked me to meet him in his town house on Sixty-ninth Street in New York City and accompany him back to Washington. When I arrived there I chatted with Harry Hopkins, the Federal Emergency Relief Administrator, Miss Marguerite Le Hand, the President's personal secretary, and Miss Grace Tully of the White House staff. La Guardia came in. I was congratulating him on his reelection when the President's mother came up and headed for the smiling Mayor.

"Congratulations," she said. "I knew your victory was assured long before election. Nevertheless, I am much pleased that you have won."

Miss Le Hand turned to me and winked. There was no doubt where Mrs. Roosevelt had heard that La Guardia would win. The trip to the town house was regarded as having been made expressly to congratulate the victorious La Guardia.

And so it developed when the Mayor and I went in to the President a few minutes later. In the congratulations, I came in for a bit of kidding. I took the opportunity to state that I considered it unfair of the ALP to oppose Democratic candidates for the State Assembly and the Democratic slate of delegates to the Constitutional Convention, which opposition had strengthened Republicans. La Guardia said he had wanted to go to the Convention and we Democrats would not send him, so he had no other choice. I said it would have been a travesty for the Democrats to send him.

The next afternoon I attended one of the most interesting Cabinet sessions during my years in office, one on which I dictated voluminous notes. The meeting got under way slowly in the long Cabinet room with tall windows looking out on the rose garden on the right of the south portico of the White House. We were seated at our regular places when the President entered, sprinkling cheery greetings. He took his place at the head of the table with Under Secretary of State Welles, acting for Hull, on his right and Secretary of the Treasury Morgenthau on his left. The rest of us were seated alternately on either side of the table in the order of the creation of the Cabinet positions. In accordance with established procedure, the President called upon each department head in order. Welles briefly discussed the situations in the Far East and in Spain. It was not until the President reached the last member of his official family, Secretary of Labor Perkins, that the meeting really got under way.

When the President questioned, "Well, Frances, anything on your mind?" she pulled out a memorandum, prepared by Isadore Lubin, Labor Department statistician, which reported a decline in employment in October of about two per cent where, ordinarily, she said, the month shows an increase of two per cent.

"This is the first real sign of a falling off in employment, which might be serious and even dangerous in view of conditions," she said. "The report shows the falling off is greatest in heavy industries such as steel plants, rolling mills, foundries, and automobile plants. In connection with the automobile industry, I have no direct information as to the result of the automobile show, but I do not believe sales following the show were up to expectations, because they are laying off workers in so many auto plants."

Others chimed in with gloomy reports of the business picture. The President listened until these were ended and then called for suggestions. Welles passed, evidently holding that the domestic situation was outside the purview of the State Department.

"I think you ought to issue a statement comparing business conditions of today with what they were in the early days of your administration," said Morgenthau, who was next in line. "Then you could talk frankly about the general tax situation. You know business is

moaning that the capital gains and undistributed profits taxes are retarding recovery. But I think it would be heartening for you to show
how far better off we are today than we were four years ago."

"Oh, for God's sake, Henry, do you want me to read the record
again?" the President asked with no attempt to conceal his irritation.

Morgenthau reddened. The President glowered. The silence became
as awkward as it was cold and heavy. Finally I spoke up:

"Boss, I think Henry is right." Henry looked surprised and pleased;
the President merely looked surprised. "I think the situation would
be helped materially if you did say something to alleviate the fears
which no one can deny exist in the business world today. If I may speak
frankly, my contacts with people around the country lead me to believe that business people feel you have taken a stubborn attitude. I
quote exactly when I use the word 'stubborn.' The impression has been
created, rightly or wrongly, that you have no interest in business. I
may not be making myself clear, but there is a feeling you have
no sympathy or confidence in business—big or little . . . Now,
even . . ."

"That's not true . . ." he began.

"Let me finish," I begged. "I am not saying it's true. I had intended
to finish by saying that in spite of all your endeavors to clear the situation, the fact is that the impression still remains you are against business and this impression must be cleared away. I think Henry is right,
you should make a quieting statement."

"There are altogether too many statements being issued now and too
much talking," the President said. "The Department of Agriculture
has issued a statement saying that the national income will be less
than it was a year ago and the Department of Commerce has issued
a statement saying it will be greater than it was a year ago."

"Since my father's time the Department of Agriculture has been
getting out such a statement," Wallace said. "It was thoroughly
checked before release and we feel it is correct in its figures."

"I am satisfied the Agriculture estimate is correct," said Perkins.
"We have checked its figures and are in agreement with the estimate."

The President glared at Roper with a what-have-you-to-say-for-
yourself look. When the Secretary of Commerce launched into rosy

predictions, the President cut him short. It was evident to everyone at the table but Dan that the Boss was most annoyed at him.

"There are a number of things which must be done," the President began, leaving Roper floundering in some circumlocution about cycles. "There's housing and railroads and utilities."

"I have reason to believe the utilities would spend a lot of money if they knew where they are heading," I broke in.

"That's what they say," he went on. "But take a typical example, Niagara–Hudson. The real trouble with them is they were and are over-capitalized for three times their real worth. And they want the government to extend consideration to them based upon the over-capitalization instead of sitting down and admitting their real worth and then trying to work out their problems in an honest manner. In other words, they want to charge the consumers for power based on a false capitalization. In the case of Niagara–Hudson, they sold their stock at $20 a share to the public and it is now down to $8 and seven-eighths a share.

"Every time you do anything for them they want something else. I am ready to sit down and work it out, but you can never pin them down. I had Wendell Willkie of the Commonwealth and Southern in here for a talk, but I couldn't get anywhere with him; you can't get anywhere with any of them."

Someone brought up the plight of the railroads.

"All right," the President said, "let's take the railroads. They want higher freight rates and higher passenger rates. Some months ago when the rates were reduced, over the opposition of the railroads, the result was increased volume of business. Only one railroad, the New York Central, admitted the decrease was justified by the returns."

"Boss, I've talked to a number of railroad executives around the country and they are not sure whether a freight rate increase will solve their problem," I said. "They feel as soon as they get an increase, labor will demand additional consideration. Take the 70 car bill. The unions want freight trains limited to 70 cars which means more crews for them, whereas trains of 100 cars are more efficient from the standpoint of the operators."

"I know, I know," he said. "I realize the situation is a bad one; many of the roads are in a bad financial condition, and some are in poor physical condition. A lot of this has been due to inefficient management, particularly in eastern roads, and failure to go along with the times.

"Finally, there's housing. Speeding up of housing will go a long way toward adjusting the present business situation. An increase in construction will give considerable help to the industry itself, which has been in a bad way for a long time. Its stimulation will help, naturally enough, all industries engaged in supplying materials and also will help the transportation industry."

Morgenthau and I did most of the talking for the Cabinet at first. Then Perkins and Secretary of War Woodring joined in. We had some help from Wallace and a little from Roper. More than once I stepped in to help Morgenthau. The President blamed the recession on Wall Street.

"I get all kinds of criticism and complaints about the economic situation," he said, "but few people come in to see me with any concrete suggestions as to how the situation can be alleviated. It's easy enough to criticize, but it's another thing to help.

"I want all of you—every one—when offering criticisms to make suggestions which are constructive. I am fully conscious of the situation which exists; I have been studying it for a long, long time.

"And I know who's responsible for the situation. Business, particularly the banking industry, has ganged up on me. They are trying to use this recession to force me to let up on some of my program. They want to get back the control they had in the past, to get back what they feel is theirs. They want to increase the power of wealth without government restriction in the future. There is no doubt what they want, although they won't admit it and they are taking it out on the present situation to put over their own ends.

"In my talks with businessmen and people generally, I have brought up the question of wages and hours and labor limitations. I am proceeding on the theory that better conditions among working people are absolutely necessary. Legislation is vital because in some sections of the country wages are pitifully small.

"I have found that businessmen in one section of the country are not concerned about conditions in another part of the country. In other words, they are concerned about their own particular business and they are not interested in anything else. They are a pretty selfish lot. I feel there is a bitter, selfish attitude on the part of all businessmen, big and little; for example, newspaper editors and publishers are concerned only with their own welfare. That situation makes it difficult to do the job right and to help all elements of our population. I am willing and determined to use every prerogative at my command to do the right things and to bring us along to a better way of life."

At the conclusion of the meeting I remarked that it was one of the best we had ever had. The President agreed. The next day Morgenthau called to express gratitude for the way I backed him up, saying he would never forget it, because he felt the President was annoyed at his persistency, and added that he would not have gone on had I not stepped in as I did and given him courage to go on. He was never more friendly in all the years I have known him than he was that morning. Morgenthau said the discussion was certain to produce favorable results.

On the day Franklin D. Roosevelt, Jr., and Ethel Du Pont were married in Wilmington, Steve Early told me, Morgenthau called during the height of the festivities and excitedly demanded that Roosevelt be put on the phone so that he could give the American government's position on the French franc. The President was relaxing at the reception in the Du Pont home when Henry called seeking approval of the position which was about to be announced. Steve found the Boss sipping champagne. When he relayed the Morgenthau message, the President frowned at the interruption and said, "Tell Henry I don't give a good damn what the government's position is on the French franc." Steve carried the message back to Henry word for word, because the White House staff was finding Henry's worries tiresome.

CHAPTER TWELVE

NEW YORK GOVERNORSHIP

AROUND THIS time Walter J. Cummings, Chicago banker and former treasurer of the Democratic National Committee, called by phone quite distressed because he had heard Senator Harry S. Truman of Missouri was about to make a speech attacking the receivership of the Chicago, Milwaukee, St. Paul & Pacific Railroad. Cummings was disturbed because he was the receiver. He wanted me to call up Truman and ask him not to do so. I said I did not feel I had any right to call off the Senator but I would try to find out if Walter's information was correct. I did call the Senator and found that while he was going to speak he was not going to attack the railroad or its receivership.

Truman was under the impression, and with some reason, that he was not being treated fairly by the administration, because of his connection with Boss Tom Pendergast of the Kansas City machine. On November 19, 1937, he came in to see me to ask if the Attorney General would appoint a United States District Attorney in Missouri to succeed Maurice A. Milligan, who prosecuted Pendergast. Truman said he did not want to submit a name unless the appointment was to be made. I found both the President and Cummings cold toward any change in that office.

The same day I saw the President. I had had an appointment hanging fire for a couple of days, but he was ill and I was put off. I went to the White House proper. I was ushered through the oval study above the Blue Room and into the President's bedroom. I was shocked by his appearance. His color was bad; his face was lined and he appeared to be worn out. His jaw was swollen as a result of a tooth infection. During the entire interview he kept an ice bag to his jaw to relieve pain. In addition to the infection, he told me he had an intestinal disorder and a fever. His spirits were excellent.

"I'll be all right, if I can get away," he said. "If the doctors let me go, I'll head for Warm Springs. What I need is a bit of rest." "Why don't you take a fishing cruise?" I suggested. "They seem to do you a world of good. If I were you I'd head for warm waters and let Congress wrestle along with the legislative program."

There was no doubt in my mind that the President had suffered a great deal more than was indicated in the press. He told me that he had lost a great deal of sleep as a result of the infection—an infection which made it necessary to delay the extraction of the tooth. The fever lingered on for weeks. And I learned there was worry over strain on Roosevelt's heart.

The President's condition so concerned me that I had a long talk five days later with Admiral Cary T. Grayson, White House physician to President Wilson, about Roosevelt's health. He told me he was in daily touch with Jimmy Roosevelt on his father's condition. I told him that while I had a great deal of respect for White House physician Ross T. McIntire, I thought it highly essential that some prominent physician be called in to go over the President thoroughly. Grayson said it was important not only to get a good doctor, but one who would not talk, recalling that when Wilson was ill outside doctors were called in for consultation and some of them talked.

I gathered he was aware of the worry regarding the President's heart. I told him nothing I knew, however, and he told me nothing he knew. There was no immediate concern, I had been told, but Roosevelt's condition was such as to bear watching. Grayson said it might become serious. There had been many rumors in New York and elsewhere about the President's health. Most of these had no basis in fact whatsoever.

At my conference with the President, we discussed various appointments. At this time I was being mentioned prominently in polls and various articles in magazines and newspapers as a Presidential possibility in 1940. While I was highly pleased to fall under such consideration, I did not take it seriously. The President had never mentioned this although I was subjected to much good-natured kidding from others on the matter.

"Jim, before you leave, I want to talk to you about the New York State situation," he said, taking the ice bag away from his ailing jaw.

"I've talked to Ed Flynn about it. He's very much hurt by the attitude and actions of the American Labor Party and is in a bad mood generally. I realize the situation is a difficult one, but one that needs straightening out—needs it badly. Now, Jim, I want you to give some thought to the situation, particularly I want you to give some thought to running for governor."

He put the ice bag back and studied me.

"I'm not keen on living in Albany," I sidestepped.

"I suppose Bess would not like it either?" he asked.

"I'm of the impression she wouldn't."

"I don't blame her for a minute. However, serious attention should be given to the New York situation. If you would take the nomination, you could get the support of the CIO and the AFL, as well as the American Labor party and undoubtedly La Guardia."

"That last statement is somewhat amusing," I said. "I can see the Little Flower on the stump for me."

"Seriously, Jim, I'm certain that La Guardia won't oppose you unless Dewey should happen to be the nominee."

"What about Bob Jackson?" I asked.

"He isn't well enough known and I question whether he could build himself up enough to run by next year," he answered. "If you don't run, the only other person available would be Senator Wagner. And then, Jim, you could run for the Senate. At the same time you could keep any position in the business world, which would take care of your private financial situation."

"Bess doesn't think much of Washington either," I volunteered.

"You know, before I left Albany," he went on, ignoring my interruption, "a bill was passed where an appropriation of some kind had been arranged for an additional contribution of $10,000 a year for the support of the Executive Mansion so that the Governor now receives $35,000 instead of $25,000 as I did. This would enable you to carry on the functions of the Mansion without having much of a deficit."

"All right, granting that is so, it still would not take care of my personal situation. There would be no chance of relieving the difficulties of the accumulating deficit I incur by service here, and there would be no chance of saving money for myself and my family. Frankly, I would love the place, but I do not see how in my present position I can give serious consideration to it."

"Well, think it over," he urged. "Think them both over—Governor and Senate."

One other subject of general interest was considered in the conversation. The President expressed disappointment that Hull had not received the Nobel peace prize that was awarded to Lord Cecil. He said Hull did not want his name entered as a candidate again next year, but he had instructed Welles to do so anyway. He said, "You know, there's a cash prize of $40,000 that goes with the award." I said, "Cordell could use it."

Three days later I repeated much of this conversation to Vice President Garner at luncheon in his office at the Capitol. He smiled at the Presidential insistence that I run for Governor or Senator in New York, saying that it looked as though Roosevelt were trying to get me out of the way in 1940.

"Quite frankly, I don't think the boss looks on me as a qualified candidate," I said. "Not that I have any feeling in the matter."

"Well, I do," Garner broke in. "I recently told a friend of mine that I have never known a man who had grown more in stature than yourself during all my years in Washington. I never knew you until 1933, but after having seen you in action at Cabinet meetings, I have acquired a high regard for you and know you are big enough to be President.

"And, I want to tell you something in the strictest confidence. Well, I made a bet with Silliman Evans—100 to 1—that I could name the next President. He wrote out a check for $1,000 and I wrote one out for $10 and we turned them over to the Missus with the name I wrote. And—not to be repeated to a living soul—the name I wrote was yours."

"Why didn't you speak for yourself, John?" I quipped.

"I don't want the Presidency under any circumstances," he said. "Silliman was very anxious to find out the name I wrote, but I wouldn't tell him. He thought it was Wallace and offered to bet another $50 that was the case, but I wouldn't bet. No, I don't want to take the job. I would hate to have to take over the reins of government. It's a tremendous responsibility. I hope to God the Boss keeps his health. I'm worried about him now."

I told him there was nothing to worry about, nothing immediate. He said he was glad to hear it. I gathered he, too, had heard about the concern over the President's heart.

The night before, I had run into Marvin McIntyre in coming out of my apartment. Mac said the third term was out of the question. I said I considered Hull the logical candidate. "Don't be foolish, Jim," Mac said, "you are the outstanding candidate."

Garner's suspicions that the President regarded me as a 1940 contender and wanted to sidetrack me to Albany were verified to my satisfaction by Basil O'Connor at a lunch in his home in New York City. "Doc," as the President's former law partner is known, told me Roosevelt had mentioned the prospect of my running for Governor of New York in 1938. "Doc" told him I was not interested. The President acknowledged to "Doc" that I had said I was not "particularly interested." "Doc" said he could go farther and say I was not interested at all. At this, he said, the President looked at him and asked, "Is Jim anxious for 1940?" "Doc" said his answer was that he didn't know about that.

Soon after that the President took a fishing cruise. When he returned, much rested, I called the White House to inquire after his health. He reported he was feeling fine; that the dentist and doctor had said it would no longer be necessary to scrape his jaw bone where the abscessed tooth had been, and the condition had improved greatly in the past thirty hours.

I saw the President a few days later. He told me about the impending appointment of Joseph P. Kennedy of the Securities and Exchange Commission as Ambassador to Britain. I asked him whether Joseph E. Davies, then Ambassador to Russia, would go to Berlin. He replied that Joe would be shifted to Brussels, that Berlin needed an experienced diplomat. Then he brought the conversation to New York State politics.

"Jim, I'm very much concerned about New York," he said. "The simple fact is that whether we like it or not, the American Labor Party holds the balance of power and our nominees must have their support in order to win at the polls. Ed Flynn is very much against the ALP, but we must deal with them.

"You and I are practical fellows, Jim, and know we must approach the situation in a practical manner, regardless of personal feelings. There are certain conditions to be worked out to meet the approval of the Labor party for our tickets. I list them as: Wagner for Senator and Farley for Governor, or Farley for Senator and Wagner for Governor."

"We have already talked this over before," I said. "My mind has not changed in the slightest. Either post would be a great honor, but I just can't consider them because of my personal problem."

"Well, don't dismiss them entirely from your mind. I want to talk to you about this again. I understand your personal attitude. I have some other ideas on the ticket. What do you think of Wagner for Senator and Jackson for Governor, or Wagner for Governor and Jackson for Senator, or Wagner for Senator and La Guardia for Governor, or La Guardia for Senator and Wagner for Governor?"

"I just can't believe the Democrats would turn over the party to La Guardia," I said. "I think the party would rather lose than do this. Now, don't get me wrong, speaking from the national point of view, I don't care whether La Guardia runs as a Democrat—we have a majority in the Senate anyway. As a Democrat, I'm heart and soul against it. La Guardia is an opportunist and would desert on a moment's notice if he thought it would be to his advantage."

"Yes, La Guardia has a swelled head," he said slowly, "and it's my guess he has presidential aspirations. He's very friendly with the La Follettes; Bob La Follette is a nice fellow, able and honorable, but I never thought much of Phil."

I told the President that Hull was of the impression that he (Roosevelt) did not consult him enough, that the Secretary had intimated as much to me, though not in so many words. I told him Hull had much Capitol Hill experience in tax problems and his advice in that field might be invaluable.

"Why, I'm very fond of Hull," he disclaimed. "I see him at least twice a week. However, he's a free trader at heart and for that reason his views can't be accepted in their entirety."

This brought up a general discussion of the Cabinet, which was extremely intimate and frank. It was the first time the President had taken down his hair with me on my colleagues in his official family.

"What do you think of Homer Cummings?" he asked.

"I think Homer is all right," I said. "He has been extremely loyal and cooperated in every way. If he has any weakness, it is due to the fact that instead of advising you about what you should do, he is always trying to find out what you want to do. In other words, he's always trying to go along with your views. I think you might have a chat with him and try to impress on him that he must make his own decisions."

I knew the President got this as a reference to the fact that many people blamed Cummings for the ill-fated Court plan. The full blame had been placed on Homer's doorstep when the truth was the President only consulted him in preparation for the program. I understand Judge Samuel I. Rosenman was also in on the hatching.

The President said nothing, but from his manner I gathered that Homer's days were numbered. I knew Cummings was anxious to leave the Cabinet and was disturbed by stories that Jackson was to succeed him. Jackson had accompanied the President on the recent southern cruise.

"What about Dan Roper?" he asked. "I am thoroughly dissatisfied with Dan but don't know how I can get rid of him. Maybe I could give him a diplomatic post of some kind."

"I think that if Dan did leave the Cabinet, he'd want to remain in Washington rather than take a diplomatic post, but he is so fond of honors he might accept anything in the diplomatic line," I said.

"Well, we'll try," Roosevelt continued. "Do you think Claude Swanson will resign?"

"If his condition gets any worse, I think it would be the proper thing to do," I said. "Up until six months ago he was clicking all right mentally, but it's pitiful to see him at Cabinet meetings now."

"Yes," he agreed, "it's too bad. He was a grand old man. I'm afraid his number is up."

"Speaking of the Cabinet, Louis Johnson is expecting to be named Secretary of War any day now," I said.

"I wouldn't name Louis under any circumstances," he replied. "I've talked to Harry Woodring, who understands he will get a diplomatic post and that is entirely satisfactory to him."

"I think Harry is doing a good job," I put in. "I think he worked hard to make good because of the criticism directed at him before you took him in."

"Yes, he's done a much better job than Dern. What do you think of McNutt?"

"I think McNutt has a lot of ability," I answered, "but he's ambitious and we can't be sure of him. I have told you many times before that he prevented you from getting the vote of Indiana in 1932."

"I think Henry Morgenthau has tried to carry out my plans in every respect," Roosevelt said. "I couldn't put Joe Kennedy in his place, for example, because Joe would want to run the Treasury in his own way, contrary to my plans and views."

We talked of Frances Perkins and I got the impression that he would be pleased to have her resign. I gathered he would appoint Edward McGrady in her place. Ed might not have wanted it, but it is rather difficult for any person to refuse the President and I don't think Ed would have in the end. Roosevelt changed his mind on Frances, and rightly so. She took many a blow for him and served him loyally and faithfully at all times.

We did not talk of Ickes and Wallace at that time. I did mention later that Ickes's speeches were causing trouble because of their bitterness and that I thought he was casting an acquisitive eye on the Forestry Bureau in the Agriculture Department.

A few days later politics was blasted from the President's mind when the U.S.S. *Panay* was sunk by Japanese aircraft on the Yangtze River. At the Cabinet meeting there was talk of the possibility of war. The President closeted himself with the army and navy high command. Hull reiterated his gloomy warnings of the danger existing in the Orient due to the aggressiveness of the Japanese. On first receiving news that the gunboat had been sunk, the President by memorandum directed Hull to make strong representations to Japan. Hull needed no urging, but swung into demands for apology, reparations, and guarantees against repetition of the attack. All this was duly reported to the Cabinet. The President kept his finger on the public pulse; when he found that the incident brought no demand for war, he sent the military back to their offices and the threat of war passed like a lacy cloud over the moon.

Another incident brought the President abruptly back to politics. Late one night the House finally came to a vote on his Wage and Hour bill. The bill had been hamstrung by amendments and was hardly recognizable, but it would have been acceptable. The vote was not on the bill itself, but on a motion to recommit the bill to the House Labor Committee for further study and revision. The motion was carried by a vote of 216 to 198, the Republican minority being swelled by a bloc of Southerners. The vote ended a seven months' struggle over the bill, which had been passed by the Senate in June. The vote was the first conclusive action taken by Congress after five weeks of struggling on the five-point program the President had presented in his call—crop control, wages and hours, government reorganization, resource planning, and modernization of antitrust legislation.

The President was furious over the vote. He muttered against southern betrayal, then declared he would see that the legislation would be introduced early in the regular session of Congress a few weeks off. He was not as angry as he had been over defeat in the Court fight, but only slightly less so. He was bitter in references to those who had betrayed him. He said the people wanted the program and he was determined that they should have it.

The President was not to show his hand to me for another month, however. It was the Christmas season and politics were pushed into the background. I called him from New York to wish him a merry Christmas. He expressed hope that I, Bess, and the children would have "a grand Christmas."

New Year's Eve I reached Washington to find that the President had been trying to call me. When I returned the call he was at dinner. I tried again between the acts of a show I attended, but found he was in his study. The next morning he reached me at my apartment. Before he had exchanged more than a perfunctory New Year's wish, he said he had called to talk about Bob Jackson's speech at the New

York City Jackson Day dinner on January 8. I told him the arrangements were satisfactory. Later in the day I was talking with Senator Wagner and Vincent Dailey at headquarters when the President called again and appeared to be put out about the arrangements. The President was most anxious that everyone be fair to Bob Jackson.

After the call Wagner and I agreed that the President had evidently decided on running the head of the antitrust division, who was soon to be named Solicitor General, for the governorship of New York. Wagner said there was no chance for Jackson, which was my opinion, too. At the time, concern was being voiced over speeches delivered by Jackson and Ickes. Many felt, as I did, that these speeches were retarding recovery and rendering a delicate economic situation more acute. Some felt that Jackson and Ickes were letting off blasts the President hesitated to deliver himself. Jackson had accused business of conducting "a strike of capital" against the New Deal and held that the only criticism which could be leveled against the new philosophy of government was that "it set out a breakfast for the canary and let the cat steal it." Ickes was more savage, carrying on a war against business, while the President was seeing more leaders of industry than he had ever seen, in a desperate search for a way out of the slough of recession into which his New Deal was sinking.

In his Jackson Day address, the President echoed the Ickes and Bob Jackson blasts at monopoly by reporting that of a total of 13 billion dollars worth of electric utility securities, owners of less than 600 million dollars exercised control of the industry. He told celebrating Democrats throughout the nation, "Here is a 96-inch dog being wagged by a 4-inch tail." The next day on the telephone I found him still chuckling over his joke. He wanted to know what I thought of his "dog" story. I replied that over the radio he seemed to be getting a good laugh himself.

I reported Oliver Quayle, party treasurer, estimated we would make up to $450,000. "Great," he enthused. "But that's not what I called you for, Jim. I need your help. The Ludlow resolution calling for a national referendum before a declaration of war is coming up for a vote in the House. I'm told the vote is very close. I wish you would do all you can to help defeat it. Call Hague and Kelly and get their delegations lined up. We must beat this resolution as it will tie our hands in dealing with international affairs." I promised I would come down to do all I could.

Monday I spent the entire morning on the phone calling Congressmen and urging them to support the administration. I talked to seventy-eight men. All but two or three had signed the petition, circulated at the time of the *Panay* crisis, to bring the resolution to the floor for a vote. I was unable to reach 32 others for whom I had placed calls. Later I was satisfied that most of these were evading me, because only four voted with the Administration. I succeeded in inducing a large number to change their vote. Hull was most grateful, saying my efforts had undoubtedly led to defeat of the resolution by the narrow vote of 209 to 188. I sent a complete report of my calls, including those to Frank Hague and Edward J. Kelly, to the White House, where the President found the list interesting. At a Cabinet meeting, Garner credited me with turning the tide.

The next day, at a morning conference in the President's office, we talked about the recent resignation of Supreme Court Justice Sutherland. The resignation cut the Old Guard of the high Court to two and gave the liberals, counting the successor to Sutherland, a majority as effective as any the President would have received under the Court plan. I was hopeful he would forget those Democrats who had opposed his scheme. In the interest of healing the breach in the Democratic party, I thought a bit of humor might not be out of place.

"I have a candidate for the Supreme Court for you," I offered.

"Who's that?" he asked.

"Burton K. Wheeler."

"Where'd you get that idea?" he snapped.

"I don't remember at the moment. Someone gave it to me. When it comes to me, I'll send you a memorandum." Later I remembered it was Representative William I. Sirovich of New York City and I forwarded this information to him.

"Wheeler's trying to use his vote on the Supreme Court bill as a springboard to the Presidency," the President said.

I saw that my joke had missed fire. Without asking him whom he had in mind, I urged him to make the appointment as soon as possible. He promised to do so by the end of the week and eventually sent up the name of the Solicitor General, Stanley Reed, which choice was expected and applauded.

CHAPTER THIRTEEN

PURGE PRESCRIBED

LATE THAT January I got definite indication of what I had long feared—that the President's hate for members of the party who had opposed him on the Court fight had not cooled by the lapse of time, but glowed as fierce as ever under the ashes of the past six months. By the tone of his references, I knew he was still bitter; but such references had been fewer and less heated, so I had high expectations that all would be forgotten for the all-important Congressional elections ahead—elections made more important because the recession was unquestionably strengthening the opposition. While I was uneasy, I had no actual indication of the purge that was on the way, beyond vague threats uttered immediately after the defeat, until January 27, 1938.

That morning I received a call in New York from James Roosevelt, son and secretary to the President. He said candidates for the Senate were going to file in Illinois the next day and wanted to know if we had said anything publicly on the Administration's attitude. I told him we had not; but I thought it advisable that I issue a statement immediately declaring that the administration was not going to become involved in primary fights in the Congressional districts. I said I would be in Washington the next morning and bring a statement to the President. Jimmy said we should not wait until tomorrow and asked that I dictate a statement over the phone. This I did as follows:

In the course of political events we have reached that stage in which ambitious men of the Democratic party are launching their campaigns for nomination or renomination for Governorships and to the Senate and to the House of Representatives. As usual the newspapers are carrying a great deal of gossip that this or that candidate is favored by the Democratic National organization, which moves me at this time to repeat what I have so often said on these occasions; that is, that the job of the Democratic National Committee is to work for and to assist in every way possible in the election of the party candidates. It denies to no man the right to aspire to

office and it has absolutely no concern with, or in, the primary or convention struggles for these nominations. As individuals, the members of the
National Committee may have their favorites, but as a body the organization's hands are off and will continue to be off. These nominations are entirely the affair of the States or the Congressional districts, and however
these early battles may result, the National Committee will be behind the
candidate that the people themselves choose. This goes for every state and
every Congressional district.

Jimmy thanked me. I had the statement transcribed as dictated. Ten
minutes later he was back on the phone again saying everything was
fine except for the last two sentences. I said they had been included to
quiet fears expressed to the Committee and argued for their retention
since they expressed sound party doctrine. He flung an irrefutable answer at me with "Father has struck the last two sentences out." Out
they went and in came a flock of troubles. An albatross, not of my own
shooting, was hung from my neck. From that time on I knew no political peace. I have the copy of the statement before me now, the one
from which I struck the two sentences by order of the White House.
It seems as though it were yesterday that I was looking at it for the
first time and saying to myself, "It's time to stop feeling sorry for the
Republicans."

My worst fears began to be realized at the White House conference
the next day. From that time conferences were latticed with a pattern
of purge talk. From the beginning I made it clear that I could not as
Democratic chairman drop the reins of the party band wagon to whip
the boys hitching a ride on the tail gate. The President agreed that I
should keep my hands off because of my position. It was my contention that it was perfectly proper for the people, in their wisdom, to
punish those who had voted against him on the Court bill, wage and
hour legislation, and the like; but quite another thing for the national
organization to call for their defeat. He expressed himself confident
that the people would support him by defeating his opponents, adding
that he might, like the schoolmaster, have to apply the political birch
to teach refractory members of the party the three R's—Regularity,
Right, and Reason.

In the next month he went over the whole political field as he prepared to distribute patronage rewards for "going along" and punishments for not "going along" to twenty-seven Senators and some three hundred Representatives. One of the President's first concerns was the senatorial nomination in Illinois. The situation was complicated by the internal strife between Governor Henry Horner on one side and Mayor Kelly and the National Committeeman Patrick Nash on the other. Horner wanted Congressman Scott Lucas and the Kelly–Nash machine, United States District Attorney Michael Igoe. Neither faction wanted Dieterich. The President said he had asked the warring groups not to become involved in a public fight because of Dieterich's loyalty to his administration. Their differences could not be reconciled, however, and Dieterich was forced to withdraw from the race.

In Georgia the President wanted Senator Walter F. George defeated. He was particularly anxious to make an object lesson of George because he thought such a defeat would furnish a lasting lesson to the southern bloc in Congress which had been opposing his social reforms.

"We've just got to beat George, Jim," he said.

"Boss, I think you're foolish," I said. "I don't think George can be beaten. The only man who could possibly defeat George would be Governor E. D. Rivers and I don't think he could do it. In fact, I'm not sure Rivers thinks he could do it. I don't think he would run. And, if he did, he might do you more harm than good. Rivers's nomination would raise the Klan issue and I don't think you want to go through that again so soon. Don't misunderstand me; he's a fine fellow and a personal friend of mine, one for whom I have a genuine regard, but you must face the facts."

"We'll have to talk about it again," he said.

He was no less eager to defeat Senator Tydings in Maryland. "I've had a talk with Bill Stanley (former Assistant Attorney General) and he thinks our best candidates would be President H. C. Byrd of the University of Maryland and Attorney General Herbert O'Conor for Senator," he said.

"I'm sure O'Conor would like to get into the Senate, but I think he's made some sort of commitment to run for Governor," I said. "I'll talk to Howard Bruce, Maryland's National Committeeman, and to

Byrd, and let you know. I've been seeing Byrd about Federal aid for the University."

"Oh, yes, I've taken that up with Ickes, but haven't received a report yet."

He asked me what I thought of running Paul V. McNutt for the Senate against Senator Frederick Van Nuys in Indiana.

I said, "Boss, there's no use going into that again. McNutt was responsible for having the Indiana delegation vote against every Roosevelt proposal in the convention. Why, if he had had his way, you wouldn't be here today."

"Now, now, Jim," he counseled, "I know Paul is a hot presidential candidate, but so is Tydings."

"McNutt's a red-hot candidate," I said, "but I don't think he can be nominated. He won't have any delegates with him but the Indiana delegation."

In this connection I could not fail to mark how conscious the Boss was becoming of political ambition. He had gone out of his way at various times to tax me, La Guardia, McNutt, and Tydings with nursing plans to redecorate the White House. In the months to come, I was to find this thought was never far from the front of his mind whenever he undertook even a casual appraisal of almost anyone in political life.

Returning to the Indiana situation I gave it as my opinion that Van Nuys would run independent if he lost the Democratic nomination and thus assure the election of a Republican. The President remarked that he was aware that Van Nuys was "vindictive."

"What do you think about Iowa?" he asked.

"Frankly, I am quite disturbed about it," I said. "Iowa has always been Republican and seems to be slipping back."

"I don't think Senator Gillette is a strong candidate," he said. "If we could get a real liberal, we would have a strong ticket."

Thus, Gillette was marked for purging. It was my opinion he could get the nomination, but I was not so sure of the election. The President asked about Senator Augustine Lonergan of Connecticut and Senator Bennett C. Clark of Missouri. I told him that both men were acceptable to all elements within the Democratic party in their states and would be renominated. I made it clear there was nothing he could do about it. He asked about Senator Alva B. Adams in Colorado. I replied that I thought Adams would win. The President said he thought Mayor Stapleton of Denver could beat Adams. I said there was no chance because the Adams forces would be joined by those of Senator Edwin C. Johnson. Adams had not taken an active part in the Court fight but would have voted against the plan had it reached that stage. The President asked what chance there was for beating Senator Pat McCarran of Nevada or Senator Ellison D. Smith of South Carolina. To my curt "none," in each case, he offered no comment.

We discussed the situation in Pennsylvania where, I said, conflicting personal ambitions were injuring the Democratic cause. In California he said he was hopeful Senator William G. McAdoo would be reelected and signified he was willing to help. In Ohio he expected Senator Robert J. Buckley would beat former Governor George White. Neither of us thought Charles Sawyer, National Committeeman from Ohio, would take the Democratic gubernatorial nomination from Governor Martin L. Davey. The President said he had tried once to persuade Congressman Wesley E. Disney of Oklahoma not to run against Senator Elmer Thomas and hoped to convince the Representative, in another interview, to let his senatorial ambitions sleep awhile.

"And that brings us to Kentucky," the President said. "I am very anxious to have Barkley reelected. If Barkley loses the fight, Pat Harrison will become majority leader and I'm afraid Pat won't go along on liberal legislation."

"I'm sure that Pat is loyal and will go along," I said. "You will find that he will go along like Senator Robinson—to the last breath. There are stories that Robinson was not too strong for the Court plan, but went along anyway."

"They just aren't true," he snapped.

"I am not saying they are," I reminded him. "I am just passing on what I hear. I have been told that Senator Wheeler was advised every night, with the knowledge of Robinson, what fellows were weakening on his side and what fellows were weakening on our side."

"I just don't believe it," the President said. "You know, I have come to the conclusion that Wheeler is not a progressive or liberal at heart, but a New England conservative, the same as Calvin Coolidge. He moved out to Montana and had to go along with the progressive ideas that were in evidence in that section of the country, but his heart was never in them. I have known him a long time but I have never really known him well. Of course, he is tremendously ambitious and wants to be President. His wife is even more ambitious for the White House and it's a well-known fact that she runs him. He can't control her."

"I've never known Wheeler well," I answered, "nor Mrs. Wheeler; but more than one man has had trouble controlling his wife on political matters. But getting back to Kentucky, at present it looks as though Governor Chandler is in the lead. 'Happy' is an able campaigner."

"I realize it and that is the reason why we should put forth all our efforts for Alben."

"It has been brought to my attention that Barkley thinks I am against him," I said. "I must see him and correct this impression. In accordance with our agreement, I am keeping my hands off primary fights. I am fond of Barkley and Chandler. I wish they could both win."

"Barkley must win," Roosevelt said earnestly. "Harrison would repeal the Capital Gains Tax. He would do it now if he could."

The last state discussion in our political review was our mutual native state of New York. The Jackson bubble had exploded and Jackson had been kicked upstairs by being named Solicitor General.

"Bob lacks political experience," he shook his head sadly. "Such a nice fellow, too."

"You just couldn't get anywhere with him," I said. "I'm satisfied of that. I think Governor Lehman might want to run again."

"I think so, too," he said. "Mrs. Lehman likes to be first lady of the state. But he's not working so hard as he did. He spends a lot of time in Westchester and doesn't work like he did."

"He's too busy writing letters," I put in facetiously in reference to the Governor's letter to Senator Wagner against the Court plan. He ignored my reference to the letter which had put a beautiful friendship on ice. Later Roosevelt forgave Lehman.

I asked whether he had any new legislation to propose to Congress.

"No, I haven't anything on the fire for this session," he said, "but I will have for the next. I have to do something about housing. Unless private capital steps in hurriedly and starts spending money, the Federal government will have to lend assistance. J. P. Morgan and Company and Thomas W. Lamont agree with me on this. So does Owen D. Young. I have some definite ideas in mind for a road program—some transcontinental highways, Boston to Atlanta and others."

We talked about finding a place for Frank Murphy in the administration, because the latter was doubtful of reelection in view of his record against sit-down strikers in Michigan. The President said he planned to name Harry Hopkins, then recuperating in Florida, First Commissioner of Public Welfare when such a department was approved with the passage of his reorganization program.

"By the way, do you think Dan Roper is willing to resign?" he asked.

"I think he will resign if you suggest it," was my answer.

"Maybe I could send him to Canada and put Joe Kennedy in his place."

"I don't think Joe would be satisfied with anything less than the Treasury," I said. "Don't you expect him to stay abroad?"

"Only about a year," he answered. "I'd like to get him in Commerce."

"Or get Dan out," I interjected.

"You have something there," he laughed. "But Joe is an able fellow. You know, I've been annoyed by stories that I appointed Joe before Robert Bingham resigned. Actually the late Ambassador had said he wanted to resign. He telephoned from abroad saying he wanted to come home for a physical examination and would resign, but wanted to defer his resignation until the check-up. He wanted to go back to close his affairs at the embassy. Actually I had his resignation but did not make it public. The story by Arthur Krock in the *New York Times* was annoying to me and to Bingham in the hospital where he died."

Not long after I discovered the Krock story came directly from the

White House, but without the President's knowledge, then or afterward.

At this time it was my belief that the Democrats would not lose more than two or three seats in the Senate and about fifty in the House. I based this estimate on the inevitable return pendulum swing of an off-presidential year, the general recession, and the fact the Democratic machine was not functioning as smoothly as it might because of the split within the party. I considered this a most serious deflection and was striving as best I could to quiet party fears. My efforts were being pointed at the November elections, in the belief that once the primaries were out of the way, all would be well. I little knew what was ahead.

In these days I was spending more and more time with members of Congress. The President had asked that I help in the drive to put over his governmental reorganization bill. On Capitol Hill I ran into the trails of Harold L. Ickes, Harry Hopkins, David K. Niles, Joseph B. Keenan, Thomas G. Corcoran, and James Roosevelt, all of whom were expressing the displeasure of the President with those who had opposed him. On every hand I heard complaints that the vast power of the administration in the manipulation of patronage and funds was being mobilized to purge the party of all but one hundred per cent New Dealers. There was much grumbling that while the President was proclaiming hands-off in the Democratic primaries, he was writing letters endorsing the candidacy of his friends.

There were innumerable murmurings from Congressmen that these advisers were displacing me and that presidential purgers had taken over the party machinery. I was doing my best to laugh away these fears when a blast of presidential displeasure came up out of the South with a terrible roar. I had seen the President off on a spring vacation to Warm Springs. On his way down he paused at Gainesville, Georgia, to dedicate a public square named after him. He was introduced to a sizable crowd by Senator George. The President ignored the Senator but beamed over Governor Eurith D. Rivers.

The words the President spoke were not many but they were as heavy with ominous portent as the chains that Marley's ghost dragged to the bedside of Ebenezer Scrooge. The halls of Congress echoed his blast against representatives of the people "who vote against legislation to help social and economic conditions, proclaiming loudly they are for the objectives but do not like the methods, and then fail utterly to offer a better method of their own." He laid the South's difficulties to old-fashioned feudalism, adding: "When you come down to it, there is little difference between the feudal system and the fascist system. If you believe in the one you lean to the other." What was even more galling to southern members of Congress was the inference that those who had opposed him had been purchased by the vested interests. I found members of Congress seething. Garner told me that the speech had made a solid bloc that would vote against almost anything the President might propose. He labelled the purge "as unnecessary as hell," predicting it could do nothing but harm to the party in November. He stormed against the President's advisers, saying they had crept up on the Boss's blind side.

The next week the President threw Congress into another dither by an extraordinary announcement, released to reporters at two o'clock one morning at Warm Springs, castigating those who were opposing his reorganization bill. He characterized the opposition as "an organized effort on the part of political or special interest groups" and then expressed personal disinclination to become a dictator with:

"I have no inclination to be a dictator.

"I have none of the qualifications which would make a successful dictator.

"I have too much historical background and too much knowledge of existing dictatorships to make me desire any form of dictatorship for a democracy like the United States."

The statement was a calculated reply to the flood of hundreds of thousands of telegrams against the plan, which poured in upon members of Congress, at the inspiration of the Rev. Charles E. Coughlin, radio priest, and Frank Gannett, publisher. The Senate supported the measure and the President hailed the action as evidence that the Senate cannot be purchased by organized telegrams based on direct misrepresentation. The use of the word "purchased" was resented in Congress where administration spokesmen were offering all sorts of promises for votes. While the bill would not have made Roosevelt a dictator, the overzealous activity of White House agents gave members of the House considerable reason to believe so when the measure came up in that body.

On the President's return from Warm Springs I found him in excellent humor, nearer what he had been in his earliest days in office than I had seen him in some time. I saw him at a bedside conference that morning.

I grasped the opportunity to deal quite frankly with the problem of Congress and the business recession. I revealed myself as hopeful there would be no more clashes with Congress.

"In other words, I hope this session of Congress will soon adjourn and that we try, if possible, to get away without having any more legislation proposed," I said.

"Lord, Jim, so do I," he said with a flash of old time candor. "I feel just as you do. I want to get them home as soon as possible. We might need some money for relief and possibly tax legislation. Might need a billion or a billion and a half for public works."

"Well, I hope that they move it as soon as possible. The atmosphere here and around the country is none too good, if you know what I mean."

"I certainly do, Jim. I'm fully aware of the situation that has been created around the country through propaganda and by other means. Every time I ask for more legislation they raise the cry of 'dictator' and, apparently because of the situation that exists in Europe, they frighten the people in this country over such a possibility. I mean a possibility of dictatorship. This has had its effect on legislation. The people are unnecessarily disturbed about it as in the case of the reorganization bill. This bill doesn't really mean very much. You and I know it. The teeth have been taken out and there really isn't very much to it except the principle of the thing."

For some time I had been worried about the President's attitude on the recession. There was an honest doubt in my mind as to whether he realized the seriousness of the situation. However, in our talk I found him fully aware of the problem and preparing to take steps to meet the crisis.

On April 8, 1938, I got busy with the telephone to aid in the reorganization fight, determined to help the President emerge as the master of his party. Everywhere I found members of Congress committed against the bill. I was surprised at the strength of the opposition, particularly since the bill as passed by the Senate was a mild one. I got a number of Congressmen to go along, but many refused to be budged. I worked right up to the night when the bill was defeated by a vote of 204 to 196.

The next day I had lunch with the President. I rode over from the Post Office Department expecting to find him in a lather similar to those he worked up over defeat of the Court plan and the wage and hour legislation. Before I went in to him I had a chat with White House Secretary Early, who told me that an effort was being made to have the President fire a critical salvo at deserting Democrats by writing a letter to Congressman Rayburn congratulating him on his effort in the losing battle. I guessed that Early was referring to Ickes, Corcoran, Hopkins, and the rest of the White House clique. Early said he had argued for a more conciliatory tone and showed me the copy of a letter he favored.

When I went in I found the President in a mood to talk and more hurt than angry over the latest defeat. I took the bull by the horns by stating that I had seen the Early letter, thought it was a good letter, and considered it expressed the proper attitude for him to take.

"Jim, I'll tell you that I didn't expect the vote," he said. "I can't understand it. There wasn't a chance for anyone to become a dictator under that bill."

"The best thing to do is to forget it," I said, embarrassed by his confession of bewilderment. "The important thing to do is to get people to work. It is essential to get the relief legislation moving as quickly as possible and get Congress out of here by May 15, if possible. I think you should do as much as you can for the Public Works Administration because the people regard that organization highly."

We shifted to a discussion of politics. He asked for a review of the situation beginning by saying he did not think we would lose more than five or six seats in Congress.

"I think we might lose two or three in the Senate alone," I said.

"We can hold our own in Massachusetts and Rhode Island and we might have a loss in Connecticut. That takes care of New England," he said.

"Well, we might be all right in New York, but we may be seriously affected in Pennsylvania because of the unfortunate fight within the party," I said. "We will lose some seats in Illinois. We might also lose in the Midwest generally. We may lose in Delaware. The Ohio situation is not good. I don't think there's much danger in the western states. The border states are safe. At present I would say we may lose about fifty seats; but then the situation may clear up by election time."

"Seems to me you're getting to be a gloomy prophet," he laughed, "and I'm getting to be more optimistic than you."

"See me in October; I can call them better when we come down the stretch." I joined in his laugh.

"Jim, why don't you run for the Senate?" he asked.

"Boss, I just wouldn't like it," I said. "Whatever ability I have is executive, and it would just drive me mad to sit up there every day and listen to speeches."

"I can understand your attitude, but we just can't close the matter by leaving the ticket at Bob Wagner for Governor and Jim Mead for the Senate, if Lehman won't run again," he said. "By the way, I saw La Guardia the other day and he isn't strong for Lehman. He doesn't want to support him."

"He will, because the American Labor Party is for Lehman," I put in. "There's no doubt in my mind that La Guardia would support Lehman before he would throw in his lot with a reactionary Republican."

"Well, La Guardia suggested that the three of us sit down and arrange for a ticket that the American Labor Party would like," he continued.

"I'm out," I said with no little finality.

The next few days were occupied with the planning and writing of the presidential message which officially acknowledged the United States was in another depression. The solution to be offered Congress was five billion dollars of pump priming in cash and credits, including $1,250,000,000 for the Works Progress Administration, $1,450,000,000 for the Public Works Administration, $462,000,000 for housing, flood control, and federal buildings, and $300,000,000 for the Civilian Conservation Corps. He had been voted an authorization of one and a half billion dollars in new Reconstruction Finance Corporation loans the week before.

I had dinner with the President April 12, during which I sought to impress upon him that speed was the essence of his pending program; that every effort should be made not only to halt the downward spiral but to move it back up again. He was in a good frame of mind, but I could see by the jut of his chin he had made up his mind and was determined to go through with what he had already decided on. In the talk the name of Henry Wallace was brought up.

"Henry would like to run for President," he said slowly. "However, I'd rather have a fellow like Ickes named, who, at least, is a fighter. Ickes will go through with whatever he has in mind. But you never know what Henry will do. He's in favor of one thing today and something entirely different tomorrow."

Around 8:15 P.M. Ickes and Wallace came in along with Hull, Morgenthau, Harry Hopkins, Jesse Jones, Jimmy Roosevelt, and Steve Early. The President read his message to the assemblage. Some suggestions were offered. The next day Jesse, Harry, Steve, Jimmy, and Paul Appleby of the Department of Agriculture met at the White House in the morning for another round of suggestions. At five o'clock that afternoon the President had me back for another reading, this time with Senators Glass, McKellar, Wagner, Barkley, Hayden, and Byrnes, and Congressmen Rayburn, Taylor, Woodrum, and Cannon. There was general approval of the message, although Glass was cold to the WPA proposal.

The message was well received as was another, somewhat later, asking for a Congressional investigation of monopoly which did much to undo the harm wrought by the Jackson and Ickes diatribes against "economic oligarchy," and the "60 families." A third and unconventional message to the Congressional Conference Committee, seeking to reconcile Senate and House views on taxation, was not so well received. It was the President's position that business would be hurt, not helped, by the Senate's slash of the administration's pet measure, the undistributed profits and capital gains taxes. The conference ultimately brought about a compromise, but the President's message did not sit well in the memory of the conservative wing of his own party.

With these matters off his desk, the President once more turned his hand to politics. In Illinois the result had been unfavorable but not too bad. Igoe, who had White House support, was defeated by Lucas, who had voted against wage and hour legislation. The New Deal lost this state earlier, however, when Dieterich withdrew after he was turned out of the Kelly–Nash and Horner factions.

In a series of conferences in late April and May, the President reiterated his desire to defeat Clark, McCarran, Smith, Adams, Tydings, Gillette, Van Nuys, George, and Lonergan. Each time, I gave him the best information I had, but kept myself aloof from the primary battles. I tried to tell him why this or that candidate could not dent one of his targets, but each time I found him determined to go through with the purge.

I did make an exception to my rule in Pennsylvania, where a violent primary campaign, best described by the President as reminding him of Dante's "Inferno," gave concern that factional feuding might cost us the state in November.

At the President's request I issued a statement in favor of Governor George Earle for the senatorial nomination and Thomas Kennedy for governor.

But Earle repudiated our support. The next day Pennsylvania voters turned thumbs down on it decisively by nominating Charles Alvin Jones over Kennedy, and Earle over Samuel D. Wilson. A few days later I found the President smoldering over Earle and the Pennsylvania setback.

"Earle has killed his chances for the Presidency," he said, "unless he comes to the Senate and makes a reputation that would nullify the primary results."

The state went Republican in the November election.

The President was most anxious to defeat Senator George in Georgia, but was having difficulty in finding a candidate. He was gleeful over reports that George appeared to be worried.

"I am going to endorse someone, if I have to pick my tenant farmer,

Moore," he said one day. "Rivers is definitely out, but will support whoever is picked. He's out because of the Ku Klux Klan business and because Eugene Talmadge would beat him."

He was equally firm about getting a candidate against Tydings in Maryland. There was some hope that Congressman Goldsborough, a power on the eastern shore, and Congressman Lewis, a power in western Maryland, could get together to block nomination of Tydings. The President said he wanted to name Goldsborough for a judicial post and might have to pick Davey Lewis for the Senate race if O'Conor would not pull out of the race for Governor in behalf of President Byrd of Maryland University.

Senator McAdoo had given me the draft of a letter he wanted the President to write for him. The President made a wry face as he read the glowing tribute McAdoo had composed for himself. He said he couldn't write the suggested letter, but would write a "Dear Mac" letter that would be satisfactory to the Senator, but not "so sugary."

We talked about the Missouri situation, where I said Senator Clark was bulletproof against purging. In this connection I reported that Senator Truman wanted to name the United States Marshal in the western district of the state and felt entitled to the post because he had consistently supported the administration. Roosevelt said he would have to consult Governor Stark. I protested that I did not think Stark should be consulted because it was a Federal appointment. He countered by saying Stark and T. J. Pendergast would have a battle for control this fall and the Governor might win.

"Jim, I'm going to go to Kentucky to help Barkley," he said. "I'm going to make a speech for him."

I said frankly that his appearance there was the only thing that could help Barkley, as Chandler was a formidable campaigner. I was not sure the visit would turn the tide.

In Idaho I told him Senator James P. Pope, who had supported the administration, would have his hands full with Congressman Worth Clark running on an anti-New Deal program.

During this period he discussed the Cabinet quite frankly. Dan Roper was beginning to feel the blasts of presidential coolness at Cabinet meetings and had asked W. Averell Harriman whether he should resign. I said I was sure Dan would accept another appointment or be content to retire to private life if the President so wished.

"I'll be glad to consider him when I get around to him," he said. "But we have to find someone for his place. We might take Frank Murphy, who is worried that he will be defeated for Governor this fall."

"Why not give the spot to Jesse Jones?" I asked.

"I don't want to do that," he said, "because just as soon as Jesse would get into the Cabinet he would try to use his office to get elected President. And he would make a bad President, Jim; he's too old and in bad health."

The President said he didn't know what to do with Secretary of the Navy Swanson, who was getting feebler every day. Nor did he know what to do with Secretary of War Woodring.

I asked the Boss whether he had read the book, *The 168 Days*, by Turner Catledge and Joseph Alsop, which was the story of the Supreme Court fight. I remarked that it contained mention of many inside discussions that could have come only from participants in various conferences.

"There's nothing I can do about it," he said. "It's a shame the way stories leak out. Frankly I think Harold Ickes is responsible for many of the stories that leak out of Cabinet meetings. I think he tells them to Drew Pearson. I arrive at this conclusion by a process of elimination. Hull and Morgenthau don't give them out, I'm sure Woodring, Cummings and you don't leak. Swanson doesn't see anyone. Neither Perkins, Wallace, or Roper would carry tales. That leaves Harold."

I asked about Morgenthau, who had been ailing.

"Oh, Henry works himself up into terrible stews," he said lightly. "When I was away, he was terribly concerned about the tri-partite agreement between the United States, France, and Britain on money stabilization. He was calling London every other minute and sweating over developments. You know when Henry is under a strain, he gets terrible headaches and really is in a very, very bad way. Now he's distressed about the relief program, not being in sympathy with it. I'll have to rub his brow and he'll be all right."

At this time I was working on my book, *Behind the Ballots*, with

Eddie Roddan. The President asked me particularly to mention that he had built up Lehman in New York.

"Jim, do you remember in 1929 when I told you I didn't want two terms as governor and should be looking around for a successor?" he said. "And do you remember in 1930 I definitely told you Lehman was the man? I did everything possible to put Lehman in the limelight and saw to it he was sent to different places throughout the state so he could be better known. The trouble with the Democratic party now is that they haven't built anyone up, particularly upstate."

CHAPTER FOURTEEN

PURGE FAILURE AND NEW DEAL ROUT

DURING THIS period the President was in excellent physical condition. Following his Warm Springs visit he went on a fishing trip along the Atlantic coast on the shakedown cruise of the U.S.S. *Philadelphia*. His mental attitude was up to par. He was undaunted by the Illinois and Pennsylvania setbacks and was sublimely confident that he could reform his party through the purges. He was not a whit less confident that the depression would be solved, if Congress would only follow his lead.

Jack Garner took a more realistic view of the situation. I had lunch with him and a number of Senators, including Minton, Lee, Byrnes, Barkley, Schwellenbach, Burke, and Truman. There was considerable good-natured kidding about the purge. After lunch Garner took me to his office where he gnawed angrily at a cigar as he gave vent to his analysis of the situation.

"The Boss has stirred up a hornet's nest by getting into these primary fights," he said. "There are now twenty men—Democrats—in the Senate who will vote against anything he wants because they are mad clean through. The feeling is becoming intensely bitter. It's downright unhealthy. Jim, I think you ought to take exception to the President's attitude. I think you should do so for the good of the party and this country."

"John, I just can't do that unless I resign from the Cabinet and the Democratic Committee. I don't like the purge any more than you do, but the situation won't be helped by my breaking with the Boss. I think I can render the best service by carrying on impartially until after the elections are over, and then determine what is best for me to do at that time. Until then there is nothing for me to do but go on as I have been doing. I will do my best to hold the party together."

"That's my concern," he said. "I'm interested in the continued success of the Democratic party. I've spent too many years working to get the party in power to enjoy the prospect facing us now. We are throwing away what we have gained. I have no further political ambitions. The party has been good to me. When it's all over, I want to go back to Uvalde and live to be a hundred. I don't think the Boss has any definite program to meet the business situation. I don't think much of the spending program. You can't keep spending forever; some day you have to meet the bills."

Political thunder came from the right in the primary campaign. Out in Iowa Gillette and Wearin waved their arms among the rows of tall corn. Gillette denounced "this gang of political termites . . . boring from within . . . planning on taking over . . . the Democratic party" and publicly acknowledged his opposition of the Court plan as "my crime, which has brought down on me . . . this pack of political wolves." Wearin played up the endorsement of Harry Hopkins and Jimmy Roosevelt. Gillette handily won renomination. I saw the President the day after the Primary. I showed him a wire I was sending congratulating Gillette on his victory and he approved it. I suggested that he see Gillette soon in the interests of promoting party harmony. He was not warm to the idea, but said he would see what could be done. Subsequently he extended the olive branch by offering a luncheon invitation.

June and July found the purgers working assiduously, but getting no pay dirt. In Indiana the state organization handed Van Nuys the nomination on bended knee. In Colorado Senator Adams licked his chops over Judge Benjamin Hilliard, who launched his unsuccessful candidacy practically from the front porch of the White House. In Texas three one hundred per cent New Dealers—Maury Maverick, Morgan Sanders, and W. D. McFarlane—bit the dust, and five Texas Congressmen blacklisted by the CIO, including Hatton W. Summers, vigorous foe of Court packing, were renominated. The score for the purgers was a succession of defeats. Senator Elmer Thomas won in Oklahoma with the White House blessing and Senator Claude Pepper won in Florida, but neither of these contests figured in the purge fight.

Meantime, the purge strategy board was turning up candidates against the men marked for extermination, but they didn't look like winners. The President dispatched White House Secretary Marvin

H. McIntyre to Georgia to survey the thinning crop. Mac didn't recruit tenant farmer Moore, but came up with Lawrence Sabyllia Camp, United States District Attorney at Atlanta. After many false starts the purge got under way in Maryland with sixty-nine-year-old Davey Lewis running against Tydings. In Missouri Senator Clark faced three candidates without more than a ripple of worry. In Nevada Pat McCarran was unruffled by the opposition of Doctor John Worden, one-time Socialist turned New Dealer, and Albert Hilliard, son of the man who failed to budge Adams in the Colorado race.

In the House the President was most anxious to defeat Smith of Virginia, O'Connor of New York, and Cox of Georgia. Against the Virginia Congressman the purgers pitted William E. Dodd, Jr., son of the former ambassador to Germany. Governor Price of Virginia told me Dodd hadn't a prayer. I had a conference with Corcoran, Keenan, Lowell Mellett, and Charles Michelson of the Democratic National Committee. Corcoran and Mellett were enthusiastic over Dodd's chances. I told them there was no use kidding themselves; their candidate hadn't a chance. Keenan and Michelson agreed with me that Dodd was a lost cause.

The President selected James Fay to run against O'Connor in New York. Fay had run against O'Connor a few years before. I saw O'Connor at this time. He was aware of the campaign being directed against him from the White House, but was confident of his own strength. He did not believe Fay could be persuaded to run against him. To protect himself he went after the Republican nomination as well as the Democratic selection.

At this time the New York situation was complicated by the death of Senator Copeland. The good doctor, who had sent chills up and down the spines of his colleagues after the death of Joseph T. Robinson when he took the Senate floor to say he could see the mark of death on the brow of many of his colleagues, was unable to see the sign on his own. I attended his funeral at Suffern, New York, where Governor Lehman told me he was going to make an announcement of his candidacy for the Copeland vacancy. This was a surprise because ordinarily he should have given state leaders the courtesy of a conference before making any announcement. Ed Flynn was irked and I didn't blame him. The same was true of Frank Kelly of Brooklyn.

Back in Washington I approached the President with the Lehman story by saying I had interesting news. He said he could tell from the way I was approaching it, that it was not pleasant. I reported my brief conversation with the Governor. He said he was sorry that Lehman had handled it that way; he said the Governor should have had more confidence in us and should have come to us with his desires. We agreed that there was little we could do beyond seeking to persuade Lehman to sit tight and not rock the boat. The Lehman announcement was made before any move could be made. On the day Lehman announced, the President called me to say that the news was broken to him by his colored valet, MacDuffie, as the latter brought in his breakfast. MacDuffie said, "Mr. President, I notice that the Governor announced for the Senate before the other man had a chance to lie down." The President enjoyed the remark immensely.

Early in July the President left on his western trip, stopping in Kentucky to do his best for Senator Barkley. Before he left, the President delivered a "fireside" chat on one of Washington's warmest nights, but the speech had more than enough heat for Democrats, for he frankly acknowledged he was out to purge his party.

"As head of the Democratic party, however, charged with the responsibility of carrying out the definitely liberal declaration of principles set forth in the 1936 Democratic platform, I feel that I have every right to speak in those few instances where there may be a clear issue between candidates for a Democratic nomination involving these principles, or involving a clear misuse of my own name.

"Do not misunderstand me, I certainly would not indicate a preference in a state primary merely because a candidate, otherwise liberal in outlook, had conscientiously disagreed with me on any single issue. I would be far more concerned about the general attitude of a candidate toward present day problems and his own inward desire to get practical needs attended to in a practical way. We all know that progress may be blocked by outspoken reactionaries and also by those who say 'yes' to a progressive objective, but who always find some reason to oppose any proposal to gain that objective. I call that type of candidate a 'yes, but' fellow."

There was more about Copperheads and the campaign of defeatism against the President, Congressmen, and Senators. On the whole, however, he found that the Seventy-fifth Congress had done better than any Congress between the end of the World War and the spring of 1933 even though it had failed him on the Supreme Court and reorganization. There was more, as I said, but the fact that he had been won over to the purge wholeheartedly was enough for me. I prepared to go to Alaska with Eddie Roddan and Ambrose O'Connell, where I hoped it would be cooler. As I surveyed the coming primaries, certain that the purgers were headed for trouble, I wondered if Alaska was far enough.

In Covington, the irrepressible "Happy" Chandler plumped himself into the President's automobile between Roosevelt and Barkley although he knew the President had come to throw the weight of his favor in the scales for the Senate's Majority Leader. Not even after the President had declared he had no doubt that Chandler would make a good Senator but . . . was the smile tightened on "Happy's" face. That night the President, from the rear platform of his train, pulled the rug from underneath the Governor by praising Senator M. M. Logan for standing "square like a rock" when Chandler came to the White House with a proposal that Logan be made a federal judge, so that Chandler could go to the Senate. Logan and the President had refused "to traffic in judicial appointments," said Logan, who also spoke. The President's Special left Kentucky a few minutes later, certain that the day had been saved for Barkley; and so it developed.

In Oklahoma Senator Thomas was called "my old friend." In Texas the President caused Senator Tom Connally's face to drop into his lap when he announced from the rear platform at Wichita Falls that he had offered Governor Allred a federal judgeship. Connally was not consulted on the appointment. Neither was Garner, who had a candidate and did not greet his chief during the latter's visit. In Colorado, Roosevelt gave Adams the silent treatment. In Nevada, McCarran, marked for the same treatment, maneuvered skillfully to turn a Roosevelt reception at Carlin into a rally for himself. McAdoo was hailed into the "old friend" tribe at Los Angeles. All this made interesting reading in Alaska. From San Diego the President embarked on a fishing trip down the west coast through the Panama Canal and to a dock at Pensacola, Florida. On his way to Washington he stopped off at Athens, Georgia, to accept an honorary degree at the University of Georgia, where he avoided politics. He more than made up for the omission the next day at Barnesville.

A goodly crowd heard him refer to George, who was on the speakers' platform along with his opponent, Camp, as "my old friend" and then proceed to excommunicate the senior Senator from his party. George was uncrushed. He reached over to take the President's hand, expressing regret that the Chief Executive had seen fit to attack his standing in the party and accepting the challenge. George reported that the President accepted this gesture with, "Let's always be friends." And George was sure he heard him add, "God bless you, Walter."

I did not see the President until August 25 when I went up to the family home at Hyde Park. I had talked to him on the phone August 20, when I mentioned the victory Worth Clark had won over Senator Pope, who had the White House blessing (which was rapidly becoming a kiss of death). After the call I advised Clark, also by phone, to send the President a wire and letter explaining his vote in the House on different measures, telling him I thought it would help and might eliminate the possibility of Pope's entry into the field as an independent in the election. Such a move by Pope would certainly bring a split in the party in Idaho, which I was determined to avoid.

At the family estate I had lunch with the President, Mrs. Roosevelt, Mrs. James Roosevelt, Jr., Mrs. Ellen Woodward, and four or five women who were regional WPA directors. In the evening we had dinner at the home of Mrs. James Roosevelt, sister-in-law of the President. In the afternoon we took a drive to the retreat the President was building for himself. We had a long conversation in his study.

"Jim, why don't you run for Governor?" he began. "Now, hold on a minute." This cut short an interruption he saw was coming. "I'm sure you can be elected. You know anything can happen in 1940 and I think you ought to take the chance and run for Governor now. You would make a good governor, Jim. And by taking the proper position in relation to power, electric light, and utility interests; and urging reorganization of the government, eliminating towns, and cutting municipal costs; and getting down overhead expenses of government, you could go a long way, Jim. You could become a very positive governor and get the proper background for 1940."

"Frankly, I'm not interested in 1940," I said. "I can't afford to be interested."

"A lot of other people are interested in you for 1940, Jim; and I'm not sure whether as Postmaster General and Democratic National Chairman you have sufficient background to be nominated and elected President."

"The White House is the least of my troubles," I told him. "I just can't think of it, even though the governorship might be a step in that direction. The plain fact is that I have reached the age in life where I should be thinking of myself and my family."

"The governorship might not be as expensive as you think, to say nothing of the White House," he said.

"Regardless of the money involved, Bess would not want to go to Washington even if you gave her the Capitol," I said. "And she has no use for Albany."

"The social life isn't so strenuous," he said. "There are only three dinners during the year—one for the Court of Appeals, one to the Cabinet, and one more. I'm speaking of Albany, of course. And then it's necessary to be up there only one afternoon a week to see callers, who occasionally drop in around tea time. The governor's wife can devote as much or as little time to social life as she wishes."

"Boss, there just isn't any use in talking further about this," I said. "As much as I would like to be Governor I just can't do it. Let's forget it for once and for all."

"Well, if you feel that way . . ." He left the sentence unfinished and assumed an injured look.

In a discussion of the political situation, I attempted to persuade him to make a swing around the country in behalf of Democratic candidates after the primaries. He put me off saying if he went into one state he would have to go into another.

In our mention of Kentucky he was furious over the conduct of Chandler, because the irrepressible "Happy" had bowed to the right and left, acknowledging applause of the crowd when he drove with the President and Barkley to the Latonia Race Track. I was surprised to find the President feeling so deeply about homage he felt was his.

The President reported he had made up his mind to put Harry Hopkins in as Secretary of Commerce when Roper submitted his resignation. He wanted to know if it would be all right to name Louis Johnson Secretary of the Navy in case anything happened to Claude Swanson. He said he had not removed the ailing Swanson because the Secretary and his wife were without income other than that he had as a Cabinet officer.

The defeats followed in the next week. In South Carolina "Cotton Ed" Smith had little trouble winning renomination. The President had a one-sentence comment, "It takes a long, long time to build the past up to the present." In California "Dear Mac," Senator McAdoo, was soundly trounced by Sheridan Downey and his pension program. The President accepted Downey as a liberal. As National Chairman I offered Downey election support.

That week end the President, bloody but unbowed, set out to do battle in Maryland in behalf of Lewis against Tydings. On September 4, 1938, we motored down to Morgantown, Maryland, with candidate Lewis and Governor Nice riding with the President. I rode with Senator F. Ryan Duffy of Wisconsin. That night was the only night I ever spent on board the presidential yacht *Potomac*, except the night we went down to Jefferson Island near Washington for the harmony meeting after the Court fight.

The next day, Labor Day, the President delivered what he termed a "sermon" on the courthouse lawn at Denton, eastern shore home of Congressman T. Alan Goldsborough. The President pointed an accusing finger at Tydings as one of "those in public life who quote the golden rule, but take no steps to bring it closer." Lewis beamed.

"It's a bust," I confided to reporters.

On September 8, I received a phone call from Miss Le Hand reporting the President was in low spirits because of the illness of his son Jimmy, who was suffering from a stomach ulcer. She suggested I call around 5:30 that afternoon, which I did. I inquired about Jimmy's health, and he confessed himself upset over it. Otherwise he was in a good frame of mind and asked about the Maryland situation. I said it was bad, noting that those supporting Lewis against Tydings had been unable to raise money because those from whom they might get money were not in sympathy with what was being done there.

That night I called Vice President Garner to suggest he wire the President about Jimmy's health. He said he would do so and then asked, "How do things look?"

"All depends on which side you're looking from," I countered. "From your side and mine the whole situation is most aggravating. I've gone through a number of hectic weeks, but am doing my best to keep my feet on the ground."

"I think the Boss is making a great mistake," he said. "Don't you?"

"I agree with you one hundred per cent," I answered.

"Are you still a Democrat?" he asked.

"Yes, and I have my flag flying," I replied. "After my church, my family, and my country, the party comes next."

"That's the way I feel about it," he said.

"And after the primaries are over, I'm going to try to put the pieces of the party together again," I said.

"More power to you," he exclaimed. "Remember me to the family and God bless you."

"Thanks and my best to Mrs. Garner."

On the night of September 13, 1938, I called the President at Rochester, Minnesota, and, after inquiring about the condition of Jimmy, who had undergone an operation, I reported that the Maine election was disappointing in showing Republican gains and that Maryland had come out even worse than we expected. Tydings was renominated by a thumping three to one majority.

"Boss, it's necessary for me to send a congratulatory wire to Tydings," I said.

"I don't know why it should be," he retorted.

"I think I should at least express hearty congratulations," I persisted.

"Leave out the 'hearty' and all the other adjectives," he snapped.

"Boss, I think I ought to send him the same kind of wire I've sent to all the other successful primary candidates," I said.

"Suit yourself but leave me out of it," he closed.

The next day I had lunch with Secretary Morgenthau who, to my surprise, expressed himself very much opposed to the purge. He said he had received calls from Hopkins and Corcoran asking him to get internal revenue collectors to come out for Fay against O'Connor in New York, which he refused to do. This led to a discussion of Hopkins's role, and I said I was convinced that the President would like to run him in 1940, but it just was not possible to do so. He said the President was very fond of Harry. The same day I saw Jesse Jones on his return from Europe. I kidded him about the endorsement of the Texas convention of Garner, rather than Jones, for the Presidency. After some banter I told him I was sure Garner did not want the nomination himself but was willing to take the delegation so that he could swing it any way he wanted to go in the 1940 convention. Jones agreed with me. Jesse was very much opposed to the purges and, like Henry, felt that they would be harmful to the President in the next Congress.

That week the purge campaign blew up completely. In Georgia first returns put Camp in third place and he never got out of it. George won and anti-New Deal Eugene Talmadge was second. In Colorado, Adams was nominated without opposition. In Connecticut Lonergan was renominated by the Democratic state convention. Of those marked for purging only Representative O'Connor still was to face the voters. Of others so marked, Senators Gillette, Smith, Tydings, George, Van Nuys, Clark, McCarran, Adams, and Lonergan had all come through unscathed. Representative Smith won in Virginia and Representative Cox in Georgia. Along the line the President suffered minor rebuffs. His victories—Barkley, Pepper, Thomas, and others—were not involved in the purge.

When the Georgia results were in I was asked by reporters to comment on the primaries.

"Well, they are about over now," I said.

"Did you say, 'Thank God'?" I was asked.

"All right, make it 'Thank God,'" I said and I meant it.

Although I am not a political philosopher, but one schooled in practical politics, let me pause here to point a moral. I knew from the beginning that the purge could lead to nothing but misfortune, because in pursuing his course of vengeance Roosevelt violated a cardinal political creed which demanded that he keep out of local matters.

Sound doctrine is sound politics. When Roosevelt began neglecting the rules of the game, I began to have doubts. When he persisted in violating the rules, I lost faith in him. I trace all the woes of the Democratic party, directly or indirectly, to this interference in purely local affairs. In any political entity voters naturally and rightfully resent the unwarranted invasion of outsiders. The attempt to establish a personal party, the neglect of party leaders, the assumption of control over the judiciary and Congress, and the gratification of personal ambition in the third and fourth terms—all were the evil fruit of his breaking the rules of the game. Party leadership has its obligations as well as its privileges. He should have kept his hands out of regional matters; he should have observed the regularity, which is the essence of the two-party system, and he should have encouraged other men in the party to grow as tall as himself. This is as sound in business and labor as it is in politics.

The end of the month found me at the New York State convention in Rochester working to persuade Governor Lehman to reconsider his decision to run for the Copeland vacancy and to seek reelection against Thomas E. Dewey. In the convention and conferences I assumed the responsibility and was in complete charge. Old timers noted it was a long time since the state chairman had so dominated a convention. Lehman was finally persuaded to accept the nomination but insisted on the nomination of Charles Poletti, as Lieutenant Governor, instead of M. William Bray. I was in communication with the President during the negotiations. He expressed pleasure at the outcome. Wagner and Mead were named for the Senate. I felt we had a strong state ticket.

In the next few weeks I was busy doing all I could for Democrats everywhere. On all sides reports gave cause for concern. I reported faithfully to the President. He pitched in to help, avoiding the unpurged Democrats, however. On election eve, speaking from his home at Hyde Park, he did a stint over the air to elect Democrats who would help him carry out his program.

"If American democracy ceases to move forward as a living force, seeking day and night by peaceful means to better the lot of our citizens, fascism and communism aided, unconsciously perhaps, by old line Tory Republicans, will grow in strength," he said.

In my drive to leave no stone unturned to help put over the ticket, I went to Al Smith to ask him to support Lehman. I knew this would not only have a salutary effect on the state ticket but would help the Democratic cause throughout the country. He said that while his family was going to vote for Lehman and Wagner, he could not offer public support. He said he was very fond of Wagner, that he had roomed with him for years. He said he would not change his mind if the Governor were to make a personal appeal.

During an hour's chat in Al's office, he said he never had any feeling about my activity in behalf of Roosevelt, saying there was nothing else I could have done or should have done except follow my judgment. He revealed he never expected to be nominated in Chicago in 1932, especially after the two-thirds rule was invoked. He said he had no feeling against Roosevelt personally, but could not agree with many New Deal policies or with a lot of things that were going on with his knowledge or acquiescence.

Election night I was at my offices in the Biltmore. From the first it was evident that the tide was ebbing and it was a question of how far out the Democrats would ride. In New York the governorship was nip and tuck with Lehman finally squeezing out ahead by over 68,000 votes. Mead and Wagner both rode through. But elsewhere there was little to rejoice about. The Republicans won 81 House seats, 8 in the Senate, and 11 governorships. It was a great turnover, but the Democrats were still comfortably in control. During the long night I spoke several times to the President. He was surprised at the extent of the sweep, far more surprised than I was. He was by no means stunned, however. I joked with him about defeat of some of his New Dealers. He took it well enough. It is not in my nature to cry over spilt milk, so I found what humor I could in the situation, remarking that while it was a defeat, it was still far from final and we had two years to build up the party. The President said that he had expected to lose one Senator and perhaps sixteen Representatives, but was not prepared for a deluge.

That was his public face. On November 11, 1938, he let down his hair at a Cabinet meeting. The session opened with a discussion of the foreign situation. Politics were not discussed until the President reached me in going down the line of members of his official family.

"Have you got anything to say?" he asked me almost accusingly.

"No, sir," I answered. "Nothing in particular."

"Well, I've been giving a lot of time to the study of the election returns and I find they demonstrate the result around the country was due in every case to local conditions," he declared challengingly. "Take Massachusetts—our losses were due to Curley. The people didn't want him back as Governor so we lost all down the line."

Everyone at the table nodded as he seemed to demand some expression by the vigor of his statements.

"It was the race track scandal in Rhode Island," he went on. "And in Connecticut it was the Merritt Parkway squabble. In New Jersey defeat could be attributed to Mayor Hague. In Pennsylvania it was brought about by the trouble within the party. And in Ohio Davey was to blame."

I interjected a note of agreement on the last state.

"So it goes everywhere you look into the real causes," the President continued. "In Michigan the defeat of Murphy was brought about by the Dies Committee and its sensationalism in investigating the sit-down strikes. Murphy had not recovered from the loss he suffered in the strikes.

"The Minnesota defeat was caused by the opposition of the churches. They were aroused by reports that Governor Benson had the support of people with Communist leanings."

"Also Benson had three or four Jewish assistants and they were responsible for giving him advice that hurt him," Wallace put in.

"In the farm belt the result was due to farm prices," the President went on. There was a general nodding in agreement.

"We lost the small businessmen in small towns and every effort should be made to get them back for the next campaign," Wallace said.

"In Iowa the Maytag strike hurt Krashel," the President said. "And in Wisconsin the Democrats voted Republican to get rid of La Follette."

No explanation was offered for Wyoming or Colorado, where we lost. Harry Hopkins sat in on the Cabinet meeting, but did not participate in this phase of the discussion. I debated asking him to discuss the contribution of the purge to the defeat, but thought better of it. There was nothing to be gained by churning up unnecessary hates. I could afford to swallow the injuries done me by the purgers, if the attempt to build up a personal machine was to be abandoned and we were returning to the building up of the Democratic party. However, I was soon to find that the White House crowd looked on the purge as a mere training lap and they were off to a new start in whooping it up for a third term. From that time on the President began to see less and less of me, as if I were to blame for the defeat I had counseled against, and to see more and more of those actually responsible for the November rout. My appointments became further and further apart. I was no longer consulted on appointments. And I found myself without a voice in political policy. Yet, there was nothing I could put a finger on. Outwardly we were as friendly as ever. It was just that I found myself outside the White House door. True, it had not been slammed in my face, but it was locked and barred nonetheless.

CHAPTER FIFTEEN

THIRD TERM BEGINNINGS

I NOW COME to the story of the third term. This is not an easy story to tell. I shall tell it as fairly to all concerned as I know how. Wherever I can, from my voluminous notes, I shall tell in his own words how Franklin D. Roosevelt put by third term suggestions "each time gentler than the other," then entered on a long period of enforced silence, and finally engineered his own nomination. I want to be fair to myself, for, had it not been for the man many have credited me with putting in the White House, I might have been Vice President or even President. I say that without rancor because I believe what has happened to me has happened for the best. I am now providing for my family, which I could not have done if I had remained in public life to preside over the Senate, or even if my address were now the White House.

As a matter of cold fact, I have only one regret about public service and this is that I did not participate in the war effort. I offered to forego politics at the outbreak of the war to devote myself to organizing the nation's productive capacity. I was confident I could do a good job, but my offer was ignored. Again, after Pearl Harbor, I volunteered to serve in any capacity where I might be of value, but my opposition to the third term evidently induced the President to turn his thumbs down on me. This action of the President hurt me deeply. After all, I had a right to serve my country and, in all modesty, I could have been useful. The loss of political advancement has not troubled me, as no one is more aware of my shortcomings for the Presidency than I am. I would have tried my best had the office fallen to me, but my best might not have been enough.

I have been widely criticized for remaining with Roosevelt as long as I did. Let me say I had faith in the man. This was shattered in 1937 and 1938, and I made up my mind that I was going to carry on into 1940 for the country and the party. I felt I could be helpful. I also felt

I owed it to those who had confidence in me to remain as long as I might be of help.

The third term issue began simmering almost before the second was assured in the 1936 landslide election. A presidential denial of third term ambitions did little to discourage the political hot stove league which runs the year round. In June, 1937, the question was dramatically thrust before the nation at a White House press conference when Fred W. Perkins of the *Pittsburgh Press* asked, "Mr. President, would you care to comment on Governor Earle's suggestion that you run for a third term?"

"The weather is very hot," the President said laughingly.

"Mr. President, would you tell us now if you would accept a third term?" spoke up Robert Post of the *New York Times*, who was to meet death heroically as a war correspondent on an air mission over Germany.

"Bob Post should put on a dunce cap and stand in the corner," was the presidential answer which was to become celebrated in stories and cartoons.

"Mr. President, did your statement last winter fully cover the third term situation?" came from the undaunted Perkins.

"Fred Perkins should don a dunce cap likewise," he retorted.

This incident provoked more third term speculation than it quieted. While some professed to see in it a renunciation as final as William T. Sherman's "If nominated I will not accept; if elected I will not serve," it was more widely interpreted as a nimble evasion or colorful postponement of the issue.

From the election of 1936 on, Roosevelt was concerned with his succession. After the Democratic reverses in the 1938 election, he became increasingly interested in the 1940 Democratic national convention and the presidential campaign to follow. He saw his successor in every man to achieve stature in the country but found each one wanting in White House qualifications. He became more critical of others as the campaign approached until, at length, he let himself be persuaded there was only one man possessing both the qualifications and the experience necessary to administer the nation.

Men are not, as a rule, nominated for the Presidency because they are the outstanding men in the party from the standpoint of ability and experience. Many fine men, who would have made great Presidents, could never be nominated. This was true in the past and it is true today. National conventions of both parties usually pick a man who is considered the most available from a vote-getting point of view with a secondary emphasis upon his competency as President if elected.

At the end of 1938, it appeared that the Democratic nominee for President would be Garner, Hull, or myself. This was the verdict of many polls, the consensus of political leaders, and the judgment of political writers. Of the three, I had reason to believe Roosevelt would have preferred to see me nominated. This does not mean I was his choice, except in that group and at that particular time. I don't think he would have taken Garner under any circumstances. I think he would have preferred Hull to Garner, although he believed Hull would have made a poor Chief Executive because Hull, he said, pondered long and moved slowly. He objected to Garner's conservatism. As for myself, I am sure he felt my religion and my background would be a handicap if I were the nominee. I can perhaps best give the picture of that period as it looked to me, by quoting from a memorandum I dictated at the beginning of 1939:

"I am satisfied in my own mind that the President will not be a voluntary candidate for reelection, but might be willing to listen to argument. I don't know if he has anyone in mind, definitely, to succeed him. If he had to make a selection at the moment, I believe he would select Harry Hopkins, Robert Jackson or Frank Murphy, in the order named.

"But a situation can develop in 1940 whereby the nominee will be either Garner, Hull or Farley, in the order named. There isn't any doubt in my mind that if I assist in bringing about Garner's or Hull's nomination, I can have second place with either man, if I want it. I think the President, if he doesn't take the nomination and run himself, is going to be placed in the position of choosing among those named. But Roosevelt is a very strong character, and he might insist on naming his successor." If a choice had to be made, I am sure he would have selected Hull.

Following the 1938 Congressional election I wrote to Democratic leaders throughout the country. I called on every county chairman to write and give me his reasons for the defeat. I received hundreds of letters, which I passed on to the President. The reasons they gave for the Democratic reversals were:

1. Criticism of the administration's spending program.
2. The battle between the AFL and the CIO.
3. Widespread feeling that the CIO exerted tremendous influence on the administration.
4. Low farm prices.
5. Dissatisfaction of WPA workers with their rate of pay.
6. Public dissatisfaction with the WPA program.
7. Discontent among those receiving Federal bounty in the form of loans when called upon to make payments.
8. The protest of business—large and small—against regimentation.
9. The business unrest created by the administration in its regulatory programs.
10. The continued pounding of the New Deal in the press.

With all this information in his hands, the President nonetheless persisted in viewing the adverse results of the 1938 election as due in every case to local conditions. While I was certain that deep in his heart he knew better, he never admitted it to me.

I did not see him alone after the election until November 15, 1938. Before going to the White House for dinner I had a visit from Henry Wallace, who was very much disturbed about the New Deal. He expressed the belief, which surprised me, that the President was leaning too much to the left and expressed the hope that we could persuade him to do differently. I told him I was having dinner at the White House and would talk to the President. I gathered Wallace had done so without effect.

At the White House I found the President preoccupied and somewhat distant. He talked less than he had at any time I had been with him. He ate slowly. He kept looking about as though he would welcome an interruption. I waited for his mood to pass; but when it did not, I carried the conversational ball.

"Boss, if you wouldn't mind, I'd like to offer a little advice," I began. "I just want to give you an idea or two, based on the way things look from my corner and I hope you won't misunderstand me."

"Shoot, Jim," he invited.

"Well, I think the thing for you to do when you come back from Warm Springs is to get together with members of Congress. I'm speaking particularly of the Senators and Congressmen who were opposed to you on the Supreme Court, wages and hours, reorganization, and the like. . . ."

"I'd like to see them all . . ." he interrupted.

"Wait!" I urged. "Hear me out. I don't want you to make up your mind now. Just think the matter over. I'd like to talk this over in detail with you later on. Right now I'd like to have you think over the necessity of securing a friendly attitude toward you and your program in Congress. I am convinced that the present condition is detrimental to you and to the party. I don't know what you are being told by others, but I think you ought to know this."

He was silent.

"That's all I want to say at this time. I want you to know how I feel. I think the situation can be corrected and forgotten, if you take the initiative. I would like to see you avoid any arguments with Congress over patronage. Such wrangles could only bring you a loss of dignity."

"I just won't go along with Carter Glass on any appointment in Virginia." He was almost peevish. "And I won't go along with Walter George in Georgia. That's final."

"Well, then you just won't get any appointments by the Senate that Glass and George label personally obnoxious."

"We'll see about that," he said with a determined thrust of his chin. "I don't anticipate any trouble from Congress. Reorganization is now in the lap of Congress and I am willing to let the farm bill go along as it is to see whether it will work out."

"I have one thing more on my mind in connection with Congress and that is the Vice President," I said. "I think Jack Garner could be most helpful to you. He's looked up to by everyone in Congress and he could do you a lot of good. I'd see him as soon as he gets back and have a long talk, if I were you."

"Yes," he said vaguely. I knew from his tone that he did not have too much confidence in Jack and that he felt that Garner was opposed to his legislation. While he did not say so, I was fully aware he still blamed Garner for the final defeat of the Court bill, when the facts were there was nothing Garner could do but throw in the presidential towel.

We talked about a successor to Cummings, and a successor to Roper, and a possible successor to Woodring. Roosevelt could purge his own Cabinet if he couldn't purge Congress. Even so, he was proceeding most slowly about the shifts, being one who was forever putting off anything distasteful.

I did not see the President again for more than a month, except at Cabinet meetings. During this period the situation was growing more critical in Europe. Renewed persecution of Jews in Germany by Adolf Hitler brought Ambassador Hugh Wilson home for a consultation which proved to be a recall. William Phillips was summoned home at the same time from Rome. Cabinet meetings were solemn considerations of the Rome–Berlin axis, larded with gloomy predictions of what the Tokyo partner might do. I did not keep notes of these fateful meetings, feeling that what was said concerned the country and the world so deeply that it should not be carried from the room. While I regret that this chapter of history, a most important chapter, is missing from my files, I would probably not make the notes if I had it all to do over again.

While I contributed to the discussion, feeling that war was close, I realized that the conduct of international affairs was in the province of the White House and State Department and I did not want to run the danger that my notes, if I kept them, might get out and possibly embarrass my country.

Thanksgiving Day, November 24, 1938, I talked with Arthur Krock of the *New York Times*, who was still engaged in controversy with Harry Hopkins over the remark, "We will spend and spend, and tax and tax, and elect and elect." The remark, carried by Krock in a Washington report, was widely quoted by the opposition. Hopkins had denied it and was still denying it weeks after the election. Krock told me the story of the remark and how he got it. I must respect his confidence, but I am satisfied it was made as quoted. I have every reason to believe it was said by Hopkins to Max Gordon and at least one other person at the Yonkers, New York, Empire Race Track in August of 1938.

On December 1, 1938, I had luncheon with Wendell Willkie, president of Commonwealth and Southern Corporation. In a general discussion of the political situation, Willkie professed great admiration for the President and his program. He said he disagreed with him only on the power question, where Willkie felt Roosevelt was being led astray by Thomas G. Corcoran and Frank McNinch of the National Power Policy Committee. Willkie told me he was a firm Democrat and had cast his vote for Governor Lehman and the rest of the Democratic ticket.

Early in December the New York election had a most interesting aftermath, which offers a pertinent sidelight on the Roosevelt character. The close race made by Thomas E. Dewey against Governor Lehman clearly made the former a contender for the Republican nomination in 1940. George Holmes of the *International News Service*, president of the Gridiron Club, invited the New Yorker to deliver the opposition speech at the select gathering of newspapermen, an occasion which blends humor and gravity in skits on domestic and foreign affairs. When Roosevelt heard that he was expected to meet Dewey in the political debate, which is a part of every Gridiron dinner, he first employed persuasion and then exerted pressure on Holmes to withdraw the invitation. When Holmes rightfully refused, Roosevelt said he would not speak at the dinner. I was drafted. Dewey made a bright, graceful address. I did not do so well. I should have spoken extemporaneously, instead of attempting to read a witty speech, which is not my style.

On December 16, 1938, the Cabinet meeting was devoted to the foreign situation and the resignation of Dan Roper. The President was most generous in his remarks about his parting servant, paying tribute to Dan's long and valuable service to him and the administration. He expressed the hope that Dan would still remain a member of the family even though he would not be sitting at the Cabinet table. Homer Cummings, soon to go himself, paid a warm and graceful tribute to his associate. Dan had an appreciative word for everyone in a friendly farewell.

CHAPTER SIXTEEN

MORE RUMBLINGS

Two DAYS later I found the President extremely cordial and pleasant in a luncheon conference at his desk.

"I saw Jack Garner as you suggested, Jim," he began, "but I'm afraid we didn't get anywhere. Jack is very much opposed to the spending program; he's against the tax program, and he's against the relief program. He seems to be pretty much against everything and he hasn't got a single concrete idea to offer on any of these programs. It's one thing to criticize but something else again to offer solutions."

I had talked to Garner about the visit. Garner said he had urged a friendlier attitude toward Congress and had spoken rather plainly about opposition feeling on the administration program. From the two accounts I was satisfied that, while the visit was pleasant, the two did not get anywhere because they held decidedly different views.

We discussed a number of appointments. When I brought up the name of Franklin B. Lane, son of the Secretary of the Interior in Wilson's Cabinet, he waved his hand in dismissal and said, "Nothing doing." He gave no explanation. The President was a nurser of grudges. Those about him felt that his coolness toward Bernard Baruch was due to the fact that Baruch, as head of the powerful War Industries Board in the first World War, had been rather casual with Assistant Secretary of the Navy Franklin D. Roosevelt.

In turning to foreign affairs, Roosevelt discussed the increased persecution of Jews in Germany. He said the international situation was most delicate, but he thought it could be handled by a show of firmness.

"Have you had any conversation with Ambassador Kennedy?" I asked.

"Oh, yes, we've had a very pleasant conversation, without any friction. Of course, Joe is very definitely of the opinion that we will have war in Europe and everything will go to pot. He's very gloomy."

"Things don't look any too well over there to me and I'm no expert,"

I said. "Russia's the big question mark to me. She can make war or keep the peace. By the way, have you made up your mind on the ambassadorship to Moscow?"

"No, I haven't got around to that yet," he answered. "I'm going to wait until Hull returns from the Lima conference."

I brought up the name of a prominent lawyer for the vacancy on the Court of Appeals for the District of Columbia. To my surprise the President waved dismissal.

"I will not appoint a Jew on the District Court of Appeals," he said. "I can't do it. There is a strong feeling throughout the country, a feeling against the Jews."

"Well, you don't have to decide now," I said. "We can let the matter go over until we have more time to discuss it."

"That's all right with me," he ended the matter.

I spent an hour and a half with the President. At the end of the meeting we made plans to continue our discussion a week later at dinner. On the evening of December 28, 1938, I went to the White House and found the President's mother, his half-brother's widow, and Daniel Roosevelt, a cousin, in the hall. While we chatted, Mrs. Roosevelt came up and said the President was waiting for me in his oval study. There we had dinner.

I found the President looking tired and drawn. He said he had not been feeling well, but felt he was improving. I never saw him in such good humor, so I decided to let down my hair on the election. He took no offense at my remarks, nor did he sulk as he had before. He was more open-minded on the defeat than I had ever seen him.

"Boss, for a long time I have wanted to give you my observations on the election and I feel there's no time like the present," I began. "I don't know whether you agree with me or whether you want to agree with me, but I would be less than frank if I did not tell you that the results gave very definite signs of dissatisfaction with the Federal administration, although not with you personally. You are personally as popular as ever, if not more so. If the election were held tomorrow, it would be another case of 'As Maine goes, so goes Vermont.' "

He laughed, puffed at his cigarette and quoted, "You may fire when ready, Gridley."

"There are several fundamental factors, which in my judgment were responsible for the results," I continued. "Whether we agree or not there is a definite feeling against the spending policy and the resulting increase in the national debt. Whether we like it or not, there is resentment and it had its effect at the polls. The supposed influence of the CIO on the administration—and I say 'supposed' advisedly—had its effect, particularly with farmers and small businessmen. This especially so because Frances Perkins is being tied in with the CIO. I don't say she is, but that's the impression."

"I hope that it may be possible to effect a reconciliation among the labor groups and clarify the situation," he said. "God knows, it needs clarification."

"Then there's the WPA," I continued. "Those on the rolls are dissatisfied because they are not getting more, and the rest of the public feels they are getting too much. Nobody is satisfied and as a result we lost votes. I don't know whether the name should be changed or not, but something ought to be done."

"Yes," he agreed, "there's a lot of dissatisfaction there. I think a lot of it is due to the supervisors, about whom there are many complaints. The situation is something like the feeling against draft boards in the war."

"Well, I think a lot of our trouble comes from the type of person on relief," I said. "In every section of the country there are those who might best be described as the ne'er-do-wells, who never worked steadily in their lives and who are now drawing a larger monthly wage from WPA than they ever did. Most of these are lazy and would not work regularly if they could. And if they did they would not do a good job. They are not desirable anywhere."

"That's so," he acknowledged. "We have that kind in Dutchess County and even in Hyde Park."

"I admit I don't have the answer to the situation, or even a suggestion as to how the lazy can be sifted from the deserving needy," I said. "Right now I was merely making an observation as to the cause of our defeat. I have no remedy at the moment. And to continue the analysis, there has been widespread dissatisfaction with farm prices from cotton in the South to grains in the Middle West and cattle in the West."

"I know, I know," he said. "If the Supreme Court had not ruled out the AAA, the farm problem, particularly in relation to cotton, would have been solved. We were on the way to solving this when the Court threw a monkey wrench in the machinery."

"I can't set myself up as a farm expert, but I have been interested in the situation because it affects the country," I said. "I have talked to many people. Now as to cotton, Garner feels . . ."

"Jack wants to throw all the cotton into the market," he broke in. "Well, you just can't do that. If surplus cotton is dumped out on a sick market, it will drive the price of cotton down no matter what is done. This will have the effect of breaking down Hull's reciprocal trade treaty program and then where are you?"

"I have not studied the situation to the extent that I have any firm opinion," I said. "I am merely gathering information. I hope that something can be done about farm prices or we will be face to face with trouble in the next election."

We switched to a consideration of appointments. I had a long list of judges, marshals, collectors of internal revenue, collectors of customs, and other posts.

"I want to take up each case individually as they come up," Roosevelt said. "I want to talk particularly about the collector of customs in Savannah, who worked for George. I don't want him reappointed."

"I think that's just foolish," I said. "That's all water over the dam."

"I won't appoint him again," he affirmed.

"What about the judgeship in Virginia?" I asked. "I don't need to remind you that Glass won't confirm just anyone you might appoint. That is, he will block confirmation of someone not agreeable to him."

"Then I'll appoint my selection's law partner and if the latter is not confirmed, I'll appoint the cousin of the man originally selected or the cousin of the second choice and so on," he declared. "I am not going to let Glass or Byrd make any appointments in Virginia. And that goes for a lot of Senators."

I saw his chin was all the way out, so I decided not to pursue the subject. I shifted the conversation by asking, "What about the Supreme Court?"

"I'm having a difficult time there," he said. "Felix Frankfurter wants to get on in the worst way. Some months ago I had to tell him at Hyde Park that I just couldn't appoint him for many reasons. In the first place, the appointment has to go west. In the second place, I told Felix that I could not appoint him in view of the anti-Semitic feeling. I couldn't appoint another Jew, but if Brandeis should resign or die, I told Frankfurter I would appoint him that same day without hesitation."

"What about Sam Bratton out in New Mexico?" I asked. "That's far enough west."

"Bratton belongs to a judicial school of thought that ought not to be represented on the bench," was his comment.

"You could give some consideration to Joe O'Mahoney of Wyoming," I suggested.

"Black has dissented many times since I put him on the bench, but his dissents would be a drop in the bucket to what O'Mahoney would do if he were on the Court," he smiled.

"What about Burt Wheeler of Montana?" I asked.

"I won't appoint Wheeler." There was no smile on his lips or in his eyes.

(Later as I was leaving the White House, Mrs. Roosevelt said she would not be surprised if the President appointed Wheeler "or someone like him.")

"What about Harold M. Stephens of the Court of Appeals for the District of Columbia?" I persisted in my questioning.

"I have given considerable thought to him, but I just can't make that appointment because it doesn't seem to be the right one."

After some discussion of lesser appointments, the President reached into a drawer of his desk and brought out a draft of his message to Congress. He read excerpts at length from one of the most memorable of his annual reports on the state of the Union. In the quiet of the study I heard him read, for the first time, his warning of "storm signals from across the sea."

This brought us to a review of the world-shaking events of the closing year—the annexation of Austria, the partition of Czechoslovakia, the Japanese invasion in China, the Spanish Civil War, Germany's domination in central and eastern Europe. We agreed it was not a happy picture. He said the answer was adequate defense, amendment of neutrality legislation, and serving notice on dictators that "if another form of government can present a united front in its attack on a democracy, the attack must and will be met by a united democracy." The message was well received before a joint session of Congress.

As I went to my apartment, I made up my mind not to press him on appointments lest he get the idea that I was trying to control delegations and votes. I decided I would make no recommendations and indicate no preferences, but rather let him do whatever he saw fit. If I should start pressing him, I decided, he might get the erroneous idea that I was working for myself rather than for him. After all, I was in his Cabinet and was not going to use or abuse my post for personal advantage, when there were men in the party who had claims above mine.

Between the opening of Congress and the Jackson Day dinner, January 7, 1939, the President named Frankfurter to the high Court. The appointment came as a complete surprise to me. I checked at the White House and learned that it was made just as Black's had been. The President secured a blank appointment, filled the name in himself, and sent it up to Capitol Hill so that the first news of the selection came from the reading of the appointment on the floor of the Senate.

At the Jackson Day dinner, seated between the President and Garner, I questioned Roosevelt about his selection, asking if it was made because the fellows out west did not measure up to his qualifications. He said that was so, but did not elaborate. I did not want to press him because I thought he might not want to speak frankly in front of the Vice President. There was a lot of good-natured kidding during the dinner. In the course of this, Garner, at one point, shook his finger at the President.

"If it were not for your damned Dutch stubbornness," he laughed, "we could all do more with Congress. We could handle the Senators and the Congressmen. We could get bills passed. We could even get that fellow Carter Glass is fighting appointed Federal judge. Then we could all go home and go fishing."

We had to laugh at that.

"The judgeship isn't all of it," Garner continued. "There is no sense to playing with the Governor down there because he won't control the delegation in 1940. It will be controlled by the Glass–Byrd crowd. They have a machine down there which compares to a large city machine in solidarity of organization. It is a 'one man' organization. It was Senator Martin's, then Claude Swanson's, and now it belongs to Glass and Byrd. They are in control and the Governor is not."

The President said nothing.

I did not see the President's speech in advance of delivery. He told us that he thought Garner and I and the crowd generally would be pleased with his speech. We were especially interested in the line, "If we Democrats lay for each other now, we can be sure that 1940 is the corner where the American people will be laying for us." Later Garner confided to me that he crossed his fingers on that remark. I had a hearty laugh on that because I was forced to acknowledge that I had mentally crossed my fingers at the same time, as I could not help but contrast his words with his vehemence against Glass and George a few days before.

Without reference to anything in particular, he launched into a lengthy discussion of Martin Van Buren in conversation with Garner and myself. He said that Van Buren was a smart fellow but a poor President; that while he carried out Jackson's policies and wishes, more or less, he got into difficulties because he was not running the show completely in sympathy with Jackson. With the latter statement it became apparent that the President was telling Garner and myself that Jackson should have picked someone more in sympathy with him than Van Buren, if he was not trying to tell us that Jackson should have run again himself. He was trying to point out that the 1940 Democratic nominee must be a real liberal, I felt at the time. I also felt the President's selection of a liberal would make little difference at the convention, because I was sure the delegates would want a real Democrat to head the ticket and not someone who would run out on the party after he was elected, like Wallace or Hopkins.

On January 2, 1939, I had attended the inauguration of Governor Lehman at Albany. It was the twelfth inauguration I had attended and I found less enthusiasm than at any of the others. The fact that it was Lehman's fourth may have accounted for it. On January 11, I attended the inauguration of Governor Herbert O'Conor at Annapolis, where there was much enthusiasm. On the way back I rode with Under Secretary of State Welles, who amazed me by stating that affairs had been mismanaged, in his opinion. He expressed himself as convinced that unless Hull or I should be nominated, the country would be in serious trouble. He was very much against the nomination of either Hopkins or Wallace, as against the best interests of the party and the country. This was the first time he had ever indicated any interest in me or in politics as such, and I found it surprising to say the least.

On January 29, 1939, the day before the President's fifty-seventh birthday, I called him from New York to congratulate him on the eve of his impending anniversary. I always called him and sent him a congratulatory message on his birthday, just as I always called him and sent him a message on Christmas, New Year's Day, and St. Patrick's Day, his wedding anniversary.

"Thanks for your good wishes, Jim," he said when I called. "Tomorrow I'm going to be fifty-seven and I guess I'm old enough to pack away with Heinz's pickles."

"Well, I see you've imported fifty-seven varieties of beauty from Hollywood," I quipped on the motion picture performers moving into Washington for the President's Birthday Ball.

"They're on my 'must' program for tomorrow," he laughed. "I'm going to devote tomorrow to the female stars, but I don't know what to do with the male stars."

"Turn them over to Grace Tully," I suggested. "And you might turn the female stars over to Marvin 'The Hunter' McIntyre."

He roared with laughter over this play on his secretary's middle name—Hunter.

"That's simply grand," he said. "I love it. I'm going to steal it, Jim, and pass it off as my own on Mac."

"You can have it for what it's worth," I said.

From the first of the year I scarcely saw the President except at Cabinet meetings. Meantime, my name was being featured more and more, along with those of Garner and Hull, as his successor in 1940. From all over the country political leaders came in to pay respects and stay to pledge support. Many of these were genuinely friendly and earnest. Others were merely building up character with me against the day when lightning might strike and they would be looking for jobs for themselves or their constituents. When he isn't mending fences, the average politician is putting up lightning rods.

Those who came to see me were organization leaders and office holders. Governors, Senators, and Congressmen filled up my daily list of appointments. There were hordes of newspapermen and a variety of federal office holders. All were looking for the answer to 1940. By far the majority were out of sympathy with the third term or said they were. They held it would be a mistake. My invariable answer was that nothing could be said about 1940 until the President spoke and, as I saw it, there was no necessity for him to speak until early in 1940.

At this time I made several long trips, during which I sounded sentiment on the administration and on 1940. Leaders all spoke of the chances of Hull, Garner, and myself. In consideration of my position, leaders indicated that my religion might be a factor, but not as much as it was against Al Smith because I had broken down a great deal of the prejudice against a Roman Catholic. I was pleased to hear this. I must confess I was pleased at being considered a presidential possibility along with men of the stamp of Garner and Hull. It made me feel good to know that the rank and file of the party would support me, if I were to be the candidate. I was satisfied I could receive support in a number of states, even if I wanted to contest selection of either Garner or Hull, which I had no intention of doing.

At this time Roosevelt was also doing a bit of traveling. He went south for the fleet maneuvers and a fishing trip in February. In April he went to Warm Springs, partly to recuperate from a persistent cold which threw his temperature off normal for weeks, to the concern of physicians. He made frequent week-end trips to his family home at Hyde Park. In this period he was beset by foreign and domestic troubles. On the foreign front, Hitler's partitioning Czechoslovakia was an ominous warning; on the domestic front, he was occupied with tax legislation, WPA appropriations, the national defense, and the national income, and he was concerned with neutrality legislation.

I did not see him for a chat alone from January until March, although I talked to him by phone at least once and took part in Cabinet discussions. On February 12, 1939, I called him to advise him that New

York Congressmen and leaders were complaining that he was giving most of the city's patronage to Representative Fay who had beaten John J. O'Connor. O'Connor was the only member of Congress purged by the President.

"You can just tell them I'm not going to give any patronage to any leader who supported O'Connor and that's that," he said.

"But there are plenty of Congressmen in New York City who went along with you and they are annoyed because they feel they are getting no consideration," I protested. "The situation could go along the way it has been going in the city, except that if you feel the patronage in Fay's district should not go to the leaders, you could turn it over to Fay to handle in any way he wants to."

"That's not the point," he said. "I don't want to give a single job to any leader who was with O'Connor. If some Congressmen are hurt by this, it's too bad."

"I can't argue with you about Fay's district," I tried again, "but I would argue about the other districts, particularly where the Congressmen have been with you all along."

"I don't want Curry (John F. Curry, former Tammany Hall leader) or his leaders to have any jobs," he said.

"There are no more Curry leaders," I insisted. "Curry was defeated by Jim Dooling and Christy Sullivan succeeded when Dooling died. Curry's men are gone."

"Well, that's the way I feel," he said. "And in view of the trial of Jimmy Hines, nothing should be given to the Hines district in the way of appointments."

On March 29, the President called me over to the White House where we talked about stamps and patronage and finally about 1940 politics. At that time the topics intermingled, as was the case with stamps. I urged consideration be given to the inclusion of Frances E. Willard in the great American series as a friendly gesture to the drys.

"That's a perfectly wonderful idea, Jim," he said. "The drys might be friendlily disposed toward us if we honored her. I'll give you a decision as quickly as I can."

He asked me about the Legislative Correspondents' dinner at Albany, particularly after the speeches made by Lehman, La Guardia,

Al Smith, and District Attorney Dewey. I told him Lehman, La Guardia, and Smith did all right in short speeches, but that Dewey talked for seventeen minutes and took some pot shots at Republican leader Simpson, which I considered unwise from Dewey's point of view. I added that I couldn't be fair with Dewey because his attitude irked me.

"That's exactly how I feel about him," the President said. "He's arrogant and ambitious. He wants to be President, or thinks he can be."

"I understand Ed Birmingham, state chairman for Iowa, was in to see you," I switched the subject slightly.

"Yes, he asked me what would have to be done for 1940 and I told him it was too early," he answered. "I did tell him that the Democrats would have to have a liberal platform and a liberal candidate."

"Boss, I am constantly being interviewed by newspapermen about 1940 and I have told them consistently that anyone who made an announcement before you have spoken ought to have his head examined."

"That's right, Jim," he observed.

"Boss, when you get back, I'll be glad to sit down and discuss the 1940 situation with you in a general way," I said. "Meanwhile, there is nothing to do but let matters take their course."

"I'll be glad to, Jim," he said. "What do you think of Garner's candidacy?"

"To be wholly frank, I don't think Jack is a serious candidate at this time," I answered. "Naturally, he is flattered by the attention he is receiving in the press, but I don't think it has gone to his head. I think the people around Garner are more concerned with his candidacy than he is. For your information I talked to him recently and he brought up, entirely of his own accord, the Presidency. With tears in his eyes, he told me he hoped that nothing would happen to you so that he would have to take over the reins of the government. I know that he was absolutely sincere. He has a very deep affection for you, Boss."

"I'm glad to hear it," he said. "I feel the same way about Garner's candidacy that you do. I'm sure Garner is speaking from his heart when he says he doesn't want to succeed me."

On June 7, 1939, I was called by the President as I was having dinner in my Mayflower Hotel apartment in Washington. He was in the friendliest of moods.

"Jim," he began, "I'd like to have you and Bess join me over the week end on the *Potomac* for a cruise."

This was the first invitation Mrs. Farley and I had received for a cruise aboard the presidential yacht, although I had been in Washington for more than six years. But I had to refuse.

"I'm sorry, Boss, but I agreed a few weeks ago to present a watch to Joe McCarthy, manager of the Yankees, in a ceremony at the home plate in Yankee Stadium Sunday. I appreciate the invitation a lot, but I don't feel I can change my plans at this late date, much as I'd like to."

"What about the next week end?" he pressed.

"I have a lot of work cut out for me that week end," I said. "I'm going to attend a postal convention in Maine a week from Sunday. Maybe I can pull the state into the right column in 1940 and leave Vermont all alone."

On June 23, 1939, I was called to the White House for a conference. As usual we began by discussing stamps. I reported receiving a letter from a Mrs. Casper Whitney suggesting a Cape Cod postage stamp.

"Jim, there's not a Democratic vote at Cape Cod," he laughed. "I think the next stamp we issue should be for Farley and Roosevelt."

"Just a minute," I cut in with a laugh. "I don't know how you feel, but I'd just as soon that stamp won't be issued for a long, long time. Unless, of course, you could have the law amended to permit living persons to be portrayed on stamps. Then it would be all right with me."

"Objection sustained," he chuckled.

I told Roosevelt I was being pressed by Charles Harwood of New York for a judicial appointment. I knew nothing of Harwood's $25,000 loan to Elliott Roosevelt, or the $200,000 loan of John Hartford of the Atlantic and Pacific Tea Company, until the story became public in 1945.

"I'd like very much to help Charlie, but I just don't know where to turn," he said. "I am anxious to find something for him and will get around to it."

There was no mention of politics in our talk except when the President brought up his one and one-half billion dollar pump priming

Lend–Spend program. The theory was to advance loans for self-liquidating projects, so that the Federal budget would not be further unbalanced by administration spending.

"I think it's all right and the one thing necessary to win in 1940," he said. "If the program is not passed, we Democrats will have plenty of trouble."

A few days later, when he was entertaining King George and Queen Elizabeth, he was cold and distant. Along with other Cabinet members and their wives, Mrs. Farley and I went down to Mt. Vernon aboard the *Potomac*. The day was hot, but there was ice in the President's manner toward me. I enjoyed the visit of the King and Queen and thought they handled themselves extremely well under difficult, or let us say trying, circumstances. I laughed heartily at the famous British Embassy garden party when Jack Garner slapped the King on the back in telling him a story—not so much at the gesture or the story but at the looks on the faces of the astounded Britishers.

In July, as I was preparing for a European tour with my daughters, Betty and Ann, and Edward Roddan of the Democratic National Committee, the third term talk was boiling under Capitol Dome. In fact, it boiled over, sweeping down Pennsylvania Avenue into all executive offices and departments. Various Democratic Senators and officials up to Cabinet rank came to me declaring themselves against the third term, predicting it could bring nothing but disaster to the party. I advised them all there was no necessity for my getting into a row with the President about a situation which might clear itself in a few months.

On July 6, Paul McNutt came to see me and talk about the number of candidates for 1940 if the President did not run. I said there was nothing to be done until the President made known his intentions around the first of the year. He agreed. A few days later McNutt was named Federal Security Administrator, which occasioned no little surprise in official circles, but was no surprise to me, because I saw in the move an adroit maneuver to silence Paul's campaign for the nomination. As a member of the President's official family of near Cabinet rank, he was bound not to campaign unless he had the blessing of the President.

That noon I went up to Capitol Hill for a lunch with the Vice President, at his invitation. He was preoccupied during a pleasant meal. I had an idea of what was on his mind, but said nothing, as I wanted him to approach the problem in his own way at his own time. After dessert, Garner pulled out one of his long cigars, lit it carefully; through the smoke and from under his picturesque eyebrows he studied me and then plunged into the heart of his subject, which I had expected him to do.

"I have no intention of playing poker with you, Jim, but will lay all my cards on the table," he began. "You don't have to commit yourself one way or the other. I want to let you know just where I stand and exactly how I feel. I mean on this third term business. Jim, I can't support a third term and will fight any third term bid for the good of the party. First off, I want you to believe me when I say I don't want to be President. God knows how true that is."

There were tears in his eyes and his voice was charged with conviction.

"Jack, if you tell me you don't want to be President, then I do believe you," I said. "Your word is good enough for me."

"Thanks," he said. "Mrs. Garner would like me to give no consideration to the Presidency because she would like to go back to Uvalde. She has no liking for the third term. I'm sure she wouldn't vote for Roosevelt, Jim."

"I don't think Bess would stay away from the polls," I laughed. "If I would get back to private life, I think she and the children would be happy. Sometimes I wonder if we in politics neglect our families to our own disadvantage."

"You may have something there," he agreed, "but I have been in politics for forty years and at this stage of the proceedings I can't let down the people who have helped me. I particularly can't let them down by silence on such a vital and far-reaching issue, the third term. At the moment, I feel I'm the only one who can head up any opposition. I owe it to my friends and to the party."

"That is so," I acknowledged. "However, I'm not sure when any decision has to be made. Early in the year, I thought August 1 was the deadline on which the President would have to declare his intentions. Since then I have changed my mind and now feel that we might wait until January."

"On the strength of that 'we,' I want to ask you a question," he said. "If it's out of order, you don't have to answer. Jim, are you against the third term?"

"Yes," I answered, "but don't tell a living soul."

"I won't and I appreciate your confidence," he said earnestly. "The two of us can pull together to stop Roosevelt."

"I'm not sure that we will need to," I said. "If the President doesn't talk to me by the early part of January, I'll have to go to him as Chairman of the National Committee and ask him what his plans are. I don't know whether I should announce my own candidacy. Frankly, I have no feeling at all about the nomination for the Presidency or the Vice Presidency, but I am concerned over the precedent that might be established by a third term. And no one can question my loyalty or faithful service to the President. I must confess I am a bit piqued over the neglect and the kicking around I have been getting."

"Why, Jim, you mean to say you don't know why you are out in the cold?" he asked.

"Truthfully I don't," I said. "I'm deeply grateful to the President for the opportunity of serving in his Cabinet and as party chairman, and I have returned thanks by performing as well as I know how. But I feel I am entitled to a few thoughts of my own on matters of concern to the country and the party."

"The plain and simple truth is that he's jealous of you, Jim," Garner said. "No chairman has ever made the contribution to the party you have, nor could any chairman compare with you in party achievement. You have grown tremendously in office and before the country, and he is just downright jealous of your popularity."

"I find that hard to believe," I said.

"Well, just think it over," he said. "He's jealous of Hull for his standing before the public. Cordell and I have talked that over. And he's jealous of me for my popularity in Congress. He ought to be glad to see men in the party coming along and fancies that he is glad, but actually he doesn't like it."

A few days later I was in Columbus, Ohio, for a postmasters' convention. When I put in my daily call to the Post Office Department Bill Bray, my administrative assistant, told me that Cardinal Mundelein of Chicago was having lunch with the President and had asked to see me. He had my call switched to the White House where the Cardinal asked if I could call on him. I said I would be in New York on July 12, 1939, and would be glad to visit him. He told me to come to the Vanderbilt Hotel, where he always stayed when in New York City.

CHAPTER SEVENTEEN

THE CARDINAL AND THE PRESIDENT

I FOUND THE Cardinal reading his breviary in his hotel room. He laid it aside, tucking in a ribbon to mark his place. We were left alone after I was ushered in. We exchanged greetings as old friends. I inquired as to his health and, without much more ado, he came to the point of the meeting.

"I had a most enjoyable visit with the President," he said. "Although he must be extremely busy he spent two hours or more with me. I found every minute enjoyable. He is truly a great man. I find more to admire in him at every visit. I think it is most fortunate that he is where he is and I hope he remains. It is my belief that he will run for a third term."

"Did he say so?" I asked eagerly.

"No," he said slowly. "No, but I hope that you will support him if he does. The President was extremely generous—I feel that I can tell you this—in his reference to you and spoke of you in very flattering terms."

"I am glad to hear it," I said. "I wouldn't mind hearing it from him. There is no reason why he should not be generous to me; I have always done what he has asked me to do, and I certainly have given him no cause for complaint."

"James," he studied me earnestly, "you have always been most frank and open with me, so that I feel entirely free in broaching a most confidential matter to you. It is my sincere feeling that a Roman Catholic could not be elected President of the United States at this time or for many years to come. I hope, therefore, that you will do nothing to involve the Catholics of the country in another debacle such as we experienced in 1928."

At the tone of his "James" I braced myself for what was to come and resolved that I was not going to be persuaded into taking a course contrary to my better judgment.

"Your Eminence, I have my own views, definite views, on the third term, but I do not think this is the proper time to air them if for no other reason than that I do not think you are the proper person to hear them, although you are a respected friend. I do not feel at liberty to discuss my views until the President has told me what he will do.

"Last winter he indicated strongly he would not be a candidate again. A week ago Friday he told me how often he had supported Democratic candidates for the Presidency when he knew there was no chance of their election; that he plumped for Bryan in 1908, Cox in 1920, Davis in 1924, and Smith in 1928; that he had run with Cox in 1920 when he knew it was hopeless, and that he had run for Governor in 1928 only to help Smith out. He said he had worked for all the party nominees on losing tickets and yet maintained that if a losing ticket should be nominated in 1940, he did not feel obligated to support it. I told the President he did not have to do anything he did not want to; but I find such an attitude difficult to understand, particularly in that it comes from one who has twice received the greatest gift the party can bestow. I cannot imagine him upsetting party tradition to be a candidate for a third term."

"I am satisfied he is going to run," the Cardinal said.

"I can't believe it, and my belief is based on his own intimations and hints. Not that there isn't plenty of activity for a third term on the part of a lot of the fellows who are close to him and want to stay close to the White House. But I can't imagine a third term happening without the President's full knowledge and approval. It may be that he is willing to let it develop and see if it is possible and then announce what he will do. Perhaps he might even blow on it as one would blow on a dying fire to kindle it into flame. Until he speaks, as I think he will speak and as he should speak, I must rely on his intimations.

"Now, for myself, I frankly do not care what happens to me politically. A place on the national ticket does not concern me too much. My wife and children would be far happier, and without a doubt better off, if I forgot all about public life. I hope you will believe me."

"I do."

"Now I want you, as an old and respected friend, to know I have been kicked around by the President and the so-called New Dealers for some eighteen months. I do not deserve such treatment. I have done much, certainly too much to deserve such treatment. It is not a matter of great concern to me that Roosevelt does not regard me as qualified for the office of President. It would be difficult for him to find anyone qualified but himself. I do not say that unkindly, because it has been so with every President, Democrat and Republican, Federalist and Whig. There are many other people of intelligence, wisdom, and ability, whose judgment is above question, who believe I am qualified. I do not think the President should take the position that I am not. I am not asking him to do anything for me. He certainly should not be the one to say I cannot win, if nominated, in view of what I have done for him."

"Why don't you tell the President how you feel?" he suggested.

"I would and will if he ever raises the question."

"James, I do not believe a Catholic could win."

"A great many people, among them the Vice President, Senators, Representatives, and party leaders, feel differently. Men who know something about politics. Conditions are not the same as they were ten or twelve years ago. When Smith ran, the Democratic party was not in power; Smith was in the front in the fight for repeal of the prohibition law; the country was prosperous; Smith's choice of Raskob, a Republican, for National chairman was an affront to the old time Democrats; Smith's conduct of the campaign was anything but skillful and diplomatic; it was doubtful that any Democrat could have been elected in that year, and the religious issue alone should not be blamed for Smith's defeat.

"On the other side of the picture, there is no reason to believe that the Democratic party will not win in 1940; the party is now in power; there are hundreds of thousands of Democrats on government pay rolls and whether or not they like the name Farley, they would not vote themselves out of office just because the candidate happens to be a Roman Catholic. There are thousands and thousands of persons working for the government of no set political affiliations, who would vote for me feeling reasonably certain they would keep their jobs if the Democratic party remains in control. I travel at least 75,000 miles a year around the country; I have been in several thousand communities and I have personally met hundreds of thousands of persons and shaken their hands—I have a larger acquaintance than any other man in the country.

"I have contacts with members of the national committee, with state chairmen and other party workers. Regardless of what anyone may think, I am known, respected and trusted; and I have no hesitancy in saying, and I say it without egotism, that no other Democrat has any better chance than I have. In view of this, the President has no right to be against me. I said I don't care what happens to me—actually I am not planning to secure the nomination for myself. Time will disclose my plans. Nonetheless, I am not going to take this lying down. I will not let myself be kicked around by Roosevelt or anyone else.

"Loyalty is not all on one side," I continued. "For the last year and a half he has not consulted me on appointments. Within six months, two appointments have been made in New York, my own state, which have been most displeasing to me. There is no reason why the loyalty should be all on my side. It is time that the President be loyal to me. I have been loyal in the face of a most trying situation. I have been made some very attractive offers 'if I would forget Roosevelt,' and a huge fund could be mine if I would get out and fight Roosevelt, which I do not for a moment propose to do. I am still being loyal, and loyalty should work two ways, even if Roosevelt doesn't recognize that principle."

The Cardinal repeated that I should talk to the President. He said that he was interested in me and, as a friend, felt he could speak frankly; that he hoped the situation could be settled so that I would support the third term he was certain the President would attempt.

"If I talk to the President, Your Eminence, should I tell him that you have talked to me?" I asked.

"I hope you will not do so, James," he said.

I do not know whether he talked to the President about me. I feel that he did in view of what happened, but I have no way of knowing. Even as we spoke, I had the feeling the President had asked him to speak to me.

"Before I go," I said, looking him full in the face, "I want to be free as I know how, Your Eminence. I want to be perfectly frank. Perhaps you will not like this, but it is in my mind and you should know it. You are the first person in the Church who has ever attempted to influence me on a political matter and I have been in politics for thirty years."

"It is only because I am interested in you and because you have always been considerate of me," he said. "I have heard something, which I hope you will not object to my mentioning. I understand there has been some criticism of Mrs. Farley—some things she has said, or is supposed to have said, about the President."

"That is perfectly all right," I said, wondering if he was carrying this complaint from the White House itself. "I'm glad you brought it up. Mrs. Farley is a loyal wife and feels strongly resentful of what has been done to me. She has never forgotten the way the President acted when Huey Long attempted to bring about an investigation of me. Long was not aiming at me, but was trying to get at the President. He chose me because I was the most vulnerable to pick on, in view of my dual role as Postmaster General and party chairman. Long was aware he would injure Roosevelt if he could tear me down.

"Mrs. Farley could never condone the President's silence in the face of Long's accusations. Even after the Senate had vindicated me—and splendidly they did so—Roosevelt said nothing in my defense. She felt that in view of my services, he should have rallied to my support, even if he were not moved by loyalty and friendship. Apparently I am a bottle of tonic to be taken when needed and then shelved until needed again. Now I have come to the point where I don't care to be shaken well before or after using. The President has never written me a word of appreciation or thanks for what I have done since 1930 and I have given freely of my strength, my time, and my ability at great personal sacrifice."

"I can't believe that," he exclaimed. "I mean I couldn't if you hadn't told me it was so."

"It is so, more's the pity," I said.

At the conclusion of the foregoing discussion, we had a very nice chat about the current situation and the world generally. He was extremely well informed on all matters, and it was always a delight for me to visit with him. Our friendship was not at all disturbed by the discussion we had, and from that day until his passing we remained close, intimate friends. I very much resented the President's suggestion to His Eminence, my close, personal friend, that he try to change my course of action on a matter of principle which the President himself should have freely discussed with me. There was no reason for a third person to be brought in for such a discussion.

Some months later, at Cardinal Mundelein's funeral, one of the priests who had accompanied him to New York at the time of the meeting which I have herein related told me that after I left the hotel that day, the Cardinal told him that he appreciated the candid way in which I explained my position and that his regard for me was greater than ever.

CHAPTER EIGHTEEN

HYDE PARK CONFERENCE, 1939

IN THE DAYS that followed, the newspapers and magazines were filled with stories of a rift between the President and myself. Editorial and news columns were heavy with speculation that I was dissatisfied at the way things were being handled, which was an understatement, and that I had quarreled with the President, which was wide of the mark. As evidence of a rift, my infrequent appearances at the White House were cited. When the speculation showed every sign of increasing rather than abating, the President sent for me, summoning me to his home at Hyde Park for dinner and to spend the night of July 23. Later, I understood Norman Littell of the Department of Justice, who was most anxious to avoid a party split, had been active at the White House with other mutual friends in promoting the conference. I visited my son, Jimmy, in camp in New Hampshire that Sunday, leaving about noon to drive down to Hyde Park by way of Vermont.

I arrived at Hyde Park about four-thirty in the afternoon. The President was not at the family home, but at the field-stone cottage retreat where he had served hot dogs to King George and Queen Elizabeth a few weeks before. Monte Snyder, the President's chauffeur, started to drive me over along a winding dirt road between acres of young Christmas trees. At a fork in the road we were flagged down by able, efficient Michael Reilly, Chief of the White House Secret Service detail, who said the President was coming. In a few minutes he came whirling down the lane in his hand-braked Ford. Missy Le Hand was at his side. He beckoned to me and I climbed into the back seat.

"Hello, Boss," I said.

"Glad to have you aboard, Jim," he greeted.

"I guess I'm safe in Republican Dutchess County," I wisecracked, "inasmuch as I just left Vermont without getting into difficulty. You know, ever since Vermont and Maine got out of step with the rest of the country in 1936, I don't like to walk around up there, especially after dark."

"Why, Jim," he laughed, "I believe you've inherited the prejudices of your Irish forebears against the north country."

"Only in the electoral college," I said. "And speaking of politics, you may be interested in a conversation Jimmy and I had under a tree at his camp. We were talking about this and that, when, out of a clear sky, he asked me, 'Dad, what's this I see in the papers about you and Roosevelt?' I had to laugh, because Jimmy at his age isn't much of a hand at reading the papers."

The President threw back his head in hearty laughter and exclaimed, "I love it! I love it!"

By this time we reached the graveled driveway, curving in front of the house. We had iced tea and cake on the porch. Missy was with us almost continuously during an hour and a half of conversation. Once or twice she was called to the phone. At seven we had dinner, being joined by Laura Delano, a cousin of the President; Aunt Polly, sister of his mother; Harry Hooker, schoolmate and former law partner of the President; Mrs. Roosevelt, and the President's mother. Dinner conversation was general.

After dinner Roosevelt and I headed for the small study in the north wing. The night was hot but not unpleasant. A light breeze set the massive trees awhispering and the hum of insects could be heard during lulls in the chat. The President toyed with a bottle of Danziger Goldwasser, watching the gold flakes dance as he poured a thimbleful every now and then.

He hopscotched over the political situation. He talked about the purge, explaining that he started it because conservatives were hamstringing his program and he felt the Democratic party must be liberal to be successful. He told me he wanted Alben Barkley of Kentucky as Senate Majority Leader because he felt Pat Harrison of Mississippi was against his tax and spending policies.

"Let me interrupt you right there," I broke in. "I think you made a mistake by projecting yourself into what was the Senate's affair. I would not have opposed Pat Harrison's candidacy, although I have nothing in the world against Alben Barkley. He's my close friend.

The simple fact of Harrison's service before and during the Chicago convention in 1932 would have moved me to hold my hand if I had been in your shoes. You may recall that on the third ballot the Mississippi delegation was within a vote or a fraction of a vote of leaving you, due to tremendous pressure within the delegation. Pat got out of bed, came to the convention hall late at night and stiffened the delegation into holding the line for you. Had they shifted their vote, disastrous shifts might have followed in other delegations. I told you before and I repeat now that, in my opinion, his action placed you under everlasting obligation to him."

He was frigid during my remarks. I filled in a conversational gap by saying that I thought he had made a mistake by interfering in Ohio, and expressing regret at my small part in the attempt to purge Senator Tydings, saying I should always be sorry that I let him talk me into accompanying him on his purge tour into Maryland. He was quite bitter against Tydings, but admitted there had never been much chance for Representative David Lewis to beat the Senator, adding that the Lewis candidacy was the best thing that could be done under the circumstances. He then drifted into consideration of his fight against John O'Connor. He said he had seen O'Connor a number of times, when the New York Congressman was opposing his wage and hour legislation and during the contest for House leadership against Sam Rayburn in 1937, but had been unable to get anywhere with him. I knew nothing of these visits and said so, adding that I thought the situation might have been handled differently, because O'Connor was disposed to be friendly.

The misunderstanding arose when Senator Guffey of Pennsylvania had the state's delegation support Rayburn, which, I said, naturally enough led to the assumption that the President was behind the Texan. The President confirmed this assumption by saying O'Connor could not have led Congress the way Rayburn had. I did not argue the point, because it was all water over the dam. I repeated that I thought the situation could have been handled better had there been a little give and take.

"Jim, you know Tommy Corcoran feels you did not go along all the way in the fight against O'Connor." He cocked his head and measured the effect of this shaft out of the corners of his eyes. From the tone it was evident that he was attributing to Corcoran what he himself felt.

"To be entirely frank, I didn't," I acknowledged. "You recall I explained my position at the time of the purge and you approved my determination to keep my hands out of the fighting within the party. Getting back to Corcoran, there is no reason why he should expect the party chairman, whose first consideration is to maintain party harmony, to do his dirty party-splitting work.

"Mr. President, John O'Connor is my friend and he was your friend, too, in Chicago and before Chicago. As you know, John F. Curry, then leader of Tammany, tried to deprive him of his seat in Congress, because of his work on your behalf. The truth of the matter is that he would have won renomination if it wasn't for the financial assistance and campaign direction given his opponent, James Fay, by Corcoran and Ed Flynn.

"Between you and me I'm getting a bit fed up with Corcoran and his crowd. They have not been fair with me. I know they have inspired stories against me. I think they have done you and me a great disservice. I know definitely they haven't got the influence with you which is attributed to them, but I don't think it healthy that such an impression of their influence prevails. I'll be able to handle them in my own way and at my own time. They're merely peanuts in a sugar barrel."

Roosevelt was silent for a few moments, evidently turning over in his mind what I had said. I was glad to have a chance to speak out as I did, because I wanted to set myself straight with him and because I was hopeful that I could help him to a realization of the damage some of the brain trusters were doing. There was always the possibility that he might be induced to veer away from them and steer in the direction of those who had been truly helpful to him, including myself. At heart the President was a boy, sometimes a spoiled boy. Although he had tremendous charm and vitality, he had a few petty attributes which were continually getting him into trouble. One of these was that he was forever trying to get even with someone for some slight, real or fancied. Another was that he was motivated on decisions, large or small, by his heart rather than his mind, all too frequently, and by hunches rather than by reason. Surrounded by genuinely loyal and able people, he would have encountered far less trouble.

Roosevelt was slow in getting to the point, which I knew must come. The thing I was determined to do was to impress upon him that I would follow whatever course of action I decided was right and honorable. He knew, for example, where I stood on Hull, but was not sure, I believe, where I would stand on a third term. Also, he was not sure how far I would go with him in supporting any candidate he might suggest. He began by considering the candidates.

"To begin with, there's Garner," Roosevelt said as though he were counting on his fingers. "He's just impossible."

"Just a minute," I cut in. "I am sure Jack is not interested in being a candidate. I am certain of this. He is willing to let his name be used, if necessary and only if necessary, as a candidate by those opposed to a third term. He is being encouraged by about a dozen Democratic Senators, including Byrnes and George and Bankhead."

"Maybe so," he acknowledged. "Then there's Senator Byrd, who would not be acceptable, nor Senator Tydings; and I think Senator Wheeler is a candidate."

"I know it," I contributed. "While I have no feeling against Wheeler personally, I'm not entirely sure of him because he voted against me when Huey Long was attacking me in the Senate. Incidentally, if you are concerned about the stories which have been appearing about me casting my lot with Wheeler, because I had lunch with him on the Hill the other day, you should know that there isn't a word of truth in them. I was not Wheeler's guest as the papers had it, but Guffey's. Wheeler just happened to be one of the party and we talked casually."

"Glad to hear it," he said. He went on telling off his fingers. "Then there's Wallace. What do you think of Henry? I don't think he has *It*."

"I don't think he has balance and judgment," I said. "I have a personal liking for Henry and we have always been friendly, but I frankly don't know where he stands from day to day. I must confess I share the feeling around the country that he's a dreamer. I don't like to say it and I wouldn't want it carried back, because I would not want to hurt him. However, you asked my opinion and there it is."

"Next we come to Governor Stark of Missouri," he went on. "Somehow or other I don't know much about the Governor."

"Well, personally I'm much incensed at Stark because at the time of the Pendergast investigation I had a visit from the Kansas City leader's nephew, who asked me to intercede in the tax case. The nephew was sent to me by Senator Truman. In justice to Harry I must report that when he found out what the young man had been up to, he called me and apologized at length, saying he would never have sent him if he knew what the nephew was going to ask me to do. I told Harry to forget it.

"Well, to make a long story short, I told the nephew that the case would have to take its course, that I could do nothing even if I were disposed to do so. A few days later Stark called me and in no unmistakable terms intimated that I was interfering in the case. I burned him up. I'm telling you this because I want you to know that I'm not interested in that case or any similar case."

"I do understand, Jim," he said. "Stark called me to express dissatisfaction with the way the Treasury Department was proceeding. I told him the department was proceeding along regular lines and there was nothing to worry about, which was true."

He then brought up the name of Paul McNutt and slowly turned down the thumb of his right hand. He did not mention Hull, Jesse Jones, Robert Jackson, Frank Murphy, Harry Hopkins, or myself as candidates. Finally, we reached the third term issue.

"We must save democracy," he said in ringing tones as though he were on the platform. "It's the only way to save the country."

"I think it's necessary to have the Democratic party successful in order to save the country," I put in. "And I am more concerned with the country than with the party, because success will come to the party if the country is secure and prosperous as surely as night follows day or maybe I should have put it the other way around—day follows night."

"Jim," he said, dropping his voice and speaking slowly for emphasis, "you and I have got to be together in 1940 to work for the good of the country and the party, just as we have in the past."

I said nothing, waiting for what was to follow. He fixed his eyes on me most intently and set down his cigarette.

"Now, they're trying to make me run. . . ."

"Just one interruption, Boss," I broke in. "Before you go any further, I want to say that sooner or later you will have to declare yourself. Just when that day should be, I am not prepared to say at this time, because I am not satisfied in my own mind, except in the most general sort of way."

"Jim, I am going to tell you something I have never told another living soul," Roosevelt dropped his voice to an impressive whisper. "*Of course, I will not run for a third term.* Now I don't want you to pass this on to anyone, because it would make my role difficult if the decision were known prematurely."

"Mr. President, you have my word of honor on that," I said as solemnly as I could, little expecting that he would repeat the same words to others within a few days.

"Thanks, Jim," he acknowledged. "Now the way I'm going to handle it is this. Along about the time the North Dakota primary comes along, when it is necessary for me to file or not to file, I won't file, thereby indicating I'm not a candidate."

He smiled gleefully as though he and I were sharing a huge joke.

"That's all right in its way, but I think you ought to say something one way or the other at that time," I said. "I think you should write a letter to the state chairman of North Dakota saying that you are not a candidate."

"Yes, that would be another way," he agreed. "The thing for us to do now is to get friendly delegations. You and I must work together for the party, the same as we have in the past."

"The friendly delegations are all right with me, too," I said lightly. "Who are they supposed to be friendly for or against?"

He laughed.

"I suppose the Georgia delegation will be for Walter George," he said. "Do you think the Florida delegation will be friendly?"

"I think so."

"And what about Alabama?" he asked again.

"I think they will be for Speaker Bankhead," I said. "And I think

Tennessee will be for Hull, Arkansas for Bailey, Byrd and Glass will control Virginia, and Ohio will be for Senator Donahey."

"That's the way I size them up," he said. "But you must understand one thing, Jim. *I do not want to campaign for a losing ticket.*"

"Boss, as the party's leader, you'll have to campaign for whatever ticket is selected," I argued. "We cannot compromise on the platform; it must be a wholehearted endorsement of your administration. In turn you will just have to go along with the party. Cox and yourself received such support from the party and its leaders, although it was known that it was a losing ticket. The same goes for Smith and Robinson in 1928. Frankly, the party would be disappointed and rightfully so, if you did not support the ticket, particularly if it is a ticket that you could support."

He made no answer. He switched the conversation to an entirely different subject.

"Jim," he said, "you're the only member of the Cabinet I have no reason to criticize for any public utterance. And you're the only one who, at some time or other, has never asked for anything from some other department. And I want to say, here and now, that I appreciate it more than you know."

Later, I had cause to believe his immediate reference was to Solicitor General Robert Jackson, because Harry Hooker, the President's one-time law partner, told me the next day that Mrs. Roosevelt was displeased with Bob's speeches against business, believing they had done the President much damage. Hooker described her as very much against Corcoran and Cohen, the Gold Dust Twins, as they were called.

In reply to the President's generous remarks about my official conduct, I told him there was nothing any other department had that I wanted. As for my own department, I went on to say that there was one agency which should never be touched and that was the Postal Inspection Service. I had appointed K. P. Aldrich as Chief Inspector without ever having seen him. When he arrived to take over the post, I called him into my office and told him that I wanted it thoroughly understood he would get no interference in the conduct of his office from me. The President said he was glad to hear it, adding that he respected me the more for it.

I brought the conversation back to 1940, asking bluntly what kind of a candidate he wanted. His answer was, "All I have to say is that I hope they don't nominate just a yes man, but pick someone who is sympathetic to my administration and who will continue my policies."

Since he had solemnly assured me that he was not going to be a candidate, I gathered the impression that he had not anyone in mind for the Presidency at the moment. It was only natural that he should feel that it would be difficult to find a successor to himself. Presidents, surrounded as they are by flatterers, are not prone to underestimate their influence on history. As a dynamic and dramatic Chief Executive, Roosevelt had attracted more than his share of flattery.

At this point he switched to a consideration of the picture in the Republican camp. He named Dewey as the most important figure in that party. I disagreed, feeling that the Republicans would not nominate Dewey, but would choose Senator Vandenberg.

"Dewey might get second place," I said, "but I can't see him in first place, because he is such a middle-of-the-roader, a liberal when among liberals and a conservative when among conservatives. I have a feeling that the Republicans will not take a chance with him because they don't know whether he'll jump right or left."

"You've got him figured just about right, but I still think it will be Dewey and he will make a formidable opponent," the President said. "That will make it all the more necessary for you and me to work together in 1940."

I made no answer to this. It was my turn to change the subject.

"Boss, before we get off politics I want to show you something which may give you a laugh," I said, reaching into my brief case for some correspondence I had with Oliver Quayle, Treasurer of the Democratic National Committee. "Here's a letter from Quayle to Ickes asking for a $100 donation to the party, and here's Ickes's answer saying he could not afford such a large donation and asking that all further correspondence should be addressed to him at his office."

"Don't you just love it?" he laughed. "And isn't that just like Harold? You know he is serving his purpose as far as the administration is concerned, because his speeches are of a kind no one else can make;

but sometimes I think they may be more detrimental than helpful. And the same goes for him."

The President mentioned the Hatch bill, which was popularly supposed to clean up politics, saying that Charley Michelson had urged him to veto it on the ground that it should never have been passed on for signature.

"Personally, Boss, I feel the same way," I said. "In my judgment it will turn out to be another Volstead Act; it can't possibly be enforced and can only promote hypocrisy rather than honesty. If I were you I'd get an opinion from the Attorney General's office before acting either way."

"I'll do it," he promised.

Roosevelt confessed disappointment over his failure to get the neutrality legislation through the Senate, declaring his defeat would only serve to help the aggressor nations. He summarized the conference he had with Garner and a bipartisan group of Senators, saying that he and Hull had painted a sombre picture of the situation in Europe, predicting that war might come at any time. Senator Borah, he said, took exception to the prediction, maintaining the information he received was just as authentic and, in many instances, came from the same sources tapped by the State Department. Hull deeply resented Borah's attitude, Roosevelt said.

This brought up consideration of my impending European tour. I explained I had taken up the itinerary with Hull and had been advised that it would be all right to see Mussolini, but that I should find some excuse for ducking Hitler, should the latter extend an invitation to me. It was my intention, I said, to head off an invitation by announcing I was going directly through Germany into Poland.

"Good, good," the President approved. "Be my eyes and ears on the trip, Jim, and pick up as much information as you can for me. See as many people as you can. See Winston Churchill. See Chamberlain or anybody in his Cabinet. You know there are many people in the country who, for various reasons, do not approve of our dealing with England, but it is necessary to stand firm against the aggressors."

Conversation began to lag. Taking a hint from a long silence, I remarked it was getting late and rose. He stuck out his hand. I grasped it.

"Keep everything under control," I said. "Take it easy while I'm away."

"We'll have another nice, long conversation when you get back, Jim," he said. "I have been waiting a long, long time to hold this one —too long a time."

"Don't take any wooden nickels," I was in the hall before his chuckle died away.

"Take keer of yourself, Jim," he quoted in farewell.

I spent a little time with the family, before I went up to a guest room for the night. Waiting for sleep, I mentally reviewed our conversation. I was glad no argument had arisen and that I had not committed myself to any course of action. I was grateful there was no unpleasantness. I had demonstrated my willingness to talk freely and frankly, and without any bitterness over his neglect of me. On the other hand, I felt he was a bit ill at ease, so to speak, in trying to clarify a situation without admitting that he had been guilty of any offense toward me. He was fully aware of the stories in the press about his failure to confer with me and of the significance attached to the whole situation. I was sure that he wanted to have the appointment with me behind him, before I went abroad, so as to give the country the impression that all was well in our relationship and we were as friendly as ever.

Considering his statement on the third term, I figuratively crossed my fingers. Except for Hull and myself, he had more or less effectively disposed of all the candidates who were leading all polls, and who were most frequently mentioned by the party faithful. I had never indicated to the press my position against the third term, as he knew. I had said repeatedly for publication that I had definite views and that when the proper time came I hoped to express them in a way which would not lessen my standing before the American people. Privately, I had clearly intimated my opposition to the third term. I know that my words were frequently carried back to the White House, and that was all right with me.

I was sure that the third term issue could not be settled until the President declared himself one way or the other, and that it would remain a riddle until he chose to speak. I remember that I remarked to myself that I would have to cover a lot of ground, literally and figuratively, before I had to meet the problem. I took solace from the fact that I had kept my temper and had conducted myself to the best of my ability in a trying period. I had not once publicly expressed dissatisfaction or disapproval. And so to sleep.

The next morning I was up early and slipped out for a walk, as is my custom. When I returned, Mrs. Roosevelt was at the breakfast table. I joined her.

After breakfast I went to say good-by to the President and found him about to hold a press conference. I remained for the show. He was in high spirits and handled the questions very well indeed, particularly when he was asked if I were going to resign. He tossed his head back and snapped, "He is not!" as if the suggestion that there was any friction between himself and me was the most ridiculous idea in the world. I could not help but consider how the reporters would have loved to have sat in on the conference of the night before and how the country would have relished the story.

Our farewell was brief. I took Hooker down to New York with me. I did not see the President again until after the outbreak of the war. At my sailing with my daughters and Edward Roddan, I received the following wire from him:

NBQ72 20 THE WHITE HOUSE WASHINGTON DC 26 1035 A
HON JAMES A FARLEY
       SS MANHATTAN
A GRAND TRIP TO YOU, THE GIRLS AND EDDIE. WISH I WERE SAILING WITH YOU ALL. BRING ME A SHAMROCK.
                              FRANKLIN D. ROOSEVELT

CHAPTER NINETEEN
POLITICS TAKES A HOLIDAY

B Y UNANIMOUS consent, politics took an enforced holiday at the outbreak of the war in Europe. With war immediately at hand and with the presidential campaign more than a year away, no motion had to be put for an adjournment of politics.

While we had talked of the possibility of war frequently at Cabinet meetings, the conflict seemed very far away, indeed, as the S.S. *Manhattan* of the United States Lines sailed at noon, July 26, 1939.

The holiday mood was nipped for me by the frost of war in the air when we docked at Hamburg, Thursday, August 3. I can best describe my journey through Germany at that time by saying there was a mounting apprehension that something fearful was about to happen. In Berlin, American Chargé d'Affaires Alexander Kirk was gloomily apprehensive, wanting us to get out of Germany as soon as possible. He sensed trouble ahead and warned me his influence would be pretty ineffectual as war fever mounted in German blood.

In Poland uniforms were everywhere but there was none of the grim purpose of Germany. And there were almost no planes in the air and no ceaseless shuttling of military equipment. On every side there was calm resignation to what was considered inevitable.

At a garden party given by Anthony Drexel Biddle, Jr., American Ambassador to Poland, and his wife, I had an opportunity to converse with Poland's leaders, President Moscicki, Premier Beck, and Marshal Smigly-Rydz. At one point Beck, Biddle, and I were together.

"Mr. Premier, I am going to ask a rather presumptuous question, which you need not answer," I said. "What do you think of Hitler and Mussolini?"

Beck looked at me, turned to Biddle, and then chuckled. "The question isn't indiscreet, but the answer would be," he said.

I then asked about Poland's situation in the event of war.

"What Poland needs is money," Beck said. "We have received credit in England, but we need cash to keep our factories turning out our war equipment. We must have arms, because Hitler will attack. I became convinced of that at our conference last January. He would not look me in the eye, as in former meetings. He kept looking around the room, at the floor, at the ceiling, at the walls, at anything but me. I realized then Hitler meant no friendship toward Poland. We have been preparing as best we can since then."

I asked why the Poles were so certain Hitler was bent on war.

"We feel that Hitler is not getting the true picture of the position of other nations," he answered. "I know just what the attitude of Great Britain, France, and the United States, and other nations will be in the event of war. I doubt if Hitler knows."

I had interviews with Moscicki and Smigly-Rydz and Beck, privately as well as at the garden party. All told me the Poles were aware that Hitler would attempt to kill Poland by killing all Polish males—Jews and Gentiles alike—although he would probably begin with the Jews. All said alliance with Russia would be "walking into a bear's mouth to escape a wolf." Russian demands would be so great, they said, they could not live in peace and freedom. The General appeared confident in the face of odds and said the Poles would fight to the end, aware that Germany would be defeated eventually, and peace and freedom would certainly be restored to their country, although it might take many years.

From Warsaw we journeyed to Cracow, where we placed a wreath on the tomb of Marshal Pilsudski. In this ancient city I visited the Jewish settlement, where I saw Jews living more closely after the customs and traditions of their ancestors than it has been my privilege to see anywhere else on my travels. I was greatly impressed. I found them no less determined to resist the Nazis than their Gentile compatriots. In the short stay, I developed a tremendous respect and affection for the Poles in Warsaw and Cracow. In notes dictated at the time I expressed the hope they would be victorious. I noted, "People with the spirit they have, never die." Many of them did. I shudder every time I consider what happened to that unfortunate nation, especially in the Cracow ghetto.

Leaving Poland we halted briefly in Austria and then proceeded on
to Italy. The highlight of our Italian journey was an audience with
His Holiness, Pope Pius XII. I had twenty minutes alone with him and
then Eddie and the girls joined us for about ten minutes. We talked
of the trouble facing the world—the war.

"I am more concerned now than at any time before," the Pope said
solemnly. "I am doing everything I can to avoid a conflict by prayer
and by diplomacy."

At this point the Holy Father astonished me by posing a third term
question.

"Will the President run again?" he asked.

"I do not know," was my reply. "It will all depend on circumstances.
Personally I do not think he would want to run and, if he does, he
would be breaking unwritten law, because no one has ever done so
within our party system."

The Pope laughed quietly and then said, "You know, I am the first
Italian Papal Secretary of State to be elected Pope."

I have often thought since that on that day he was a far better political prophet than I was.

In Rome, Phillips was gravely concerned over the impending prospect of war. In Paris war clouds were so low one could almost touch
them. Ambassador Bullitt was busy holding the hands of Daladier,
Reynaud, Paul-Boncour, Blum, and the rest. The embassy was a bee-
hive. All diplomatic messages from the State Department to con-
tinental embassies and legations funneled through the structure at
the Avenue des Champs Élysées and the Rue Boissy d'Anglas. Bullitt
dispatched couriers throughout Europe, as telephone and telegraph
wires were known to be tapped. The embassy had a direct wire to
Washington through which Roosevelt and Bullitt maintained constant communication. From what I saw, Bullitt was closer than anyone in the diplomatic service to the President. Bullitt's capacity for
work impressed me tremendously.

We sailed from Le Havre for Cobh. In Ireland I found Premier
Eamon De Valera, an old friend, certain that war was on its way.

"It will be a long war," he told me, "but in the final analysis, the allied powers should win. From our point of view it will be best to stay out of the war. By so doing we will be able to keep intact and at the same time be friendly to England. We are desirous of being helpful, in this or any other crisis in so far as we are able, short of actual participation in war. That would be ruinous for us and injurious to England."

Poland was invaded September 1, 1939. On September 3, when Britain declared war, we were homeward bound. Upon arrival in this country, I caught the first train for Washington after a family reunion breakfast, and went to a Cabinet meeting. When it came my turn to talk, the President said, "Now, Jim, please tell us all about it." However, before I could get under way he started with questions and I could not give a connected account of my trip. For fifteen or twenty minutes I answered penetrating questions about the temper and character of the people as I saw them and about what I had been told by the various leaders I had seen. He then shut me off with, "I want to see you next week."

I had lunch with the President September 13. We paid very little attention to our food, which was a typical desk luncheon of clear soup, chops and peas, a salad, dessert, and coffee.

"Boss," I opened, "before you say anything, I want you to know we are to all intents and purposes in a state of war. That I hope we can stay out goes without saying. I think that at this time politics should be adjourned. The people aren't interested in politics; they are interested in their country and in their families."

"Jim, you have hit the nail right on the head," he replied with hearty cordiality. "You were never more right. I feel exactly the way you do. The reason I didn't say anything before—in the months behind—was that there was a doubt in my mind as to what would happen abroad. Now what I expected to happen has happened."

I was not clear as to his exact meaning and waited for him to explain himself. When he showed no disposition to do so I turned to the domestic scene and asked, "I haven't made up my mind as yet myself, but I wonder whether it would not be a good idea to cancel the Jackson Day dinner?"

"I don't think there will be any necessity for that," he answered slowly. "We could bring in a few Republicans and make it a bipartisan affair."

"I'm afraid it might look as though we were trying to talk politics at a time when we were urging national unity, but there's no need to make a decision this minute," I said.

"Jim, we are on a day-to-day basis now at home and abroad," he said seriously. "Our foreign policy may shift within twenty-four hours or within an hour. The same is true of domestic matters. Everything depends upon the course of the war. Problems will have to be met as they come along, including politics. You remember, before you went away, I said I would have to make my position clear on the third term by passing up the first presidential preference primary— in North Dakota, I think it is—early in the year. Now it looks as if I could do nothing until the spring, March or April.

"That makes sense to me," I agreed. "I think it would be a mistake to have anyone connected with the administration make political speeches at this time. I think you were wise in not making your scheduled speech before the Democratic women recently. If anyone in the administration has engagements, they should keep them, in my opinion. I don't see any objection to officials talking about departmental problems, but they should not bring politics into it. In this connection I think Assistant Secretary of War Louis Johnson's speech at Boston was bad. It reeked of war, and such speeches are bound to be detrimental at this time."

He nodded. Taking advantage of his good humor, I decided to risk advice.

"Boss, I want to say something you may not like," I said.

"Go ahead, Jim; I can take anything these days," was his invitation.

"Well, I think the time has arrived to forget bitterness," I said. "The time has come for everyone along the line to forget the past and try to help in every way they can. I think that you'll find those in Congress who opposed you in the past more than ready to do so and I think you should meet them more than half way. I have Senator Walter George in mind for one. He has undergone an eye operation in New York. I think it would be a fine and helpful gesture if you were to write him a note wishing him well."

"I'll send him a telegram," he promised.

"And I hear Senator Pat Harrison is ill in Biloxi," I said. "I've talked with George and he tells me Pat is suffering from high blood pressure. I think you might write him."

"Good idea," he said.

"Speaking of health, how's Harry Hopkins?" I asked.

"In a bad way, I'm afraid," was the reply. "When he comes back to Washington, it will probably be to die."

"And Marvin McIntyre?" I asked, having been told by White House physician Ross T. McIntire that the President's secretary would never be able to fulfill his duties again.

"Mac will be all right in a couple of months," he said.

I reported on my observations abroad, noting, in particular, the work being done by Bullitt, Phillips, Kirk, and Cudahy. I told him Phillips was one of the first to see how things were going to go, having been low in spirits over the world picture for over a year.

"You know he has wanted to resign as ambassador, but I won't let him," Roosevelt confided. "He can't resign now even if he should want to, because if Bill Phillips resigns I would have to appoint a new ambassador whose credentials would recognize the conquest of Ethiopia. I can't do that at present at any cost.

"I'll tell you a story about Bill you don't know. About the time of the Munich conference, I sent a message for delivery to Hitler and Mussolini through our ambassador. Phillips had gone to Florence to visit his wife when it came in; late at night, Alan Rogers, the second secretary, took the message down to Count Ciano at the Italian Foreign Office. Very cleverly Rogers told Ciano he had a message to deliver to Mussolini in person and that he (Rogers) would lose his position in the career service if he failed to do so. Ciano said Mussolini couldn't possibly see Rogers, and the second secretary had to be content with Ciano's promise of delivery. Phillips felt very badly about it, thinking Mussolini might have seen him, which I doubt.

"And my story has a happy ending, because I am sure that Mussolini had the message before him when he talked to Hitler the next morning by telephone. And I think the message prevented Hitler from marching as he doubtless intended."

I said I was aware of the delicate situation involving Ethiopia.

"The Italians know my views, whether they understand them or not," he said. "I told the Italian ambassador my position. You know I inherited from Herbert Hoover what I call the Stimson (Henry L. Stimson, former Secretary of State) policy, under which this country would not recognize Japan's conquest of Manchuria. If I recognize Italy's conquest of Ethiopia, which was made in a regular fashion, I would have a Japanese problem on my doorstep. I told the Italian ambassador to so advise Il Duce, that time would take care of the situation."

I did not understand what the President meant by "regular fashion," but did not seek an explanation. I reported that I heard praise for his policy on every side except in Germany and Italy. I told him there was criticism of him in Germany for failure to return Ambassador Hugh Wilson.

"Is that so?" he asked. "I wanted to return Wilson, but Cordell Hull was opposed to it."

I had not heard that before. I told the President the German people were grateful to Hitler for many things, but bringing them into the war was not one of them, so far as I could learn from Americans in Germany. I told him the Italians were speaking rather openly against Germany and gave it as my opinion that Mussolini was sitting on the fence as far as the war was concerned.

"That's exactly what he's doing," the President said. "If it looks as if Germany will lose, he will go in with the opposition; if it looks as if the Germans will win, he will pitch in with them."

I told him I regretted that I had not had a chance to visit England; that I should have liked to have called on Winston Churchill, to whom he had given me a letter, and others. I asked how Ambassador Kennedy was getting along. As usual he was critical of Joe, whom he never liked.

"I want to tell you something," he confided, "and don't pass it on to a living soul. Some weeks ago Joe had tea with the King and Queen, who were terribly disturbed about the situation. Afterwards he saw Sir Samuel Hoare and several others connected with the British government, and they, too, were quite worried. After his talks Joe sat down and wrote the silliest message to me I have ever received. It urged me to do this, that, and the other thing in a frantic sort of way."

Here the President grabbed his phone and asked that Under Secretary of State Welles be put on the wire. When he had Welles he asked him to send over a copy of Kennedy's message and the White House reply for the presidential files.

"You know," he explained confidentially, "Joe has been taken in by the British government people and the royal family. He's more British than Walter Hines Page (American Ambassador to Britain in World War I) was. The trouble with the British is that they have for several hundred years been controlled by the upper classes. The upper classes control all trade and commerce; therefore the policy of the British government relates entirely to the protection of this class."

The President was never very generous before me in his reference to the British in the prewar days. He was forever expressing doubt that Britain would ever go through for anyone else, declaring they were for England and England alone all the time. However, he always had the highest admiration and respect for Winston Churchill.

The President switched the conversation to a consideration of the War Industries Board, headed by Edward R. Stettinius, Jr., son of a former J. P. Morgan and Company partner.

"When they turn in their report, I think I'll put them on the shelf," he said musingly. "I realize fully that they are under the Morgan influence. A number of people have told me this, thinking I was unaware of the situation. Of course, if the war industries are dominated by the Morgan crowd, they would do all the business and make all the money. The Morgan crowd have been bitterly opposed to me and all I have advocated. I'll take all the necessary steps. Henry Morgenthau made a mistake in naming one of an associated crowd and there's someone else definitely of Morgan influence . . ."

He left the sentence hanging in the air and went into a brown study. My mind raced. Here was the opportunity I was looking for.

"Boss," I began lightly, "I'd like to say a word for a fellow I know quite well—James A. Farley."

"Why, Jim," he laughed.

"If you set up any organization to control the activities of government and business, I believe I could head it up and do as satisfactory a job as anyone else you might select. Boss, I'm deadly serious. While I am ordinarily a modest fellow and find it hard to talk about myself, I say to you I have the qualifications to do a good job."

"Jim, I think you have something there," he said.

"Further, as a member of your Cabinet, I would be sitting in on the policy meetings and would be able to report on the organization's activities," I went on. "You know how I can work for you. Anyone on the outside might not have the same attitude and might want to run the whole show."

"What opposition would come from your being Democratic Chairman?" he asked. "I wouldn't want you to give that up."

"I don't think there would be any objection, although I'd be glad to step out," I said. "I could handle the matter by saying politics had been adjourned as far as I was concerned. I think the people and the press would have confidence in me and believe me, even though they might disagree with me politically. And I would see to it that confidence was not abused."

"I think it might be worked out," he said.

"I'm sure I could handle the situation efficiently and satisfactorily," I went on. "I would bring into the organization the right businessmen and get the thing rolling in no time."

"Jim, I think it's the ticket," he said with enthusiasm. He picked up a pencil and began outlining an organization on paper. "At the top we have you. Let's see, we could call you Coordinator. How's that, Jim?"

"I don't think the title means a thing, except that you will have to have a name for the organization and for the man at its head."

We talked about the steel industry, railroads, machine tools, rubber, tires, and nearly every important line of industry. He went over his Cabinet to see if anyone else could handle the post. Hull he dismissed as having too many duties. Morgenthau had enough to do with financial problems. The War and Navy secretaries had their own problems. Ickes was not the man for the job; business would have no confidence in him. Wallace had his own problems. Secretary of Labor Perkins was not discussed. Secretary of Commerce Hopkins was too ill and Attorney General Murphy would be occupied with prosecutions and espionage. I told the President the affairs of the Post Office Department were in good order and did not need my attention every moment. I asked him not to give his decision at once but to give my suggestion every consideration. He said he would do that, making a note of my initials at the head of his diagram. I never heard of it again.

That same afternoon I had a long telephone conference with Secretary of Agriculture Wallace, who was disturbed by the influence and interference of Tommy Corcoran, of the White House "palace guard," with the government. He said Corcoran had pipelines in every department of the government. I was not quite sure just what Wallace's complaint was. He closed by saying he was going to take the matter up again with the President and also with Secretary of State Hull.

CHAPTER TWENTY

POLITICS RETURNS

O N SEPTEMBER 16, 1939, I received a phone call in my New York office from General Edwin M. Watson, Secretary and Military Aide to the President. He said the President had asked him to talk to me about the situation in the New York City district in which Congressman James Fay was running against William Kenneally for the Tammany district leadership. Watson said the President was disturbed because Steve Gibbons, Assistant Secretary of the Treasury, had promised to put up several thousand dollars to aid Fay but had not done so. I told Watson that the President had told me politics were to be forgotten during the war. Watson replied he had just talked to the Boss and received his instructions, the President being very definite on the point that he did not want Tommy Corcoran to come up to New York and get the money. I was not clear on Tommy's connection but said I would call Steve. I felt that it was best to do so, though I had no wish to take even such an indirect part in a primary fight, because I was aware the President bore me resentment for my refusal to take part in the successful purge of Representative John J. O'Connor. Fay defeated O'Connor without any help from me. From the information I had, Kenneally was facing certain defeat anyway and the situation wasn't worth a quarrel with the President. I called Steve, who told me that Victor Emanuel, the utility man, was to put up the money. I suggested Steve call Watson. Meanwhile, I called the White House myself and told the general what I had done, expressing myself certain Steve would take care of the situation as desired.

The President had asked me to talk to members of Congress in behalf of neutrality revision. On September 22, 1939, I went to the White House to report that there were about sixty votes in the Senate for the repeal of the Neutrality Bill. I said that I had no advice on Senators Donahey of Ohio, Gerry of Rhode Island, or O'Mahoney of Wyoming. I also said I had no line on Ed Johnson of Colorado or Wheeler of Montana. He made a wry face at the mention of the latter name.

"Boss, if I may say so again, I wouldn't let my personal feelings interfere with my relations with Congress," I said. "All your friends will be for repeal. I think it is absolutely necessary that you carry on at a high level and do everything possible to avoid friction in order to have a united country behind you. And to be perfectly frank, it will strengthen the Democratic party. I think you made a good start seeing Senator Glass."

"Yes, I had an interesting talk with Carter," he said. "You know, he's going to make a short speech in favor of neutrality repeal. That's real progress."

We talked about a number of routine appointments. I did not bring up our conversation about war industries, feeling it best to let the situation ride, certain he would talk to me about it before he made any move as he had promised the week before. He was slightly less cordial than he had been the week before, but I attached no importance to this fact, being aware that he was under considerable pressure by virtue of the war.

"Boss, I was delighted when you called in Senator Bailey during neutrality debate," I said.

"Yes, Bailey is going to go along and he will be very helpful," he laughed.

"How are you getting along with O'Mahoney?" I asked.

"Splendidly," he said. "Joe came in and asked how he could help on neutrality repeal, then answered the question by saying he thought he could help by talking to Senator Maloney of Connecticut. I said he had me there. You know Maloney hasn't made up his mind yet and he's really quite sincere about it. I saw him before I saw O'Mahoney. Maloney is worried about the attitude of the Church. I told him I felt the Church would not oppose it."

"I think you should see some of the others who have been on the other side of the street," I said. "How about seeing Senator Tydings?"

"I would be glad to if there was something we could discuss," was his answer.

"Well, I had a talk with Senator Wagner the other day," I said. "Bob says Tydings is strong for national defense and that might give you a common ground to meet on."

"That might fill the ticket," he said.

On October 2, 1939, I called former Governor Alfred E. Smith to congratulate him on the radio speech he had delivered the night before in behalf of neutrality revision. He said he was glad I liked it and bowled me over by reporting he had received a congratulatory message from Roosevelt.

When I next saw the President I reported my conversation with Al. Before I went into the office, General Watson showed me a letter acknowledging the congratulatory wire in which Al wrote, as nearly as I can remember, "Thank you very much for your kind wire. I am sure you will win your fight." In a few minutes I seated myself at the President's desk.

"You know, I'm getting suspicious of what is going on around here," I said laughingly. "There are some mighty strange faces running in and out of this office. There seems to be no dull moment around here. Bailey and O'Mahoney and Glass are trooping in here regularly, and now I suppose you'll throw out the welcome mat for your old friend 'Happy' Chandler."

He joined in the laugh. I told him that Governor Chandler, whom he had defeated in a race against Senator Barkley, would succeed Senator Logan, who had just died. In this connection I remarked that I planned to attend the funeral of Cardinal Mundelein in Chicago. He urged me to do so by all means.

I was most pleased to see the President so interested in healing the split within the party. He told me he had had a very nice chat with Senator Walsh of Massachusetts during my European tour. The other day, he continued, Walsh made a speech against the neutrality revision, which was most annoying. He asked that I see the Senator, which I promised to do, though I said I was not sure it would be of any avail.

I went to Chicago, where General Watson was the President's personal representative at Cardinal Mundelein's funeral. On my return I found that with winter settling over Europe and the Nazis making

no conquest after dividing Poland with Russia, politics again became a topic of conversation in Washington. House Majority Leader
Rayburn was certain that Roosevelt would be a candidate and would
win reelection. If the President turned down the nomination, Rayburn
said he thought it would go to Garner, Hull, or me. I told him and
others, who were just as certain that the President would not run,
that the time was not one for politics. I confidently expected to be
in the national defense picture and was willing to let politics rest.

Two days later, October 20, I rode up to the Capitol to have lunch
with Jack Garner in his office. "Politics is what I invited you up here
for," he said. "I want to tell you exactly where I stand, so that you can
govern yourself accordingly. As you know, I am opposed to the third
term business. It's bad for the country and bad for the party and bad
for the Boss. I don't know what the Boss is going to do, but I know
he doesn't dislike third term talk and he's doing nothing to discourage it."

"That's only natural," I put in. "Presidents find it hard to believe
anyone can fill their chairs. Alice Longworth told me her father began to worry about the future of the country as the time came for
him (Theodore Roosevelt) to turn over his office to Taft. Joe
Tumulty said that Woodrow Wilson had similar fears, and I understand Coolidge spent restless nights in his final days down the Avenue. Not that they wanted to stay particularly; they didn't like to see
themselves replaced."

"Maybe so," he said thoughtfully. "I am not worried about the
Boss. It's those people around him. I have no confidence in them. If
he should be reelected, the situation which exists today would continue. All they are interested in is staying in power. They have no
interest in the party or the country. I don't think that they give a
damn for the Boss at heart. They would climb onto Wallace's coat-
tails without giving him a second thought, if they thought they could
sell him to the people, which, thank God, they won't be able to do.
He's a dangerous character, Jim, not because he's bad at heart, but
because he doesn't know where he's going."

"I agree with you thoroughly on the men around the President," I
said. "I am convinced that those about him have no genuine affection

for him or they would not ask him to carry them along. After all, he's had four years as Governor of New York and will have had eight years in the White House. That's twelve long, trying years. I doubt if he can stand the strain of another four years, particularly war years. Those around him shouldn't ask him to put himself in a position where he would be shortening his days."

"God knows I hope nothing happens to him," Garner said earnestly. "I don't want to have to go down there. Jim, he and I have had our differences, as you know, but I feel they have been due to bad advice he has been receiving. I have more honest affection for him in my little finger than they have in their whole bodies. I don't want to have anything happen to him and I don't want his job. But I can't swallow this third term as Vice President with him. I don't even know whether I'd vote for him, if he were nominated. I absolutely will not run for a third term as Vice President with him. I don't want to run for anything, but if no one else will come out against him for a third term, I'll do it, even if it's only for the record."

"I feel the same way; as far as I am personally concerned I would be better off if I were not nominated for either place, because I would be in a position to recoup my finances," I said. "Of course, to be absolutely frank, I would find it hard to turn down either nomination, if they should come my way. It would be a great honor and one which I just couldn't bring myself to turn down. That may not be modest, but it's truthful."

"I know," he said. "I'd like to go back to Texas and I hope I will." Tears stood in his eyes. "But there must not be a third term. However, we could go on like this all afternoon. We've talked this over pretty much before. What I want to know is a number of things. I'd like to ask you a few questions, which you can answer or not, as you see fit."

"I'll do my best," I invited.

"First, what will your attitude be if the Boss doesn't come out?" he asked.

"Well, that would be hard to say right now," I answered. "Just between us and in the strictest confidence—I have not told another soul —Roosevelt has indicated he will make known his attitude after the first of the year. Since time must pass, it's hard to say right now what I would do, as circumstances will naturally play a large part in my decision."

"Fair enough," he said. "Now then, I take it you still feel as you told me you did some time ago on the third term?"

"I think it would be a mistake," I said.

"So I gathered," he said. "Finally, can you be persuaded or brought around to the conviction that Roosevelt will have to run for a third term to keep us out of war?"

"Don't disturb yourself about me," I answered. "Just have confidence in me and trust me to make the right decision at the right time. Frankly, I'm sure the Boss doesn't want to run again, although a lot of pressure will be brought to bear by those around him, as you are aware. The whole situation may clear itself in time."

"That may be, but I am concerned about the United States, and so is Cordell Hull. He's very much worried that the President may be talked into running. Mrs. Hull had talked very frankly to Mrs. Garner about his concern for the country."

"I know how Cordell feels," I said. "Just as you and I do. None of us can help but be concerned. I must say, however, that there is only one thing that would cause me to change my mind about the third term and that is if the very existence of the country were threatened. I don't mean a threat, but actual danger."

"I don't want him to run again—nohow," Garner said. "I don't want him to run, whether we are at war or not. I don't foresee any possibility of our national existence hanging by a horse's hair, but I do see dangerous precedent in this third term business. You know, in spite of all this talk, the Boss could never be a dictator, but someone could come along who might be."

We talked about delegates. Garner said that I would probably go into the convention with more than he or Hull, adding I would have to make the decision in time, perhaps, as to whether I should not take the nomination myself, or as to which way I should throw my strength.

"Jim, I have great confidence in you," he said earnestly. "I feel that you would probably be the best President of the three of us. I have a high regard for you personally, for your ability, for your judgment, for your loyalty, and for your integrity. Yes, you could do a great job."

I must admit I was pleased and flattered by his words, and was happy to have this great man consider me worthy of the nation's highest office. No man resents mention of himself for that office, no matter how much he may protest. I told Garner quite honestly that I was deeply moved by his confidence, but I was inclined to think that the convention would decide between Hull and himself, and that I considered it proper such a choice should be made. If a situation should develop where there would be positive strength for me for first place in the convention, that was a decision I would have to resolve for myself. It might be that I would have to take it, although I saw no reason for daydreaming over that possibility.

On October 27, 1939, I had lunch with the President, right after Henry Wallace shattered the unnegotiated truce on partisan politics. With the 1940 presidential election a year and eleven days off, the Secretary of Agriculture told an audience at Berkeley, California, "The war situation obviously makes it clear that the President's talents and training are necessary to steer the country, domestically and in its foreign relationships, to safe harbor." Republicans sputtered indignation. At the White House Steve Early told newspapermen, "It would have been kind and polite of the speaker to have consulted the victim before he spoke." I was not so sure that the President had not been consulted, feeling that Henry, although prone to fly off at a tangent, would hardly take such a step without authorization. Finding the President in an excellent humor, I brought up Wallace's third term statement.

"I see by the papers Henry Wallace is out stumping," I opened. "I wonder if you ran across the item."

The President chuckled. "What did you think of it?"

"I think it was very stupid," I said studying him closely. "I think it was unwise to talk politics at this time. He gave the Republicans ammunition by putting us in a position where it could be charged that we were the first to begin political activity in the war period. And it was bad to bring up the third term question, just as things were moving so well within the party."

"Yes, I'm satisfied with the present situation in the party," he said.

"The situation will continue all right, too, if you don't introduce anything controversial in the next Congress, and if there is no more bad political timing on the part of Wallace and others."

"Oh, Henry means well, but he just isn't politically minded," Roosevelt said airily.

"If you just confine yourself to defense matters, Congress will get along all right," I said.

"You know I'm a bit disturbed about that," he said. "Congress would like to run away with appropriations for defense. I'm worried about the budget. I don't want to give the Republicans an issue by having it get too far out of line, as it will if Congress takes the bit in its mouth on defense appropriations. We ought to have some sort of plan to keep the Republicans from making an issue of the budget. Maybe we could get some additional funds by raising income taxes for the fellows in your class and mine."

"Boss," I said jokingly, "I don't care what they do about the fellows in your class, but I'm in trouble in my class as it is now. I had to borrow money to pay my taxes this year."

"I didn't have to borrow this year," he said, "but I did last year. We ought to have a plan of some sort, though, to make it easier for the party nominee, if Congress runs away on defense appropriations; and there has been some suggestion of readjusting income tax brackets to get more revenue, without dipping into the mass of people in the lower brackets."

The President said nothing about his own candidacy and neither did I. I went away feeling that he had not been entirely unaware of what Wallace was going to say, although he was apparently a bit annoyed over its reception. If he had sent up a trial balloon, he must have come to the conclusion that the move was ill-timed.

The Cabinet meeting was given over that afternoon to a lengthy consideration of the case of the United States freighter *City of Flint*, which had been overhauled by a German warship and made a prize of war because it was carrying a large quantity of oil to Britain. The Germans put it into the Russian port of Murmansk, posing a neutrality problem for the Soviets. President Roosevelt called for a strong hand in dealing with the Russians, not only because the lives of the American crew would be endangered if the Germans decided to attempt running the British blockade, but because he held it necessary to be firm with Russia, which he then regarded as an aggressor nation. At this meeting the points of the indignant note, ultimately sent to the Kremlin, were outlined.

Early in November I dropped in on Secretary of State Hull and found him exercised over the proposal to transfer American ships to the flag of Panama in order to circumvent the Neutrality Act. He said that the President was in favor of making the transfer, disclosing he had argued that to do so would be an indefensible violation of law. Hull said he had told the Boss that the party situation was all right again, with the passage of the joint resolution lifting the arms embargo, which had been signed a few days before as Congress wound up its work. Hull had warned that transfer of American ships might stir up everything again.

"His mind is evidently made up," Hull said. "Apparently he has been listening to those people around him again. I made no impression on him—not the slightest dent. My situation is not good to say the least."

"No matter what situation develops between you and Roosevelt," I said, "under no circumstances should you resign in protest. You have carried on for almost seven years in the face of many disappointments and now is not the time to be getting out of the picture. That would be surrendering to that group, and the country needs your advice and counsel going into the White House, whether or not it is followed."

"It is my intention to follow all international phases and developments as I have in the past and to report as well as I can to the White House," he said slowly. "I am pleased that you do not want me to leave the picture at this time. I hope I can maintain that confidence."

I was satisfied that Hull would stay. We discussed the political situation. I told him quite frankly that he, Garner, and I might have to sit down some time and decide upon a course of action. He agreed that such would seem to be the case. In his round-about way, he made it clear, as he had in the past, that he had no sympathy with a third term.

On November 10, 1939, President Roosevelt asked me to stay after the Cabinet meeting. He asked what was being done about the Jackson Day dinners, saying again that it would be a good idea to have Republican leaders present to give evidence of united national sentiment in the face of the European war. He said the presence of Republicans would have a wholesome effect on the defense program. I said I would have to take the question up with Charley Michelson.

I did not like the idea. I felt it was a shallow subterfuge at best, but he would not let me forget it. He went so far as to suggest names, including Senator McNary of Oregon and Congressman Joe Martin of Massachusetts. On November 21, 1939, he called me into his office for a brief conference on the invitations. I told him I would try to handle the matter by phone as the situation was delicate and one which required tact. He approved.

"By the way, Jim, I've been thinking about the meeting of the Democratic National Committee," he said. "I think it would be all right to have it in January. You could then pick the convention city. I think it would be a good idea to have the convention after the Republicans hold theirs. We might postpone our convention until the Republicans meet."

"I think that's perfectly silly," I said. "The leaders won't stand for it. As it is, it will take all of July to get in shape for opening the campaign in August. If we wait until August, we won't be ready to open the campaign until the first of September."

"Well," his face fell, "don't say a word about this to anyone. Maybe we can talk about it later." I said I would keep his suggestion to myself. "Incidentally, who do you think the Republicans will nominate?" he asked.

"At the moment it looks like Taft or Vandenberg," I said. "I don't think Dewey will make it."

"You may be right," was his only comment.

As I was leaving the Cabinet meeting on December 8, 1939, the President beckoned to me, signaling I should remain behind.

"Jim, I've got quite a problem on my hands," he said after the others had left. "It's the appointment of a new Secretary of the Navy, to succeed Swanson."

"What's wrong with Charley Edison?" I asked in surprise.

"Nothing, exactly," was his answer. "I have a high regard for him and he's done a good job as Assistant Secretary. But between you and me, Jim, it is rather difficult to carry on with him because he's so hard of hearing. He's a perfectly wonderful fellow and I wouldn't hurt him for the world, but I'm afraid he won't do."

"I'm sorry to hear it," I said. "Have you anyone in mind?"

"What do you think of Frank Knox?" he asked.

"Do you really want to know or have you already made up your mind?" I countered.

"I want to know, really," he said.

"Frankly, I am not keen for bringing a Republican into the Cabinet at this particular time, or I might say, at any time," I said. "There are qualified and able Democrats for the job. But while I feel strongly on that, let's look at the difficulties in the way of the appointment of Knox."

"They can be taken care of," he broke in.

"Maybe they can, but there's a question as to whether you would want to do it," I persisted. "If you name Knox, you would have to have Edison's resignation, because I'm sure he expects the appointment. If he is let out, it might have a bad effect. You might be subjected to considerable criticism."

"Oh, I have that all figured out," he said lightly. "There won't be the slightest trouble. The best way to handle it would be to have Frank Hague name him as a candidate for Senator or Governor and he'd resign to run for office."

"Have you talked to Hague?" I asked. I could think of nothing else to ask at the moment, because I was thrown for a loss by the boldness of the scheme.

"No, but that's where you come in, Jim," he smiled engagingly. "You call him up and tell him I want it. I'm sure he'll go along."

"I suppose so," I acknowledged. "I understand he's away, but will be back by Christmas."

"That's too late, Jim," he said. "I want to do it this week. You find out where Hague is and get him on the phone."

"I'll talk to Hague," I promised, "but I just can't see the appointment, Boss. Knox was Landon's running mate, and you'd have a Republican observer in your Cabinet."

"Aw, come now, Jim," he chided mockingly. "Republicans aren't that bad. Remember that under our democratic form of government they have votes too."

"Yes, but they only count in Maine and Vermont," I said jokingly. "Why, Knox may be a candidate for the Republican nomination and participate in party primaries."

"Oh, I'll tell him beforehand that if he participates in Republican primaries, he'll have to get out," he looked at me out of the side of his eyes. "Besides, I don't think he'd get out and it would embarrass the Republicans a lot."

"Boss, he just couldn't do that," I said. "After all, he was nominated for the Vice Presidency by his party and owes the party strict regularity for that honor. He's under obligation to the party. Anyhow, I think it would be a great mistake."

"Well, you'll call Hague," he said. "By the way, I meant to tell you about this some time ago, but it just kept slipping my mind. Get it in shape for next week."

I had a little trouble reaching Hague. When I did, Jersey City's Mayor agreed to nominate Edison for governor if that was what the President wanted. I called Roosevelt by phone and reported Hague's willingness.

"Fine, Jim," he said. "Good work. Now I can go ahead."

"Boss, if I could say a word—and I have given this thing a lot of thought—I wish you wouldn't do it," I said. "You know how I feel about the Republican end of it, although I have nothing against Knox personally; I don't know him."

"Knox might not accept, but I think he would," he said.

"If Knox wouldn't take it, that would be good news to me," I said. "I think you should give the job to Edison. I think he deserves it. He won't hear any better in Trenton than he does in the Navy Department and New Jersey is an important state. I want to remind you that Hague is a hard taskmaster and he might want Charley to keep certain obligations that Charley wouldn't want to fulfill. I don't think it would be fair to Charley to get him involved. He's an honorable fellow."

"Well, we'll see," he said.

Shortly afterwards, Ickes and I had lunch. He sought the meeting in order to talk over the candidacy of Paul McNutt, which was apparently distressing him. He could not see McNutt for first place, or for Vice President in the event the President tried for a third term. Ickes was bitter in his references to McNutt, and held the latter's selection for either place would be "a terrible thing," and "the worst thing in the world that could happen to the country." He declared himself for the third term. He said he would hate to see Garner nominated, but I gathered he would support Hull.

Ickes volunteered that the thing that disturbed him most about the President was that he would make promises and not keep them. Ickes said the one ambition he had when he came to Washington was to have the Forestry Service shifted from the Agriculture to the Interior Department. The President, he said, blessed the proposed shift and promised to support it. He said he had asked Roosevelt to speak to Wallace about it and the President said he would. But the bill authorizing the transfer died. Some time ago, Ickes said, he asked Wallace if the President had spoken to him on the matter. Wallace said the President had never mentioned it, Ickes concluded.

On December 8, 1939, I spent an interesting hour with Hull. I told him that a situation could develop at the convention where Garner, Hull, and myself would have most of the delegates in the convention no matter what the President did.

"Now, I want to be entirely frank with you," I said. "I will do all I can to get delegates for myself. At least that is what I think would be best. I think you and Garner should do the same. Then the three of us can sit down and determine what is best for the country and the party."

"I've done nothing, but I think that after the Jackson Day dinner I'll let my friends speak," he said slowly.

"Neither have I, and I don't think I will do anything until the spring," I said. "I have said nothing publicly that would permit anyone to do anything for me. Nor have I been active privately. I have been getting a line on the situation, so that I will be ready to act. I will talk with you and Garner again in January."

"Jim, I find myself in a most delicate situation," he said. "Above all things I do not want the impression created that I am trying to get glory out of my handling of the situation abroad, nor do I want it to appear that I am capitalizing on my achievements in the State Department. I am content to let all credit go to the President as is fitting and proper, because it is his administration after all. If he chooses to acknowledge my services, that is another thing. So far, he has shown no disposition to do so."

"That is not surprising, because that is his way," I said. "From my attendance at Cabinet meetings I know the great part you are playing in the international situation. I am aware of the value of your contribution. In time, I am confident, the country will know whether or not the President chooses to speak out. I think there is a growing realization of your worth, as is evidenced, to be entirely frank, by the widening mention of you for the Presidency."

I feel certain that had Hull declared himself, and permitted his friends to work for him, he would have secured the nomination hands down. A boom for Hull would have gathered the momentum of a landslide and the President could not have opposed him. I could have done a job for him as I did for Roosevelt in 1932. Without the slightest shadow of a doubt, in my mind, Hull could have been elected in 1940. I am equally convinced he would have made a great President.

On December 14, I had a half-hour conference with the President, largely given over to consideration of appointments. I found him chuckling over clippings of editorials taking McNutt's presidential candidacy over the jumps.

"Paul seems to be getting into trouble in a lot of places," he said. "He's getting a general razzing around the country."

"I hate to say, 'I told you so,'" I said.

"Paul didn't make a very good impression at the Gridiron Club dinner either," he laughed. "Well, he's getting a lot of experience in running, even if he isn't getting any place."

Supreme Court Justice Pierce Butler had died, which placed a Court seat at the top of the list of unfilled jobs.

"What about Senator O'Mahoney?" I suggested.

"Joe is your friend," he countered.

"Of course, but don't hold that against him," I laughed. "What about J. F. T. O'Connor of California? He's another friend of mine."

"I don't know that he'd be for us," he smiled. "I guess there is nothing for me to do but to appoint Frank Murphy."

CHAPTER TWENTY-ONE

GARNER'S HAT IN RING

O N THE MORNING of December 16, Jack Garner called me from his Washington Hotel apartment, saying he had arrived in town in advance of the opening of Congress and that he wanted to see me before he went to the White House, where he had an appointment. We had breakfast and explored the political situation for almost two hours.

A day or two later came real action on the political front. Vice President Garner tossed his familiar Stetson into the 1940 ring with, "I will accept the nomination for President. I will make no effort to control any delegates. The people should decide. The candidate should be selected at primaries and conventions as provided by law, and I sincerely trust all Democrats will participate in them."

Hull called me to get my reaction. I told him I thought the timing was bad, that it would receive a bad press and that I didn't think it would help Jack's position. I told Garner the same thing by phone. On December 22, the Garner statement came up as I sat with the President between the silken American and presidential flags flanking his desk.

"Now that Jack Garner has become an author," I said, "I think you ought to let him make the Jackson Day speech. You should yield to younger men."

"Frankly, Jim, what do you think of Garner's chances?" he asked.

"Meeting frankness with frankness, I don't think Jack wants to be President," I answered. "I am convinced he made his announcement only because of his opposition to the third term. I think he just wants everyone to understand that he is willing to let his name go before the convention, if necessary, in order to stop a third term."

Roosevelt was thoughtful. Finally he shook his head sadly. "I just don't understand Jack," he said. "And I'll tell you why, in confidence. Once when he was in the White House attending a lunch-

eon we discussed 1940. The luncheon was with Congressional leaders. After all the others had left, with the possible exception of Barkley,
Jack came over and patted me on the shoulder asking, 'Are you going
back to Hyde Park after 1940?' I told him I was. Then Garner said
he was glad because he was going back to Uvalde. Now, in view of
that, you'd think he'd understand I was telling him, in so many words,
that I was not going to run. I have proceeded on the theory that he
would not, in view of his words. I think he should have accepted my
assurance, provided he was thinking clearly."

"Boss, I have known Garner a long time and I have never seen
him when he was not in full possession of his faculties," I said. "He's
very careful of his health, as you know, and is a nine o'clock fellow."

I did not reveal that Garner had told me the story himself, because
the Vice President had repeated the conversation in confidence.

Roosevelt said he was going to name Myron C. Taylor, retired head
of United States Steel Corporation, as his personal representative at
the Vatican, to work for peace in Europe. I told him the appointment
was satisfactory in every way to me and bound to be well received.
He also told me that he had definitely made up his mind to put Frank
Murphy on the Supreme Court and to move Robert Jackson, present
Solicitor General, in as Attorney General.

"Boss, to return to politics," I said. "I think that sometime after
the first of the year you and I had better have a talk on the political
situation."

"Grand idea, Jim," he agreed. "Suits me to a 'T' and I hope we can
make it a long one."

"I haven't discussed the conversation we had last July in which
you confided you would not be a candidate," I said. "People have
been asking me for advice—Senators, Congressmen, national committeemen, state chairmen, and other leaders. I have been stalling them
off. But there will come a time when we have to face the facts, and
the sooner you and I clear up the situation, the better it will be all
around."

"I agree one hundred per cent," he said.

"I think that there will be plenty of time after the Jackson Day
dinner," I said.

"Oh, I'll want to talk to you before that," he said thoughtfully. "We ought to get it out of the way before that time."

That same day I visited Harry Hopkins in his Georgetown home. When I called, Miss Marguerite Le Hand, the President's personal secretary, was also paying a visit. Hopkins looked pale and feeble, but his eyes were alive with energy, which gave indication that he might return to his post, though none of us had expected him to sit in the Commerce chair of the Cabinet again.

In a jesting way I told Hopkins that I was managing Garner's campaign, but was wondering whether I should not shift to McNutt.

"McNutt is at the bottom of my list," he said somewhat shortly.

"You are quite complimentary, because he isn't even on mine," I laughed.

"He had no business going around telling people he had the Boss's blessing," Harry said. "He hasn't had a kind word."

A week later I reported to the President that I had called a meeting of the Democratic National Committee for February 15, 1940, to select a convention site. He approved and was pleased at my further report that the Jackson Day dinners were getting along all right.

"By the way, Jim," he said, "rumors are reaching me that Senator Wheeler and your friend, McNutt, are giving the impression that the administration is for their candidacy."

"I thought McNutt was your friend," I countered.

"Yes, just as close a friend as Burt Wheeler," he laughed.

On December 30, 1939, Edward J. Flynn, Bronx leader, told me he was of the opinion that the President would not run. He said I should let my name go before the convention. He said the President could not fail to support me for the Vice Presidency, if I were nominated with Hull.

On the last day of the year, the President appointed Charles Edison as Secretary of the Navy, which was pleasing to me. I called to congratulate Charley and learned that the President had sent for Edison and at the end of a chat, told him he would be named to the Cabinet. Edison expressed appreciation of my efforts in his behalf.

On January 3, 1940, I had a visit with Anna Boettiger, the President's only daughter, and her husband John. They asked me how I thought the President looked. I said I thought he looked tired, that the strain was telling on him. Anna said that when she first came east on vacation, she thought her father looked well, but when she saw him under pressure in Washington, she thought he looked tired. John and Anna said it was quite apparent to them the President was anxious to get away from Washington.

Later in the morning I received a telephone call from Malvina Thompson, Mrs. Roosevelt's secretary, saying Mrs. Roosevelt would like to see me. My afternoon was full and I so reported. After this was relayed, Mrs. Roosevelt came on the phone and asked me to come to dinner for a discussion of Democratic women's plans. The President, Missy Le Hand, and some young fellow connected with the Navy Department were at the table, along with Mrs. Roosevelt and myself. The Boss was in high spirits.

"Jim, I have the grandest joke for you," he confided. "I had Garner, Barkley, and Rayburn in this morning for a conference on the anti-lynching bill. And you'll never guess what Jack said. Very seriously he said that he had given considerable thought to the legislation and that he felt that the colored vote in the border states and in northern cities was such that he thought the legislation had to be passed."

Roosevelt threw back his head and laughed till tears came to his eyes.

"Don't you love it?" he asked. "Jack has done a complete about face on it now that he's out looking for votes. Don't mention it to a soul, though."

"Boss, it's really childish not to mention it," I said. "You are going to be reading about it, because some of the Congressional leaders are bound to talk."

After Mrs. Roosevelt and I had disposed of the women's problems, I went upstairs with the President to listen to a rebroadcast of his message to Congress on the state of the Union. He enjoyed every bit of it. I have never been able to listen to my own voice with any enjoyment, but he was his own best audience. He relished every bit of Republican applause for his statement on budget balancing.

"That shows you can have your cake and still eat it," he said. "I put them into a hole with that one."

He was delighted with the shot he took at Senator Borah by his reference to people who professed to have more and better information than the State Department and were positive there would be no war.

"Well, Jim, a while back I told you we'd have a long talk about the political situation. What do you think about a date for the convention?"

"Boss, I think it would be a mistake to set it back too far," I said. "I don't think it should be in the latter part of July."

"Let's see, the boat races will be on in Poughkeepsie the last week in June and I hope to be at Hyde Park then," he mused. "Maybe it could be about July 15 or July 8. Set it when you like. What about the city? I prefer Chicago."

"So do I, but I don't know if Chicago will give us the money," I said. "I think Philadelphia and San Francisco will offer more money. I'm not keen for Philadelphia, but if they put up more money, I don't see anything to do but take it."

"Possibly so," he agreed. "I'd like Chicago and a late convention, after Congress is out of the way."

"Congress was in session during the 1932 convention," I reminded him. "Again, I must say we can't hold a convention too late, because, while we can set up a headquarters, we can't put it in operation before the convention because we don't know who the nominee will be."

Then I looked him square in the eyes and said, "And there will be a new national chairman and the new chairman will want to set up his own show."

He made no comment on my announcement that I did not expect to remain at the helm of the party organization. We talked about a temporary and permanent chairman. I maintained that we would have to consider Senate Majority Leader Barkley and Speaker Bankhead because of their positions in Congress.

"Barkley's long-winded and will have to be told to hold himself in," he said.

On January 17, 1940, I had lunch with Jack Garner. He reiterated his opposition to a third term and again said he had no desire to be President, but added, "No man could refuse the call of his party and his country, if it should come." He said he preferred to go back to Uvalde and live for ten or twenty years. The next day the President and the Vice President sat one on either side of me at the Jackson Day dinner. We chatted lightly during the course of the meal. Roosevelt's laugh rang above the rest when I opened my remarks with, "Fellow candidates."

CHAPTER TWENTY-TWO

FARLEY'S HAT IN RING

IN THE NEXT few weeks I saw literally hundreds of persons, all of whom had the same major concern—the 1940 presidential nomination. There were members of Congress, political leaders, businessmen, professional men, and newspapermen by the score. It seemed to me that the time had come for a showdown with the President, since my friends in Massachusetts were pressing me to enter the state's preferential primary. I sought an appointment and saw the President at lunch the day after his fifty-eighth birthday.

"Boss, a situation has arisen which I must discuss with you," I said. "I am going to be frank with you and I want you to be equally frank with me."

"Sure thing, Jim," he invited.

"I don't want to get into a discussion as to what will happen next month or in March or in April. I am now confronted with a proposition on which I must make a decision. I want your approval of whatever position I take. The Massachusetts and New Hampshire primaries are coming up."

"Is Garner going to enter?" he asked eagerly.

"That I don't know," I said. "I imagine he will enter if I don't."

"I don't think Garner could win in Massachusetts," he said.

"I don't either," I agreed. "The problem is, however, whether I should enter my name. I propose to file in both states unless you have any objection."

"Go ahead, Jim," he laughed. "The water's fine. I haven't an objection in the world."

"Now, Mr. President, do not say yes to this arrangement unless you are thoroughly in accord with the course of action, which is suggested by William Burke, Democratic chairman of Massachusetts," I cautioned. "Burke says that if a delegation is not filed, a half dozen sets

223

of delegates would enter the primary and disturb the party's position in the November election."

"I think it's a grand idea," he said.

"I don't want you to say so unless you are thoroughly in accord," I persisted. "I don't want somebody coming to me a couple of weeks from now saying that you said you could not say no at the time."

"I am in accord, Jim," he said. "Go to it. Nobody will be running to you with anything different."

(Within two weeks of the conversation, Senator David I. Walsh of Massachusetts came to my office saying he wanted to discuss the state's delegation. He said he had just seen the President and would like my side of the story. I gave the story as I have told it. When I came to the final words, Walsh interrupted me.

("Stop, Jim," he said, putting up his hand like a traffic policeman, "that's exactly what happened. His version was not quite the same as yours, but he did tell me that he could not say no to you.")

I must make it clear that I did not regard the President's approbation in any degree as approval of my candidacy, although I did regard it as in line with his statement that he would not be a candidate. As a matter of fact, I was not asking him to approve my candidacy in seeking his approval to enter the Massachusetts primary.

We discussed the convention date, agreeing that it would be best for me to appoint a committee to set the date, with the understanding that it would come a week after the Republican meeting. We also discussed the place and he declared himself against New York, San Francisco, and Philadelphia, regardless of what money they might tempt the committee with. He said he was for Chicago for a number of reasons, including the fact that Mayor Kelly would be able to control the galleries. I gave little thought to the remark at the time, but it was brought home to me in Chicago in July. We then came to the candidacy of Wheeler.

"If Wheeler should be nominated for President, I'd vote for a Republican," he said.

"Boss, you couldn't do that as the head of your party," I interjected.

"Oh, yes, I could," he snapped.

A few days later Senators Clark of Missouri and Johnson of Colorado came to sound me out on the possibility of a Farley–Wheeler ticket. I said I could not make a combination with anyone.

My filing provoked quite a flurry in the press, as was to be expected. It was considered in some quarters that I had New England's 82 convention votes in the bag. Hardly had I acted when the third termers got busy. Pressure was brought to bear on Democratic leaders. Some yielded and hastened to get in line, with what they considered might be the trend, by announcing various votes were pledged first to Roosevelt and second to Farley. The efforts of these leaders to "get right" were more amusing than anything else. They were in a bit of a panic, being desirous of holding White House favor and yet having no desire to offend me.

I was unmoved by praise or criticism until Ernest K. Lindley, the President's official biographer, published an article purporting to be the answer to the third term riddle. Supposedly, the President was answering direct questions from a Democratic stalwart. I understand that the article was inspired by an exchange between the President and veteran Congressman Bob Doughton of North Carolina. I want to be most fair about this episode because nothing which ever happened to me politically so wounded me as this article, not so much for itself but because it was generally believed that it had been inspired by the President, and he took no step to offset that impression.

The article said the President had declared he would not run again unless Britain were overrun by Nazis, that Hull was his choice for his successor, that the Vice Presidency lay between Jackson, McNutt, and Wheeler, and, finally, that I was not a sound vice-presidential candidate because of my religion. Roosevelt was reported to have said that he owed more to me politically than to any other person, not even excepting his wife, but in the event of my nomination, people might say "we were using Cordell Hull as a stalking horse for the Pope."

At his press conference the President was asked to comment on the article. He said he had not read it. Newspapermen felt this was not true. If he hadn't, he was the only person concerned who had not done so. A dozen people called it to my attention before eight-thirty o'clock the morning it appeared. It is hard to imagine the White House people had failed to bring it to his attention at once. What was harder to understand was why, once it had been brought to his attention, he did not do something about it.

As I said, I want to be as fair as I can. Many of my friends were convinced that the President had deliberately inspired publication of the story in order to take me out of the picture, either by giving the story to Lindley or by sending Lindley to get it from Doughton. I would prefer not to know the worst. I have never asked Doughton about it; nor did I question Lindley as to the source of his piece. I did tell him I believed his story was accurate. I do not say that Roosevelt inspired it. I sincerely hope that he did not. If he did, I say that he was guilty of one of the most unfriendly acts in politics. If he did not, I say he should have moved to correct the impression the story created. And I say this, aware that the story probably did me more good than harm as it rallied the forces of toleration to my defense.

I went over to see Hull, feeling I had to talk out the situation with someone. I found him puzzled.

"Cordell, I want to be as objective as I can about a matter which touches me deeply," I said. "I do not believe the President told the story exactly the way it was published, but I believe that, in general, the story presents his view. I can't conceive of him . . . no, let's say I don't want to think of him as counting me out on religious grounds; but I can believe he discussed it. What I can't understand is why he didn't say something after the story was printed."

"Without doubt the President should have done something about it," Hull said.

"Well, one thing is definite," I said. "I'm sure the President will try to prevent me from having a place on the ticket. I want you to know I understand that and want you to govern yourself accordingly. We have had no understanding and that is just as well in view of this situation."

"Jim, I want you to know that I do not share . . ."

"Let's not go into that now," I broke in. "I want to be able to say I have made no commitments and I want you to be able to say the same thing. I'm not sure but what this thing is being shaped against us from across the street."

Involuntarily, we both looked in the direction of the White House. "What I don't understand is the story that Roosevelt is for me," Hull said. "I am sure he doesn't want me."

"With that I agree," I said. "But the situation may move beyond him. Unless he takes it himself, which he has told me he will not, then he can't in all likelihood put over one of his own group like Wallace or Jackson or Douglas. Most of the delegates will be for Garner, Hull, or me. He won't take Garner; he won't take me; that leaves you."

"I find it difficult to understand his turning against you," Hull said. "He owes you so much."

"Since 1928 I have given unceasingly of my time and loyalty to advance his cause, even to my personal disadvantage," I said. "Through the years I have been told how ungrateful he is. You are aware of that, too." Hull nodded. "I dismissed all those observations, feeling that things would work out all right in the end. Now this has happened. Well, I don't propose to go off the track. I will do all I can to keep the party on its traditional course. I hope you will do the same. But I want you to know that if I think that the proper course is to let my name go before the convention, all the Roosevelts in the world couldn't stop me."

Former Governor Cox of Ohio told me he had mentioned my name for second place to Roosevelt, and the President had said he was not afraid of the religious issue but felt a Hull–Farley ticket would not be pleasing to liberals. At this time Ed Flynn had talked with the President and reported that Roosevelt told him he wanted to retire to Hyde Park, as of the moment, but that a situation could develop abroad which might cause him to change his mind.

At first I was for a showdown with the President, but as my mind cooled I decided the proper course was to keep my temper and bide my time. I resolved, however, to let him know I was annoyed.

At the Cabinet meeting of March 8, 1940, I made no comment until the President got to me. I said I had nothing to offer, in such a way as to indicate I wanted no conversation with him. He remarked, rather vaguely, we were getting out a lot of interesting stamps and made some comment on the Pan-American stamp which he had designed. I studied the table in front of me. It was obvious to all that I was irritated. He talked about joining in the celebration of penny postage in Canada, mentioning that he and I could participate in an international broadcast marking the event. I was as cold as ice, saying I thought he should go on the program alone.

"I'll see you tonight, Jim," he said after an awkward pause. It was evident to all I was resentful of the situation which he had allowed to develop.

"Mr. President, you are not going to see me tonight," I said. "I must go to a social gathering of Democrats in Queens Borough and I am going to broadcast in connection with the anniversary Farm Dinners from New York."

He shrugged and went on to Secretary of Navy Edison.

On March 16, 1940, I talked to Frank C. Walker, who had assisted in the financing of the Roosevelt campaign for the nomination in 1932. In discussing the President's failure to repudiate the Lindley story, I said I wasn't going to say anything about it to the President, but would handle it in my own way at my own time. I told him I wasn't going to get angry but I did feel very much hurt. I was aware he would carry back what I was saying to the White House, so I told him I would follow a course of my own after proper consideration of the picture with those I considered my friends.

That Saturday night I made the principal speech at the annual banquet of the Friendly Sons of St. Patrick in the Mayflower Hotel in Washington. The society, as some may not know, was founded by men of Irish descent back in colonial days, to give comfort and aid to Irish immigrants, regardless of religion, on their arrival at American ports. George Washington was an honorary member of this organization of good Samaritans, which is now a social organization in Boston, New York, Philadelphia, Cincinnati, and Washington, meeting every St. Patrick's Day except, as was the case that year, when the day of the gentle Patrick falls on Sunday. I took the time and the occasion to answer the Lindley article in my own way. Before that friendly group and over a nationwide hookup, I said, with all the sincerity in my soul:

We must never permit the ideals of this Republic to sink to a point where every American father and mother, regardless of race, color, or creed, cannot look proudly into the cradle of their newborn babe and see a future President of the United States.

As might be expected, the sentence rang from one end of the country to the other. It was not new, but it was a truth that needed restatement. I had uttered the right words with the right accents and they could not fail to find a warm reception in all hearts and minds. Monday morning White House Secretary Early called me to give the President's congratulations on my remarks, adding that Roosevelt was preparing to answer the Lindley article at his next press conference. I told him that it was too late, that too much time had elapsed for a denial to carry any weight, that the harm had been done and the entire matter could be forgotten, as far as I was concerned. Nonetheless, at his next press conference, in answer to a "planted" question, the President belatedly said that not one word of the story was true; that "it was made out of whole cloth." He grasped the opportunity to hit at columnists generally, saying that they were right only twenty per cent of the time and soft-pedaled their errors. Lindley stood his ground, as well he might, because he knew he was voicing the sentiments, if not the actual words, of the man in the White House.

I did not see the President again until April 16. We had lunch. I found him studiously cordial in manner and overly friendly. He began by mentioning that he was prepared to appoint my brother, Tom, as Federal marshal for our district in New York. He had promised to make the appointment earlier in the year. After the Lindley story I discussed the matter with Tom and we agreed it might not be a good idea to accept it in view of the circumstances. I told the President Tom was perfectly satisfied on the Boxing Commission and advised him to forget the appointment.

We talked about everything and nothing. It was evident the President wanted to talk to me more about the situation but he didn't know how or where to open up. I studied him closely. He appeared to have lost much of his former fire. He looked tired and his color was bad. I remember thinking that it was a crime that the people around him were urging him to be a candidate again. After all, he had or would have had twelve long years in Albany and Washington, which had taken their toll, and he should not be called upon to face another four years, possibly more exacting than all those which had gone before.

We talked about routine appointments. He mentioned Senators Barkley and Byrnes for temporary Chairman of the convention. I told him I thought the place ought to go to Speaker Bankhead.

"Jim, have you heard talk of giving Governor Lehman the complimentary vote of New York State at the convention?" he asked.

"It hasn't been brought to my attention," I reported.

"Several people have talked to me about it," he said. He lighted another cigarette. I thought his remark was going to lead somewhere so I waited.

"You know," he resumed, "I think there are about ten or twelve men who have a good chance of getting the nomination. I'm going to put the names in an envelope and take them out after it's all over."

"There's no sense in putting more than six names in it," I said. "Will you put down Garner's name?"

"He can't be nominated," he said by way of dismissal. "I think the whole thing is just balmy."

"Maybe so, but I hear efforts are being made to take the Texas delegation from him, and I think that would be a mistake," I said. "I think he is entitled to the vote of the delegation, a courtesy vote in recognition of his long service to the party and the nation."

After lunch we went to the opening ball game. I rode out to the park with him. As we passed the Washington Hotel, where the Vice President lived, he brought up Garner again, saying the Vice President didn't have a chance. Then he lowered his voice to confide that he was for Hull.

"That's one candidate you and I can agree on," I said. "You couldn't find a better choice."

I reported the conversation to Hull, who told me that once, late in 1939, when he and Roosevelt were discussing some problem, the President said, "That is something the next President will have to worry about, and that will be you, Cordell." Hull said he was going to sit tight and rely on the President's word. I agreed that was the only thing to do. I understand Roosevelt never discussed the Presidency with Hull again until the day he told Hull he was going to run for a third term and asked Hull to take second place on the ticket.

In this period Mrs. Farley happened to be seated at the President's left at an official White House dinner one night. He remarked to her, "I'm having a terrible time, Bess; they're trying to make me run and I don't want to." He looked at her with an engaging smile.

"Well," Mrs. Farley answered, "you're the President, aren't you? All you have to do is tell them you won't run." He blinked surprise and turned to the lady on his right.

On April 30, 1940, Basil O'Connor, former law partner and close friend of the President, came to see me, saying that he had attempted to patch the rift between the President and myself.

"I talked with him about what I called the Farley situation," O'Connor reported. "I asked him why he did not sit down and talk things over with you. I told him that he could explain his position to you. He answered that there is no reason to do it now. I must admit I didn't do anything about the situation; I got just exactly nowhere in my efforts."

O'Connor said the President indicated he would reluctantly take Hull. Roosevelt talked about Jackson and Wallace for the Vice Presidency, mentioning Rayburn as a possibility. O'Connor was of the opinion that Roosevelt would not be a candidate unless an unforeseen situation should develop abroad.

What Basil told me confirmed my suspicions that the President never wanted me on the ticket. O'Connor said that the President had not asked him what he thought of running for a third term. Basil said that had Roosevelt done so, he would have told him frankly that it would be a terrible thing. I know he would have done so, because O'Connor never hesitated to speak the truth to his long-time friend. He did so to the end. I feel he was possibly the only person who did so in Roosevelt's last years.

From the time of the Lindley story the President virtually ignored me. I was not invited to the White House except when my position in the Cabinet made an invitation imperative. Taking a cue from the White House were many who had professed to be my friends. They avoided me as though I were the plague. Some channels of information dried up. One of the most amazing evidences of the extent to which I was cut off came from the State Department. Some time back, an Assistant Secretary of State had promised to help in the preparation of a couple of speeches, one which I had promised Senator Truman of Missouri I would deliver at Fulton, Missouri. Another one was to be on foreign affairs. The Assistant Secretary reported the speeches had been sent to my New York office. They did not show up. Finally, Ambrose O'Connell, First Assistant Postmaster General, went to the official, who frankly confided he was under White House orders not to help me and asked that I should not embarrass him by calling on him. I sent word that I would not.

I was no longer consulted on even the most trivial of appointments. I found the White House was dealing directly with political leaders and members of Congress and members of the Cabinet on these matters. It was evident that the President didn't want to talk to me, that he was going out of his way to avoid any meeting that might lead to a discussion. I met the situation by staying away from Washington as much as I could. I made up my mind to keep my sense of humor and not to lose my temper. Stories and editorials began to appear in the press about neglect of me. Housing Administrator Nathan Straus brought me word that the White House "palace guard" realized the anti-Catholic campaign against me had failed and that they were going to take the slant that I was not a liberal. He was one of many good friends who remained faithful in spite of the fact I was out of favor. The antiliberal campaign gave me a laugh, because I had supported the President faithfully on all legislation, and a great deal of it might never have been enacted without my efforts.

On May 9, 1940, I had another long talk with Hull, who said he was so worried over the foreign situation that he had no time to give to politics. He said he was naturally grateful for the many generous offers of support and approval he had been receiving from people throughout the country. We talked about the Gallup poll results, which showed Hull stronger than Roosevelt. He disclosed that he had learned from sources within the White House that the President was not pleased over them.

"The President has never talked a word of politics to me," Hull said. "He may be assuring others that I am his choice, but I find it hard to believe."

"I am sure that he will accept you, if he is not himself a candidate," I said. "I am not going to tell you that he prefers you, but I think he will have to take you. Meantime, there is nothing for you to do but go along as you have been and see what happens. I think you should go along, unless you decide to announce yourself or let your friends announce you. Should you do that, which you have shown no disposition to do, you would get the nomination, as I have indicated to you."

"Jim, I've told you that in view of the world situation I do not feel I should use my position to seek office," he said. "I can only put my trust in what the President is telling everyone, even if he does not see fit to confide that trust in me."

"There's no denying it; Roosevelt is a strange man," I said. "He's the author of all my present troubles."

"God, Jim," Hull exploded with feeling, "you don't know what troubles are. Roosevelt is going directly to Welles and Berle. I was never even consulted on the Welles trip to Europe. Then he's by-passing me by going to ambassadors. He's in communication constantly with British leaders and others. He doesn't consult with me or confide in me and I have to feel my way in the dark. I have the devil's own time keeping him from issuing statements that would be most detrimental. He only discusses matters with me when he feels that he is obliged to do so because of their importance. Troubles! You don't know what they are!"

I was forced to laugh at myself and acknowledge that there was much truth in what he had to say. I told him to keep the flag flying, and went on my way comforted, but regretful that so splendid a character was receiving such treatment.

In the middle of May I went out on post office business to Detroit and Milwaukee. I stopped in Chicago, where I received a visit from Mayor Kelly. Kelly expressed himself convinced the President would be nominated, and urged me to remain so I could maintain a position of influence during the next four years. He wanted to know if he could talk to the President for me. I answered bluntly I knew where to find Roosevelt, and added that no real friend would urge him to run again for many reasons. I said he could retire to Hyde Park to a well-earned rest and maintain a position of great influence, confident of having earned a great place in history. Kelly said Roosevelt could win. I acknowledged this, but said his victory would not be as easy as that of 1936. I also said that Hull could win more easily than Roosevelt.

The Cabinet meeting of May 17, 1940, was concerned with the situation in France. Roosevelt said there was about a fifty-fifty chance the French would hold out. He brought up the possibility of a German victory and what our attitude might be if a German purchasing commission came over in search of materials. He did not reach any conclusions, but contented himself with making observations on the possibility. It was evident that the President was running the Army and the Navy, and that he would try to direct all the efforts which would be made in connection with the coordination of government and industry. I dictated my observations of that date as follows:

"I think the President is getting jittery. I am really fearful that if the President is elected for a third term he may not be able to stand up physically under the strain and he will let those around him get into a situation which will be bad for the country and himself."

After the Cabinet meeting he asked me to talk to him about George Starr, postmaster at Seattle, Washington, who was up for reappointment. He said he understood there were some objections to the reappointment of Starr. I said there were none, except that Starr and John Boettiger, Roosevelt's son-in-law, had had some differences over newspaper mail charges. I showed him a report of the inspection division of the Post Office revealing Starr's office was one of the best conducted in the country. He brushed this off by saying inspections didn't amount to much. I said that Starr's rating was high and that there was no valid excuse for not reappointing him. Roosevelt went into a long involved story, which I did not consider to the point. He then suggested giving consideration to Howard Costigan of the Washington Commonwealth Federation.

"Mr. President, while I don't think Costigan is a Communist, he's way to the left, as has been brought out in Hugh De Lacy's campaign for mayor of Seattle in the last few weeks," I said. "And the Commonwealth Federation has tried to usurp functions of the state Democratic organization. I don't think that should be tolerated."

Somewhat grudgingly he acknowledged that was correct.

"Personally, I have no interest in Starr, except that you would be doing a faithful servant a grave injustice if you do not reappoint him," I said. "All you have against him is the complaint from John Boettiger. If John had not complained, he would have been reappointed without question."

"Well, a lot of objections have been raised against Starr," he said doggedly. "One of them is that he didn't cooperate politically."

"What about the Hatch Act?" I challenged.

He had no answer for that. I left after he said he guessed he would have to reappoint Starr. I said he wouldn't regret it. (The appointment was made.)

Before I left we talked about Speaker Bankhead for temporary chairman and Senate Majority Leader Barkley for permanent chairman. He had told Charley Michelson they would do.

"Charley told me you are satisfied with Barkley and Bankhead," I said. "They are fine with me, because we will be taking the two top men in the party."

"What do you mean, 'top men in the party'?" he snapped.

"The two top men in the legislative branch of the government," I amended.

"That's better," he said.

CHAPTER TWENTY-THREE

MAKING MY DECISION

IN THESE WEEKS and the weeks before the convention just ahead, I was called on to make the most difficult decision I had ever faced in my life. It was evident to me that the President was going to run again, or rather that he was going to permit himself to be persuaded to run by those about him, on the ground that he was an indispensable man. I find it hard to say just when this realization dawned on me. As far back as 1937 I was suspecting things from the way he spoke of possibilities for a successor. Then I had his personal assurance he would not run. Still I was not easy. Suddenly, the fact was before me and I had to decide my course of action.

My decision was not an easy one. There was no doubt that if I came out against the third term, I could make myself a big man in the eyes of the country. But I was not seeking personal aggrandizement. I knew that if I left the Cabinet I would be deserted by many who professed to be my friends, and that I would have to ask true friends to stay away from me for fear that I might injure their futures. Days stretched into weeks as I turned the problem over in my mind. Nightly I walked the streets of New York and Washington debating with myself. I tramped miles around the reservoir in Central Park. I paced the reflecting pool from Washington Monument to the Lincoln Memorial for many more miles in Washington. I took to dropping into churches at late hours. I must have aroused much conjecture from many who recognized me. For a tall man, I have a short stride, but make up for it by a rapid pace. I must have appeared to the casual watchers to be going somewhere, when the truth was I had no idea where I was going.

I was and still am opposed to a third term. I honestly do not believe that any real friend of the President should have urged a third term upon him. I was aware that the Republicans could conduct a formidable campaign on the third term issue. A most bitter campaign could bring about his defeat, although I felt that at that moment he could be elected, provided the war continued. The Republican candidate had not been selected, but it appeared to me then it would be Senator Taft or Senator Vandenberg. I did not want Roosevelt to place the party in jeopardy by running for a third term, when a candidate like Hull could have been certain of victory. Modestly, I say I could have helped Hull if I were on the ticket as Vice President, but I believe Hull could have made it with any one from a field of candidates.

On May 21, 1940, "Chip" Robert, Secretary of the National Committee, went to the White House for a chat with Harry Hopkins, who was regarded as the master mind of the third term drive. Chip was as much in the dark as I was about what was going on of a political nature in the White House. He told me the story of the meeting.

"Is Jim still running for President?" Harry asked derisively.

"I don't know," Chip answered. (And he honestly didn't.) "Whatever happens, Jim will be all right and can't be criticized."

In a more pleasant tone Hopkins told Chip that he regarded the situation between the President and Farley as "an appalling thing." He then proceeded to blame Tommy Corcoran for the situation and was bitter about Ben Cohen, Corcoran's partner in the administration. Hopkins said it was "too bad Farley's brother had not been named a judge." (Of course, my brother Tom was not aspiring to a judgeship but to be a United States marshal, an ambition which he had voluntarily abandoned.)

I had lunch with Garner on May 28, two days before my fifty-second birthday.

"Jim, what's the Boss going to do?" asked Garner.

"Your guess is as good as mine," I answered. "I've given up guessing."

He looked at me sharply and read what was in my eyes. I was smiling.

"I guess he's going to run," he said.

"Well," I laughed, "to quote our old friend Cordell Hull, it begins to look that way."

"Hell, he's fixed it so nobody else can run now," Garner said. "I wouldn't have gotten in myself or I wouldn't have handled myself . . . Ah, well, there's no use watering spilt milk."

"I went along with the assurances he gave me that he wouldn't run," I said. "So did you and so did Cordell. And we are all left high and dry. Al Smith warned me never to rely on Roosevelt's word. I laughed at him. So did others and I laughed at them. Now he's laughing at me and at us."

Garner ripped savagely at his cigar. "What are you going to do if the Boss wants the same ticket reelected?"

"I'll answer that with a question: Are you going to let your name be presented for President?" I asked in turn.

"I certainly am," Garner said. "And for two reasons—I really want to go back to Uvalde, and I am against this third term business. What about you? Are you with me?"

"I'll know better when the President makes his decision," I answered. "The way I feel now there is only one honorable course in front of me and that is to register my protest against the third term without injuring the party. I'm not satisfied how that is best to be done. Put your trust in Farley, though."

We shook hands on it.

Senator Chandler of Kentucky was called to the White House at this time for a bedside conference with the President. Roosevelt told him he was not going to run, but was in search of a good, strong candidate. "Happy" suggested I be given consideration, reporting to me that this suggestion awoke no presidential enthusiasm. I thanked him for advising me of the conversation, and told him I hardly expected enthusiasm for anyone from that quarter short of one man—Franklin D. Roosevelt.

On June 5, 1940, I had visits from Ed Flynn and Frank Walker. Both argued at length that I should manage the Roosevelt campaign, if the President should decide to run. They acknowledged I had been treated badly, although I said I was not complaining.

"I'm going down to the White House and demand to know what Roosevelt is going to do," Flynn told me. "I'm not going to take orders from Hopkins, Ickes, Wallace, Corcoran, Cohen, and the rest of them."

"Maybe he'll tell you what he's going to do, but he won't tell me,"

I said. "I'm not sure whether I'll ask him or wait and let him tell me. I'm not going to make any decision today that I can put off until tomorrow."

Walker told me he would hate to see me break with Roosevelt, although he wouldn't blame me a bit for doing so. He said a break would be bad for the party. I acknowledged that it would not be pleasant for me to break with the President, but one of these days I would have to make my decision.

"I'm not going to kid you, Frank," I said. "The President's attitude has made leaders feel they can do nothing but string along with him. They don't want him for the candidate—many of them don't—but they have no choice unless he makes an announcement of his attitude, which apparently he doesn't choose to do, which in itself is an undeclared candidacy."

On June 12, I asked Frank Kelly, Brooklyn leader, what he thought I should do. I expected him to follow the Ed Kelly–Frank Hague line that I should overlook all that had happened and take over the conduct of the campaign for the sake of remaining in the national scene and retaining my Cabinet post and party leadership.

"I'm not one given to passing out advice unless it is asked," he said. "Straight from the shoulder, Jim, I'd hate to think of a national campaign being run without you. Of course, the organization you have built will run along for some years yet, but it won't be the same without you in the driver's seat. But, and a big 'but' it is, Jim, if I had been kicked around the way you have by Roosevelt and his crowd, I would no more run the campaign than I would jump out of this window."

He looked down into Vanderbilt Avenue. I followed his gaze and had to laugh. I appreciated his frank statement more than he ever knew.

On June 14, I ran into Henry Wallace on the six o'clock train from Washington to New York. We had dinner together.

"Jim," he said, "I don't like it. I want the President to run again and I think he will run, but I am very discouraged at the way the thing is being handled. Harry Hopkins, Ben Cohen, and Tommy Corcoran are doing the contact work for Mayor Hague, Mayor Kelly, and the other bosses. They have a group working out the details in an office in the Interior building. You know Ben Cohen has an office there as counsel for the Federal Power Commission."

I told Wallace that I didn't feel that the third term was for the best interests of the country or the party. I said I had not been taken into the President's confidence so I did not know his plans, but I had my suspicions.

"There's no justification for the way you have been treated," Wallace said. "It is difficult to understand. Many things are difficult to understand with Roosevelt. There's Ickes trying to grab my Forest Service, and I'm not sure which way the President is going to decide in the final analysis, but I'm not going to take it lying down. I don't understand what he is going to do politically either. In my own case he told me over the phone and in writing—maybe I should say indicated, but he practically told me—that it would be all right to have the Iowa delegation for me. A few days later he talked to Senators Gillette and Herring, Congressman Jacobson, and State Chairman Ed Birmingham and told them I was a nice fellow, but I didn't have a chance."

On June 19, 1940, when I was in Chicago making convention arrangements I received a call from the President saying he had had a meeting with Congressional leaders the day before and Speaker Bankhead had remained behind to make a request.

"The dear old Speaker wants to make a speech as temporary chairman of the convention, Jim," he said, "and you know the dear old Speaker doesn't make a very enthusiastic talk."

"Well, Boss, you will remember that you and I had an agreement that Bankhead and Barkley would be temporary and permanent chairmen respectively," I reminded him. "Bankhead may make an uninteresting speech but it will be a Democratic speech."

"Sure, sure, but maybe we could get someone to make a good talk along the line," he said. "Maybe we could get a fellow like Senator Byrnes, or possibly Senator Josh Lee."

These were the first words we had exchanged privately in a long time.

While I was away Frank Knox and Henry L. Stimson were named to the Cabinet in what was widely regarded as a maneuver calculated to upset the Republicans in the midst of their selection of a candidate to oppose the third term, a project which was becoming more obvious as each day passed. I returned to Washington June 21 and received a visit from Harry Woodring, who was ousted from the War Department to make room for Stimson.

"It all started with a phone call I got from 'Pa' Watson (Edwin M. Watson, Military Aide and Secretary to the President), a few days back," Woodring began. "Watson said the President wanted me to get together with Morgenthau to sell or transfer some army planes to England. I told Watson right off that I could not go along with it unless the transfer could be made without affecting our defenses. I took the matter up with the department and told the generals that whatever decision they made should not be changed later on, but should be made in the best interests of the country's defense and should be rigidly adhered to. I promised I would stand my ground.

"Watson called several times, urging me to sit down with Morgenthau and give the British the planes. This I refused to do. Then next day I received a letter from the President, written in longhand, telling me how much he appreciated what I had done in the War Department, but stating that things were moving fast abroad and he wanted to make some changes, particularly in the War Department. He wound up by saying he would like to have my resignation. I took the letter home, and that night I sat down with my wife and we wrote the answer. I wrote it in longhand, too. I told him that inasmuch as he wanted the resignation, I was happy to give it to him. I thanked him for his past expression of confidence. Among other things, I expressed the hope he would continue his policy of nonintervention because I felt it was the best thing for the country. I told him, too, that I was satisfied to resign because I did not want to be a party to some of the things I saw in the offing. I made that very clear, Jim. I don't like it.

"As soon as I had prepared the letter, I called Assistant Secretary Louis Johnson on the phone and told him I had sent in my resignation and advised him to take the necessary steps to protect himself. I sent a memorandum to the President saying I was not going to release anything from my office on the resignation, and stating that it would have to be done from the White House. I asked that it be done at once because I was planning to leave my office immediately and was in the process of moving out. I said I would not do anything that would embarrass the President.

"Then I received another letter from the President which was typewritten. This, as you probably saw, was a conventional letter designed for public release. He offered me an ambassadorship or the Governorship of Puerto Rico, but I told him definitely I would not take it. That night when I got home, I got another letter from the President. This third one was again in his handwriting and begged me to reconsider my decision not to take another job. I did not answer it and will not. I am going to get out of Washington by the end of this week or next.

"I have not seen Roosevelt or talked to him. All our communication has been by correspondence or through Pa Watson or Steve Early. I got a White House call asking me over to the Cabinet meeting. I said I wouldn't go. Watson asked me if I was sore, and I told him I was not but I didn't want to attend the meeting. Just before Stimson's appointment was announced, Early called Louis Johnson and told him the President was appreciative of his loyalty and service and hoped he would carry on if it would be agreeable for him to do so. Later Roosevelt called Johnson to the White House where he did not indicate whether or not he had anyone in mind, but made it rather plain to Louis that he would not get the place."

I listened to Woodring's story with great interest. I was impressed with his exhibition of courage and his stand for principle. He refused to go against his convictions even though he was aware it would mean the end of his Cabinet career.

Vice President Garner, with whom I lunched, told me that the Cabinet meeting was concerned with the transfer of fifty American destroyers to Britain, to be conveyed from New London, Connecticut, to a British port. These were the destroyers in exchange for which the United States secured the right to lease and build bases in British possessions from Newfoundland to New Guinea. This transfer was being worked up at the same time the White House was seeking to give army planes to Britain.

"The Boss said that the transfer had been cleared legally by the Attorney General, and Charley Edison spoke up and said the transfer was being arranged over his protest," Garner told me. "The Boss didn't like what Edison said, any more than he liked what Woodring did. The interesting part is that after the meeting, Attorney General Jackson came to me and said that in spite of the statement made that he had approved the sale and held it to be legal, he had not made such a decision. I told him that he should have so declared himself at the Cabinet meeting and I say now he should have said he had not held the transfer to be legal, if he did not."

Woodring's handwritten letter of resignation was never made public. Edison, who also was moved out for opposing White House policy, had expected to go sooner or later and did not write a scorching letter. However, he was no less firm against a policy which he did not believe to be in the best interests of the country. I am satisfied that Edison and Woodring would have been eased out on one pretext or another to bring men into the Cabinet, who were convinced that the United States should enter the war and would work toward that end, while the President was treading softly in the campaign year. I do not say this critically, but state it merely as a fact.

In a few days the Republicans nominated Wendell Willkie at Philadelphia. I must confess that I was surprised by the nomination. I thought the regular Republican leaders like Taft, Dewey, Vandenberg, Joseph Pew, and the rest would not possibly go along with him. Yet he was nominated. I was not in on the inside of that nomination and I cannot speak with any accuracy about it, although I have heard many stories about the capture of the GOP by a man who had been a Democrat up to two years before the convention met and had told me he was a member of my party at our only meeting.

On the day of the nomination Steve Early called me and read a statement the White House had prepared for me to release. It read, "The nomination greatly clarifies the issue before the nation—which is a good thing. The question is, of course, what sets of forces, economic and social, are to conduct our government—the historic American processes or some new and somewhat foreign methods of concentrated control. Most of the rank and file Republicans will understand this as well as most of the rank and file Democrats."

I objected to the use of the word "foreign," but there was no arguing with the White House.

That afternoon, June 28, 1940, at the Cabinet meeting, politics replaced the foreign situation.

"We will have to try and break down the aura they are trying to build up around Willkie," Roosevelt said. "I want the Senators and Congressmen to start in on him Monday."

Ickes said that a vigorous campaign should be directed at once against Willkie, because if the Democrats were put on the defensive, it would be a distinct gain for Willkie. The President told him to "go to it."

My contribution was that Willkie might be a formidable candidate and it would not be wise to discount him. We all agreed that Senate Minority Leader Charles McNary added strength to the Republican ticket as candidate for the Vice Presidency.

Late that same day I had a long talk with Cordell Hull. He was thoroughly disgusted with the political situation. Like myself, he had taken the President at his word when the latter said he would not be a candidate and, as a result, he had not lifted a hand. He said he also knew nothing of the Knox and Stimson appointments until he saw them in the papers. I asked him whether the President wanted him to run with him as Vice President. Hull answered, quite simply, he had no political ambitions. I am sure he would have left the Cabinet then and there had it not been for the war situation.

At this time I made up my mind on my question. I decided I would permit my name to go before the convention as evidence of my protest against the third term. I also decided that I would leave the Cabinet and the party chairmanship. However, I also made up my mind that I would not work for the defeat of my party. Once my mind was made up, I had no cares. I realized that I had been fortunate to play a part in the national picture. I was determined to make my exit as gracefully as I could without any sacrifice of principle or honor.

The long wait for the first move from the White House came to an end July 1. Steve Early called Bill Bray, my executive assistant, while I was on my way to Chicago. During the course of their conversa-

(*International News Photo.*)

July 7, 1940—Hyde Park, N.Y.—During our two-hour private conference in his small study, FDR first said: "Jim, I don't want to run, and I'm going to tell the convention so." But later in the same talk he volunteered, "Undoubtedly I will accept the nomination by radio and will arrange to talk to the delegates before they leave the convention hall. . . ." (See page 249.)

(*Acme Photo.*)

July 15, 1940—At the 1940 convention in Chicago, Harry Hopkins and Jimmy Byrnes set up unofficial headquarters to "draft" Roosevelt (see page 260).

(Acme P

July 18, 1940—Taken shortly after the peak of my political career, when I was nominated for president. Here, after the roll call, I am requesting the convention unanimously to nominate President Roosevelt for a third term (see page 291).

tion Steve indicated, rather pointedly, that he knew the President would be glad to talk to me. Early said that any time on Friday, Saturday, or Sunday would be agreeable. I regarded this as a command and phoned Steve to tell him I would drop in Sunday. I hadn't had a talk, a real talk, with him since the previous fall, I realized as I hung up. I didn't know what was ahead, but resolved to be as friendly and frank as I could in the discussion to come.

CHAPTER TWENTY-FOUR

HYDE PARK CONFERENCE, 1940

T HE RIVER WAS melted sunlight as I crossed the George Washington Bridge and headed north, my thoughts shuttling between the past and the present on the way to the appointment I well knew would be a chapter in my country's political history, not so much for the men involved as for the issue. For sentimental reasons I chose to proceed up through the more familiar country of the west bank, making the decision at Mass before my departure. As I drove up the Hudson River through Rockland County, I never felt closer to my native soil than in that midday drive.

Here I was born and grew to manhood; here I courted and married; here I entered politics, to achieve greater success than I had dreamed of; and here my mother and father had returned to cradling earth. From the warm kindnesses I had had in the past, I resolved to accept what was in store gracefully and calmly. I determined to keep the interview as friendly as possible. Life is too short to be scarred by furious flames of hate, which too often is sparked by hot, heedless words. I can truthfully say I hate no man, living or dead.

From time to time I turned my eyes to enjoy the grandeur of the Hudson, but for the most part my attention was on the impending meeting. I made up my mind that I would not take exception to anything that might be said, nor would I rake up irritations from the past. I further made up my mind I was not going to hurl recriminations over acts I considered unfriendly, nor would I conjure up unfavorable statements attributed to the President about me from various quarters. I wanted him to tell his story in his way and I was anxious to tell mine. I determined to be friendly but firm, and not retreat from my position.

The journey passed quickly. Shortly before one o'clock the car crossed to the east bank at Poughkeepsie and along the Albany post road to the Roosevelt estate, with its curious old stone fences. The President had not returned from church when I mounted the four steps to the broad front porch from which he had joyously acknowledged the congratulations of his fellow townsmen on his election to a second term. I was met by his mother, who, after a word of greeting, said she was wondering whether there was any truth in newspaper stories that I would not be around the picture much longer.

"You know," she added brightly, "I would hate to think of Franklin running for the Presidency if you were not around. I want you to be sure to help my boy."

"Mrs. Roosevelt, you just have to let these things take their course," I answered.

At that moment Harry Hopkins came downstairs. We joined Steve Early, Missy Le Hand, and Victor Scholis, Hopkins's secretary, for a few minutes of light banter before lunch. On the way into the dining room, Mrs. Eleanor Roosevelt stopped me in the hallway beside the seated, life-size statue of the President as governor. She was "both pleased and shocked by the news" in the morning papers that I was going into business and leave politics.

"Of course, I am pleased to have anything happen to you which would be personally beneficial, but I am shocked at the thought you may not direct things in the coming campaign," she said.

Then the President came and we all went in to luncheon. There was a lot of good-natured conversation during the meal, and some serious conversation. The President talked about the complications of the French surrender. He assumed four-fifths of the French fleet had been destroyed or captured by the British.

Somehow a discussion of Andrew Jackson was raised, during which the President recalled how the hero of New Orleans was attacked on the question of the legality of his wife's divorce. The President's mother pricked up her ears at the mention of divorce and, after listening a moment or two, turned to me and said, "My heavens! I did not know they had such bad things as divorce so long ago."

While the others were talking I told her how well she looked. She regarded me quizzically and then remarked that she often wondered whether some people do not live too long. In the next breath, she thanked me very prettily for news photographs of her son I sent her from time to time.

Shortly after luncheon, Steve called me from the porch to the President's study, the narrow high-ceilinged room I knew. As I settled myself I noted "Via Crucis," by F. Marion Crawford, among the tiers of books. Before we started to talk, Steve was back to say photographers wanted a picture of the conference. After the photographers left, there was a brief but heavy silence. Occasionally I could hear laughter on the porch and the crunching of gravel as Secret Service men and New York state policemen went about their duties. It was so hot we removed our coats and ties.

For a half hour or more the conversation was about everything and nothing. It was apparent to me the President was having difficulty in approaching the subject, and frankly, I was not disposed to help him. I made up my mind that I would not open the discussion of his candidacy. Evidently he realized that, so he took the plunge.

"Jim, last July when we canvassed the political situation," he began with an engaging smile, "I indicated definitely that I would not run for a third term. I believe we decided that on or about February 1, I would write a letter to one of the states which has an early primary, stating I would not be a candidate for reelection."

"It was the North Dakota chairman you were going to write to," I said. "In 1932 you announced your candidacy in a letter to Fred McLean, then state chairman in that state."

"Well, after that conversation of ours, the war started and when it got along to February 1, I could not issue that statement," he continued. "It would have destroyed my effectiveness as the leader of the nation in the efforts of this country to cope with the terrible catastrophe raging in Europe. To have issued such a statement would have nullified my position in the world and would have handicapped the efforts of this country to be of constructive service in the war crisis.

"I must say that I am disappointed that my efforts have not accomplished what I hoped. In all probability it would have been just as well if I had made the announcement as planned. We bullied Mussolini in every way possible and tried to get the influence of the Pope to keep Italy from getting into war, but Italy went in."

The President lit another cigarette. He smiled through the smoke. I let him go on and talk without interruption, because of my determination on the morning ride that I was going to let him tell his story in his own way. I was equally determined that I was not going to succumb to the charm which had beguiled so many, when it came my turn to speak.

"So I would probably have been better off if I had said I didn't want to run. I still don't want to run for the Presidency. I want to come up here." He swung his left arm in a half circle to take in the cottage retreat and library he had designed and supervised. Then he shrugged his shoulders in eloquent indication of his conviction that the matter had been taken out of his hands by mounting demands that he remain at the helm and he said so.

"Jim, I don't want to run and I'm going to tell the convention so," he concluded, his eyes wide in apparent frankness.

"If you make it specific, the convention will not nominate you," were my first words, and I put in them every note of the conviction I had.

"Well, there could be several ways of doing it," he countered. "I could write a letter to someone like Senator Norris and decline. (I made a mental note to put in a word against employing a Republican, but didn't do so because the point was merely academic since he was going to run anyway.) Two, I could broadcast it. Three, I could issue a statement. And four, I could write a letter to be read by you at the convention.

"You know, Jim, I want to fully explain my position in order to be honest with myself about the situation, because I am definitely opposed to seeking a third term," he said. "In justice to my conscience I want that thoroughly understood by the delegates and the country."

I told him that I felt he should do that, and in such a way as to leave no doubt in the minds of the delegates or the country as to the sincerity and the honesty of the statement he issued; that it should be so worded that the delegates should be free to choose someone else, if they so desired. He seemed to agree. I then delivered what I had been turning over in my mind for months.

I began with my views on the third term, stating I was against it in principle and because the Democratic party had always opposed it. Quite frankly, I said, I felt that if the Democratic party was not able to campaign on the record it had made under his leadership in two terms—in other words that if there were no other candidate but himself—we deserved to lose. I said there were other men in the party who could be nominated and elected. If the convention was left free, I insisted, it would turn to these other men.

He heard me with attention. The smiles were gone. I was very definite in my statements as I unfolded my views at some length, views which were known to him and everyone else. I acknowledged that my views were foreign to the present discussion in view of his decision to accept the nomination. I said the time had passed when any opinion of mine could have any bearing on the convention because he had permitted, if not encouraged, a situation to develop, under which he would be nominated unless he refused to run.

"Jim, what would you do if you were in my place?" he asked.

I thanked him for asking my advice, but countered by saying I would never be in his position because I would not have waited as long as he had to make my position known. Now, I reminded him, he had made it impossible for anyone else to be nominated, because by refusing to declare himself, he had prevented delegates from being elected for anyone except Garner and myself. Many states, I said, had declared for him because there was no other course open; that leaders were fearful they might be punished if they did not go along with him. Further, I added, I would not have waited until that late day to tell a person so intimately associated for twelve years, as I was with him, what I was going to do. If our positions had been reversed, I would have told him my plans long ago, I said.

In mentioning punishment of Democratic state leaders, I had in mind the situation in North Carolina, where an agreement had been reached to instruct for Hull, but the leaders had had to do an about-face when the President and his friends took exception to a pro-Hull statement made by Governor Hoey. The President knew, of course, exactly what I was referring to. He had given Max Gardner, former governor, permission to set up a slate of delegates for Hull. Later, state leaders were told to halt instruction of the delegation.

He mopped his face with a handkerchief. I had more to mop because my hair has done more retreating. He chain-smoked cigarettes in the familiar long holder which had become a symbol for him.

"I'm answering your question," I resumed, "but you're not going to like it or pay any attention to it. In your position I would do exactly what General Sherman did many years ago—issue a statement saying I would refuse to run if nominated and would not serve if elected."

"Jim, if nominated and elected, I could not in these times refuse to take the inaugural oath, even if I knew I would be dead within thirty days," he said.

This statement made a powerful impression on me. And it has been etched deeper into my mind by what happened less than five years later. I can see him now, with his right hand clasping the arm of his chair as he leaned back, his left bent at the elbow to hold his cigarette, and his face and eyes deadly earnest. This picture has often been in my mind since his death. There was much talk of his physical condition for more than a year before his death. I cannot help wondering whether during that year he pondered the remark made to me and whether he knew he was under the shadow of the dark angel's wings. I cannot help but feel those about him knew, if he did not, and over-estimated his strength.

From this point on, the conference lost what pattern of order it had. He had made his speech and I had made mine. Now he reverted to his customary restless, rambling consideration of a problem, which so often reminded me of a pup worrying a slipper.

He talked on aimlessly about the third term, saying that Grant, who had served for eight years, could not push it aside; that Theodore Roosevelt, who had served a few months less, could not forego an attempt to break tradition; and that Coolidge debated long before he issued what he described as a "yes-no" statement. I did not press this phase of the discussion, because it was more than evident he had his mind made up and he was trying to justify his position to me, and also seeking to justify his failure to tell me he had changed his mind since our last discussion. This failure to tell me personally was serious, not only because I was a candidate for the nomination by virtue of the Massachusetts primary, entered with his knowledge and consent, but also because I was the party's chairman and should have had his political confidence or have been replaced.

From his fidgeting it was evident he knew he was in a difficult position because he knew and everyone else knew he was going to run again. I am convinced, and was during our conversation, that the reason he did not confide in me was that he was fearful I might take some action in Hull's behalf which might prevent his nomination, or injure his chances for such renomination. He evidently hoped that this problem would resolve itself, as others had with the passage of time, and, therefore, put off our conversation until the last possible moment.

"Now I am going to say something else you won't like," I told him during a pause. "I am going to be entirely frank with you. Notwithstanding the fact that you have put all the other candidates out of the picture by maneuvering delegates into a state of mind where many feel that they must nominate you whether or not you want the nomination, I am going to allow my name to go before the convention.

"I say this in all friendliness and I sincerely and earnestly hope you will take it so. My decision is the result of hours of internal debate. I walked the streets of Washington at night turning over this problem. Quite candidly all of my friends disagree with me. However, it's my decision and it is irrevocable. I feel I owe it to my party because of the principle involved and to myself because of my position before the country which, while not approaching yours, is not inconsiderable. To be fully honest, I don't think I could walk down any street and meet people, if I did not do as my conscience dictates."

During my remarks, his eyes were fixed on me. Once or twice he nodded. Again he took no exception to anything I said, although I pulled no punches. He did not comment on my statement but shifted the conversation to Willkie. He said he was not sure he could beat Willkie and asked what I thought of his chances. I replied that I was not sure either, that Willkie could become a formidable candidate, and then again he might turn out to be a flop, all depending on Willkie himself. I thought Willkie would make an active campaign, mentioning that he looked well in the newsreels, made a good speech, and seemed to have caught on with the public.

"You are absolutely right," he acknowledged. "You know if the war should be over before the election and I am running against Will-kie, he would be elected."

I asked him about the chances of Great Britain holding out and he said solemnly, "about one in three."

I went on to tell him that I was not quite clear in my own mind as to how he should make the statement of his third term position and was not sure that he was either. I charged him not to worry about my feelings in choosing among the four ways he had mentioned, that he could write to me personally as he desired, since I was not thin skinned. Again, I told him my position on the third term issue and my belief that it would injure the party. I said many of the delegates would be voting for him against their better judgment because of the situation he had created, but they would go along like good organization regu-lars. In addition to my name, I said, I was certain that Garner's would also be placed in nomination. I was not certain what Tydings, Wheeler, and the others would do.

He switched the conversation to a discussion of Hull's possible pros-pects, asking whether I thought his Secretary of State could win. I answered that Hull would have been a very strong nominee and could have been elected. I purposely employed the conditional past to chart its effect on the President. He ignored it. I went on to remind him that the last Gallup poll showed Hull to be even more popular than the President, and told him I was sure in my own mind that Hull could be elected, despite his age, by almost the majority the President re-ceived in 1936 because the third term issue would not be raised.

The conversation drifted to vice-presidential candidates. I told him that while my position on the third term was clear, I felt that as long as he was going to run, I wanted to be on record as saying I should like very much to have him take a real Democrat with him, one in whom the country had confidence and one who could carry on in case anything happened to him. I said that all the talk about Bill Doug-las for Vice President was asinine and he quickly agreed.

"Jim," he asked, "do you think Jack would run with me again?"

I imagine the surprise I felt showed in my eyes. Garner, I reminded him, was opposed to a third term. While I had no right to speak for him, I said I felt confident he would not run for the second place even if the President asked him. I told him I believed Garner was hurt over the manner in which the President had acted and that their once happy relationship had been sorely tried. I added Garner was looking forward to the close of his term so that he could return to a quiet life in Texas.

I said Senator Lucas of Illinois was a candidate. The President laughed and dismissed that candidacy with a wave of his hand and the remark he had seen some of the very attractive circulars sent out by Lucas's committee. He dismissed Governor Stark of Missouri with another laugh and asked me what I thought about Wallace.

"Boss, I'm going to be very direct," I said. "Henry Wallace won't add a bit of strength to the ticket. I say that advisedly, although my relations with Henry have always been most friendly, as you know. He won't bring you the support you may expect in the farm belt and he will lose votes for you in the East. Beyond that I would not like to see him Vice President, even though I like him personally, because I think it would be a terrible thing to have him President, if anything happened to you. He has always been most cordial and cooperative with me, but I think you must know that the people look on him as a wild-eyed fellow."

He made no comment on my reply. Now, I am convinced he had already made up his mind on Wallace and had determined not to disclose his choice until the last minute in order to keep the field of vice-presidential candidates in line for the third term.

I mentioned Bankhead, whom he dismissed as too old and not in good health.

"The man running with me must be in good health because there there is no telling how long I can hold out," he declared. "You know, Jim, a man with paralysis can have a breakup any time. While my heart and lungs are good and the other organs functioning along okay . . . nothing in this life is certain."

With that he pulled up his shirt, unbuttoned, and showed me a lump of flesh and muscle under his left shoulder, which he said were misplaced because of his affliction. He noted that he must sit most of the time.

"It's essential that the man who runs with me should be able to carry on," he emphasized, tucking his shirt back in and reaching for another cigarette.

It was the first and last time in all the years I knew him that he ever discussed his physical condition with me.

He asked me about Senator Maloney of Connecticut and went on to say that a Catholic could be elected Vice President along with him.

"That's true, but no more so than if the ticket were composed of Hull and Farley," I threw in quickly. I looked him squarely in the eyes as I spoke and he acknowledged that was so before dropping his gaze. This was a most interesting admission, since he had been dismissing Hull because of his age and me because of my religion.

I made no further mention of myself, although this was the first time I had ever brought out my position in exactly that way. In my desire to avoid the controversial I did not bring up the remarks attributed to him about the impossibility of my election because of my religion. I felt any reference to that might lead to a quarrel, which I wanted to avoid.

I brought up the name of Jesse Jones and he countered that Jesse's health was none too good, that he had not fully recovered from the effects of the airplane accident he was in during the spring of 1938. I was aware that this was an excuse, because I knew Jesse's health to be good and knew also that he was never strong for Jesse. When I tried almost two years before to have him name Jesse to succeed Roper as Secretary of Commerce, instead of Hopkins, he bluntly told me there was no reason why he should put Jones in the Cabinet and have him start running for the Presidency. This was more than a year after he told Bob Post of the *New York Times* to "go off in the corner and put on the dunce cap," when he was asked if he would accept the third term nomination.

The President said flatly he would not take Jones, Garner, or Rayburn. Next he disposed of Jimmy Byrnes, saying Flynn had advised him it would be unwise to name him in view of Byrnes's desertion of the Catholic faith many years before. Later I was shocked and distressed to learn the President told Byrnes I was against him on this ground. In Chicago I discussed this with Byrnes, saying I was not personally opposed to him on any ground. I did say that the ticket might suffer in some Catholic centers if he were the vice-presidential candidate, but not so much as to endanger victory.

After his reference to Byrnes, I facetiously said I had a nominee for him in Paul V. McNutt, which moved him to laughter and the exclamation, "We did a good job by bringing him into the administration, didn't we?"

I told the President that, in my judgment, there was only one man with whom he should run and that man was Hull. He asked me to urge second place on Hull, but I refused, saying I knew how Hull felt about both the third term and the Vice Presidency, adding that I certainly was not going to urge him to change his attitude.

Deep in my heart I feel that Franklin Delano Roosevelt deprived Hull of the Presidency. I think I can say that in all honesty, having been in intimate touch with all delegations. I say this without malice or rancor. I feel that the party would be in a stronger position today had he allowed other men to follow him in the leadership, men who deserved laurels for years of faithful party service.

At this time I brought up my own situation. I told him that under no circumstances could I run the campaign, both because of my views and because the time had arrived when I must do something for my wife and children, that I had already made too many financial sacrifices. I discussed several attractive propositions then before me, not mentioning the Coca-Cola Company because I was not at liberty to do so.

During my recital the President's face showed evident concern. He sought to get me to stay on, first by urging me to remain for the campaign and then by suggesting I continue as national chairman while in the business world, leaving actual work to a campaign manager.

I suggested Frank C. Walker as my successor because of his association with the National Committee as treasurer. The President agreed with me and then asked if I thought Byrnes would not be a good choice. I said Byrnes would do an excellent job, being one of the most able and intelligent men I had come in contact with and, from an all-round point of view, one of the most able men in the Senate. I suggested Oliver Quayle remain as treasurer, but that someone like

Joseph E. Davies be named Chairman of the Finance Committee. The President felt that Chip Robert should not remain as Secretary and spoke about criticism leveled at government contracts Chip's firm had been securing.

"Besides," he said, without a smile, "his wife, Evie, talks too much."

"I think Chip has been subjected to a lot of unfair criticism," I said. "Not the slightest irregularity has been shown against Chip or his firm. And more than one man has had to bear the cross of a talkative wife."

He then turned to a discussion of the platform, on which I said I did not think there would be any serious debate, except possibly on the foreign relations plank.

"Oh, that could be handled in a single sentence," he said. "We could say something like:

" 'We do not want to become involved in any foreign war.

" 'We are opposed to this country's participation in any wars, unless for the protection of the Western Hemisphere.

" 'We are in favor of extending aid to democracies in their struggle against totalitarian powers, within the law.' "

Conversation drifted to convention procedure. Almost as though he were thinking aloud, he said he thought that if he sent a letter or statement saying he did not want the nomination, it should be done right after my opening speech. I said most of Monday morning would be taken up with organization procedure. The next morning would be taken up with committee organization and the convention would not be functioning in order until Tuesday afternoon.

He wanted to know then whether the platform could not be read on Wednesday and the nominations be made on Thursday. That would be all right with me, was my answer; but they would want to keep the convention in Chicago, and the city expected visitors to stay through the end of the week if possible.

"By the way, Jim, the family is not going to attend the convention," he volunteered. "Undoubtedly I will accept the nomination by radio and will arrange to talk to the delegates before they leave the convention hall after the nomination."

There were times in the discussion when he appeared to be in doubt in his own mind on his position and attitude on breaking the third term precedent. On the whole, there was no doubt in my mind then that he had made up his mind long before. I am certain he had sold himself the idea that he was the only one qualified to serve during that particular period of the nation's history and, as it subsequently developed, in the next four-year period.

During the long conversation, which was carried on with studied friendliness on both sides, he was not as free as he had been in past discussions. He was ill at ease because of the position he found himself in. I am sure it did not please him to have to sit and talk with me as he did. It was uncomfortable for him as the President of the United States to have to humiliate himself by defending himself to me, particularly because he had brought himself into the embarrassing position by not being frank with me.

At length conversation lagged and it was evident that the discussion was exhausted. I rose to go, making a commonplace remark about having to get along. As I stood up, he thrust out his hand.

"Jim," he said with evident emotion, "no matter what happens, I don't want anything to spoil our long friendship."

"That goes for me, and I mean it sincerely," I said.

"So do I, Jim."

I left him studying what he called the "jimcracks" on his desk. Personally I was glad the interview was behind me. More than ever I was convinced of the wisdom of my course of conduct, and I was happy that all had gone off without any bitterness or clashes. I had lived up to my resolve to avoid a quarrel.

CHAPTER TWENTY-FIVE

CHICAGO AGAIN

ONDAY EVENING, July 8, 1940, I left for Chicago and the convention, fully aware of the strains and stresses awaiting me. I knew my role would be taxing physically, but was resolved to tread it out on the convention stage like a good political trooper. I realized that pressure would be exerted from every point of the political compass to make me pull out of a race which, no one knew better than I did, I had no chance of winning.

My course was to have my name presented to the convention if it was the last thing I ever did. I was going to have my name presented —if I received only one vote. There was no other course open to me as I had promised to run in my Springfield, Massachusetts, statement early in the year; and, if I failed to live up to that promise, I felt I would lose the respect and regard of not only my family and friends, but also of everyone who knew me.

Actually I felt then and I still feel there was only one way in which I could fairly and clearly express my opposition to a third term as a life-long Democrat and as party chairman. If I came out flatly against the third term, every Republican orator in the country would have spread-eagled before audiences, using my declaration to defeat my party. It was not in me to forge a verbal dagger for my party's back. The fact that I had managed every Roosevelt campaign for Governor and President and was entering my name against his third term candidacy, I felt would be sufficient evidence of my position.

Many of those friendly and sympathetic to me were fearful, I know, that I would make some mistake which would react against me; they were terribly concerned over the possibility that my pride would be mortally wounded. I know that because of the way they approached me and eyed me as they asked, "Are you all right?" Knowing what they meant, my reply was invariably, "Everything is under control."

I arrived in Chicago Tuesday morning and went with Oliver Quayle and Chip Robert to look over hall arrangements. The earliest of the party faithful were gathering for the exciting days ahead. Old political fire horses come out to rub against political hacks at conventions. Men who are big fish in their communities and states, but small fry nationally, like to look over the candidates. The high moments of bygone conventions are lived over again by the veterans. There is much dark whispering of trades and agreements. Even the least important of the party can pass judgment on the strategists. Everyone likes to weigh charge and counter charge. Everyone enjoys assaying rumors. Many like to hold forth on what the various contenders should do and what line the party should adopt in order to win in November. Best of all, their pleasure really begins when the show is over. They begin to shine when they get home and describe convention scenes and the part they played in the nominations. They have conversational fodder for days, weeks, months, and even years. And the stories gain with each telling.

Wednesday things began to happen. All the leaders in the country began trekking to the unofficial Roosevelt headquarters Harry Hopkins and Jimmy Byrnes had in a Blackstone Hotel suite overlooking hustling Michigan Boulevard, green Grant Park, and placid Lake Michigan. Many never came in to see me at all. A few came in to pay their respects to me, and some of those were timidly ill at ease. Others were swinging aboard the Roosevelt band wagon. This was perfectly all right with me. I had been in politics a long, long time, was well aware those things are inevitable, and was fully prepared to meet that aspect of the situation.

Even though my headquarters were very often as deserted as a church at the setting of the sun, I was not distressed. The few who came cheered me and deepened my determination.

The Hopkins–Byrnes strategy became clear that day. Every effort was being directed at winning the nomination by acclamation, in an effort to convince the country there was a real draft. They knew that Wheeler would not stay in the race if Garner and I withdrew, so they told him the party platform needed the peace plank, dear to his heart, perhaps dearer than the Presidency. I was told they were certain Garner's name would not be presented formally, although Texas could cast her votes for him, if I withdrew. That was the reason for all the succeeding pressure brought to bear on me to get out of the race.

What I did not like was the hypocrisy: the effort put forth to make it appear that the President was being drafted, when everyone knew it was a forced draft fired from the White House itself. Many delegates were sincerely for the President; but I think I can truthfully make the statement that the majority were against the third term and did not want to nominate him again. I talked with many delegates who frankly said they were going along, against their better judgment, for one reason or another.

Curiously enough the Byrnes–Hopkins suite—308 to 309 in the Blackstone—had once before made political history. It was the "smoke-filled room" in which the deal that brought Warren Gamaliel Harding to the White House had been consummated on June 12, 1920. In July, 1940, Democratic bosses succeeded the Republican bosses of the twenties in writing history. Here Ed Kelly of Chicago and Frank Hague of Jersey City and Ed Flynn of New York City's Bronx rubbed shoulders with one hundred per cent New Dealers like Leon Henderson and Claude Pepper and David K. Niles.

From the outset the temper of the delegates was bad. While many feared to come near me they were incensed over the way I had been treated. Their resentment was heightened by anger over the treatment they received at the hands of Hopkins. His manner was arrogant rather than ingratiating. He offered nothing and demanded blind obedience. Murmurings of mutiny grew until the delegates were downright ugly, but the President's maneuvering over the years saved the day. Delegates lacked a rallying point for revolt and were forced to surrender, grumblingly and glumly, on the never genuine threat that Roosevelt might not run and thus leave the party without its greatest vote getter.

Early that morning I called Hull to ask him bluntly whether he would accept the vice-presidential nomination.

"I can't take it under any circumstances, Jim," he assured me. "It would be kicking me upstairs and taking me away from the one thing I like best to do. I positively won't consider it."

A short time later mild, mellow and affable Jimmy Byrnes called, ostensibly to pay his respects. Before we reached politics, I was told Herbert Bayard Swope, who had an appointment, was outside. I asked Jimmy to step outside a minute or two and Swope came in, carrying information from Washington that the President had told Byrnes I was against him for Vice President because he had left the Catholic Church many years before. When Swope left Byrnes returned.

"Jimmy, a situation has been brought to my attention which I want to correct here and now," I began. "I have been advised that an impression has been created in the White House that I am against you because you left the Church. Jimmy, no one has any right to accuse me of taking that position, and I don't care who he is, because it just isn't true. I say to you, very frankly, I am not against you. I do think that if you are nominated, your personal situation will undoubtedly be brought to the attention of voters, with resulting injury to you in Catholic centers. I tell you this as a friend, but the decision is yours. In addition may I say, Jimmy, this would not be fatal to your candidacy, nor would it affect the ultimate success of the ticket and that is all that counts."

Byrnes said he understood my situation perfectly.

"I want to return frankness with frankness," Byrnes opened. "I hope nothing will happen here that will prevent you from running the campaign in November."

"Jimmy, you might as well know it all, if you don't already," I answered. "I have told the President that my name is going to be presented to the convention. His answer was that he hoped this would not be a real test of my strength. Now, I want you to know and him to know that I am not interested in a test of my strength. The question of votes is of no importance to me. I don't care if I get only one vote. But, I feel it is fitting and proper that all the candidates for the nomination go before the convention. And I feel very deeply that no effort should be made to shut them off. I have heard, in such a way as to believe it, that such efforts are being made. I think it will be a mistake the party may have cause to regret in November, and if not then, in the years to come."

"Whatever you do is all right with me," Byrnes said. "But I still think very definitely that whatever happens, you should run the campaign."

That afternoon Frank Walker came around. We had a long conversation covering much the same ground as Byrnes and I had.

"I am going to stay at headquarters and the Post Office until September 1," I told him. "I will certainly not stay beyond that, and any statement to the contrary is not correct. I have suggested you or Byrnes as my successor. Before you interrupt, I want you to know the President has agreed with me that it is all right to resign."

He eyed me silently, his lips set in a wise smile. He offered little that was persuasive and went his way.

Thursday passed uneventfully in routine visits and phone calls. We held the last meeting of the Democratic National Committee, as then constituted, to approve the plans of the committee on convention arrangements and to fill committee vacancies. This was followed by a press conference, marked by the usual fencing on the third term.

Friday morning Harry Hopkins called. He threw one leg over the arm of a chair at my desk. He looked tired; his eyes were sunk deep in his pallid face; his scanty hair looked as though it had been combed with his fingers. He was restless, constantly fingering a cigarette. He had asked for the interview and had dragged his drooping frame across the street, which I believe was the heaviest exercise he took during the convention period.

"Jim, I'd like to know what you think is going on," he opened almost belligerently.

"Now, Harry, you don't really expect me to answer that," I countered with a laugh. "There is no necessity for me to tell you because you are making it happen."

"Well, what I want to say is that, whatever you may hear, the Boss wants you to run the campaign."

"Be that as it may, I can't discuss it with you," I said. "I discussed the matter fully and freely with the Boss in Hyde Park and he thoroughly understood and agreed with my attitude or, at least, said he did. This I suppose you know."

He ignored this gambit.

"What do you think the President's going to do?" he asked.

"Harry, what's the use of kidding each other about what the President is going to do?" I replied, striving to keep any impatience out of my voice. "We both know very well what he's going to do."

"Jim, I want to make it clear that I am here on my own and I am not acting as the President's intermediary in this call. You have my assurance on that."

"There's no necessity for an intermediary," was my answer. I felt that he was one whether he came directly or indirectly. "If I had anything to say, I would say it to the President and no one else."

"That's right," he affirmed. "By the way, what do you think about the vice-presidential nominee?"

"I haven't given it much thought," I parried, "except that I think the Democrats should nominate a real Democrat."

"How many delegates do you expect to get?" he asked abruptly.

"I think it will be between 120 and 150 unless pressure is brought to bear," I answered, looking him in the eye. He was a bit embarrassed. "I want you to know I have never asked anyone to vote for me before coming here and I will make no effort to get any delegates. In return, I think, no effort should be made to take delegates away from me."

"Nothing will be done in that direction," he promised.

Nevertheless, much was done. I didn't ask anyone to vote for me, because I was aware of the pressure that would be brought on job holders, relatives of job holders, and others. I felt that the Massachusetts delegates should go along for me because they were pledged for me in the primary. I was disappointed, but not surprised, that many delegates were swayed from their pledge under pressure. I was mindful that some who were pledged to me in good faith, believing Roosevelt would not be a candidate, felt they were entitled to switch to him. I think the heavy effort made to swing this delegation from me was mean and petty. The third termers went so far as to phone Ambassador Kennedy in London to urge him to have his son, later to become one of the heroic war dead, break his pledge. While Kennedy and I were never close friends, I am happy to this day that he spurned the suggestion, saying the decision rested with his boy; and I remember that resolute young voice calling "James A. Farley" when the Massachusetts delegation was polled.

I could have embarrassed many wavering delegates by calling for the polling of several states, thus forcing them to go on record with me as to where they stood. Doubtless this would have added to my votes, but since there was no chance of winning, I decided against such a course as of no value except to soothe my vanity. I was finding solace enough in knowing that I was holding to principle, so I did not need to resort to blackjacking votes.

Senator Wheeler dropped in for a chat during the day. At that time I am sure he was under the impression he would let his name go before the convention, but he acknowledged that if the platform committee accepted his peace plank, he would have nothing to fight for.

"As a matter of fact, I'm in an involved position," he said. "We are having a primary in my state Tuesday and I can't say anything until it is over. If this were not an election year, I would raise hell for the Presidency."

Senator Clark came in to explain he was going to cast his ballot for Garner, but the Missouri caucus indicated the rest of the votes would go for Roosevelt. I expressed surprise, because I thought Joe Shannon would vote for me. He said Shannon was very friendly toward me, but had voted for Roosevelt at the caucus.

"I am telling you this because I'd like to vote for you, but I promised Garner a year ago that I would vote for him if his name would get before the convention," Clark said. "I am against the third term and disgusted with everything that is going on here in Chicago. But there's nothing we can do about it; the President has the votes and will be nominated. Yet, it's a great mistake; I feel it in my bones."

Silliman Evans, publisher of the *Nashville Tennessean*, came in with Congressman Sam Rayburn in tow. Both were incensed over the way Garner was being handled. I did not take Sam's tears too seriously, as he was a red-hot candidate for Vice President. He thought it would be best if Roosevelt were renominated along with Garner and I were selected to run the campaign.

"That's just impossible," was my comment.

Senator Pat Harrison came in to pay his respects. Genial Pat was one of my Democratic idols. I had no secrets from him, so I told him what I was going to do. Pat didn't say much, but what he did say made it unmistakable that he was not in sympathy with the drift of events. Of course, he could never forgive the fight made by the President to prevent his obtaining the Senate leadership.

Former Attorney General Homer Cummings came in to urge me to run the campaign. I don't know whether he came in of his own volition or whether he was sent, but I cut his slow, drawling arguments rather short.

Sunday, after Mass at St. Mary's, I again talked with Hull, who told me he was going to have lunch with the President the next day. I advised him that the temper of the delegates was bad; that the real Democrats were annoyed; that the majority did not want to vote for the third term; that if they had their way they would nominate Hull and myself; and that they resented the presence of Hopkins in Chicago. I emphasized this was not an idle impression but one gathered from talking to many delegates, leaders, and newspapermen.

Secretary Wallace called to say hello and seized on the opportunity to stress the necessity for unity after the convention was over. I agreed, adding that the fellows with Hopkins were apparently proceeding on the theory there would be no election in November, as they were scuttling party unity.

At midnight Ed Flynn and Vince Dailey came into my Stevens Hotel offices. By this time I was getting fed up with the parade of Democratic leaders, who were urging me to step aside for the good of the party. By the time Flynn appeared I was ready to get a load off my chest, so I determined to let him have it. Vincent sat stolidly in a chair at the side, looking and saying nothing. Flynn sat across from me. He was nervous and disturbed; it was apparent he had something on his mind and was seeking the best avenue of approach. He decided on a direct one.

"Jim, this isn't going to be easy to say," he began, "but for the sake of party harmony, for the best interests of the country, and in the interests of world peace, you should pull out of the convention as a candidate and continue as party chairman."

"Now, Ed," I began, "in the first place, I am not going to get out of the race. My name is going to be presented to the convention. If I withdraw my name now after telling everyone, my friends and newspapermen and women, continuously for weeks that my name is going to be presented, I would have to leave town a shamed man, unworthy of anyone's respect. I am going to keep my integrity no matter what happens. I want to have my self-respect and the respect of my friends. My name is going before that convention, as I said it would, so I can keep my head up no matter how far I fall in position.

"I am not to blame for the present situation. It was none of my making. I was led to believe by the President that he would not be a candidate. When I saw him in Hyde Park last July, before I went abroad, he told me definitely he would not be a candidate. He asked me when the first primary or state convention would come along and I said, 'The first week in February and I think North Dakota is the state.' He said, 'I will at that time write a letter stating I am not a candidate for reelection.' And he added that he would definitely make it clear that was so.

"From that day until I saw him last week at Hyde Park, he never said a word to me about his candidacy. Then he tried to explain to me why he did not issue the statement in accordance with our conversation.

"For my part, I did not comment on his explanation; I merely told him it made no difference what he did next because a situation had been created with his knowledge and approval which made it certain he was going to be nominated, regardless of what statement he made. I told him it had now become a closed case; that he had made it impossible for Hull, Garner, or myself, or anyone else to be nominated. He is to blame for the situation that exists here today. You know it; I know it; and he should know it, if he doesn't.

"Ed, I have been in politics thirty-one years. In this period I have earned the reputation of being a fellow who tells the truth. I have been telling people for months that my name would go before the convention. I have been saying it and newspapermen have been writing it. The country knows it. If I should pull out now, I could no more go to a press conference, after all was over, than I could jump out of this window this minute."

I flung my arm behind me where a window looked out on the Blackstone Hotel.

"I am not going to jump out of this window or any window. And I hope the good Lord will spare me for a few years more and that I will continue to keep the respect of newspaper folk and other people. Some day I will tell my story, this story, and I am sure it will not be without interest."

Flynn started to speak but I waved for silence.

"I'm not through yet," I said. "Some people, and you may be one of them, have the false idea that I think I am running for the Presidency. That's all past . . . it's water over the dam or ambition over the dam or whatever you will. I am not running. The President has the votes. Everyone knows he has eight or nine hundred votes pledged to him.

"Now, what they want is the few votes that have been pledged to me. Hopkins has been attempting, with White House knowledge and consent, to have those few votes taken away from me. And why? So that the outside world will think this is a 'unanimous draft.' You know as well as I that this 'draft' has been cooked up for months.

"What I am trying to let the people outside understand is that I am opposed to a third term. Many of them already know it. Many others do not. I have never said so because I did not want the Republicans to pick up any quotation of mine and go up and down the country with, 'This is what Jim Farley says,' to cause the President and the Democratic party embarrassment.

"I love the party. Everything I am I owe to the party. Most of the friends I have, I owe to the party. I am deeply aware of this, but I don't want anyone lecturing me on my party obligations. I told the President and I tell you I have thought out my course of action carefully and at length. Mine is no sudden impulse or fit of piqued vanity.

"I say to you with all the sincerity of my soul, I am opposed to the principle of the third term. I think it is bad for the party and bad for the country. And as much as I love my party, I love my country more. My family has been in America almost a hundred years. I feel we were good citizens because we were good Democrats, but it is more important to be a good citizen. The only way I can publicly show how I feel, without misunderstanding and with dignity and honor, is to permit my name to go before the convention. This is exactly where I stand and this is exactly what I am going to do.

"Carter Glass is coming on to the convention to nominate me and Pat Fisher of Rockland county is going to second the nomination. And if I only get Fisher's and Glass's votes, that is all right with me.

"I want you and the others to know I am not looking for votes. I have said that at press conferences. No one can show that I lifted so much as a finger to get votes here. Before I came here I was not seeking votes.

"The third term fellows are not playing the game on the level; every effort is being made to steal votes from me which are pledged to me. I am thoroughly disgusted with the actions going on around here. For the life of me, I can't understand this giddy performance. Hopkins's position here is beyond intelligence. There is no reason for this situation and it is all wrong.

"Finally, I have no desire to embarrass my friends. I am not going to embarrass anyone if possible. But if anyone should be found standing up carrying a banner for me, they will do so knowing I am standing up for a principle."

Flynn admitted I had a right to take the attitude I did. However, he said, he disagreed with my course of action. He felt I could not get anywhere in the convention, that my course would be harmful to me and not helpful, and that it might be made to appear that I was being prompted by some outside source to do as I planned to do.

"I don't care what anyone says or thinks about my stand," I replied, "I am acting on my own. I have been in politics thirty-one years and if I leave public life, it will be with my head high. In those years I made many sacrifices and am prepared to make more, but if I go I will be able to look into the eyes of all of my friends. And when I go down the street, it can be said, 'There goes a fellow who at least keeps his word!'"

After Flynn had left, Vince stayed on. He agreed that I had taken the only tack I could with Flynn in view of my stand and predicted that when Flynn brought that speech back to the third termers, they would know what to expect. Vince saw Flynn the next day, and the

Bronx chairman glumly said there was no sense in trying any further to get me out of the race.

Even so, the third termers did not cease their whittling at my votes by persuasion and threats. They went even further and attempted to have Glass, weak in body but stout in heart, back out of his promise to nominate me. This futile effort to dissuade a Democrat of deep conviction and high principle from his commitment I regarded then, and still do, as the most reprehensible action I have known in politics.

I told Dailey I would like to have the New York vote split so I would receive 47 votes, merely as a compliment to my party services. I felt my services to the party in New York entitled me to that much. As an officer of the state committees for twelve years, I had done everything in my power physically, mentally, and financially to advance the party. I asked Vince to deliver this message to Flynn and Wagner. I know the message was delivered to Flynn and to Governor Lehman. They did not go along with me. The reason was that the President did not want any opposition candidate to poll over 150 votes. Hopkins and the others went around with the story that if the opposition polled over 150 votes, Roosevelt would not allow himself to be "drafted."

While Flynn was waiting to see me, I learned later, he told Mrs. Jane Duffy, my personal secretary, that his one desire was to see me happy and his one hope was that I would not "do an Al Smith" and walk out on the party. This gave me a chuckle, for Flynn's idea of making me happy was for me to make him the bearer of good tidings to Roosevelt, the good news, from the viewpoint of the Blackstone suite, being my withdrawal.

CHAPTER TWENTY-SIX

1940 CONVENTION

MONDAY MORNING, July 15, 1940, just before I went out to the Chicago Stadium for the opening of the convention, I received a call from the White House. This was my first call from the President although I had been in Chicago seven days. At the moment the call was announced by Mrs. Duffy, my competent and efficient private secretary, the thought flashed across my mind that here was the final card of the third termers; the charm master was about to pull out the tremolo stops and lull my convictions so that I might be indentured to the third term campaign. While I had no intention of stopping my ears, I bound myself mentally to my mast of principle. The next moment the familiar voice boomed out with a heartiness which was a reasonable facsimile of that I knew so well in the 1932 and 1936 conventions.

"Howdy, Jim," he greeted.

"First rate," I reported. "How are things with you?"

"Fine, thanks, fine. Is everything going along all right?"

"Everything is okay with me, so far," I cautiously conceded. There was a brief silence which I broke. "I'm just on my way to the convention hall; have you got that letter we talked about ready?"

"Good thing you brought that up, Jim. I just got back from my week-end trip and am going to tackle it this afternoon. I may have it ready for you tonight."

"I'll be right here if you want me."

There was another brief pause, which this time he broke.

"By the way, Jim, there are a lot of stories in the papers . . . They are writing stories about there being no need for a ballot."

The tone of his voice reminded me of the times in my youth when I reached a testing toe into the cool Hudson. The long forgotten taunt, "Last one in's a fraidy cat," flashed into my mind. I took the plunge!

"That's perfectly silly. There just has to be a ballot. You and I both know there must be a ballot and that any effort to prevent a ballot or a roll call will be the one thing that's needed to wreck the Democratic party in November. It's just too ridiculous to discuss."

"Of course, of course," he said slowly and, I thought, somewhat regretfully. "I agree with you on the situation, but the papers are talking."

"Once again, I want to say to you that I will handle the situation along the lines of our conversation. You can rest assured that everything will be done on my part to conduct a dignified convention. Some people are trying to bully the situation and roll over everyone, and if that happens, it will be just too bad. . . ."

"Thanks," he said. "Take care of yourself."

"Don't worry about me; I'm all right."

I did not ask him about the contents of the letter or how he was going to get it to me, because I gathered that he had no intention of releasing it through me. I was sure it had been written by that time, because Sam Rosenman had accompanied him on the week-end cruise and Sam always turned up when there was an important letter, document, or speech to be written.

Before the phone call there had been another parade in and out of my office. United States Housing Administrator Nathan Straus expressed himself disturbed about what was going to happen to me. I told him not to worry. Mrs. Anna Rosenberg came in, similarly perturbed, to express the hope that I would remain for the campaign. Governor Lehman of New York came in, with dignity enough for two, to say he thought I was making a mistake, but did not remain to argue. Edward H. Crump, Democratic leader of Memphis, Tennessee, came in with Senator Kenneth McKellar. The clerical-faced "Boss" repeated the familiar arguments of the Blackstone suite crowd. I told Crump, after he had gone on and on, that I could appreciate his point of view but apparently it was impossible for him to appreciate mine.

When I told Crump I appreciated his point of view, I was not talking through my hat. I understood the position of Kelly, Hague, and Flynn as well as they did. Uppermost in their minds was the success of their local tickets. They all felt that if the President was at the head of the ticket, they would get more votes for their local tickets. It was as simple as that.

Senator Millard Tydings bounced in with William Richie, of Omaha, cousin of the late Maryland governor, full of high hopes for the "stop the third term" movement. I met his enthusiasm with reserve and, mindful of the coming presidential message, told him we might be in a better position to discuss the movement's prospects on the morrow.

Elliott Roosevelt breezed in for a talk on the situation. I explained my position and outlined my course of action.

"You are all right," he declared, "but there is a lot of guttersniping going on across the street."

In this period not all my callers were seeking to persuade me to desert to the third term. Many came to congratulate me on my stand. I shall never forget these loyal friends and concerned citizens. Many of the party's faithful came, knowing that they were perhaps marking themselves in the third termers' black books, but they walked in boldly. Others were surreptitious but nonetheless sincere.

My last act before leaving for the hall was to call Carter Glass in Washington. I was aware of the pressure being put on him by the acclamation boys to have him sit out the convention in his home, and leave me without my chosen nominator.

"How are you, young fellow?" I began.

"Never felt better," his rasping voice came over the wire.

"Are you coming to our convention?" I asked.

"It's a fight, ain't it?" he countered. "Try and keep me away."

"I'm delighted to hear it and I still hope you'll place my name in the running."

"Nothing can stop me, and I mean nothing."

His assurance was music to me, though it came in a hoarse whisper. I told him I was grateful and left for the west side.

Crowds were milling about the Stadium when I arrived. To me a convention has all the drama inside and outside of a spectacle in sports, like the world's series, a championship fight or an Army–Notre Dame game. I love the holiday mood of the crowd. I love the restless surging of the delegates, part actors and part spectators. I thrill to the marches and songs. I am fascinated by the activity in the press sections. I delight in the oratorical cadences. I love the bustle of the platform, heavy with political notables. I am enthralled by the drama of a roll call. I am carried away by the color and frenzy of a demonstration. To me the waving state standards are more beautiful than a field of tossing grain. I love the popping of flashbulbs, the endless surge of noises, and the thick and often simmering atmosphere. To me it's *the* great American show. There's not a dull moment in it.

So it was with mingled joy and pride that I raised my gavel, almost at the stroke of noon, and looked out upon the restless scene in the convention hall. In a moment I brought the gavel down, and the 1940 convention was launched into history. The invocation was followed by an address of welcome by Mayor Kelly, who seized upon the position of first speaker, which was his only by courtesy to his role as convention host, to draft the President.

Grinning broadly, Kelly thrust the name of the President before the convention almost at once. I have no doubt that the Mayor was confident that his mention of the magic name would precipitate a parade that would end in a spontaneous draft of Roosevelt. Puzzlement was stamped on his face when the expected demonstration failed to materialize and he hurried disappointedly through the remainder of his speech. His words were resented by the delegates as being in bad taste. Whatever faults the speech had, Kelly paid for them in disappointment. I was told later he had fully expected to stampede the convention and was nonplused by the lack of delegate enthusiasm. Being a man of action, he moved to correct the situation and prepared to ensure enthusiasm for the Roosevelt nomination, even if it had to be manufactured.

Following the official photograph taking, I made an opening address, which was well received. At this point the stadium organ was to have played *When Irish Eyes Are Smiling* by way of a musical tribute. Suddenly the power mysteriously failed. Well-wishers of mine later taxed Kelly with deliberately arranging the power failure, a charge which he denied. It did not happen again. The brief morning session ended with a bit of general routine business and a few announcements.

At nine o'clock that night the gavel was raised in my hand again.

A bit of pounding brought the meeting to order and the nation was listening in by radio on our deliberations. The night meeting had been set to gather in the radio audience.

"And now, men and women of the Democratic national convention, it becomes my duty to relinquish the gavel and present to you the temporary officers who will guide your proceedings until you have expressed your views as to the permanent organization." I closed my salute to the accomplishments of the Democratic party. "Mine has been a happy service. I have had the hearty support and cooperation of the national committee which now goes out of existence, and I want to thank the members from the bottom of my heart, on my own behalf and on behalf of the Democratic party whose interests they have so sincerely guarded.

"Let me thank also the delegates to the convention who have done everything possible to expedite and make easier the business of this meeting. I know that your new organization will not let the Democratic party down, and I firmly believe that every member of this great gathering will give our successors and the new national party organization the same support that was accorded to the national committees in 1932 and 1936, and, if that is so, let me promise you now another triumph next November."

Again there was generous applause. "So far," I remember saying to myself, "you have behaved in a manner no one can criticize." True, I had not mentioned the President's name, as some remarked later, but it was not my role to do so at that time and in that place.

Speaker Bankhead was then escorted to the platform in accordance with the free and easy convention protocol, and I surrendered the gavel. The Speaker unrolled a half hour of rounded sentences to strike a wartime party keynote. He said:

"The minds of the American people are now so deeply engrossed in . . . the preservation of our established order of life and institutions, that they will have no tolerance for the superficial banalities of politics. An election must be held, but . . . the major objective of both parties must be unity and solidarity of purpose."

Bankhead warmly praised Hull and Roosevelt for the formulation and execution of the nation's foreign policy. I am sure these words fell pleasantly on Hull's ears in his Carlton Hotel apartment in Washington, because I knew that the Tennessean was hurt over the President's failure to acknowledge his services to the state just as Roosevelt had been loathe to acknowledge my political services to himself and to the party.

The Speaker drew his heaviest round of applause when he quoted the President's statement, "We will not send our men to take part in European wars." A few minutes later he mopped his perspiring face as the convention marked the conclusion of the keynote with rounds of applause. He adjourned the gathering until noon of the next day.

Bankhead, I am sure, injured himself, as far as his ambitions were concerned, by his appearance before the convention. It was obvious to all that he was tired and worn. His speech lacked the fire that might have been fanned into flames of enthusiasm during consideration of the Vice Presidency. But he made his speech aware of the stakes, and my hat was off to him as a grand soldier and loyal party man.

Back in my office I put in calls to Garner and Hull. I chose to talk to the Vice President first because I knew he was in the habit of retiring early. Although it was past his usual bed time when I called, I knew that he and Mrs. Garner had their ears turned to the radio for the convention and that I would not be awakening him.

"Well," I began, "are you all set to be steam-rollered with me?"

"Looks that way," he laughed.

"For my part, I'm ready for the steam roller," I said. "I am satisfied in my heart that I'm doing the right thing and I'm glad I have played it through."

"God bless you, boy," he said in a sudden sincerity that surprised me in view of the bantering approach to our situation. "Jim, you've definitely proved to me what I always thought about you: that you are a man of character, principle, and courage. I want to wish you every success and happiness in the future and you deserve it because you're doing a brave and noble thing, Jim."

I was touched deeply. I thanked him as best I could and told him I reciprocated his feelings.

Then I put in a call to Hull. I used much the same opening with him

October 28, 1940—After I had resigned from the Cabinet, President Roosevelt,
Mrs. Roosevelt, and I met again in Madison Square Garden. He had requested me
to sit next to him in his car and on the platform during his speech (see page 336).

Aboard Presidential Special
December 3, 1940.

Dear Jim:-

Thank you for yours of the twenty-third. You know I am a funny fellow in that unlike many, many people I do not get excited by what you call an "unprecedented honor". The reason is that I am perhaps a little "queer" in never having sought public office for "honor".

To put it another way, I would have been just as content in my own heart and conscience to give service to the country as a private citizen as I would to give service to the country as a first term or a third term President.

I am off for an attempt to get two weeks of sunshine -- and I do hope you will run in and see me when I get back. I would really love to talk with you quietly about a lot of things that intimately relate today to the future generations of America.

Is it true you are going to South America? Let me know if I can help.

My best to you all,

As ever,

F. D. R.

Honorable James A. Farley,
1040 Fifth Avenue,
New York, N. Y.

December 3, 1940—The President's unsigned reply to my letter of congratulation (see page 338).

and to my amazement he replied in almost the same words Garner had used. I told him so. He said they were deserved. I went to bed contented that night, secure in the thought that if two such men thought well of me and my course, I would come through a trying time with credit and dignity, as I hoped.

Tuesday afternoon's session of the convention was routine, serving to accentuate the fireworks that were to come. That night's schedule called for the address of the permanent chairman, Senator Barkley. There was no indication that the address would offer anything unusual until the President told his press conference, in response to a probing question on politics, that the Senator would read to the convention a message from the White House that night.

While the first real news of the convention came out of Washington, it did not remain a secret until Barkley addressed the convention. Within two hours, word of the statement was echoing up and down hotel corridors and long before the night session convened, only the radio audience and the galleries were in doubt as to what the President was going to say.

Jimmy Byrnes was the first to call me with the news. His voice was charged with suppressed excitement.

"The President has released his delegates," he said.

"Finally?" I asked.

"He has authorized Barkley to tell the convention so, and to tell the convention he has no desire to run again and never had."

"Oh," I said as noncommittally as I could. "That's a brick of another color, as my father used to say."

Byrnes hung up somewhat annoyed by my unenthusiastic reaction, I think. Soon after Herbert Bayard Swope was on the phone with an entirely different version of the coming statement. His story was that the delegates had not been released. He told me he had read the statement most carefully. For the first time I learned that the words were to be the words of Barkley although the hand that wrote them was the hand of Roosevelt with an assist credited to Rosenman.

A little later Frances Perkins marched in to see me under one of her tricorne hats, which were her trademark. She came in to discuss the vice-presidential nomination, saying it was necessary to have a strong man. I told her I was for Jesse Jones, if he would take it, and I was sure he would if he got the Roosevelt nod, because I thought he would fit into the third term picture—as much as I disliked it—better than anyone I knew. She told me she thought I could name the man, if I determined to do so. Then she asked my opinion of the President's statement.

"Frances, to tell you the truth, I'm not familiar with it," I replied. "All I know about it is what I have been told by Jimmy Byrnes and Herb Swope and a few newspapermen. And I have to admit the reports are somewhat contradictory. I'd be glad to get a little information."

She studied me earnestly.

"Jim," she said at length, "has the President talked to you about it?"

"No," was my emphatic reply.

"It sounds incredible," she said half to herself. A moment later she went purposefully through the door with tears in her eyes.

About twenty minutes after eight, as I was preparing to head for the Stadium for what I recognized would be an historic session, Mrs. Duffy came in with the news the White House was on the line.

"Jim, I've been trying to get you all afternoon," the President began heartily. "And I haven't been able to catch up to you. What are you up to out there?"

As he laughed, I smiled. I had been in the office all afternoon. As a matter of fact if I had been out and word had come through that the President wanted me, everyone around me would have kept after me until I was located. Just for the record, I made a check later and found that there had been no White House call during the afternoon.

"Oh, I'm a pretty busy fellow out here," I responded somewhat perfunctorily.

"Jim, I wanted to tell you that Alben has that statement we talked about," he said. "I decided that it would be best to release it after the permanent organization was set up. I would rather do it that way than the ways we talked about up at Hyde Park. I think you'll agree when you think it over. It's short and to the point."

He did not read the statement. I did not know what was in it until

I got to the convention hall and Barkley read it. I have in my possession the original copy Barkley read.

At the hall I ran into Miss Perkins, making her way through the police lines to the platform. As we were being swept along the aisle below the platform, she smiled at me.

"Did you get a call from the White House?" she asked archly.

"Yes," I acknowledged. "And I could make a good guess as to who was responsible for it."

"You'd be right," she said as we separated at the head of the stairs.

I am satisfied the President would not have called me if she had not prodded him into it. I told the story to Frank Walker the next day, and he said he had discussed the matter with the President on Monday, suggesting Roosevelt should talk to me the moment the statement was drafted. Walker said he was assured the President would do so.

I confidently expected that the statement would be the signal for a demonstration; such tactics appeared to be elemental. I was surprised, therefore, when Barkley mentioned the President's name after the first fourteen minutes of his address. Barkley is a born orator of the southern tradition and scarcely begins to get under way in the first fourteen minutes. He is one of the best orators of our time, not only in my opinion but also in that of others competent to judge.

A demonstration started spontaneously in several delegations. In no time banners were dancing down the aisles. Cheers echoed. The organ whooped it up with the tuneful *Franklin D. Roosevelt Jones*. Here and there could be noted a tussle over a state banner. I saw Senator Tydings, standing with out-thrust chin, grimly hanging on to Maryland's standard and stoutly resisting every attempt to wrest it from him. The Garner delegation hung on to one Texas banner. In the Massachusetts delegation, one was held by my crowd.

As the delegates filed past the platform in a joyous snake dance, my eyes popped in surprise to see the austere, impeccable Under Secretary of State, Sumner Welles, jogging along. I could have been no more surprised if General MacArthur had trotted by in full dress uniform. Welles's creased trousers were getting a collection of wrinkles and his collar was wilting. He was going through the motions, but his wan smile was ample evidence that he wasn't really enjoying himself.

Barkley began pounding for order early in the demonstration, so I realized this outburst was entirely genuine. He was able to restore order only by shouting for a doctor, stating that a lady had been injured. Throughout this demonstration the galleries were strangely silent. Once order was restored, Barkley droned on with his speech.

Now preparations went on in earnest for a demonstration. Gradually the aisles of the convention were filled up by strangers with concealed cardboard banners. They united in the jammed aisles, shifting from foot to foot as the Barkley cadences rolled on.

At length he produced what I was waiting for—the statement:

"I and other close friends of the President have long known that he has no wish to be a candidate again. We know, too, that in no way whatsoever has he exerted any influence in the selection of delegates, or upon the opinions of delegates to this convention.

"Tonight, at the specific request and authorization of the President, I am making this simple fact clear to this convention.

"The President has never had, and has not today, any desire or purpose to continue in the office of President, to be a candidate for that office, or to be nominated by the convention for that office.

"He wishes in all earnestness and sincerity to make it clear that all of the delegates in this convention are free to vote for any candidate.

"This is the message I bear to you from the President of the United States."

Barkley gave the statement to the full of his resonant lungs. Then he turned away to await the roar of applause. There was no applause! The delegates stood pat. The strangers flashed their banners, which read "Roosevelt and Humanity" and began shuffling through the aisles. The organ pealed. But the delegates stood silent in their places, eying the marchers with distrust.

Suddenly, from over the loud-speakers throughout the hall came a bellow:

"We want Roosevelt."

Surprise was registered on all faces. Mayor Kelly beamed. The thundering voice went on at intervals for forty-five minutes chanting:

"Chicago wants Roosevelt!"
"The party wants Roosevelt!"
"New York wants Roosevelt!"
"The world needs Roosevelt!"
"Illinois wants Roosevelt!"
"America needs Roosevelt!"
"Everybody wants Roosevelt!"

Every now and then Barkley would give the voice added steam by yelling into his microphone, "We want Roosevelt!" He kissed the Kentucky banner in the parade. Few delegates, except for the most earnest New Dealers, like Senator Pepper of Florida, were in the parade. Once when the demonstration was fading, Barkley gave it new life by roaring, "Will the galleries remember they are our guests here and conduct themselves accordingly?" The laughter came from the marchers. Those in the gallery were quiet, strangely enough. Many left and there were huge gaps of empty red chairs. On the floor the Kellyites worked on and on, encouraged by smiling approval from their boss as they passed his box. One of the marchers yelled, "Hey, Ed, we planned it that way!" as he filed past the box, a witticism widely quoted throughout the evening.

Those on the platform were as bewildered over the identity of the loud-speaker voice as the delegates. Reporters finally tracked it to a small basement room where the amplifier circuits were centered. There enjoying himself immensely was leather-lunged Thomas D. Mc-Garry, Chicago's superintendent of sewers. He had been selected for the job by Kelly himself. A half dozen times he darted out of his basement cell to bask in Kelly's approval and to see the scene; then he would go back to his chant.

During the machine-made tumult, I studied the President's statement. Now and then I looked out on the scene myself and pondered my words, that we Democrats would make the convention as dignified as possible. The statement itself was inconclusive and certainly did not approach what the President promised at Hyde Park. It was apparent he did not want me to know what was in it, because I would have been frank in my opinion of it. But like everything else at the convention, it was not brought to my attention. Apparently no one except the President was satisfied with the statement. Everywhere it was regarded as misleading and evasive.

Back in my office, I called Hull. He told me about his luncheon conversation with the President, saying he had assured the President solemnly and finally that under no circumstances would he permit any consideration to be given to his name before the convention. He begged me to head off any effort in that direction, if such effort appeared.

I made what had by this time become a nightly report to former Governor James M. Cox at Dayton, Ohio. The head of the 1920 Cox–Roosevelt ticket understood my position and sympathized with my purpose.

CHAPTER TWENTY-SEVEN

NOMINATION FOR PRESIDENT

J ULY 17, 1940, in one respect the political pinnacle of my life,
dawned brightly enough. Before leaving for the convention, I
called Bess, who was in our suite across the street, to assure
her "everything would be all right." She went out to the convention
hall with a party of friends. I went to the Stadium with my daughters.
Quite honestly I wanted them to hear their father nominated for the
Presidency. Bill Bray, my executive assistant, and Tom Davis, of the
Democratic National Committee, went along. When I reached the
hall, I was told that Mrs. Roosevelt wanted me on the phone. I put
through a call to her at Hyde Park, New York, from the stadium
press office.

"Frances Perkins has called me and insists that it's absolutely necessary I come to Chicago," she explained her call. "Frances doesn't like
the looks of things out there and feels that my appearance would do
a lot to straighten things out. Now, I don't want to appear before
the convention unless you think it is all right."

"Why, it's perfectly all right with me," I said.

"Please, don't say so unless you really mean it."

"I do mean it and I am not trying to be polite," I declared. "I feel
and mean what I am saying. Frankly, the situation is not good. Equally
frankly, your coming will not affect my situation one way or the
other. From the President's point of view I think it desirable, if not
essential, that you come."

"Thanks, Jim," she said. "I appreciate this. I'll come."

Back on the platform I went over to shake hands with Carter Glass
and his wife. He had come to nominate me. I told him how deeply
I appreciated what he was about to do and what a great honor I considered it to have so great an American present my name to the convention. He waved my emotional gratitude aside kindly.

"Senator," I shifted to a lighter vein, "I think it is rather bad taste for a man whose name is going to be placed in nomination for the Presidency to stay on the platform during the proceeding."

He looked at me sharply and smiled his crooked but illuminating smile.

"Jim, if I were you, I wouldn't be too modest about anything I did in this convention."

As I left him I'm sure my affection stood out in my eyes. It was a moment of great happiness and elation. I looked out over the scene satisfied in my soul that I was doing the right thing. Before I left I nodded to friends in the press box, glad to be able to meet their eyes and smile the smile of the quiet in heart.

Under the platform, I made my way to a stadium office and seated myself with Bill Bray and Tom Davis beside a radio. Senate Secretary Edwin Halsey was in and out. Alabama was called in the roll of states and Senator Lister Hill nominated Roosevelt in a speech that was later appraised as more noisy than distinguished.

Then came my greatest thrill in politics. I have known many moments of exultation in politics. The thrill I received when Roosevelt was first nominated in 1932 was tremendous. I was thrilled by his election. I was thrilled at his inauguration. I enjoyed a great personal thrill that afternoon when I took the oath of office as Postmaster General. I was thrilled by the second nomination in 1936. And on election night that year when my prophecy of 46 states to 2 came true, I thought I had experienced more thrills than any man has a right to expect in politics. But that night in the dingy old stadium office, all previous thrills paled into insignificance.

Arkansas yielded to Virginia and Barkley introduced Glass. In my mind's eye I could see the frail but vital figure advancing to the rostrum. I would have given anything to see the Senator, one of the nation's truly great statesmen, stand before the crowd. I would have loved to watch the unfolding of the greatest scene of my life, but I felt it proper to remain out of sight. I was brought sharply out of my reverie by a rather faint, rasping voice.

"Mr. Chairman," it began, "and members of the National Democratic convention: There is no material consideration and few spiritual reasons that can draw me from a sickroom halfway across the continent to speak a brief word to this national convention of the great Democratic party."

I thought Glass's gravelly voice had failed and I was nervous for him. I got up from my chair and began pacing. Then came a few boos, which swelled into a chorus. For the first time in that convention, I became fighting mad clear through. Bray and Davis later told me I stopped my pacing, clenched my fists, and set my jaw as though I were going to stride out and take on the hoodlums. I felt that way. Here was one of the greatest Democrats in the country, a man who had made a reputation in a long and successful public career, being booed by Democrats because he had the courage to stand before a Democratic gathering to present my name and because he felt I was representing the best in the Democratic tradition. We both knew the presentation was merely a gesture; that the votes would not be forthcoming. We knew also, and everyone in the hall knew, that the convention was not a free and open convention, or his speech might have had added significance.

The boos churned anger and indignation and injury within me, not only because of Glass's position in the party, but because here was a venerable old man, who had left a sickbed to do what he believed to be right. He was entitled to respectful attention because of his years, position, and services, and he was being booed by a lot of political riff-raff who had no right to the convention floor, and perhaps a few misguided zealots. I am not a man who hates; I have no capacity in my soul for hate; but I can never feel kindly toward those who prompted and permitted the booing of that gallant gentleman. I was fearful that something might happen to Glass. I knew he was not feeling well, and with his advanced years and with the excitement, I was worried that he might be stricken in his tracks. This fear erased my anger and I prayed, as hard as I knew how, that he might carry on and finish what he had to say. I did not know a word of his speech before delivery; I did not think it proper that I should.

Quite abruptly the faint voice surged into a fighting roar. I did not know until afterwards that they had failed to lower the microphone for the Virginia gamecock. I hung on his every word. When the disgraceful booing ended, Virginia's senior Senator continued:

"But among these spiritual considerations, first of all, is a desire to present to this convention the name of an incomparable Democrat, who has conducted the affairs of the Democratic party for seven years in a way that no other man within my recollection of forty years of public service has ever done.

"Always eager to be an intense partisan, always eager to have his party win, nevertheless he was a man of such a type of patriotism as always to put his country above party considerations, a genius in matters of a political nature, so thoroughly well versed in the sentiment and observance of the action of the people of the United States as to have twice predicted the success in this party so accurately as that he claimed but two states in the Union would go against his party.

"He is not only a man of loyal attachment to the Democratic party, but there is no manner of personal or political reward that would sufficiently secure him for the sacrifices he has made to his party. A man of character and intelligence, a man on whose word every human being can always rely, a man who never in all his lifetime ever violated a pledge once given, a man who believes in the unwritten law and traditions of the Democratic party as advocated ever since before the days of Thomas Jefferson, who less than three years before his death appealed to the party which he established never to nominate a man for the third term for the Presidency; and Virginia, always mindful of the principles enunciated by Thomas Jefferson as immortal, stands today unmoved, from any source, from the principles advocated by the founder of the Democratic party; and through consideration for the party itself, for its success and perpetuity, I have come from a sickbed to present to this convention the name of a great Democrat, James A. Farley of New York. If nominated by the convention, there will not be a shadow of a doubt as to his election next November.

"Let me say this word in conclusion: since I have been sitting on this platform I have had two anonymous communications objecting to Jim Farley because he is a Catholic. When I reflect that one of the three achievements of Thomas Jefferson which he most valued was the Virginia statute in favor of religious freedom, it made me more determined to present his name than I otherwise would be."

During this speech I thought of my dead mother and how proud she would have been had she been able to be present. I thought of the father I hardly knew. In my mind's eye I could see Bess in her box and Betty and Ann on the platform. I was happy to have them hear my name presented and I hoped Jimmy was listening to the radio, as I was. I welled with sentiment. Never in my wildest dreams had I thought I would live to see the day when my name would be seriously presented to a Democratic convention for the office of the President of the United States. And to be presented by such a magnificent American character and in so critical an hour in the nation's history filled my cup of happiness. Tears came to my eyes and spilled over. And I am not ashamed of a single one of them; I would have been less a man, had I not been moved at that hour.

A short ovation followed. I remember it was short, but at least it was genuine. Everyone in that vast hall who cheered for Farley meant it. Not a single one was paid and not a single one did it to keep a job. There were some boos and I took them all on my shoulders, dividing the cheers with Glass, because I felt that the demonstration was for him, too. Mayor Kelly's organist was silent; the band forgot to play, and in a few moments my "parade" was over. Bess's box, which she occupied with several New York friends, was near that occupied by Mayor Kelly, his wife, and others. She said Kelly and those with him were glued to their chairs during the Farley flurry. As Mayor of Chicago, he was host to the convention and, despite the fact he was going down the line for the third term, which was his privilege, common courtesy demanded that he rise for other demonstrations. I rose when I was on the platform during the Roosevelt demonstrations, both genuine and staged.

Glass's voice was not the only one raised for me that evening. Pat Doyle of Massachusetts strode purposefully to the rostrum to deliver a seconding speech, and, in his winning Irish way, drew no little applause.

Doyle was followed by Pat Fisher, my dear old friend. Pat was holding my old job of Rockland County chairman. I knew I could count on him, if everyone else deserted me. I could understand how Pat felt as he stood in front of that great body. I was proud with him. I knew the folks back in Rockland were listening in for Pat and myself. They were hearing the seconding nomination of one they had known through his entire lifetime by another they had known equally well. I thought of various friends, especially those who had known my father and mother, who would be listening in to hear how Jim and Pat were doing. Again my heart swelled and my throat choked and my eyes filled.

Pat's speech was a nice little speech, and nicely delivered, if I, who perhaps shouldn't, do say so myself. The final seconding speech—and I permitted only three instead of the allowed four—was that of Mrs. L. O. Keen, national committeewoman from the Canal Zone.

At the conclusion of the nominating speeches, I started for the platform. On my way I saw handfuls of puzzled men, clutching Wheeler banners, around the entrance aisles. Edward J. Colgan, Jr., of Baltimore was nominating Tydings. Booing had by this time become a habit. There was a cheer, not a loud one, but Tydings had had the courage to voice his opposition. Then silver-haired Wright Morrow was at the rostrum nominating Garner. It was hot in the hall. Delegates became drowsy. But the booers lost none of their bad manners. The Texas delegation bravely trooped around the hall to the tune of *The Eyes of Texas Are upon You* and Cactus Jack had demonstrated his courage to stand for conviction.

"The roll call is concluded," Barkley announced in stentorian accents. "The clerk will now call the roll."

One hour and ten minutes later at 10:38 P.M. CDST the third term tradition was broken. The vote was: Roosevelt 946 and one-half, Farley 72 and one-half, Garner 61, Tydings 9 and one-half.

CHAPTER TWENTY-EIGHT

THIRD TERMERS TRIUMPH

D URING THE nominations and roll call, I remained out of sight at the rear of the platform. Before my nomination I went to Barkley and Byrnes and told them I wished to move that the nomination be made unanimous after the roll call. I wanted everyone to know that my course was one of principle, that I was not trying to throw a monkey wrench into the proceedings, and that I was not a sorehead. They told me I would be recognized but that Sam Rayburn had already asked permission to move that the votes of Texas, recorded for Garner, be shifted to Roosevelt, which, in effect, would be to move unanimous nomination. I told Barkley it was perfectly satisfactory with me that Rayburn be recognized first, but that I would be appreciative if I could be recognized after Rayburn. That he promised to do.

When I was introduced by Barkley I moved down the aisle with Eddie Roddan and Bill Bray. Eddie had been my close friend during the time he had been associated with the committee. While he was not in sympathy with what I was doing, he had asked particularly to walk down the aisle with me, because he wanted everyone in the convention to know that he was my friend. It was a splendid evidence of friendship, and I shall always cherish it. I am afraid Eddie paid dearly for it, because I am sure it cost him a place on the Federal Communications Commission, which he had been promised. Mrs. Roosevelt, Steve Early, John and Anna Boettiger, and Ed Flynn were all for him, but the President put them off with one excuse after another and Eddie never got the post. The irony of it was that Eddie was a staunch believer in the third term, and the party had no more faithful or valuable worker in the third term campaign. I also deeply appreciated Bray's presence at my left hand. While Bray was my secretary at the Post Office Department and could have been expected to appear with me without arousing wrath, others with less to lose had shunned me and dodged me on the platform, in the streets, and at the hotel. Among these were many for whom I had done much.

At the rostrum I was greeted by a standing ovation from the delegates. The little army of well-disciplined booers remained silent. The galleries displayed enthusiasm for almost the only time during the convention. I was touched by the reception. As I responded by waving my right arm, contentment grew within me. I knew my course had been right. I could see the ovation was genuine and I accepted it as vindication of my stand. I realized that I was in a delicate position. Everyone in the hall was undoubtedly wondering what I was going to say and how I was going to say it. Millions were listening in. Those who knew me, of course, and those who knew anything about my record, were confident I was about to make the nomination unanimous. Nonetheless, I believe there was doubt in the minds of many people as to just how far I would go, doubt raised, perhaps, by the recollection of what Al Smith had done eight years before.

There was never any doubt in my mind for months before as to what I was going to do at that particular moment. More than once since, I have had occasion to recall Mark Twain's famous line, "When in doubt, do the right thing." I was full of doubt, but I knew what I was doing was the right thing. I knew I had to let the convention know my convictions or I would not be true to myself, my party, or my country. I did this in allowing my name to be presented. Now it was up to me to accept the will of the convention and move the nomination be unanimous.

I had prepared the speech I was about to deliver before I left the hotel. Roddan worked it over with me, but most of it was mine and the sentiments were all mine. During my long years in public life I have received help from many persons with my speeches. I have never been ashamed to own this. Charlie Hand, Vincent Dailey, Raymond Moley, Adolph Berle, Ambrose O'Connell, Claude Bowers, Charley Michelson, Eddie Roddan, and others have dressed my ideas, and I have been and still am grateful to them. While I am no great author, and no orator, I have come a long way from the tongue-tied town clerk elect, who practiced unappreciated in the back yard of his Grassy Point home. I can get to my feet and unburden myself extemporaneously. There are those kind enough to say that some of my best thoughts have been expressed without preparation and without aid. Be that as it may, I never took more care with an address in my life, so that there would be no question about the delivery itself or the sincerity back of it. I said:

"Senator Barkley and fellow Democrats, you have given me on two occasions the highest honor in your gift, chairmanship of the Democratic national committee. I ask you now for a further courtesy. I ask your indulgence so that I may deliver without interruption a brief message to this great convention."

I paused for effect. I could see I had the attention of the delegates. The hall hushed.

"I have pursued a course here that has been dictated by the deepest convictions, and when a man fails to follow his sincere convictions, no matter how unpleasant the consequences, he is false to himself, false to his party, and false to his country.

"I wanted this convention to proceed as Democrats should proceed, to nominate its standard-bearers in keeping with the high traditions of our party. That is the only democratic method and that has been observed.

"My name was placed in nomination for the Presidency of the United States by a great and noble American. As long as I live I shall be grateful to Senator Carter Glass, of Virginia. I am grateful to those delegates to this great convention who voted for me and to those delegates who would have voted for me had they not been otherwise pledged.

"Down through the years I have always given my best efforts to advance the cause of democracy, and I want this great convention to know that I will give that same support to the nominees of this convention.

"It is, therefore, a great pleasure for me, Senator Barkley, to move to suspend the rules and declare President Franklin D. Roosevelt nominated for President of the United States by acclamation."

There was a tremendous roar from the convention. The organ, Mayor Kelly's organ, had no trouble with *When Irish Eyes Are Smiling*. I acknowledged the salute and turned away from the rostrum.

That session of the convention ended with acceptance of my motion by a roaring of "ayes." I choked up when I heard Betty say to Ann, "We certainly can be proud of Dad tonight." That was my highest praise.

Many crowded to the platform to shake my hand. As I went through the hall there were cheers on every hand. The crowd knew they were cheering a loser, but they approved my courage to stand up for what I believed in.

I went back to the Hotel Stevens with Betty and Ann. I was relieved that it was all over and that I had come through as well as I had hoped. Actually, the strain was terrific. I felt that a great load was off my shoulders and that once more I was a free man—free to do the things I wanted to do, free to make my own decisions without regard to the feelings and ambitions of others, free to do what I thought was best for myself, and free to do the things for my family that a man in my position should be doing.

When I started for my rooms in the Blackstone Hotel, it took me a half hour to get through the lobby of the Stevens and another half hour to get to the elevator in the Blackstone. Hundreds struggled to grasp my hand and congratulate me on the attitude I had assumed and its successful outcome.

In the privacy of our suite I learned that all in our box had tears in their eyes when my name was offered, and Betty and Ann had cried on the platform. I confessed to my own tears. It was a great thrill for them as it was for me and their tears were salted with joy. None of them wanted me to win. Neither Bess nor the children wanted to live in the White House or for me to be elected Vice President. They wanted me to take myself out of politics and get back into private life so I could enjoy the pleasures that come to a man with a devoted family. They rejoiced that I was leaving with my head and heart high, and with my eyes lowered to no man. They delighted in the reception accorded me and the honor which went with the presentation of my name, but their greatest pleasure came from the knowledge that I would soon leave political life and be with them.

The family's attitude is best illustrated by a phone conversation I had the next morning with Jimmy, whom I reached at his New Hampshire camp.

"Hello, champ," I greeted.

"How are you, Dad?" he piped. "How did you make out?"

I told him.

"Good, Dad," was his reaction, "Mother will be very happy."

Thursday morning, July 18, 1940, the President called me early. He was as gay and bright as he had been after the 1932 and 1936 nomination. His manner was as warm as it had ever been.

"Now, Jim, we have to give some consideration to the selection of a Vice President, and I have thought it all over and have come to the conclusion that Henry Wallace is the best man to nominate in this emergency," he said breezily.

"Mr. President," I replied, "I am going to be for Jesse Jones and I think the best thing that can happen to you is to have Jesse Jones on the ticket with you."

"But Jesse's not in good health since that plane accident a couple of years ago. If anything should happen to me—if I should be bumped off—or if I should be hit with a bomb—I would want to feel that there is someone in the White House to carry on. One who would be able to do it. Anything can happen to Jesse at any time."

"I know nothing about Jesse being in poor health," I said. "He looks good to me. But be that as it may, I will be for him and will second his nomination. I sincerely believe he is the best man for you to nominate."

"I think Henry is perfect," he said doggedly. "I like him. He's the kind of fellow I want around. He's honest. He thinks right. He's a digger."

"Mr. President, there is no use fooling yourself. The nomination of Wallace just won't help the ticket any way. While I have a personal regard for Wallace as a man, for his integrity, for his courage, and for his energy and the rest you say, the people look on him as a mystic and I think you'll regret it. I think you are unfair to your country and your party in forcing Wallace's nomination, and you'll live to regret it."

"He's not a mystic," Roosevelt snapped. "He's a philosopher. He's got ideas. He thinks right. He'll help the people think."

"I'm merely telling you what the feeling is, I'm not arguing."

"Wallace will help in the farm belt."

"Maybe so, but he'll hurt in other places. This is your ride, Mr. President, and it is up to you to select the man you want alongside you. Jones would offset the lack of business support, big and little, which will come if Wallace should be the nominee."

He was silent.

"Mr. President," I went on, "I think you should know that Jesse would offset the arguments which are coming from all over about the influence of the Hopkins–Corcoran–Kelly–Wallace–Hague–Byrnes group and the others responsible for the silly performance out here."

The cordiality died out of his voice.

"Jim, Cordell won't take it," he said in aggrieved accents. "I pleaded with him yesterday, but he wouldn't take it under any circumstances."

"I thoroughly agree with Hull. He would be getting kicked upstairs. I talked with him and know how he feels."

"I had a talk with Jimmy Byrnes. Of course, the Catholic issue would hurt there. You know, he had been a Catholic until he reached the age of twenty-one and had graduated from college and law school, and then when he started going around with the girl who became his wife, he began attending a Protestant church, finally becoming a member of it. Jimmy realizes that this would affect his candidacy."

I could not suppress a smile. Jimmy had seen no more of the inside of a college than I had. Roosevelt found it hard to believe that those about him had risen without his educational advantages. Jimmy and I have done all right with colleges in another way. We each have about a dozen honorary degrees from a scattering of institutions who honor credits won in life. I told him what I had told Byrnes.

I thought it was time that the conversation took a lighter tone, so I reported that Assistant Secretary of War Louis Johnson was around telling everyone, "The President has given me the green light."

"Oh, my God," was his rejoinder.

"Looks like Louis will run into a red light," I laughed.

"He'll run into a red light at the next block."

"I want to talk to you about the situation that developed here and about my resignations," I said.

"Hold them off as long as you can, Jim."

"September 1 is the deadline and I can't wait beyond that under any circumstances. You know my financial situation. And I want to sit down with you and discuss the performance of some of the fellows you sent out here; their actions were incredible."

"Eleanor is coming out there," he sidestepped.

"I know it; we had a talk about it last night."

"Well, Jim, be sure to make it certain the vice-presidential nomination is unanimous. By the way, you were grand last night, Jim."

I talked with Hull, who seemed delighted that he came out of it without being forced to accept the Vice Presidency. He applauded my performance of the night before and the position I took in the telephone conversation. I then called Garner.

"They licked the daylights out of us last night, Jim," he chuckled.

"Well, John, I wouldn't have changed my position for anything in the world."

"I know."

"Have you any idea who your successor is?"

"I'll give you a guess as to who it is."

"I know; you guess."

"Well, who is it?"

"Between you and me, it's Wallace."

"No!"

"Yes, and I told him if he was thinking about the November election not to take Wallace, because Wallace is regarded as a mystic. I said I am going to be for Jones."

"More power to you."

"Well, I am playing it out, John, and I'll go down with colors flying."

I called Jesse Jones on the phone and then walked over to his hotel. I found him dictating a statement he was going to release to the press, declining the vice-presidential nomination. Jones looked up at me and smiled, "My heart ain't in it, Jim." Colonel Joseph M.

Hartfield, New York City attorney, was with him. I went over the statement.

"Jesse, I'm with you if you stay in the race," I said. "But I'm not here to advise you. That's something for you to decide. I'm going to make my decision, but I don't advise others unless they ask for it."

"What would you do, Jim?" he asked.

"Jesse, if the President did not want me, I wouldn't run."

"He doesn't want me because he thinks I'm not well."

"Jesse, that's not the real reason; he just doesn't want you, and you might as well face it. I'm telling you that because I would want a friend of mine to tell me the truth under like circumstances. Now, I'm for you. If you change your mind and stay in the race, you have my vote and support. I think you can be nominated with my support. I say that in all modesty. I told Roosevelt I'd be with you and I will."

"No, Jim, I guess I'll let this statement go. I won't change my mind."

On my way back to my office, I stopped by to pay my respects to Senator Glass. He was all smiles and reading over a handful of congratulatory telegrams he had received.

"How did I do last night, Jim?" he asked.

"You were great!"

"Well, it went all right except for the beginning. My voice gave out. But I was choked with emotion."

"That was nothing to worry about; it came out all right. If you had only stood up there and said, 'I place the name of James A. Farley in nomination,' that would have been enough for me. The fact that you presented my name is the greatest tribute I could personally have and I will remember it to my dying day."

"It was a real pleasure, Jim."

"The younger you get, the better you get."

Almost six years later I stood beside his grave with Senator Byrd. As the frail body of my friend, wasted by a long illness, was lowered, my mind flashed back to a visit Glass and I paid to the grave of Thomas Jefferson. As we looked through the iron fence at the resting place of the founder of our party, Glass said:

"Jim, I have always abhorred the thought of being buried in the ground, and I have been trying to persuade my Presbyterian wife (the first Mrs. Glass) to permit me to build a mausoleum to house my remains when I pass on."

I never mentioned the incident to any member of his family. While Glass spoke, Mrs. Roosevelt was laying a wreath on Jefferson's grave and President Roosevelt sat near by in his car. The President spoke that day at Monticello.

During the afternoon I could not resist calling up Ickes and congratulating him on Wallace's coming nomination. A couple of weeks earlier I had written him a facetious letter saying I was managing Wallace's campaign for the Presidency and giving some thoughts to Works Progress Administrator John Carmody for Vice President. Ickes was feuding with the pair and had long been at odds with Hopkins.

"Wallace's nomination is a damned outrage," Ickes sputtered.

"Seriously," I said, "what do you think of things?"

"What do I think of them?" he roared. "Who cares what I think? Here I led the whole third term movement while Hopkins was in the hospital and they thought he was going to die. Then he comes out to the convention and I'm not consulted at all. I know nothing about the program. I can keep a secret. I've been keeping secrets for years. Hopkins never even attended a county meeting and wouldn't know how to get into one. Now here he is taking over a national convention. It's disgraceful."

Ickes indicated he didn't know whether or not he would make any speeches. He told me he appreciated my position and admired the way in which I handled myself. It was rather amusing to see the New Dealers fighting so bitterly among themselves.

Senator Wheeler called me to say that he had decided to withdraw from the presidential race because he couldn't even hold his own delegation in line. I recalled the sad knots of men with his banners. Also I remembered running into Senator Bennett Clark, who was to have nominated Wheeler. Bennett pulled the speech from his pocket laughingly and told me, "This is the best speech I never made at a convention."

One of the most amusing incidents in the Chicago convention

came when Delegate Francis W. Durbin of Ohio, in a light interlude, made a speech nominating Bascom N. Timmons, one of the nation's ablest newspapermen, for Vice President. It was extremely hot and Fran peeled off his coat and handed it to Barkley. The Chairman obligingly held the coat while Durbin extolled the candidate of the press corps.

Several days later the Texas newspaperman encountered Wallace on the train which was carrying both of them back to Washington. "Mr. Wallace, when we came to Chicago, we each had one man behind our candidacy," Timmons drawled dryly. "I had Fran Durbin, but you had Franklin D. Roosevelt."

CHAPTER TWENTY-NINE

WALLACE SECOND CHOICE

ELLIOTT ROOSEVELT dropped by Thursday afternoon, July 18, 1940, to say he thought "it would be a great mistake to nominate Wallace." I told him I was for Jones. He met this with "If you nominate Jesse, I'll second it." I told him that was all right with me and that we would talk it over when his mother arrived. It was arranged that Arizona would yield to New York so that I could deliver the nominating speech.

I drove out to meet Mrs. Roosevelt at the airport. She had said I was the only person she wanted to meet. Her plane was on time. She was accompanied by Franklin, Jr. After she had given a brief press interview, we got into the car and headed for the Stevens Hotel, where she had rooms engaged.

She asked about my position and I outlined it quite pointedly. She said she felt as though she had always known me, that she could always turn to me for advice and assistance, and that I could always be depended upon. She said she would miss me in the campaign and had hoped there was some way my financial situation could be worked out. She was kind enough to say the campaign would not be the same without me, when she became convinced I would not change my mind. We then switched to discussion of the Vice Presidency. I said it was a mistake to nominate Wallace. She agreed, as did Franklin, Jr.

"Henry is a nice fellow," she said, "but people just don't become enthusiastic about him. His personality doesn't impress people."

"Looking at it practically," I said, "this fellow Willkie will get liberal financial support. It should be important to attract contributions to the Democratic campaign. And I don't know where they are going to come from with Wallace on the ticket."

"I agree with you, Jim," she said.

"The trouble is," Franklin, Jr., said, "that Father is making these

299

decisions while he is tired and there is no strong person around to argue with him."

Mrs. Roosevelt nodded.

At the hotel, Mrs. Roosevelt put in a call to the White House.

"Franklin," she plunged to the point, "I've been talking to Jim Farley and I agree with him Henry Wallace won't do. . . . I know, Franklin, but Jesse Jones would bolster the ticket and win it business support and help in many directions."

I also suggested Bankhead and Barkley and she relayed the suggestion. He did not take kindly to them. Finally, he asked that I be put on the phone. He appeared to be irritated. Regardless of that, I told him I had not changed my mind since morning and that I was still for Jesse.

"But I've given my word to Wallace, Jim." He was impatient. "What do you do when you give your word?"

"I keep it," I answered quickly, perhaps too quickly and too sharply, so I softened it. "If you gave your word to Wallace you should keep it; but it was a mistake to give it. I want to be frank with you. I am going out and vote for Jones if he will run, and if he won't, I'll vote for Bankhead; but I feel the Democrats want a Democrat and I do not consider Wallace one."

"I am committed," he said.

"Why not Paul McNutt?" I suggested.

He laughed. "Apparently, you still have your sense of humor."

"If I ever lost that, there will be no point to my being around the convention."

Mrs. Roosevelt and I went out to the convention together. At the hall we met Elliott, who was determined to see Jones nominated. She urged him not to do anything for Jones, because if he did "Father would feel very, very badly."

Time was growing short. Sam Morris of Arizona was already on the platform to waive to New York when Arizona was called. I signaled for him to pass and then sent for Jesse. I took him under the platform. I told him about my conversations with the President and with Mrs. Roosevelt. He had with him the statement he had prepared that morning. While we talked, Jesse's name was presented

by Howard Bruce of Maryland, at my suggestion. I had told Bruce that
if anything happened, we could take it up with Jesse before the roll
call and decide upon a final course of action. And here Jesse and I
were deciding in the office below the platform. Jesse was much hurt
by the President's attitude, but felt there was only one course he
could take, and that was to withdraw his name. There was nothing
I could do under the circumstances.

One by one the field of some seventeen vice-presidential candidates was narrowed to three men. Those who were dropped or who
withdrew included Hull, Garner, Jones, Byrnes, William O. Douglas,
Robert H. Jackson, Louis Johnson, Culbert Olson, Lloyd C. Stark,
Sam Rayburn, Charles Sawyer, and Scott Lucas. The latter at least
told the truth in eight words; the Illinois Senator stepped down in a
brief speech which began, "Had this been a free and open convention."

Only Speaker Bankhead, Wallace, and McNutt were left in the
race. Wallace had no more than a handful of personal votes when the
convention opened. Bankhead's candidacy had not been launched
too seriously. McNutt was strong only because opposition was fading. To give him his due, McNutt had an opportunity to upset the
presidential apple cart, if he remained in. He could have divided the
New Deal vote and thrown the nomination to Bankhead, if he did
not capture it himself.

The delegates were ugly. They did not want Wallace. Not all their
resentment was personal, however. They were showing their resentment against "bossism." Mrs. Wallace was on the platform through
it all. I felt sorry for her, but she did not need my sympathy to take
it bravely. McNutt had some difficulty in getting the attention of
the convention in order to withdraw, which he did most unwillingly,
I'm sure. There was nothing else he could do under the circumstances.
He was trapped by the President's adroit maneuvering like everyone
else. No one who studies this convention can deny that the President
showed himself to be a master of political rough-and-tumble with no
holds barred.

At length McNutt was allowed to withdraw, leaving the contest
between Wallace and Bankhead, and the balloting began. The voting

was made possible to a considerable extent by Jimmy Byrnes, who
went weaving in and out the delegations on the floor pleading, "For
God's sake, do you want a President or a Vice President?" It was third
term strategy to claim FDR would not run if he could not have Wallace as his running mate.

An amusing convention incident occurred when Governor Rivers
of Georgia, who was seated in his state's delegation, turned to ask
Governor Phillips in the Oklahoma delegation what the latter thought
of Wallace. "Why, Henry's my second choice," said the Governor
of Oklahoma to the Governor of Georgia. "That so?" said the Governor of Georgia to the Governor of Oklahoma. "Who's your first
choice?" Phillips fixed a beady eye on his colleague and answered
without the ghost of a smile, "Anyone—red, white, black, or yellow
—that can get the nomination."

The final vote brought Wallace only 627 votes out of 1,100. This
was almost an even division. There is no doubt in my mind that Mrs.
Roosevelt's appearance and her speech about the burdens of the Presidency in critical times saved the day for the President.

I cast my vote for Bankhead. Incidentally, I did not vote for myself;
I let my alternate vote on the presidential ballot. I suppose if I had ac-
tively supported Bankhead, I might have swung the nomination to
him in view of the closeness of the vote. I feel certain I could have
nominated Jones. However, there was no reason why I should have
fought Roosevelt on the Vice Presidency as I had on the Presidency,
especially since Jones withdrew. I always like to place myself in the
other fellow's position, whether I agree with him or not, and there are
certain rules that must be followed.

After the Wallace nomination, the President delivered the acceptance speech he had postponed until the work of the convention was
done, which (at the time he said so) meant until Wallace was nominated. Henry, who was on the platform, had an acceptance speech,
but was persuaded not to deliver it because of the temper of the delegates. Henry accepted this decision reluctantly because he is by no
means lacking in courage. He wanted to brave the delegates' wrath.

Angrily and sourly the confused delegates broke up. It had been a
long, hot, and tiring session. Many felt that the party had been split

and the Democratic ship would founder in November. Bad as the confusion was, there were those who would have added to it by presenting my name for the Vice Presidency, unaware that the Constitution provides that when electors cast their votes for President and Vice President "one at least shall not be an inhabitant of the same state with themselves." It would have been a pretty pickle, indeed, if my name had been presented and approved by the disgruntled delegates, because the New York vote could not have gone to Roosevelt and to me.

Many of the party faithful left the convention bruised in mind and disgusted in heart. That was true on the part of Senators, Congressmen, Governors, and old line party men. This worried the New Dealers not a bit. As a matter of fact they wanted nothing but one hundred percenters. The New Deal ranks were by no means solid. Ickes and Jackson were not pleased. Hopkins was in the saddle. Corcoran appeared to be on the way out.

The Democratic National Committee gathered the next morning at the Stevens Hotel. My statement of resignation was read shortly after the committeemen and committeewomen—about 110 in all—gathered in the hotel meeting room.

"Eight years ago in this city I was elected chairman of the Democratic National Committee," it read. "In the intervening years I have had the happiest associations with Democrats all over the country, and my debt to the party can never be repaid.

"I have remained in public life at great financial sacrifice, because I love politics. I have an opportunity now to accept an attractive offer in business, and in justice to my family, because of my financial situation, I am going to accept.

"Before leaving, I shall cooperate to the fullest extent with my successor as national chairman in setting up the machinery for the coming campaign. I have said repeatedly that the American people want the Democratic party to remain in power. My opinion has not changed and again I pledge my full support to the Roosevelt–Wallace ticket."

I was glad to get that pledge on the record and out of the way to head off an accusation of my being a sorehead. But I was sad as member after member of the committee, on the reading of my resignation, stood up to deliver impromptu expressions of appreciation for my services. Flynn submitted a resolution calling for the appointment of a committee to select a new chairman. It was one of the few times in my life I had difficulty in controlling my emotions. Those present appreciated this, I am sure. Tears glistened in the eyes of a number of men and streamed down the cheeks of several women.

That afternoon the newspapermen and women gave me a reception in the ballroom of the Stevens. There was a large photograph of me in the center of the south wall. There was also a five-foot Statue of Liberty of cake icing. On a table in the center of the room my name was spelled in letters of ice two feet high. A trio went around strumming Irish tunes. There was what my Gaelic ancestors call "Biadh and Deoch"—food and drink. No convention of any party has ever known such a gathering of newspaper people to pay tribute to a politician. I was deeply touched as I shook hands with between two and three hundred members of the working press who came to wish me well.

But there was more to come. To my surprise, I was hauled to a small platform. Walter Trohan of the *Chicago Tribune* was called on, representing the White House Correspondents' Association, who said, "It is only a heart as big as the heart of Jim Farley that can hold affection for the entire newspaper corps," and he tossed me a dummy baseball which contained a list of the names of those contributing to the affair. Esther Van Wagoner Tufty, of the Lansing, Michigan, *State Journal*, said, "Jim, we want you to know that the women of the press love you too," and she handed me a wooden plaque on which was mounted a first baseman's mitt. Turner Catledge, of the *New York Times*, speaking for the Capitol press galleries, said, "Fellows, we have listened for years to people getting up . . . to tell about how we never have broken a confidence with them . . . today we are here to pay a tribute to a man who has never broken a confidence with us," and he handed me a beautiful wrist watch, which I wear to this day.

The reaction of newspapers as well as of newspapermen to my course at Chicago was almost unanimously favorable. The stories of the men covering the convention were favorable even in the Republican press and the editorials were of the head-turning variety. Naturally, I was very happy for this. The radio commentators were also kind; I found myself looked upon as a statesman rather than as a politician.

Many callers filed through my offices during the day. A surprise visitor was Henry Wallace. He came in with a shy, boyish grin. I greeted him warmly. I was genuinely pleased by his courtesy call.

"Henry, you might as well hear this from me," I said. "You're not going to like it, but I want to assure you there is nothing personal in what I said or did. I sincerely hope that it will have no effect on our friendship. If our friendship can't survive an honest difference of opinion, well, it's just too bad.

"I suppose you know I voted for Bankhead. Now, you must know I didn't do this out of any fit of pique against the President. I did it because I honestly thought he would be the better man. Before that I was for Jones. I told the President I was for Jones. I thought that the nominee should be a real Democrat and one who would add strength to the ticket."

"Jim," he said simply, "I appreciate your frankness. I believe you when you say there was nothing personal in your objections. I think your frankness is one of the reasons why everybody likes you."

I thanked him for the kind remarks in his undelivered speech.

"I wanted to deliver it," he flashed. "They wouldn't let me."

"I'm sure of that."

"Jim, I hope we can bring unity within the party. I wish you were staying around because I know you could do it."

"That's water over the dam; my decision was made long ago."

"Well, I've got a press conference and have to run," he said as he rose. "But I didn't want to miss saying hello."

"When I return to Washington, I'll talk to you further. I'll be glad at any time to give my advice for what it's worth."

"Thanks." He bounded out the door, a happy man indeed.

Politics can lift men higher and faster than a rocket flames its way into the sky. It can also plummet them down to earth, never to rise again. Each man must learn this for himself.

It has been said that Roosevelt demonstrated himself to be a master politician at Chicago, outsmarting such opponents as Garner, Hull, Jones, Wheeler, Tydings, McNutt, Bankhead, and the rest. I must acknowledge that a good case can be made on his behalf. But those interested in fairness should be aware that he told each one at one time or another that he was not going to run—positively would not run—and that he could make no announcement of this because of the war situation. All who believed him were not fools; some of us were putting the country above politics. History will deliver its judgment when all the testimony is in.

CHAPTER THIRTY

ROOSEVELT PLEADS

AFTER THE convention, I did not see the President until July 26, 1940, at the first Cabinet meeting held after his renomination. The President was wheeled to his place at the head of the table. Almost at once, he looked down at me and said, in the friendliest of tones, "Hello, Jim, how are you?"

"As well as a fellow can be, in view of what's been going on for the last couple of weeks," I answered.

That eased the tension. Everyone joined in the laugh. Later, when the President got down to me, he asked, "Jim, have you got anything on your mind today?" I said lightly I had plenty but did not think this was the time or place to express it.

Somehow or other a discussion arose as to how long Congress would remain in session. The President said probably until sometime after Labor Day or September 15, and then it would recess until after the election. He added that members wanted to stay on during the emergency period to make statements which would help them in their campaigns.

"In other words, Mr. President," I quipped, "it is frequently easy to find those who serve their country before their party."

I turned around and looked at Hopkins. The President's laugh rang out above the rest. Hopkins enjoyed the remark as much as anyone. It was really very amusing and all in clean fun. The Cabinet meeting proceeded along general lines. As we broke up, the President asked me to step in and see him for a few minutes. It was the first time he had made such a request in a long time. I waited in Miss Le Hand's office with Grace Tully.

At his desk he handed me a letter that Mrs. Roosevelt had received from Queen Elizabeth. It was one of the nicest and saddest letters I have ever read. In simple language she expressed gratitude to the American people for sympathy and kindness. She told how the British people were fighting for the things they held most dear and the things they believed in. I wondered whether the President wasn't trying to get me into a receptive mood. I remarked that the letter was one of the finest I had ever read and depicted the fine character of a truly gracious person. He brushed the letter from his mind with a toss of his cigarette holder.

"Jim, everything came out all right in the convention," he said. "In the past there have been difficulties at conventions, which we have escaped. In 1896 the Palmer–Buckner ticket followed the Bryan nomination. You will remember that many party conservatives objected to Bryan's first nomination and broke away to nominate Palmer and Buckner. My own father supported the latter ticket. I remember the campaign well, although I was only fourteen at the time."

"The Palmer–Buckner ticket didn't get much support outside of your father," I threw in pleasantly. "Less than one per cent of the total vote, if I remember correctly."

"That's right," he laughed. "Now, Jim, there is a general sentiment on all sides—why, it's unanimous—that you participate in the campaign. Everybody's for you. Me, most of all.

"I realize, of course, better than the others, that you have to go out in business to do something for your family. And you should do it. But you can still do it and help the party. You could let someone else be appointed campaign manager and still hold the chairmanship in name, while actually you would be working for your family. It's as simple as that, Jim. It would mean a great deal to the party. Otherwise, there might be serious repercussions within the party and I know you would be the last one to want that."

He cocked his head and awaited my reply with his most engaging smile.

"Mr. President, that just can't be done," I answered. "You can't have divided authority around a campaign headquarters. There must be only one man in control and that one man must dominate the situation. If I can help in other ways I shall be glad to do whatever I can, but I don't want to be publicly connected with the national committee in any way."

"All you have to do, Jim, is have your name on the letterheads as chairman and that will be helpful," he suggested.

"It just can't be," I said. "There are times when all of us do what we believe is right, whether or not others agree; we have stood for things we believe in, while others have disagreed, and in this particular situation my mind is made up. I fully explained in Hyde Park what I was going to do, and there is just no point in arguing about it."

The conversation shifted to the convention again and Roosevelt said the only thing "which made me mad" during the whole convention was Glass's reference to the religious situation. I remarked that Glass felt I was being discriminated against because I was a Roman Catholic. I asked FDR not to harbor hard feelings. I told him I did not want him or anyone else to criticize Glass in my presence, because he had done something for me I could never forget. I added that a lot of things happened at the convention which had made me mad.

"Oh, the newspapers said this, some people said that, and you were supposed to have said thus and so," he said airily.

"If you will tell me what I am supposed to have said, I'll tell you if I did say it," I offered.

He said nothing.

"It was just too silly for words the way Kelly and Hague acted," I went on. "Kelly acted as if he were running a ward caucus. The performance of 'the voice of the sewers' was beyond all decency."

I then told him a story relayed to me by a newspaperman, that after the vice-presidential nomination, Hague was asking what kind of a fellow Wallace was. Hague said he did not know him very well. He urged this particular friend of Wallace's to get word to Henry that he should have some practical political advice and the best place to get it would be from Kelly and Hague.

"Frank is muscling right in as usual," he laughed.

"I want you to know that I feel deeply there was no justification for the pressure that was used to bring those Massachusetts votes to you from me," I said solemnly. "They were pledged to me in good faith and I should have had them. It's a little thing, maybe, but I want you to know how I feel."

"I didn't know about it."

"Mr. President, you did know about it because I talked with you about it over the phone," I said. "I told you what Hopkins and the others were doing, and you told me you would take steps to stop it. I didn't ask a living soul to vote for me in Chicago, despite the advice of some of my friends. I didn't permit the New York delegation to be polled, although pressure was exerted on the New York delegates to be polled. Frankly, I think the pressure was unfair. I didn't want to embarrass anyone. But the fact is, I had been strongly urged to call for a showdown and resisted the pressure. My position was difficult, but I did the best I could. And I wouldn't stoop to the level of some of the other fellows working for you because it wasn't worth it."

He said nothing one way or the other about this complaint.

"Jim, I've told the family I want them to vote for me, but I also told them I wanted them to pray I will be defeated," he said with the air of one imparting a great secret, and then he grinned impishly.

"That is the best thing that could happen to you," I said seriously. "And I'm not certain it won't happen. If anyone considers this one a walkover, he is crazy."

"I am not going to do any campaigning, Jim, except over the radio. I don't propose to mention Willkie's name."

"You won't have to," I put in. "Ickes and the others will take care of him."

He nodded.

"Frankly, Mr. President," I said, bringing up his statement to the convention, "I don't think your statement was a good one; I don't think you were frank enough. I think you would have been better off if you said you were against a third term, but a situation had been created under which everyone else had been eliminated and there was nothing else you could do but accept. I would have admitted responsibility and given the reasons why I did not come out before, if I had been you."

"A situation could have been created which might have made me decline the nomination," he said. "That's why the statement was issued the way it was. It left me a loophole to get out if a situation developed where I did not have to accept the nomination, and I really didn't want it, Jim."

"That may have been so from your point of view," I argued, "but I think you would have been better off from the point of view of the public if you had been more frank and had the statement issued along the lines I suggested. It would not have affected the delegates because they were for you, but the public would have accepted it in a better light. As it was, I think it had a bad effect for you. It's just an honest criticism on my part and I'm not going to tell you anything at any time that I don't think is right."

I could see from the way he reacted that he didn't like what I was saying, although he expressed no resentment. He went back to the party chairmanship, showing clearly the whole purpose of the interview was to get me to remain. Apparently it had dawned on the third termers that I had some influence with the party organization and that it had been increased by my conduct at Chicago.

"In this connection," I resumed, "I want to tell you that when the national committee met last January to select the convention site, I was apprehensive about the way Kelly would act. You will recall that it was you who wanted Chicago. For your information, Mr. President, I had about twelve proxies in my pocket I could have voted. They would have swung the convention to Philadelphia. I did not use them because I did not want to be placed in the position of fighting you."

"The reason I wanted Chicago, Jim, was that I was afraid criticism might follow the selection of Philadelphia because of the Guffey–Lawrence fight for state control."

"I don't know what your reasons were, but I was fearful of the thing which did happen in Chicago, and I want you to know how I feel about it."

I rose to go.

"Jim," he said, "you'll go down to the national committee meeting Thursday noon, won't you?"

"I'll be glad to."

"And, Jim, you'll sleep on your decision to leave?"

"I will, but it's a closed case as far as I'm concerned."

In the car, riding back to the Post Office Department alone, I was struck by a sudden thought: I wondered whether he wanted anyone in the party to succeed him as President, someone who might be successful and might clear up some of the disturbing problems, causing his record to suffer by comparison.

I went back to New York that night but could not escape the application of presidential pressure to keep me in as chairman. On Monday, July 29, Frank Walker called, urging me to reconsider. He said he would not take the post under any circumstances. In the afternoon Edward J. Flynn came into my office at the Biltmore and pulled up a chair. He asked me to lay my cards on the table on the New York vote.

"Well, Ed, to make a long story short, I expected more votes and I was entitled to more votes," I said. "I sent Vince with a message to you fellows, saying I was not asking anyone to vote for me; that I would be as pleased with 40 votes as I would with 94. And you should have let me have them."

"That was so," Flynn acknowledged, "but for some reason or other Joe Boyle insisted on a poll of the delegation. Under the circumstances Lehman wouldn't go along so. . . ."

Flynn shrugged his shoulders and threw open his hands.

"I might have been told," I complained.

"Yes, but you know how those things are."

CHAPTER THIRTY-ONE

MRS. ROOSEVELT PLEADS

THAT AFTERNOON I received a telegram from Mrs. Roosevelt, which read: "Can you meet me for luncheon tomorrow, Tuesday (July 30, 1940) Biltmore 12:30." We met in the lobby of the hotel and went to the roof. Neither of us was much interested in the menu or the pleasant dining room.

After a few commonplaces, she turned to me with, "I'm not much for beating around the bush, especially with you. Isn't there some way you could remain as national chairman and arrange for someone else to run the campaign?"

I started in to speak but she checked me with an admonishing finger.

"Hear me out, Jim. I know your private situation and I'm asking that you let your name remain—that you merely be nominal chairman of the committee. I am going to be terribly frank with you, Jim, and I know you'll understand. The simple fact is you have a better hold than anyone else has on the leaders, including the great rank and file of party workers, a better hold than, possibly, Franklin. You have been a great help to the party leaders—big and little. They all know you. They all have a high regard for you. Your influence with them is very great. I know the high affection in which you are held throughout the country. I have followed you into many of the communities you have visited. In every single one people are enthusiastic over you. They regard you as a friend, almost at sight. It means a great deal to have close contact between headquarters on the one hand and the party leaders and workers in the field on the other. You could assure this, and if you do, it would certainly be for the best interests of the party, and everyone would appreciate it."

"I am going to return frankness with frankness, Mrs. Roosevelt," I began. "I have made up my mind, and that's the long and short of it. In my own mind I am convinced that it would not be fair to myself

313

to change my decision now and it would not be fair to the party."

I looked at her earnestly as I resumed:

"And I'm going to tell you more than that. I think you are entitled to know it. For some time, for some reason, I don't understand . . . I know I'm not making myself clear, but the gist of it is that I feel that the President has lost confidence in me; and to be very frank, I have lost confidence in him. He has failed for a long time to consult with me in the way I believe he should consult with me. In view of that lack of confidence, for want of a better term, I could not change my course of action."

"I've felt there was something wrong," she hesitated. "I felt myself there was something wrong in the situation, but I wasn't sure about it. I wasn't sure because there was no reason for the existence of such a situation."

"Well, there it is," I said. "Naturally, it is disappointing to me that the President did not have, or rather, showed a lack of, confidence in me. This is especially hard to take, in view of the fact that down through the years I have given him the best of everything I have. You mentioned my travels; I have been in 1,500 communities in this country. In each and every one of them I have tried my hardest to say and to do that which would reflect credit to his administration."

"I know, I know," she nodded.

"I don't know whether you know it or not, but the President never discussed his candidacy with me until that Sunday I saw him at Hyde Park," I said.

"I never knew it either, believe me, until that afternoon," she cut in. "After you left, Franklin told me that he assumed he would have to run."

"What did he say of me?" I asked, but before she could answer, I went on, "I have no right to ask that, so let's skip it. That's neither here nor there, and besides I have a good idea. What I'd rather know is, what do you think of the third term?"

"Dead in the room, as you say," she looked up and laughed. I had to join in. "I don't know why anyone would want to be President during the next four years. However, inasmuch as Franklin wants to take the responsibility, and the decision is all his, it is my duty as a wife to try to see him reelected. There is simply nothing else I can do."

She sighed. I gathered that deep down in her heart she felt he and the family would be better off if they did not have a campaign ahead; at least she felt that way at that particular moment.

I told her that I felt, truthfully, that if she had not come to Chicago, the President would not have been able to get Wallace; that the convention would have named Jones.

"It was a mistake for the President to send Hopkins out to Chicago and set him up as third term consultant," I said.

"Franklin insists that he didn't send him there for that purpose," she interposed.

"Mrs. Roosevelt, let's keep this conversation on a reasonable basis," I said. "Everything at Chicago was directed by Hopkins. It would be ridiculous to maintain he did that on his own and without, let us say, White House knowledge. I told the President he could count on me to see to it that everything was done properly; but I had very few calls from him during the entire time I was in Chicago."

"I've always consulted with you, Jim."

"That's so," I acknowledged.

"And I've always held you in high regard and respect," she said. "Undoubtedly you're the most popular man in the party, Jim. If you don't associate yourself with the campaign, it will be construed as a break with Franklin."

"I'm sorry, but if that viewpoint should prevail, well, it will just have to prevail, that's all. There is nothing I can do; there is no point in pressing the subject further. What I did in Chicago was not easy, and I did it the hard way."

"I'm sorry, more sorry than you know, but I understand how you feel," she said. "By the way, you will be receiving a letter from Franklin's mother about giving up the management of his campaign. She doesn't like the idea and is going to tell you so. You must brace yourself for a letter telling you what she thinks; the old lady does not understand anyone refusing a request from the Roosevelts."

The letter came the next day from Hyde Park. It read:

Dear Mr. Farley:

I think I wrote you to thank you for your kind letter after my sister died.

Now I want to tell you that I *do hope you* will manage my son's campaign. I have such confidence in you!

Ever sincerely,
Sara Roosevelt

I replied August 3, after Flynn had been named my successor. I wrote:

Dear Mrs. Roosevelt:

Thank you very much for your kind letter of July 30.

As you have noted in the newspapers, our friend Ed Flynn has agreed to take over the Chairmanship; and I am sure he will carry on in an eminently satisfactory manner. The President fully understands my position, Mrs. Roosevelt, and I am sure when you discuss it with him, you will understand it too.

It was indeed nice of you to write such a friendly note, and I shall always be grateful to you.

James A. Farley

The question of my nomination came up, when Mrs. Roosevelt and I were discussing Garner and Hull.

"I don't think Garner would have made a good candidate," Mrs. Roosevelt said, "because of the difference in his viewpoint. But I would be happy to support you for any office; you would make a good President. Of course, I realize that the Catholic issue would be a problem; but if anyone could overcome that, you are the man. You are so well and favorably known."

"I want you to understand I had no serious ambitions for the Presidency at the convention," I said. "If I had had sufficient votes in the convention for the nomination, I would have been for Hull and would have been happy with the vice-presidential nomination. I believe in letting men come up in the party and would have taken my chances at top billing later.

"Honestly, my first concern was for my country, and my party came second; and I was determined not to be swayed by any feeling against me to the detriment of my country. Anyone who knows me knows that. I have received nearly six thousand messages from all over the country from people sympathetic with my stand at Chicago; and I would be less than honest not to acknowledge I am flattered by such an expression of confidence. This makes it all the more difficult for me to understand the President's lack of confidence and the things that went on at Chicago."

"Jim, I'm going to tell you something I have discussed with no one but Franklin," she said. "Harry Hopkins has complained to Franklin that he didn't like the way I talked to him at Chicago. You will remember I went directly to the Stevens with you and then to the convention hall, so that I didn't see him. From the Stadium I went directly to the airport.

"He called me at the airport, to say how sorry he was that he did not get to see me. I told him that I was sorry I didn't get to see him because there were some things I wanted to talk to him about—that some things were going on that were not right. He said he realized that some things had happened of which he did not approve, but he hoped no one was hurt about it. I told him quite frankly I did not think he had political judgment and that he had helped create an unfavorable situation."

She accompanied me downstairs, looking for Charley Michelson, who, it developed, had returned to Washington. She told me she didn't think the President would make an extensive campaign; that his electioneering would be done by radio and short trips. I agreed, adding that I thought the campaign would be unorthodox in a great many respects and there might be a very close fight in key states.

I summed it up: "It all depends on the way Willkie handles himself."

CHAPTER THIRTY-TWO

MY LAST CABINET MEETING

THURSDAY, AUGUST 1, 1940, I came down to Washington for the meeting of the committee which had been named to pick my successor as chairman of the Democratic National Committee, as I promised the President I would. Members of this committee were Flynn of New York, David Fitzgerald of Connecticut, W. W. Howes of South Dakota, Mrs. Mildred Jaster of Ohio, and Miss Beatrice Cobb of North Carolina. Others present were the President, Wallace, and myself. We took chairs around his desk.

"You all know," he started off, as "Pa" Watson closed the door to the reception room, "there is an unusual situation existing in the country today as a result of the war in Europe. This makes it highly important that there be unity in the country and in the party. During the seven and a half years I have been in office, the Democratic party has made a great record as a party. That has been due in a large measure to the splendid record Jim Farley has made as national chairman.

"Everybody feels this. Henry and I have talked it over several times. Of course, we will talk with Jim about it. I know how Jim feels about his financial situation, and he is perfectly justified in wanting to take care of himself. But, and a great big but it is, we all feel it would not be the same if he does not take the chairmanship. In view of the world and national situation, he should be willing to carry on until the campaign is over; and if not that, he should at least act with the committee in an advisory capacity, giving them as much time as he can, in order that the committee may be benefited by his efforts."

The President was in his best form. He was charming, disarming, persuasive, and intimate. His smile flashed on all, but the warmest smiles were directed at me. Wallace was seated at his left hand. I was to the left of Wallace; then came Fitzgerald, Howes, Mrs. Jaster, Miss Cobb, and Flynn. I'm afraid I was a bit wooden because I knew I was being given the works, as he frequently termed his persuasive best. He went on:

"Sentiment has developed in every section of the country for you to retain the chairmanship. From every state—north, east, and west—and also from the South. Everybody appreciates what you have done for the party. Everybody in the party knows you, Jim. And to know you is to love you. Your efforts have been appreciated by the rank and file and by the Committee as well. Why, 'Jim Farley' is practically a household expression. The party expects you to do your duty, Jim. The party needs you. The success of the party in the coming election and campaign would be assured with you at the helm, Jim."

Dave Fitzgerald told me afterward that during this final plea the President kept looking at me almost beseechingly. I purposely looked away because I was fearful that I might show some of the resentment within me, with the result that I would be thrown off my stride. I was frankly annoyed at the appeal. I regarded it for what it was—an act. This was the only time he had acknowledged my services since 1930, and then acknowledgment came only because he wanted to persuade me to his will. I am sure that he did not like this scene, that he did not like to have his importuning witnessed. It would have been all right had he won, so that he could have tossed the pleading off with a wise-crack about his power of persuasion. When he didn't win, he was humiliated. His pleading and the conduct toward me at Chicago and in the two years before did not jibe. It was too late for him to seek to recruit me aboard what he liked to term "a happy ship."

Wallace followed with a plea of his own, based on national unity. He recalled a conversation with Mrs. Farley some months before in which he told her any feeling she or I might have regarding my continuing in politics should be transcended by the situation in the country and in the world. He insisted that for that reason I should carry on.

Howes said it was essential for party victory that I carry on. Mrs. Jaster said Democrats are naturally interested in Democratic success; therefore, it was important that I continue. I said nothing.

"Jim, if you don't continue in the campaign, the impression will be created by newspaper columnists and by newspapers opposed to the administration that there is a break, and that would have its effect, a harmful effect," the President resumed.

"I am not responsible for the articles the newspapers write about you or me or anybody else," I broke in. "I certainly cannot dictate their policies and I should not be held responsible for what they say or do."

"But, Jim, your silence might give credence to the reports that have been and will continue to be circulated," he said gently. "You're silent now."

"All right, you have asked for it," I began. "I took a definite position in Chicago. I have a definite position now before the country. I took that course honestly and sincerely, and I followed it as graciously as I knew how. During the convention and since, I have tried to conduct myself as a gentleman should and as a loyal Democrat. For thirty-one years I have been interested in the success of the Democratic party, because whatever position I hold now in the party and in the eyes of the country was made possible by the Democratic party. Therefore, no one—*no one*—has any right to question my desire to see the party successful. There is no reason why anyone should make a statement regarding my activity in the campaign. All you have to do is be patient with me and let me carry on in my own way. The fact that I am willing to take care of the New York State chairmanship should be sufficient evidence of my regard and affection for the party. I am not a fifth columnist. My record down through the years ought to be ample evidence to the country concerning my party. No one should dictate what I do or say."

I told them everyone assembled must understand full well that I occupied a position of my own, in my own right, before the country and I certainly had a right to protect that position. Wallace took exception to the last statement, insisting my party obligations ranked highest. I might have slapped him down as a Johnny-come-lately who had no right to preach to me, but that would have been mean and petty.

"I certainly have the right to do what I think is proper from my own point of view, regardless of party," I emphasized. "No one has a right to complain about my services to the party. For eight years I have given freely of my services and ability, working from early morning into late night, and on Sundays and holidays. I liked to do that. In any position I ever held I tried to perform faithfully and well, because I get a great deal out of a job well done. There's personal pleasure and satisfaction in doing that. Everyone who ever knew anything about me knows that."

"I'm afraid that Willkie's election would be a terrible thing for the country, because of the influence of those who will be around him," Wallace said. "That same group in the old Republican days were responsible for the death of my father."

"That might be true, from your viewpoint, Henry," I said, regarding his statement as a most unusual one, "but, by the same token, many people feel that the reputed influence of Hopkins and others is bad."

The friendliness in the President's eyes died.

"I am glad you used the word 'reputed,'" he snapped.

"I never said Hopkins had any influence with you, but that doesn't take away from the fact that many people in the country do consider there is such an influence and, very frankly, it has a bad effect on the nation," I told him. "I don't like to say it, but it is an honest statement in answer to Henry's argument about Willkie."

"I would hate to see Willkie President," he switched the subject. "You know, all the time I have been Governor and President I never called out the National Guard or troops to suppress strikes or disturbances of any character. I didn't do it in the strike at Flint, Michigan, several years ago. I'm afraid that, should like circumstances arise in the future, Willkie would do just that."

"Willkie might be forced into that position whether he wanted to be or not," Wallace put in.

"Generally speaking, I got along pretty well with Congress and I don't know whether Willkie would," the President ignored the interruption. "I'm afraid Willkie would have trouble with Congress."

"You've had your troubles with Congress, too," I quipped.

"No, I haven't." He was plainly annoyed.

"I was just kidding!"

"It's too important a thing to be kidding about," he grumbled. "While Congress has disagreed with me about some questions, I have been on friendly terms with members on both sides. With a few exceptions, I have probably been on friendlier terms than any other Democratic President has been. The Democratic party has been successful in every election since 1932, which is a greater string of victories, I guess, than the party has had since Jackson's time."

Fitzgerald, about this time, said he understood my position full well; that he had talked to me in Chicago; that he had urged me to carry on; that no one wanted me to carry on more than himself; but that he considered it unfair to press me to carry on in view of the position I had taken.

"We could go on talking here for hours about the necessity of my carrying on, but we just aren't going to get anywhere," I continued. "I appreciate the confidence expressed in me. You have not been alone in that expression. Many Senators, Congressmen, leaders, and others have asked me to continue. I have told one and all, as I have told you, that I have made my decision. You could talk for days and not change my mind. You have to permit me to handle this situation in my own way. Any effort to force me to do what I do not want to do, or to force me to say anything I do not want to say, or to have someone speak for me, will not be met favorably by me. You will just have to adjust your minds to my position."

Flynn spoke for the first time. The meeting had been going on for fifty minutes.

"We all know Jim Farley well enough to know that when he says it is definite, we should not under any circumstances press him to say or do anything he does not want to," he said.

"We have talked this possibility over," Roosevelt said. His eyes no longer searched for mine. He looked at the ceiling, down at the floor, or on his desk. "We hoped that Jim would accept. Of course, there is no use talking about trying to find someone who will do the job as well as Jim has for the last eight years. We just won't be able to find anyone in his class, or two or three classes below. In view of the fact that Jim won't accept, we feel an Irish-American should be elected to succeed him. In view of the circumstances, we think Ed Flynn is the fellow to do it. Ed doesn't want to assume the responsibility, but we think it is the best thing to do."

I thought this was a rather derogatory introduction for Flynn, even though I was aware that the President was trying to build me up as an indispensable man, in a limited field, of course. He was flattering me and appealing to my vanity.

"Mr. President, I'm delighted with the appointment," I said. "I'm glad Ed decided to take it. That solves your problem."

"I guess I'm an easy mark," Flynn muttered.

I shook hands with Flynn, remarking, "I don't know whether to congratulate you or to commiserate with you."

"My wife will kill me for this," he said ruefully.

We all joined in the laugh that this remark occasioned.

Even now I find it rather difficult to describe the atmosphere for the split second following the naming of Flynn; I am certain the announcement was a surprise to everybody except Flynn. It was evident he and the President had decided before the meeting in the event that the final effort to land me failed. Flynn made a few remarks. He said he realized more than anyone else that it would be a difficult job to follow in my footsteps, but he would exert every energy toward another Democratic victory. Despite his claims over the years that he disliked the limelight, I felt he was rather glad to step in to take his share of honor and glory, as most of us are.

The meeting broke up almost immediately.

The next few days were busy ones for me. After a series of conferences with Robert W. Woodruff, president of the Coca-Cola Company, I decided to throw in my lot with that corporation, a decision which I have never regretted. If I pass it by lightly, it is because I regard the relationship as an intimate part of my personal life and, however important to me, not a part of the story of the politics of the day. I was also busy with the state campaign, spending hours in headquarters with Dailey and others. I was on the phone and writing letters as much as ever.

My most important letter of this period was written August 7, 1940. It was my letter of resignation from the Cabinet. This letter was, perhaps, longer than it should have been, as it was not an easy letter to write in view of the political situation. I reviewed my accomplishments as administrator of the Post Office Department, commended my associates, nodded to chairmen on the Congressional post offices and post roads committees, and concluded with the traditionally formal expressions of regret.

"I want you to know how much I appreciate the honor you conferred upon me and the trust you placed in me when you appointed me to this important position in your Cabinet when you took office on March 4, 1933," I wrote in the second paragraph. I closed with, "Again expressing my deepest gratitude at the opportunity you afforded me to serve as a member of your Cabinet, and with kindest personal regards, I am faithfully yours," and I scrawled my name in familiar green ink.

The letter of acceptance was one of the President's best efforts; every line was calculated to show there was no break. It read:

DEAR JIM:

I accept, with real regret, your resignation as Postmaster General, to become effective at the close of business on Aug. 31.

First of all, I want to tell you of my own sincere sorrow that we are losing you as a member of the official family. At the same time, as I have told you, I fully understand and appreciate the personal reasons which recall you to private business after all these unselfish years in the public service. I congratulate you on your new work and send you every wish that it may, in every way, be successful.

Under your administration the Post Office Department of the United States has made great strides in business efficiency, in service to the public, and in the outstanding morale of its more than 300,000 employes. That the post office service is on a completely self-sustaining basis with respect to that part that is rendered to the public for hire is in itself a real tribute to you and your associates.

All of us in the administration will miss you deeply; we count on seeing you often. I especially count on this after all of our years of close personal association. Our friendship will always continue.

I need not tell you that you have always my affectionate regards.

Faithfully yours,
FRANKLIN D. ROOSEVELT

A few days later Jesse Jones's appointment as Secretary of Commerce was announced. I phoned him congratulations, remarking that Roosevelt had evidently decided Jones could come in if Farley was going out, but that we couldn't be around together. He thought I had it about right.

Near the end of the month I received an invitation to lunch with the President at the White House before what was to be my last Cabinet meeting. I left on the nine-fifteen train for the Capital and dictated all the way down, clearing up a mass of correspondence. I said good-by to General Edwin M. Watson, the President's appointment secretary; Rudolph Forster, executive clerk; John Latta, his assistant; and my good friend, press secretary Early.

At this meeting I said I had a few requests to make. "Anything you want," he promised. I said I was interested in protecting three men on my office payroll. I said I was particularly interested in protecting Ambrose O'Connell in his position as First Assistant Postmaster General. He inquired after Ambrose's health, and I told him Ambrose, who had been laid up for weeks, was making satisfactory progress. I also asked him to do the same for Bill Bray, who had been my secretary and was now special assistant to the Postmaster General. I also spoke about my desire to have an executive order issued bringing Harold Ambrose, chief press relations officer of the Post Office Department, in under civil service. All these things were done promptly.

I said there was no one else I had a deep personal interest in except Eddie Roddan of the Democratic Committee. I had already spoken to Flynn about Eddie, I said, and had his promise to watch out for him. I remarked on what a good job Eddie had done with the "Battle Page," the campaign material supplied by Republicans and Democrats in the *New York Daily News* in 1936 and said he was preparing to do a better one in the coming campaign. Jokingly, I reported Eddie was worried that Willkie wouldn't give him the competition Landon had. The President laughed.

"And now," he said gleefully, "I have news for you—splendid news. I am going to send Frank Walker's name to the Senate next week as Postmaster General."

"That makes me very happy," I said. "Frank will be satisfactory to the organization as set up, and will not disturb it when he moves in."

"By the way, I am very glad about your connection with Coca-Cola."

"Thanks."

He asked about the situation in New England. I said at present it appeared bad, except for Massachusetts, but the difficulties might be worked out. He asked what was being done in New York about the electors of the American Labor Party, and I told him they would go along with the Democratic electors.

"Mr. President," I said, "I want to ask a pointed question."

"Shoot," he invited.

"What happened to Louis Johnson on the job of Secretary of War?"

"Oh," he answered brightly, "Louis talked too much. By the way, what did you think of my appointment of Jesse?"

"It was a good appointment. You must recall that I tried to sell you Jesse before you appointed Hopkins and you asked me, 'Why put Jesse Jones in the Cabinet and build him up as a presidential possibility?' It's apparent to me now you consider Jesse too old for 1944, or you have not made up your mind what to do then."

He looked at me quickly, laughed, but made no comment.

"I don't think Wallace will help much in the sugar beet country; you ought to keep him out of there," I said. "And if you have any more speeches by Ickes attacking Tammany Hall, they certainly ought to make the country safe for Willkie."

He knew I was kidding but that there was a vein of truth near the surface of the jokes. He made no comment, but asked what I thought of the appointment of Mayor Fiorello La Guardia of New York to the Joint Canadian–American Defense Commission, saying he thought it was a good one. I wanted to say, "It was good politics," but never let that one pass the tip of my tongue.

Here he remarked Joe Guffey was coming in shortly and he wanted me to stay until the Senator left.

"I ought not to be around," I laughed, "because Joe might want to talk something political."

"I think Joe wants to talk about removing the WPA administrator in Pennsylvania, some retired army officer," he said.

"This is no time to be removing WPA administrators."

"Don't I know it?" he laughed.

Guffey was announced. He came ponderously to a chair.

"Come in, Joe, come in," the President invited. "Look who we have with us. Don't pay any attention to him; he's just an innocent bystander."

He enjoyed this joshing immensely. They discussed the President's impending visit to Pennsylvania. Joe left a suggested itinerary for the "defense inspection" jaunt.

"What I want to know is," Guffey said turning to me, "who do I consult on political matters, now that you are leaving Washington?"

"Talk with Frank Walker, Joe," the President answered for me. "He's going to succeed Jim. Don't tell anyone, though, because it's a deep secret!"

When I got back to my office in the department, the big secret was already on the news ticker. The night may have a thousand eyes, as the poet said, but Washington has an ear to every keyhole.

After Guffey left, the President talked about the war situation.

"The British seem to be in a better position now. They are holding on all right. If they can get by the next month or so, they will find a great ally in the weather. They should hold on through the winter. Food is the problem. I think Europe might get through this winter, as far as food is concerned; but I don't think they can get by next winter."

From luncheon we went into the Cabinet meeting.

"Everyone knows how sorry I am Jim is leaving the Cabinet and the administration," Roosevelt said. "Everyone is sorry with me. You have made such a valuable contribution to my success, Jim, that I'm holding this chair for you to come back to again, after you make your first million."

"I'd be satisfied with a half million," I interposed, but did not say I'd come back to the chair. "I'm afraid, though, they are already beginning to sabotage my job a little bit, because right opposite me on the Cabinet table there are some matches advertising another soft drink."

Everybody craned their necks to look at the matches. There was a general laugh.

"Don't you just love it?" the President chuckled.

"Seriously," I continued, "I, too, am sorry to leave the Cabinet, but there must be an end to everything."

I shook hands all around before I left. Secretary of War Stimson told me how happy he was to meet me and know me for even so short a period. Quite candidly, he told me he thought I was a terrible person, for a long, long while; then he came to Washington, observed me, and changed his mind. I told him I was glad he put it that way and added that a great many people had said the same thing. When I first came on the Washington scene, many persons throughout the country regarded me as a Tammany Hall politician, in the worst sense of the word, which I was not. It flattered my vanity to have people tell me they had changed their minds about me, because I regarded that as evidence I was growing in stature.

Frances Perkins, who was always friendly to me and loyal to the President, was rather emotional in her farewell. She said she felt that Cordell Hull and I had saved many a situation in Cabinet meetings during the seven and a half years I was in the body; that the people of the country never realized the contribution I had made. She said the other members of the Cabinet felt exactly as she did. The place would not be the same without me, she concluded. I thanked her. It was no little tribute coming from a misunderstood and unappreciated woman, who had made no little contribution herself, even if one were to count nothing but the blows she took for others.

Just before I left I said good-by to the President.

"Take care of things in my absence," I said. "And protect my interests."

"It's not good-by, Jim, because I want you to see me whenever you pass through the city," he said. "Give my regards to Bess."

We shook hands.

I carried his words to Bess the next day.

The remaining few days were spent in farewells. My office was like a telephone booth in Grand Central Station; no sooner did one caller leave than another took his place. Most of them came just for a handshake and a good-by. Some, like Bascom Timmons, remained for a few minutes at my insistence. In his case we talked about the Vice President, because he was probably the closest man to Garner in the capital. I told him that Jack would be subject to considerable criticism if he did not return. Timmons agreed, but said Garner was so angry with the President, he didn't want to come back to meet him face to face at Cabinet meetings.

I had lunch with Speaker Bankhead, who was still very annoyed with what had happened in Chicago; and he was fearful of what might happen to the party in November. I tried to quiet him by saying that what had happened at Chicago had happened and nothing could be done about it, and, as for what was coming, the worst had never happened yet.

"Jim, there was never such downright perfidy in political history since Reconstruction," he said. "I never saw any good in Reconstruction and I guess I'm still unreconstructed, an unreconstructed Democrat, born and bred and not far from the grave. Why, Jim, do you know they gave me the green light?"

"They gave it to Louis Johnson," I smiled. "But they turned it red at the next corner."

"They didn't wait for me to turn the corner," he stormed. "This is the way it was, Jim. I wanted my name placed in nomination for the Presidency. I didn't expect anything to come of it, but I wanted that honor before I died. I've been going to conventions for years, voting for men who have done less for the party and less for the country. People out of Nebraska and people out of New York. No reflection intended against you, Jim; you act more like you came from Alabama.

"Well, Hopkins and Steagall and Lister Hell, I mean Hill, talked me out of submitting my name so the delegation could go for Roosevelt. In turn, they pledged me their word that they wouldn't interfere with me for Vice President. I meant to submit my name for Vice President. I never trusted Hopkins much, but Steagall and Hill were Southerners and from my own state, and I expected they would make a reasonable effort to keep their words. There was no question that an understanding was reached and solemn pledges exchanged.

"The next thing I knew the President was calling to ask me to stand aside for Wallace. Now Roosevelt wasn't a party to the agreement, but his men had made it, and I felt it was binding. I told him so. I told him I would present my name, because I figured he had broken his word.

"Then they called John (Senator Bankhead, his brother) and tried to get him to get me to vote for Wallace. Jimmy Byrnes did that. John MacCormack promised to vote for me and ran out. So did Sam Rayburn, who worked for Wallace.

"I don't care for myself, but I wanted a Democrat for Vice President, especially since I wasn't sure we have one for President."

That afternoon I said farewell to the Post Office employees. I shook hands with some 1,100 who filed by. I had a word of thanks for each and was glad to have had the opportunity of delivering it.

Saturday morning I went over to the State Department, wandered through its aisles of shutter-like doors and into Hull's office on the south side of that ornate granite structure. He was in excellent fettle after a vacation at White Sulphur Springs.

"Looks like you're getting out, Jim," he approached my situation cagily. "Don't know that I'll be around long myself; might not be here much longer than the end of this administration, along about next January."

"That's your decision and I don't give advice unless it's asked for," I said. "I just called to pay my respects, and to say that one of the greatest pleasures in my stay in Washington was that I got to know you so intimately and well. I am going to miss you more than anyone, and I say that from the bottom of my heart."

"That's mighty fine, Jim," he said. "You know my regard for you and it's nice to have it reciprocated."

"You're the one I would like to see running in November. I have told everyone that, including the President, as you know. I say that not only because I like you personally, but for the good of the party and the good of the country."

"Thank you," he said simply. "I haven't any burning desire to be President, although I am grateful. Some people seem to think I had such desires. Since the Gallup poll showed me stronger than he is (he looked significantly in the direction of the White House), every effort has been made to destroy me. I don't understand it. If they destroy me, they destroy part of themselves, part of the country's position before the world.

"Now that it's all over, I think I was treated unfairly by that fellow in his not letting my name go before the convention or in giving me an opportunity to have my name go before the convention. That is not so bad, however, because, as I say, I have no desire to be President. I do think I have been treated unfairly in that I have received no recognition for what I have done as Secretary of State in a most trying and most vital period of this country's history. At all times I have tried to be helpful. I have been helpful at every turn. Not one word of commendation has come my way. I've talked it over at home a lot."

"What about the Vice Presidency?" I asked.

"Oh, that," he leaned back in his chair and smiled. "He tried everything he could think of to get me to take it. He argued and smiled. Then he smiled and argued. I said, 'No, by God!' and 'By God, no!' and that's all there was to it. I felt he was trying to kick me upstairs. I'd rather go."

"Who can he put in your place, Cordell?" I asked.

"I have no idea," he replied. "He can get awful set and stubborn. I don't know whether he would name Sumner or not. I'm not going to worry about it. I am going to spend spring, summer, and fall in Tennessee and winters in Florida."

"He'll be after you to take another term, and I would be if I were in his shoes and reelected, of course," I said.

"I've got some reading I'd like to do and I'd like to write my memoirs," he said.

"Well, don't forget to mention that I still think Hull and Farley would have made a great ticket and could have won hands down," I said.

I took the two o'clock train to New York City.

CHAPTER THIRTY-THREE

THIRD TERM ELECTION

I DID NOT return to Washington for a month. On my arrival I put in a call to Garner.

"My name's Farley," I said when I had him on the phone. "I used to be in politics."

"Well, I guess I'm in the has-been class myself but don't know it," he countered. "But then, I never was as smart as you, Jim. You're one fellow who has grown more in public life than anybody I have ever known and that takes in a lot of years, boy."

"Well, don't let them get you down," I advised.

"I ain't, Jim," he said. "I'm going to live to be ninety-three. I'll live to pass judgment on a lot of these fellows around here."

"Why ninety-three?" I asked. "Why not a hundred?"

"Oh, Bascom Timmons and I picked it out, liked the sound of it."

I asked if I could see him and he told me he was going home that night.

"Can't stand this third term business, Jim," he said. "I don't want to be around for the inaugural—it would be too depressing. And I'm afraid for the President; I don't know how he'll carry on if he gets it. I'm sure I won't like the way he'll carry on."

"Don't be bitter," I cautioned.

"Me bitter?" he snorted. "A dozen years ago I gave up hating. I tried to go to bed every night without hating anybody or envying anybody. And I found I got rid of worries. Never had any since. Nearest I ever come to breaking it was when I got in an argument with the Boss on sit-down strikes. Ain't going to argue with him or anyone else. Wouldn't get much chance to argue with him, anyway. He hasn't said anything to me since I got back from Uvalde."

"That's difficult to believe," I said. "If you hadn't told me, I wouldn't believe it."

"It's difficult for me, too, Jim. It's so small," he said. "But there it is. I'm disappointed in the Boss over it. I am disappointed in the way Jimmy Byrnes and some others have acted, but I'm not mad. I'm going home to hunt and fish. Might be fishing when Election Day rolls around, but I guess I'll vote."

"I'm going to vote the ticket, John," I explained. "I owe it to the party. But I won't make any speeches."

Later I talked to Jesse Jones, who confirmed the story of the ignoring of Garner at Cabinet meetings. At the last Cabinet meeting, Jones said, Garner rushed to the head of the table, seized the President's hand and said, "Good-by, Boss. I congratulate you in advance. I am going home and, after I vote, I am going out to the bush and am going hunting."

In all this period I continued to get letters praising me for my position or taxing me for my failure to stump for the President. Disturbing reports were coming in from party leaders throughout the country. Most of the leaders were gloomy because they were being ignored by the third termers and felt that the ticket was being injured through nonrecognition of the party machinery.

On October 15, former Governor James M. Cox called me to tell of his visit with the President at Hyde Park. He said the President said I was sore and asked that Cox talk to me, which Cox said he would not do. Cox described the President as worried about the outlook and particularly worried about what deflection would result from what he termed the Farley break. I said that things were in a bad way west of the Mississippi and also said there was a shift in Willkie's favor, but could not say whether it would be sufficiently strong to carry him in. I noted Willkie was smoking the President out into the campaign, which the latter had had no intention of entering. I said New York was safe; that I knew that for certain.

On October 22, I issued the statement on which I had long deliberated. I said:

Thirty-one years ago I was elected Chairman of the Democratic town committee in Stony Point, Rockland County, New York, and down through the years I have served as chairman of my county committee, chairman of my state committee, and I am still serving as Chairman of the Democratic State Committee of New York.

It was my great honor to serve as Chairman of the Democratic National Committee during the two great campaigns of 1932 and 1936. I deeply appreciate the honors that have been paid me by my party and I shall ever be grateful for the loyalty and devotion I have always received during my years of party activities.

During the period outlined above I have preached party loyalty and pleaded for the success of my party. I did that because I sincerely believe in the Democratic party, in its principles and objectives.

At the national convention of the Democratic party in Chicago—at which I was a candidate for the Presidency—after the balloting was over, I pledged my support to the nominees of that Convention. That pledge was made in good faith. I shall vote the straight Democratic ticket on November 5, and I urge the members of my party to do likewise.

It has amazed me that some persons find my course difficult to understand. Most of these would have had me support the Republican candidate. I had made my fight within my party. I had lost that fight. It therefore became incumbent on me to go along with the majority of my party. I might have broken before the convention; but I had no right to do so after participating in the convention, which participation, to my mind, carried the obligation to go along with the convention decision. My party had not declared war on my country, nor had the country declared war on the party. I could not see that my desertion was called for or justifiable.

I spent all my time during the campaign in my office on the fourth floor of the Biltmore Hotel, performing the duties of chairman of the Democratic state committee. I was in daily, indeed continuous, contact with Vincent Dailey, whom I had appointed as campaign manager for upstate for the duration of that campaign. I conferred with, advised, and aided in every way possible, the upstate county leaders, regularly; and they all understood my anxiety that President Roosevelt carry New York State more than just substantially, so that no censure could be directed at me regarding my conduct as state committee chairman.

Throughout the campaign I was consulted by National Chairman Flynn, Mrs. Roosevelt, Miss Mary C. Dewson, and other department heads of the national campaign's activities. Whenever I was called upon to do so I gave the best advice and suggestions I could toward the successful conduct of the campaign.

On Sunday evening, October 28, I received the following wire from the White House:

James A. Farley (Personal Delivery Only)
1040 Fifth Avenue

DEAR JIM: I have been trying to get you since lunch time today. I am delighted you will be at Madison Square Garden tomorrow night and I greatly hope you will join me on train Mott Haven Yard at 8:30 P.M. and drive with me in my car to the Garden and be on the platform with me during my speech. I am looking forward to seeing you.

FRANKLIN D. ROOSEVELT

There was nothing to do but for me to accept, inasmuch as I already planned to go as chairman of the state committee. I called Ed Flynn to tell him I was coming and would bring Vincent Dailey with me. Flynn said he was bringing Tammany leader Christy Sullivan. We reached the yard at the appointed time and went to the dining room of the President's car. He was working at the other end of the car, the *Roald Amundsen*.

"Well, well, well," the President beamed, "here is the first of the four horsemen."

"Yes, and probably the last one," I answered his laugh.

"Glad to see you aboard, Jim." He pulled me down into a chair beside him.

"Jim, I've got a bone to pick with you," he said. "What do you mean by coming to Washington and not coming to see me to discuss what's going on?"

"Mr. President, I'm pretty busy and don't want to bother another busy man," I said.

"I'll forgive you this time, but next time you are there, don't fail to come and see me," he insisted.

I talked about the coming upstate trip, saying a mistake had been made in the Rochester plans, because two streets had been omitted in the tour of the city. I said "Wincent" would see that such things didn't happen; that the trip should be like a fireman's parade—missing nothing. The President said arrangements should be made to take "Wincent" along. This form of the name in referring to Vincent Dailey was a standing joke between us.

Soon it was time to leave for the Garden. The President said he was sorry there wasn't room for "Wincent." With a grin he ordered Flynn into the small seat in front, placed me beside him, and Sullivan beside me.

We did not get a great deal of talking in, as he was busy flashing his smile on the crowd and waving his battered campaign hat. In the quiet stretches of the Bronx I teased him about Ickes, saying I had been advised he was making quite an impression all over the country, especially in the West.

"My God, Jim, they don't want him in lots of places," he said.

"That's surprising to me," I mocked.

"Ha-ha-ha," he jeered. (Here he stopped to wave.) "But we are having trouble with some of the farm audiences. Have to tell you about it later."

"How's your mother?" I asked as he went on. "Please remember me to her."

"Fine, thanks," he said. "I'm trying to keep her at Hyde Park. She is eighty-six years old and will probably live longer than I."

"You should put your hat on or you'll catch cold," I said at another point.

"I like to keep it off," he said lightly.

"Yes, you always did—and in the ring," I said significantly.

He laughed, but not heartily.

We got to the Garden a bit ahead of time. A number of times during the ride he asked me about the opposition of John L. Lewis. He seemed to be worried about the defection of the labor leader. I said I did not think Lewis would sway any real Democrats but that he might have some effect in areas where whole groups do not follow a party line. He nodded.

I never could understand it, but evidently my appearance with the President was a pleasant surprise to the audience. I could see amazement on faces in the press box and a hurried beating of typewriters. Out in the audience I spotted some raised eyebrows.

It was my custom each year, starting with the 1928 campaign, to send a telegram to all of the Democratic workers upstate, a day or so prior to the close of the campaign, making a last minute appeal, urging them on to their greatest efforts on election day in getting every possible vote to the polls for Democratic party nominees. I sent such a wire on November 3, 1940, to approximately eleven thousand party workers in New York State north of the Bronx line. A copy of that wire was carried by all the press associations and appeared on the front page of nearly every daily paper in the United States, morning and afternoon, on November 3. After election I was told by countless party leaders and active Democrats that they believed that wire was extremely beneficial to President Roosevelt throughout the country, as well as in New York State, and helped materially in swelling his majority.

The wire read:

Since 1928 I have been sending last minute messages to the Democratic party workers in New York urging their efforts in behalf of Democratic party nominees. There never was a time during the years that have passed in the campaigns in which we have worked together when I have been more deeply concerned than at the present time for the success of the Democratic ticket in the State of New York. It is of the greatest importance for party success that we keep down the Republican majority upstate to the lowest possible figure to make certain that New York State will be in the Democratic column on election night. I therefore personally urge you to put forth every effort at your command and to work with those associated with you to the end that every possible vote obtainable is brought to the polls on Election Day in support of President Roosevelt and the entire Democratic ticket. This is an extremely urgent and important message and I am sure you will regard it in that light.

JAMES A. FARLEY
Chairman, Democratic State
Committee
Hotel Biltmore, New York, N.Y.

On Election night, when it became evident that he had scored another victory, I called Roosevelt to congratulate him, being truly glad the Democratic party would remain in power. He was in the highest of spirits. We exchanged only a few words. I offered my congratulations and he accepted them with joyous thanks. A few weeks later I wrote as follows:

November 23, 1940.

My Dear Mr. President,

Since talking with you on the telephone election night when I personally extended congratulations on your reelection, I have avoided writing or calling you because I realize how busy you are with the important matters confronting you at the present time.

However, I am writing you now because I want you to know I have a deep and sincere interest in the success of your new administration. In electing you for a third term the American people gave you an unprecedented honor, and I am sure you are determined that they shall never regret it. There were some who used the third-term issue as a convenient front to oppose you and there were some honestly concerned about the breaking of this tradition, and I happened to be in the latter group. Nothing would make me happier than that your accomplishments during the new term will confound the first group and reassure the second.

Again I extend my sincere good wishes for the success of your administration and for your personal good health.

James A. Farley

I did not receive a reply until the next month. It came dated December 3, 1940, from aboard the Presidential Special as Roosevelt was heading for Warm Springs. The letter follows:

Dear Jim:

Thank you for yours of the twenty-third. You know I am a funny fellow in that unlike many, many people I do not get excited by what you call an "unprecedented honor." The reason is that I am perhaps a little "queer" in never having sought public office for "honor."

To put it another way, I would have been just as content in my own heart and conscience to give service to the country as a private citizen as I would to give service to the country as a first-term or a third-term President.

I am off for an attempt to get two weeks of sunshine—and I do hope you will run in and see me when I get back. I would really love to talk to you quietly about a lot of things that intimately relate today to the future generations of America.

Is it true you are going to South America? Let me know if I can help. My best to you all.

As ever,
F.D.R.

And the letter was unsigned! It bore nothing but the typewritten initials, "F.D.R." Later I learned that the President had deliberately chosen to let it go unsigned.

CHAPTER THIRTY-FOUR

PEARL HARBOR

I DID NOT see Roosevelt again until January 4, 1941, when I was in Washington arranging a trip to South America. I phoned to pay my respects, and "Pa" Watson invited me over. The President was having his hair cut. I thought he looked pretty well and said so. He replied he was quite busy on his "four freedoms" message to Congress, but felt well. We discussed the war.

"There isn't the slightest doubt in my mind that Hitler will be defeated," he said, "but it will take more than a year to do it. Italy is considerably weakened and won't be of much use to the Axis for the balance of the war."

He then switched to consideration of the neutrality of Eire, saying:

"The Irish should give bases to England to facilitate the moving of supplies and maintenance of sea lanes. If they persist in refusing the bases, the British would be right in refusing to permit shipping with them after the war. Canada and England could get together and Ireland would suffer. De Valera is a bore and a dreamer."

I defended De Valera as a patriot and as one of the shrewdest and most honest and intelligent statesmen I had met in my travels.

He sent for Miss Le Hand and dictated a general letter of introduction for me. He said he knew President Vargas of Brazil very well, adding Vargas wasn't the least like other South American leaders, being more progressive in his view and a more capable administrator. The letter was most helpful.

On my return from my two months' tour, I had a few minutes with Roosevelt on March 15, 1941. His schedule was quite jammed so I did not linger. I conveyed personal greetings from President Vargas and reported that the attitude of our southern neighbors was for the most part friendly, although I did note some Axis influence.

I was back in the Capital in three weeks for the spring Gridiron dinner. I called upon Hull and found him smarting over the appointment of John G. Winant as Ambassador to Great Britain.

"I attribute the appointment to those I call the social welfare group," Hull said. "I'm sure Supreme Court Justice Frankfurter was instrumental in bringing the appointment about. I had recommended former Governor James M. Cox of Ohio."

"Roosevelt's lack of frankness is one thing that always disturbed me," I said. "It was serious enough before, but it is most grave now with the country in danger of war. I can only hope that he will not attempt to make any alliance with Britain without taking those in his official family and Congressional leaders into his confidence. Otherwise, I am sure strong feeling will be generated against him around the country."

"I agree with you completely," Hull said. "I don't see the President very often. Most of the details of the department are handled through Sumner Welles. Sometime in the future I'm going to set forth the position I have taken down through the years. The social welfarers might try to discredit my story, but I will tell it."

On April 25, 1941, I dictated a memorandum, based on my observations and conversations with various leaders. I wrote:

It is apparent to me that for some weeks at least, we have been drifting for lack of leadership on the President's part, and it is evident that because of promises made during the campaign he is unwilling to explain to the country just what our position is in the situation abroad. If he did, he would probably have to wind up by saying that he thinks the best thing to do is to move into war now. If he does that, he will be going back on his promises, and knowing him as I do, I am sure it is all very annoying to him.

I think the President has been very backward in not taking a more definite stand on the important issues of labor; he hates to make definite decisions, and he tries by devious means to go around them. At other times he is very courageous, but in this particular situation he certainly has not been giving the kind of leadership the country needs.

If he continues to go along this way and not definitely give some type of leadership, a bad situation can very well develop in this country. Wheeler, Nye, and Lindbergh are making speeches and apparently drawing great crowds, particularly in the Middle West. There is no doubt that the people in the East and in the large industrial centers have made up their minds to get into the war, and get it over. That is not true of the man in the street, particularly in the Middle West—nor the mothers and fathers of sons, recalling full well what happened during and after the last war.

I imagine this is giving the President great concern but the thing is, I think, he made definite promises in his campaign, and now he is faced with the possibility of going back on them. It was said he would do that and I am sure that it will be called to his attention on the floor of the Senate.

I have not been in Washington much—only once or twice for a day— but in my talks with people who are in Washington, I find they seem to think we are headed for war, whether or not the people outside know it, and there is grave doubt in their minds as to whether or not we are prepared for it.

The trouble in this whole situation is that we delayed six months in getting the defense program under way because of the President's desire to get the third term. When I came back from Europe in 1939, I asked for an opportunity to set up the defense program and get industry organized. The President promised me he would do that but he never discussed any part of it with me. If he had started out then, with a defense committee, or with someone, and permitted them to organize industry in this country, we would have been six months ahead or further in our program anyway. He did nothing about it and the reason was that he was fearful that the people would ask an explanation as to his plans on the third term—and how then could he expect cooperation? Of course, his actions in connection with the 1940 convention will be one of the things to always come back to plague any understanding I could possibly have. It is all right to say he did not know what he was going to do, but there is no doubt in my mind he knew what he was going to do. He certainly should have told me on Feb. 1, that he had changed his mind. He sent Ickes to California to stop Garner. He wanted it to appear that the convention drafted him. That in itself is significant. If he proceeded with the program in 1939 . . . we could tell Germany where they could head in and tell them so freely and frankly, and we could back up our demands with real, and evident defense—not just holding a cap pistol. That is our problem today and the reason we are in this situation is because of the President.

I was back in Washington May 10, 1941, when I had a visit with Senator Truman, who discussed his investigation of army camps. He attributed extravagance on camp sites to improper procurement organization in the Army. He said his investigation would bring out the weak points in the army set-up and prevent a recurrence of the extravagance.

I spent a half hour with Hull and found him exercised over the activities of Henry Morgenthau, Jr., on the freezing of German funds and other problems relating to the Nazis. Hull told me he had to call up Henry and tell him to keep his hands out of the State Department. Hull also disclosed that he seldom saw the President, but talked frequently with him over the phone. Under Secretary of State Welles, however, was seeing Roosevelt daily, he added.

On July 2, 1941, I visited John N. Garner in his home at Uvalde, Texas, along with Postmaster Burris Jackson of Hillsboro, Texas. I never saw the former Vice President in a better frame of mind or in finer health. When I remarked that he appeared to be extremely happy in his retirement, he said, "I ain't mad at anyone."

"I think Roosevelt will be a candidate for a fourth term," Garner continued. "There is no other way you can explain his actions. I think he will get us into the war by the back door rather than going through Congress. I'm concerned about the future of the country and the huge debt which is being piled up."

Garner said he last saw the President on January 20, 1941, the day of the third term inaugural, when he bade him good-by, saying, "Boss, there is nothing you can give me that I would ever accept, but if you think I can be of service to the country, I want you to call me." Garner said he knew very well that Roosevelt would never call upon him. I told him of the ignoring of my offer to serve on my return from Europe in the fall of 1939.

"You know, Jim, I'm entirely out of politics now, but if you ever become interested in the Presidency, I will get back in and pitch in for you," he said.

"Jack," I said, "I'm not interested in any office, including the Presidency. Some people are trying to interest me in running for Mayor of New York City or the Governorship of New York State, but I'm mainly concerned with providing for my family."

Back in New York five days later, Ed Flynn and I had lunch.

"Will you run for Mayor?" he asked.

"Ed, I would not run for Mayor if I could have the post without going through a campaign," was my reply.

Throughout the year I was busy fitting myself into my new post. My family was most happy and I found I was not missing public life nearly so much as I thought I would. I was finding retirement most pleasant.

Suddenly, like many another American, I was jolted out of complacency by the grim stroke of Pearl Harbor. I wanted to serve as best I could, so I sat down the morning of December 9, 1941, and wrote the President as follows:

DEAR MR. PRESIDENT:

Just a brief note to express the hope that your strength and energy may continue to fortify your efforts to keep our country triumphant over aggression. The righteousness of our cause should be a consolation to you in these days of heavy burdens.

If at any time I can be of service I know you will feel free to command me.

Faithfully yours,
JAMES A. FARLEY

I received a brief, but pleasant reply from the White House under date of December 10, 1941, which read:

MY DEAR JIM:

Thanks ever so much for your nice note.
I knew I could count on you.

As ever yours,
F.D.R.

No summons to serve came in the months and years that followed. Friends told me there was some discussion about putting me into "a place with a double-edged sword"—one which might cut me while I was wielding it for the administration—but nothing came of it.

Secretary of Labor Perkins recommended me for Chairman of the National War Labor Board, but it was thought by some persons that the job should go to William H. Davis because of his long service on the National Defense Mediation Board, which was perfectly all right with me. Frances also had a plan to establish a board of arbitrators to act, if the War Labor Board failed. The arbitrators were to be such persons as Charles Evans Hughes, Wendell Willkie, William Mitchell, Judge Florence Allen, Judge Learned Hand, myself, and possibly others. This idea was abandoned, she said, because the persons being considered as arbitrators so overshadowed the WLB that it was felt the board would suffer.

In the late summer of 1941, Secretary of Treasury Morgenthau wanted me to take on the chairmanship in New York State for the bond drive, but I had just completed four to five months of continuous activity as chairman of the 1941 Greater New York Fund Drive, and I told Henry it would be impossible for me to accept this responsibility at that time, and asked to be excused. I said I would be very happy to help him on it later. I recommended that Richard C. Patterson, Jr., be invited to assume the chairmanship; he accepted and did an excellent job.

That was the only time I was ever asked to assist in any of the government's programs which directly or indirectly related to the war effort, or to the emergency created by the war, in spite of having offered my services to the President immediately following the attack on Pearl Harbor.

On January 9, 1942, I was in Washington again and during a visit to Capitol Hill I had a brief chat with Vice President Wallace, who asked me if I was interested in coming into the war picture. I replied that, like all Americans, I was interested in serving my country, but I did not want a job just for the sake of a job. I told him I needed no honors—that sort of thing was behind me—but if my ability was needed, I would take some post that would bring out what qualities I possessed. He said he had been thinking of me, Joseph P. Kennedy, and several others. I don't know how the others fared, but Kennedy and I were left alone. Wallace appeared tired and worn, although he said he felt all right.

That afternoon I had a most interesting conversation with Cordell Hull, who brought me up to date on the war situation. Hull said:

"Jim, I want you to know and I hope some day the country will know, I purposely prolonged the conversations with the Japanese beyond the point where I felt it would do any good in order to enable the Army and the Navy to get men and supplies to the Far East. When the war party took control of the Japanese government in October, it was evident there was no hope for peace.

"In November at a meeting in the White House I told Stimson and Knox and their ranking officers what the President or I or the State Department could do with the Japanese situation. I warned them, Jim, that in view of the past conduct of the Japanese the Army and the

Navy should be prepared for an attack by the Japanese at any point or at many points, all at the same time, as the Japs might seek to have us deploy our forces over a considerable area.

"The situation in Singapore and other sections of the Far East is none too good. I am doing everything I can through Admiral William D. Leahy to keep Marshal Pétain on his feet and to preserve a friendly relationship with the Vichy government. I'm doing this at the request of the British. I must confess I don't feel too friendly toward them for a number of reasons. One is the interference of some Britishers with our efforts in connection with the seizure of the islands of St. Pierre and Miquelon off the Newfoundland coast by Free French forces."

"How do you look at the future?" I asked.

"I am confident of victory, but we are in for a lot of bad days, bad nights, and bad news before we get there," he said.

"Did you see much of Churchill?" I asked.

"Very little," he replied.

I did not press this line of questioning because I knew he felt he was being by-passed by the President.

I could not see the President because he was in Hyde Park, the visit being shrouded in wartime secrecy. I asked Steve Early to extend my regards. Frances Perkins told me she thought the President was worn out by Winston Churchill's visit. The Prime Minister not only kept late hours but, whenever he finished what he was doing, he invariably headed for the President's study or office, so that Roosevelt did not have much time to himself during Churchill's stay.

About this time Wendell Willkie, the third Republican standard-bearer defeated by Roosevelt, came to see me seeking to enlist my support for a scheme to effect bipartisan agreement for renomination and reelection of Senators and Congressmen supporting the President's foreign policy. I told him I was against any such agreement; that the decision should be left to the voters concerned, and that neither he, the President, nor anyone else could successfully carry out such an agreement. As he left, I was convinced that he was still working for the Presidency.

CHAPTER THIRTY-FIVE

BROOKLYN CONVENTION

I NOW COME to the story of the most important political fight I was ever engaged in, not excepting the third term. I refer to the New York State Democratic convention at Brooklyn in the summer of 1942, which I consider one of the greatest demonstrations of democracy and loyalty ever seen in this country.

In the convention in Chicago in 1940, I took a stand on the principle of the third term. I did not attempt an all-out fight in that convention because it would have been foolhardy, inasmuch as over nine hundred delegates had been committed to President Roosevelt. But, in the Brooklyn convention two years later, a different situation existed.

As chairman of the Democratic state committee, I was supporting Attorney General John J. Bennett for the nomination for Governor, with the backing of most of the upstate county organizations and the Brooklyn (Kings County) and Queens County organizations. Arrayed against me was the most powerful group of political leaders that ever faced anyone: the President, at the height of his wartime popularity; Governor Lehman, who was completing his tenth year in Albany; Senators Wagner and Mead; Ed Flynn, head of the powerful Bronx County organization, who had succeeded me as Chairman of the Democratic National Committee and was the National Committeeman from New York State; the O'Connell machine of Albany; the Utica machine; a portion of the Syracuse organization and most of the Erie County organization; and Michael J. Kennedy, the leader of Tammany Hall.

I have always been of the opinion that if Mike Kennedy had seen the light and had not gone along with President Roosevelt in his efforts to defeat Bennett for the nomination, Bennett would have been nominated unanimously and subsequently elected.

Even before Pearl Harbor it was known that Governor Lehman would not be a candidate. It was widely accepted that his successor

347

would be Bennett. New York Democrats were becoming a bit fed up with having someone at Albany from whom they could not receive consideration. Bennett had always been a strong party man and was widely favored by Democratic leaders, particularly those upstate. It was regarded as a foregone conclusion that the nomination would go to Bennett. He had sought my support and, as state chairman, I gave my word to him, feeling he had earned the nomination. Bennett had stepped aside in 1936 and 1938 at the request of the party's leaders, when the rank and file wanted him. Bennett ran ahead of Lehman in 1938, when Lehman headed the ticket, and Bennett was elected Attorney General.

There wasn't the slightest ripple on the New York political horizon until April, 1942, when, out of a clear sky, Roosevelt told Wendell Willkie that his candidate for Governor was Owen D. Young, the industrialist. The President said Lehman would be made a brigadier general, probably in the Quartermaster Corps; and Lieutenant Governor Charles Poletti would get a chance to show himself as Governor until the election. Roosevelt asked Willkie who the Republican candidate would be. Willkie said without any doubt it would be Thomas E. Dewey. The name of Bennett was mentioned, and Harry Hopkins, who was present, said that Roosevelt made a bad selection in Bennett for Attorney General. Roosevelt said that was not so, that there was nothing wrong with Bennett's record as Attorney General.

When this story was brought to me, I dismissed it, being aware that all Bennett would have to do would be to announce his candidacy, and Young would not get into the race. Bennett went ahead getting pledges from various leaders and prepared to fight for his nomination, if necessary, although he did not expect to be thrust into a battle.

Poletti came to me and expressed a desire to run. When I explained why I felt Bennett was entitled to the nomination, he said that under the circumstances there was no sense in his making a bid. I advised him to content himself with the prospect, which appeared to be his, of being governor for a few months on Lehman's resignation for Washington service. Our talk was entirely pleasant and affable.

On June 1, I received a telephone call from White House secretary McIntyre asking whether it was likely I would be in Washington in the near future. I said I had no plans for an early visit. He then said the President would like to talk to me about the New York situation, so I made an appointment to see him June 6.

Before going to the White House, I stopped in the State Department with Eddie Roddan and we paid a call on Cordell Hull. As I went in I decided to twit him about the controversy he had had with Wallace over an executive order by which Wallace had snatched some State and Commerce Department functions for his Bureau of Economic Warfare. Hull was successful in balking the raid by a second countermanding presidential order.

"Cordell, how did you manage it; did you use a gun or a knife?" I asked.

"Hell, no, Jim," he replied, "I used old fashioned methods. I gave him plenty of rope."

Hull went on to say that the President, in Hull's presence, had told Wallace that he would not have signed the original order had he known the State and Commerce Departments were opposed to the transfer, and Wallace said he had not asked the approval of the two departments because he knew he would not get it.

Hull said the speeches of Under Secretary Welles about saving the world were entirely impractical. It was clear, he said, we could not police the world and take care of its peoples.

In the course of our talk I noted pictures of Andrew Jackson and Abraham Lincoln on the walls of his office and could not refrain from commenting:

"I'm happy to see Jackson and Lincoln in your office, and I know you won't misunderstand me when I tell you what I have told many people, that I regret you are not President of the United States. I sincerely believe that you possess, in a greater degree than any man in the nation, the courage of Jackson and the humility of Lincoln. With such attributes, you could not help but be a great Chief Magistrate."

He was much touched, saying my remarks were a great compliment, that he knew how I felt toward him and that he appreciated my friendship to as great a degree as that of any man he had ever come into contact with in public life.

Hull then told a most interesting story about Russia. He said that in January, 1941, he had sent word to the Soviet Ambassador that this government had received most reliable information that Germany was likely to attack Russia. On receiving the information, Russian Foreign Minister Molotov made a speech attacking Hull for attempting to churn up trouble between Russia and Germany.

On Molotov's first visit to Washington, after the attack, he sought out Hull and said, "For my own information, after this war is over, I should like to have you tell me when and how your government first realized that Germany was going to invade Russia." Molotov told Hull that the Soviet government did not entertain the possibility of attack until sometime in May. Hull however, was of the opinion that the Russians did not know about it until June, 1941, just before the invasion.

At the White House I chatted briefly with Mrs. Roosevelt and then was ushered into the President's study. I had not seen him for fourteen months and found evidences of the strain he was working under. His eyes had heavy circles under them and his face was chalky. He was more nervous than I had ever seen him. He was continuously reaching for things on his desk and toying with them. He coughed frequently. Robert Brennan, Eire's Minister, had an appointment just before me. When I came in, Roosevelt began talking about Ireland almost from our handshake.

"You and I know," he said, "the kind of fellow De Valera is; he's not sufficiently practical; he is in the clouds most of the time and doesn't have his feet on the ground."

"Mr. President, we've discussed this before and you know I hold Eamon De Valera in high regard," I said.

He went into a lengthy discussion of Congress, holding that its members were in bad with the country.

"I don't know that Congress is entirely to blame," I said. "When they go along with the administration, they are praised by some people and severely criticized by others as being a 'rubber stamp' Congress. And when they refuse to go along with the administration, they are accused of being un-American and otherwise abused."

He nodded, but made no further comment. It was not until we had gone on for fifteen or twenty minutes that he approached the cause of our conference. Then he said:

"Of course, you know I have a great deal of regard for Jack Bennett, but I am wondering if he can be elected and if the American Labor Party would support him. I have some doubts about his standing among certain elements of the party."

"Whatever doubts you may have must come from those who don't want Bennett and are using any argument against him that comes to hand," I said. "If he is nominated and receives your blessing, there will be no question of his election."

"You know I always liked Jack, and you will recall the story of how we put over his original nomination for Attorney General against McCooey's opposition (Tammany leader John H. McCooey). I think you ought to get that story out to help John."

I took the fact that he wanted the story known as evidence he would accept Bennett.

The President told me to give the complete story to James A. Hagerty, Sr., veteran political reporter of the *New York Times*, who already knew the story. The President said he wanted it published only in the *Times*. (Hagerty did write the story as I suggested, in a full column in the Monday morning paper, following my visit to the White House. I wrote the President a letter and sent him a copy of the story, as promised, but he failed to acknowledge it.)

"Now, Mr. President, I never lied to you or misinformed you, during the long years I was associated with you," I said. "I have only one thought in mind and that is the success of the Democratic ticket. I feel that we can gain victory more easily this year by nominating Bennett than we could with anyone else. The Democratic leaders want him. He could have been nominated in 1936, but we drafted Lehman; and he could have been nominated in 1938, but again we drafted Lehman. Mr. President, all the Roosevelts and Farleys combined, with all the influence they are supposed to possess, could not stop Bennett's nomination for Governor in the coming convention, unless I decided to become a candidate against Bennett, which I haven't the slightest intention of doing."

"Of course, Senator Mead is needed here more than in Albany, because of his support of the administration," he said thoughtfully.

"That is true, Mr. President," I agreed. "Mead has strength where he is, but his vote on pensions for Congressmen has lost him support."

"While union labor is for Mead," Roosevelt said, as though continuing his train of thought, "there is a feeling among other laboring people against him, which might be harmful."

There was no mention of Owen D. Young or Assistant Secretary of War Patterson in our conversation. I suggested that Roosevelt could help the situation if he would bring Lehman down to Washington and let Poletti serve as Governor to the end of the year.

"I know," he said. "Poletti was in to see me, asking I do that. He feels he could get the nomination if he were Governor. I told Poletti I did not think he could get the nomination and that Lehman told me he didn't think Poletti could get it. I also told Charley I just can't bring Lehman to Washington at this time. As Governor of New York, Lehman is entitled to a decent place, but I must be careful because of the criticism that there are too many Jews in the administration."

I made no comment on that, feeling that Lehman would be taken care of—probably shortly after the convention. I suggested Nathan Straus, Laurence Steinhardt, or Charles H. Silver for Lieutenant Governor. He shook his head, saying Straus found it difficult to get along with people, and adding that he had trouble keeping him straight with Congress. He declared Steinhardt might be all right because of his record as a diplomat. He said he did not know Silver, and I said he was a fine fellow who would help the ticket immeasurably.

In my discussion with the President we both agreed that Joseph O'Leary should be nominated for state comptroller, and in the event Charles Poletti accepted the nomination for Lieutenant Governor, that Henry Epstein should be nominated for Attorney General. We also discussed names of several women for nomination as Congressman-at-large for the vacancy occasioned by the death of Mrs. Caroline O'Day. We had a very definite understanding on the whole state ticket.

I told him that I had only one desire, and that was to see the Democratic party successful in New York State, and that if he changed his mind in any way, I would appreciate it if he would telephone me and I would see him in Washington or in Hyde Park, publicly or privately, any way he desired, for a further discussion of the situation. He assured me he would surely communicate with me personally if he changed his mind in any way regarding our very definite understanding.

I did not hear from him directly or indirectly after that conversation and he made no effort to get in touch with me personally.

Before I left he said he had been glad to see me and chided me for not coming in to see him before. I told him I had tried, but had found him out of town. He inquired about Bess and the children. We parted most cordially.

Through June and July the New Dealers chipped away at Bennett delegates without appreciable result. On July 27, former Vice President Garner told me by phone that the fight I was engaged in was the most important of my career and wished me well. Two days later, at Bennett's suggestion, I called on Al Smith to enlist his support.

"Jimmy," he said, "I don't want to come out now, because some people are still sore at me on account of my attitude in 1936 and 1940. Anything I might do for Bennett might be more harmful than helpful. I hate to come out for anything because of the flood of letters which follows any public statement or commitment I make—most of them from fellows wanting jobs. I'm sick and tired of them."

I gave him a complete picture of the situation, expressing confidence we could hold our lines. If I found any weakness in our lines, I told him, I would be the first to offer to compromise.

"Jimmy, this isn't a fight against Jack Bennett, but Roosevelt's beginning of a fight for a fourth term for himself," Al said. "And he ought to be devoting all his energies to the conduct of the war, as people feel; instead he's worrying about control of the New York delegation in 1944."

On August 10, 1942, Roosevelt summoned Frank Kelly, Brooklyn leader, to the White House for a talk on the New York gubernatorial situation. The President did not say he would be for Bennett, but he did not say he would be against him. He did say he would make no speeches for any of the nominees and talked of Owen D. Young and General William N. Haskell.

Four days later Ed Flynn called Kelly and read a statement he had from the President in which Roosevelt said he would not make any speeches for Bennett and would not make any effort to get the endorsement of the American Labor Party for Bennett. The statement said that Roosevelt had so informed me during our conversation—which just wasn't so.

"You know," Kelly told me in repeating his conversation with Roosevelt and with Flynn, "I don't think all the trouble is in Washington."

"I don't follow you, Frank," I said.

"Well, I think a great deal of the difficulty is in the Bronx," he explained. "I think Flynn is more determined to nominate Mead than Roosevelt is."

"I can't see why he should be," I said.

On August 18, the day before the convention opened, the customary dinner conference of state Democratic leaders was held at the Biltmore Hotel. It was an extremely warm evening but grew hotter as I called on the various leaders. Kelly presented Bennett's name. Flynn offered Mead's. James Roe, Queens leader, supported Bennett. And Lehman declared for Mead. Most of the leaders spoke for Bennett. During the debate, I saw Lehman and Senator Wagner passing around a letter, but paid no attention to it until Lehman arose and announced he had a letter from the President. This stated Roosevelt was much disturbed over newspaper stories which made it appear there was a contest between Roosevelt and Farley. He said that while he had nothing against Bennett personally, he thought Mead would make a stronger candidate.

It was evident this was the last card of the Mead supporters. I went around the table asking the leaders who had declared for Bennett whether they had changed their views. Everyone was more emphatic in voicing support of Bennett. Roosevelt's letter had backfired. When the Mead forces refused to admit we had the votes to nominate Bennett, I said there was nothing to do but go to a roll call.

This was the first time since 1918, to my knowledge, where any minority group of leaders participating in a conference of New York State Democratic leaders failed to support the choice of the majority of the conference, and which was borne out by the vote Bennett received on the roll call. Smith, Roosevelt, and Lehman were selected for the nomination of governor in conferences similar to this, as were Copeland, Wagner, and Mead for the Senate, and all other Democratic nominees for state offices, including the state Court of Appeals.

An hour later Lehman phoned to accuse me of giving out the President's letter, which he had said was confidential. I cautioned him to keep his head and his temper, asserting that I had not made the letter public and reminding him that it was impossible to keep secret a letter read to twenty-five people. He made no further reference to it.

The Bennett forces, having the votes, could have railroaded the convention, but had no wish to do so. We agreed to let the nominations and roll call go over until Thursday, at the request of Frank Kelly. Wednesday morning a brief organizational meeting was held. That night at nine-thirty, Kelly called me, saying he would be right over and asking that Bennett be present.

"Jim, I had a call from Lehman," Kelly began in a strained voice which clearly showed the pressure he was laboring under. "He says that if Jack Bennett is nominated, he will not campaign for him and will not support him. When he told me that, and you know how highly I regard him, I began wondering whether I should withdraw my support and look for a compromise candidate. He'll have to be an Irish Catholic from Brooklyn."

This was a severe jolt. Kelly said he did not think there was a chance for Bennett to win if Lehman walked out. At this time Bennett and Vincent Dailey, my assistant, came in. Kelly said he would be glad to nominate Bennett for the Supreme Court, which Bennett refused. I asked Kelly if he had given serious thought to any other candidate.

"I would take you, but I know you don't want it," he said.

"As far as I'm concerned, the nomination is out," I said. "I have no candidate but Bennett, and I will never desert him. All that I have ever had is my word and I have given it to Bennett. The people in and out of the party in this state and all over the country know I think Bennett is the best man."

I felt extremely sorry for Kelly because I realized he was absolutely sincere and that he wanted to do what he considered was the right thing for the organization. I told him that if there was a runout on Bennett now, there would be a hopeless split and the party would be doomed to certain defeat. As it was, I said, the party was suffering through the interference of the Mead crowd. I reminded him Mead had declared himself out of the race several times.

"Now, Frank, you know how I feel about Bennett and I want him to know it," I concluded. "I am going to keep my word and go through with Bennett. I did not intend to make a speech, but it seems I will have to do it to nominate Jack."

We parted with the understanding Kelly would call me in the morning. The next few hours were among the most uncomfortable in my life. I could see a situation which would obviously wreck the party and, as state chairman, I was vitally interested in the party's success.

I was at breakfast when Kelly called at eight o'clock the next morning and asked me to come over to the Montauk Club in Brooklyn, where I found him with Judges John B. Johnston and William B. Carswell. I am an emotional fellow, as was Kelly. We both had difficulty in controlling our feelings during the tense conference.

"Frank, I have given considerable thought to the situation through the night," I began. "I have turned it over this morning. I want you to know before you say anything that I have not changed my opinion. I am convinced that Bennett can be and should be nominated. And I am going to place his name in nomination. When I do so, I will have to tell the reason for your leaving him. If I tell the story of Lehman's telephone call to the convention, and I will have to do so in justice to Bennett, the party, and myself, the effect will not be pleasant."

"Jim, I want to live in Brooklyn the rest of my life," Kelly responded. "I want to do what I think is best for the Brooklyn organization. I do not want to destroy it or myself. If I go through for

Bennett, I believe sincerely that I will be through politically. I say Bennett can't win with all these elements against him; but, Jim, I have telephoned Lehman. I told him when he says he can't support Bennett, that is his decision, but that I am staying with Bennett. Jim, I am willing to go to the end with you, and I will do it."

I grasped his hand and congratulated him on his courage, saying that in the days ahead he would never have reason to regret his stand, regardless of the outcome of the election. Many times before his death, he told me that if he had it all to do over again, he would do exactly what he did.

In the convention hall, just before the ballot, Lehman came to me with the plea that we recess for a conference. I took him aside, back of the press stand and gave him a brief but forceful talking to. I told him that he of all men had no right to appeal to me on the basis of party loyalty. I said he should feel grateful to Bennett and other party leaders, including myself. Finally, I said we had debated and conferred long enough; that it was evident that the majority of the delegates wanted Bennett; and that if the President, the Senators, he, the Governor, and the rest did not want to abide by the will of the conference and the convention, they would bring disaster on the party.

The rest is history. Flynn and Lehman asked to have the Brooklyn delegation polled. The atmosphere was charged with excitement as voice after voice—with one exception—answered, "John J. Bennett." It was evident on completion of the polling of this delegation that all was up with the Mead forces. The final vote was 623 votes for Bennett, which was almost on the head of the prediction of 620.

We did not make a single commitment. We had nothing to offer except a candidate in whom the leaders and delegates believed. Further, they resented the outside interference and the threat that, if Mead were not nominated, the party's nominee would not receive support. Also they resented the shotgun wedding with the American Labor Party, which they felt was being forced by the insistence that the convention should take Mead to get ALP support.

Again Roosevelt had violated the cardinal political tenet of non-intervention in local matters. Again he had stepped from the lofty national scene to exchange blows in a regional clash. Again he met with a humiliating defeat. And again he did not profit by the lesson.

Even though the contest was in his own state, he should not have interfered, particularly in time of war. As in the case of the unsuccessful purge, he did not do what party regularity demanded—support the candidate of the convention at once. Instead he sulked, as he had after the purge defeats, and withheld prompt support from Bennett. The result was that the Democrats lost New York State, not only that fall, but again in 1946.

The evils which have beset the party in New York, like those which plagued the party nationally, may be traced to violation of the rules of regularity. After the 1940 convention, in which I was a participant, I bowed to the will of the party and supported the third term, even though I had no sympathy with the precedent breaking and was certain that it would be harmful in the long run, not only because it was shattering American tradition but also because it was denying other men within the party their chance to come to the top.

If this book has no other lesson, I hope that its readers will heed the admonition of a practical politician that parties must provide opportunities for faithful workers to advance, and that its members— rank and file—must follow the rules of the game. Party platforms and principles may change, but growth and order must not, or the party will wither and die as so many have.

In the final days of the campaign, at the instance of Ed Flynn, the President sent a wire to Bennett in which he declared that the suggestion that "my support of you is formal and lukewarm is an untruth." This came too late; his tardiness cost us the election. Bennett stood up smilingly under overwhelming defeat. The one bright light in the gloomy election evening was his sportsmanlike manner and gentlemanly bearing.

CHAPTER THIRTY-SIX

FOURTH TERM

ROM THE beginning of 1943, only one topic approached the war in general interest and that was the fourth term, which everyone was certain Roosevelt wanted. It was evident that the President could and would get the nomination unless a number of Democratic leaders formed a coalition to stop him by capturing the delegations of their respective states. Such a confederation is most difficult to organize and harder to hold together, because of the inevitable conflict of personalities and ambitions. In this instance, it was never launched.

On February 3, 1943, I paid a visit to Garner at Uvalde, Texas, on my way home from a Mexican business trip. The former Vice President was much disturbed over the fourth term.

"Jim, I think it would be a terrible thing to have Roosevelt elected again," he said. "It would not be fair to the country or to him. He cannot last forever, and from what I hear he is losing ground. The possibility of having Wallace as President is repulsive to me."

"As long as you have brought it up, Jack, I must tell you that I am told the strain is telling on him," I said. "After all, he will have had twelve years in Washington on top of four in Albany. And years will take their toll. I think those about him are being most selfish and highly unfair to him, in persuading him to run."

"That's what I hear and it has me worried," Garner continued. "Anything can happen to the country in a situation like that, especially if Wallace succeeds. Why, we might have a revolution!"

"I'm afraid not only for the country but for the world," I added. "Not only is it important that the maker of decisions on the conduct of the war be fresh and vigorous, but the next term will bring the peace making, and it is vital that these negotiations be in strong hands."

Hull echoed Garner's fears over Wallace's possible succession, when

I saw him in Washington a few days later. He was smoldering over criticism from "so-called liberals," because of his dealings with the Vichy government which, he said, had made it possible to land soldiers in Africa with a minimum loss of life. "If the liberals have any criticism to make," he snorted, "they should direct it at Churchill and Roosevelt."

At Washington that May I had dinner with the Secretary and Mrs. Hull. I found him looking hearty. I reminded him of the early days of the administration, when his warning of the menace of Japan, Germany, and Italy were boring to the majority of his Cabinet colleagues. I noted that events had proved him right and asked what he believed should be done to the three nations when they were conquered.

"I told the President and Churchill," Hull said, "that what should be done is to have Hitler and his co-conspirators, Mussolini and his followers, and Hirohito and his group liquidated promptly by the allies. This will teach a lesson to those that follow them."

On May 30, 1944, Lord Beaverbrook, whom I found as interesting as he was frank, asked me point-blank, "Why did Roosevelt pick Wallace for Vice President?"

"Because there was less chance of Wallace developing into a presidential candidate than anyone else," was my reply.

"That's not unusual," he laughed, "Winston does that too." Then he added that he had seen Henry in action and found him impractical. He followed this with an amusing story of how Roosevelt and Churchill worked.

"I spent three days with them, you know," he said. "Whenever Churchill bore down too hard on what he wanted done, Roosevelt would turn to his stamp books and start thumbing through them. That would stop Winston short. Maybe he'd stalk out of the room or maybe he would bring up some subject that had no relation to what they were working on. Roosevelt would then laugh and forget his irritation. Winston is always bearing down to get over something he wants done."

Beaverbrook said Roosevelt was one of the most charming men he had ever met. I agreed, adding I was sorry I had never met Churchill, and that in 1939 Roosevelt told me he was the one man in England I should meet. I have since met the dynamic statesman and found him tremendously interesting.

June 24th found me back at Hull's desk. He did not look on the situation favorably, saying, "I feel somewhat like Pliny, when he exclaimed at the eruption of Vesuvius, 'I saw and was a part of all this.' And there are times I wish I wasn't part of it all. Down through the years I have worked for reciprocal trade agreements, the good neighbor policy, branding aggressors, and all the rest. I get discouraged at neglect but am determined to sit it out."

When I next saw him on August 16, he was in a better mood. He was busy on a postwar program which would bring not only Republicans and Democrats in Congress to the conference tables, but also men of the caliber of Charles Evans Hughes and John W. Davis. He said the British had no postwar program, but had been fiddling around the State Department trying to find out if we had one, and added, "I have kept it from them."

In November, Hull went to Moscow to establish accord among the allies, particularly between the United States and Russia. On December 9, 1943, at an interesting evening in his apartment he told me the story of his trip. He was in an excellent frame of mind, pleased over the success of his mission.

"You know, Jim, that there were stories in the papers from time to time that other persons were going to undertake the mission," he began. "I made up my mind that I would go. So I went across the street and told a certain person I was going to make the trip as this country's representative. He said, 'Grand!' and told me how delighted he was."

I did not say so, but I was not so sure that the President was convinced Hull would make the trip. I had heard that almost up to Hull's departure he toyed with sending Sumner Welles or Joseph E. Davies. I asked Hull what he thought of Stalin.

"He's a man of parts and quite practical," Hull replied. "I got along all right with him and other representatives of the Russian government."

"That's no surprise to me, because they undoubtedly have a record on every public official in this country and, while they feel you are not in accord with Russian philosophy, they at least knew they could get the truth from you on anything that might be discussed."

"It was apparent the Russians did not have too much confidence in the British," Hull continued. "At times I was quite embarrassed at the manner in which Anthony Eden and other British representatives were ignored by the Russians. Many of the things put forth by the British were rejected, whereas anything I put forth was accepted. Some of the things I handled at open conferences, and other matters, in private talks with Molotov and Litvinov.

"Jim, in strict confidence, I was assured by Stalin that there will be no difficulty when the United States gets around to the point when we will need Russian bases to fight Japan. Stalin asked me not to tell this to Churchill. I did not, but I did tell a certain person."

I have no intention of detailing other confidences on his mission, because that is Hull's story and he is writing it. He told me, and I am certain he was correct, that if he had not gone to Moscow, the Stalin-Churchill-Roosevelt meeting at Teheran would not have been possible.

"How did you make out through the drinking of vodka toasts?" I asked with a smile.

"I didn't drink any vodka; but I took red wine, and Stalin did the same thing," he replied. "I lost ten to twelve pounds, because the food was not what I am accustomed to and I couldn't get my supply of good milk."

"How did you like the flying?"

"When I stepped into the plane and was on my way, I said to myself, 'Oh, what the hell!' " he laughed. "It made no difference as long as the mission was successful, which it was. Of course there are matters like boundary disputes and other matters which can wait until the war is over. On the whole, I feel like the fellow who went in on a flush pot with a lone ace and drew three more."

I impressed upon him the importance of dictating the complete story while it was still fresh in his mind, because of its significance for future generations. I cautioned him not to let too much time pass without getting the story down, because details are easily forgotten if notes are not made immediately. I told him I had long had the practice of dictating at length and had found my record invaluable.

Hull said he would. He chuckled over the fact that the "liberals," who had been attacking him, were now trying to outdo each other with praise of him.

"The remarkable thing is that the so-called liberals do more damage to the true liberal cause than the opponents of liberalism," he said. "Well, Jim, it just goes to show you must have patience and courage to deal with situations such as I have had during the past few years. And if you give them enough rope, they hang themselves."

From the time of his return from Teheran in December, there were disturbing reports about Roosevelt's health. Hundreds of persons, high and low, reported to me that he looked bad, his mind wandered, his hands shook, his jaw sagged, and he tired easily. Almost everyone who came in had some story about the President's health —directly or indirectly—from any one of various doctors who examined him. Roosevelt looked bad in photographs and newsreels, and his voice lost much of its vitality over the radio. Members of the Cabinet, Senators, Congressmen, members of the White House staff, various Federal officials, and newspapermen carried a variety of reports on the President's failing health.

On June 8, 1944, I resigned as New York State Democratic chairman, a post I had held for fourteen years. The resignation ended thirty-five years of active service in politics. I had wanted to resign after the third term election in 1940, but various people talked me into staying for the New York City mayoralty race, in the hope I might contribute to the election of a Democratic mayor. I got into that campaign for William O'Dwyer after La Guardia had made a vicious reference to Lehman. My speeches were so strong that some have credited them with making it impossible for La Guardia to bid for reelection in 1945. That may be, but they did not defeat him in 1941. When that election was out of the way, I again wanted to retire. Again I was prevailed upon to remain for the 1942 gubernatorial campaign. I would have retired then, but the New Deal crowd decided they would try to force me out. I made up my mind I would fight them and stay, which I did. However, just before the fourth term convention, I decided the time had come to resign.

I hesitated to leave a debt behind me in the state committee. In talking this over with friends, it was suggested that a testimonial dinner be tendered to me and the proceeds should go toward lifting the debt. James W. Gerard consented to accept the chairmanship of the dinner committee. The dinner, which was held July 10, was a financial success; $20,000 was raised; and I was able to leave the state committee free of debt. I shall always feel pleased about the dinner, not only for the nice things said by the various speakers, but because men from all walks of life—Republicans as well as Democrats—came to do me honor.

I was amused when Frank Walker, whom I had favored as my successor as Postmaster General, wrote that he could not attend although I "richly deserved a tribute," just because his attendance prior to the Democratic convention "would without a doubt leave the impression that I approved your attitude which I do not." I thought he was taking himself too seriously, that his presence at the dinner would not make an impression on anyone. Secretary of Labor Perkins came, as did Ed Flynn and Democratic National Chairman Hannegan. I was grateful for Miss Perkins's statement that my contribution to the 1932 campaign "was the note of hope . . . to the despairing people of this country," and the assertion that I "stood on the right side of every question that came before the Cabinet."

On July 15, 1944, I left New York for the Chicago convention. I was a delegate and had made up my mind to vote against Roosevelt for a fourth term and to oppose Wallace for the Vice Presidency.

I talked with Senator Byrd, who had no illusions that he could block the nomination or even get a substantial vote, but he was determined that objection should be voiced against the fourth term. I cast my vote for him. I appreciated the kindly gesture of those who cast their ballots for me.

I did not roam around much during the convention. In the first place I did not want my visits and conversations misunderstood, and also I did not want anyone punished for being seen with me. Many of my friends became marked men by the White House "palace guard" just for being seen with me and for remaining loyal to me, even though they were doing all that was humanly possible to aid the administration. Judge Edward M. Curran, who was denied a seat on the District Court of the United States for the District of Columbia for years because he was known as a Farley man, is a typical example.

Many persons came to my room; I ran into others in hotel corridors and at the convention hall. Everywhere I found leaders and delegates restless but resigned to the inevitable, which, in this case, was the fourth term. Everywhere the President's health was a major topic, though it was discussed largely in whispers. In dictating my observations on the convention a few days after it was over, I wrote:

As I looked at the picture from the sidelines in Chicago, and observed the moves made by the administration forces, the thought occurred to me that those people who profess such great friendship for the President were doing not only him, but the country, a great disservice. Anyone with a grain of common sense would surely realize from the appearance of the President that he is not a well man and there is not a chance in the world for him to carry on for four years more and face the problems that a President will have before him; he just can't survive another presidential term. . . .

Therefore, I think those around the President are unfair to him in urging him to run, because if they are really honest with themselves, they would not do so, but would urge him to step aside and let someone else be nominated. And even if the party lost, what of it? It might preserve his life, and at the same time, in my judgment, would not have detracted from his position in the country nor in history. As a matter of fact, I think it would have enhanced it. . . .

The truth of the matter is, however, that he probably wanted to remain in office despite what may have been said to the contrary and that desire on his part was made easier by those around him who thought only of themselves and their desire to remain in power and bask in the sunlight, that is, of his reflected glory. If they were really on the level with themselves and him, they would have advised him to the contrary, but human nature being what it is, I suppose that is what we must expect.

Frankly, as one who has had a long, close, and extremely friendly association with the President, I hate to see him make the race again; for as I sat and watched the show in Chicago, I was convinced in my own mind it was a terrible mistake even if he is elected. The problems which will follow the cessation of actual warfare will be never-ending and the period in which reconversion must take place will be heart-breaking.

Vigorous leadership is necessary; and a man who is strong mentally and physically should be in the White House in order to direct the activities of those who must of necessity carry the burden, because the President cannot do it all himself; and unless a man is really able to exert the strength and vigorous leadership he did in the early days of 1933, it is likely to be very bad for the country. Congress will undoubtedly get out of hand. We may lose control of the House; and if not, it could be close, and with so many conservative Congressmen, he could have trouble. Undoubtedly we will continue to control the Senate, but Republicans could join conservative Democrats to oppose the President's program—and he is going to be in trouble.

Because Roosevelt's nomination was a certainty and because of his failing health, unusual interest was centered in the vice-presidential nomination. Some of the maneuvering was ludicrous, especially when an enormous field of candidates began jockeying for position, most of them convinced they had the President's blessing, and many of them having letters of endorsement from him. There were times, as wags said, when it appeared that the President's major contribution to the war effort was writing letters endorsing vice-presidential candidates.

From the outset, it was apparent a determined effort would be made to supplant Wallace. I had no doubt that he would go, but did not know who the successor would be. Before I left New York, Herbert Bayard Swope said he had every reason to believe James F. Byrnes, who was then familiarly known as Assistant President, had the green light.

I talked to Byrnes once or twice at the convention, but did not discuss his candidacy. His friends told me that he was aggrieved by the President's failure to demand his selection, turning instead to Truman. Byrnes, being a brilliant and capable man, would have made a good Vice President or President.

Democratic leaders told me that the President would not take Wallace, which was plain to me when I read the President's strange endorsement of the man he insisted on having as his 1940 running mate. If there ever was a left-handed endorsement, that was it. On the other hand, if there ever was anyone entitled to Roosevelt's support, it was Wallace, because he typified everything the New Deal stood for and never backed away from it, even when the President did. While I would not support him for Vice President or President, I must say that Wallace was treated shabbily.

I never knew why Senator Barkley was not included in the list of men acceptable to the President, which numbered Truman, Byrnes, Wallace, Speaker Rayburn, and Federal Judge Sherman Minton, formerly United States Senator from Indiana. By all the rules of the game, and by virtue of his service as Senate Majority Leader, Barkley was entitled to consideration. I cast my ballot for him, because I considered him well qualified in the field of candidates and, from a party point of view, more entitled to consideration.

Bob Hannegan asked me to vote for Senator Truman. I told him that, while I was personally fond of Truman, I had promised to vote for Barkley.

One of the most dramatic and least known scenes of the convention came early one morning when Barkley learned that he had been by-passed by the President. In righteous anger, he was about to tear up the nominating speech he had prepared for Roosevelt. The late Max Gardner, myself, and a few others, most of us having no liking for the fourth term, persuaded him nevertheless that he owed it to the party to go through with the nomination like a good soldier. This he did and no one guessed the reluctance that lay behind the address, so well did he deliver it.

Many experienced political observers were certain that Wallace had the votes and would have won, if the votes had not been taken away from him at the request of the President. Wallace had votes in New York, Massachusetts, New Jersey, Pennsylvania, and Ohio which were not recorded for him. In Illinois there were 20 or 25 votes for Wallace, which were held from him. Mayor Ed Kelly was driven to nominating Senator Scott Lucas as a favorite son in order to keep votes from Wallace. The galleries and delegates were wise to this maneuver and booed him. He was staggered for a moment and lost his head, but he recovered it. On the second ballot, the delegation switched to Truman, as the band-wagon movement got started.

As the convention ended I issued a brief statement saying, "I have been opposed on principle to a third or fourth presidential term. For that reason I voted for the nomination of Senator Byrd of Virginia. Having participated in the proceedings of the convention, I accept its decision and will support the party nominees."

I issued the statement because I wanted to have it behind me. If I had waited a few days, there would have been many articles asking, "What is Farley going to do?" Then I would have been accused of being a sorehead. I had preached party loyalty and organization for years, so I had to go along with the majority of my party.

Early in September Chairman Hannegan called on me, suggesting I might become active. He asked me to go on a radio program with the President and himself, merely to urge the people to register and vote. Quite frankly, he said my appearance on such a program would help because I had so many admirers in and out of the party.

"Bob, I just won't do it," I said. "Unless something very unexpected happens, I will not take any action beyond my Chicago statement. I think the fourth term is a mistake, as was the third. I do not think the situation demands that he run. I frankly feel that if he is the only individual capable of helping our country and leading our party, then there is something wrong with both. I refuse to believe we are that badly off. Winning isn't everything, Bob; there are principles involved far more important than victories. That's the reason I took the course I did. I'm not sore at the President or anyone else, but I have lost faith in one I honored and revered; and I do not feel I can ever regain that faith."

On September 29, 1944, business brought me to Washington again. As usual I called at the State Department to pay my respects to Cordell Hull. I was shocked by his appearance. He was pale and drawn and nervous.

"Jim, I am through," he told me. Tears stood in his eyes. "This illness has put me out. I am going to resign as soon as possible after the election. I can't make any speeches; my throat condition is not good."

He did not go into detail on his illness and I did not press him. I expressed regret that the country would be deprived of his services; but told him the important thing was to get well. He thanked me, remarking I had always been his friend. I switched the conversation, because I was deeply affected and didn't want to show my emotion for fear it might have some adverse effect on his condition. I asked about the Morgenthau plan.

"Some time ago," he said, "the President appointed a committee to handle some postwar problems. The Department was working on the matter and had the situation well in hand when the Morgenthau plan was announced at Quebec. My first impulse was to give public expression of my opposition to the plan, which would destroy Germany and put Europe out of economic balance. Then I decided to wait and let public opinion take care of the situation."

Hull said he had not talked with the President since the Quebec conference until that morning. I could tell that he resented the short-circuiting by the White House. I did not ask him whether he had been invited to the conference, assuming that he was not. I left, expressing the hope that he would be in the best of health when I next saw him.

On October 2, death took Alfred E. Smith, one of the most colorful figures in American public life. In the four years which followed my departure from Washington, I saw much of him and our relationship was exceedingly pleasant. We met at least once a week, usually in the Turkish bath at the Biltmore Hotel. I was always interested in his comments on the national and world scenes. I visited him in the hospital and gave him a fill-in on the political situation. He made no comment when I told him I thought Roosevelt would win, not so much for his popularity, as in 1936, but because of the general conviction that his defeat might comfort the enemy. I said the American people just didn't want the war to last one minute longer than necessary. He made no comment, although he was not in favor of the fourth term. He asked me to call again, but his condition took a turn for the worse and he was not permitted visitors. His name will live in history and I shall always look back with pleasure to memories of our long association.

The only surprise to me in the fourth term election was the size of the victory. I felt the President would be reelected but I thought there would be greater defections from the Democratic ranks.

These were more than offset, however, by the shift of 5 to 10 per cent of the Republicans, who voted against change in continuity of the war effort, lest it encourage the Axis to prolong the conflict.

On November 8, 1944, I wrote the following note of congratulations:

DEAR MR. PRESIDENT:

Once more the American people have shown their confidence and faith in you, and in all probability no man in the history of this Republic will ever receive their trust in a like degree.

We are living in troublous times and you are carrying a burden greater than any which your predecessors have been called on to bear. May I express the hope that God will give you health and strength, and guide you in directing our war activities, and in bringing about an early, just, and lasting peace.

Sincerely yours,
JAMES A. FARLEY

Under date of November 10, 1944, I received the following reply:

DEAR JIM:

I am glad indeed to have your letter of November eighth. Every word of it is deeply appreciated.

Always sincerely,
FRANKLIN D. ROOSEVELT

That letter was signed.

CHAPTER THIRTY-SEVEN

FINAL DAYS

EARLY IN January, 1945, Mrs. Farley and I and our children received invitations to the fourth term inaugural and to the tea that afternoon. I sent our regrets to the President and to White House Secretary Early, who forwarded the invitation.

I talked to a number of persons who were on the portico when the President repeated the presidential oath for the fourth time. Almost without exception they reported that Roosevelt looked badly. They said he appeared tired, haggard, and distraught. This did not surprise me, in view of the heavy stresses under which he had labored. His voice was not strong as it came over the radio in the briefest of his inaugurals, which was a far cry from his first and most famous one. I believe that his reassertion of faith in America, which pealed out to the land in ringing accents on March 4, 1933, will justly take its place among the greatest of presidential utterances. Timeless are his words: "This great nation will endure as it has endured, will revive, and will prosper. So first of all let me assert my firm belief that the only thing we have to fear is fear itself." They gave faith to the nation in one of its darkest hours and will be remembered with the closing paragraph of Lincoln's Second Inaugural, "With malice toward none; with charity for all; with firmness in the right, as God gives us to see the right, let us strive to finish the work we are in; to bind up the nation's wounds; to care for him who shall have borne the battle, and for his widow, and his orphan—to do all which may achieve and cherish a just and lasting peace among ourselves, and with all nations."

The inaugural was overshadowed the next day by the spectacular discharge of Secretary of Commerce Jesse Jones in order to make a place in the Cabinet for Henry Wallace, whose term as Vice President had run out the day before. Having fired Wallace during the Chicago convention six months before, Roosevelt felt Wallace was entitled to anything he wanted, and Henry chose the Department of Commerce, where he had tangled horns with Jones more than once. I came to Washington a few days later, when the President was en route to Yalta, and got a firsthand report from Jesse.

"Like everyone else I heard rumors about a change in my department, but there was nothing definite," Jesse said. "Harry Hopkins made a couple of visits and indicated I should present a resignation, but he did not say I should resign. I told him that if I were going to be fired, that was all right; but I insisted on being fired by the Boss and no one else. Nothing more came of it.

"I saw the President privately at the Cabinet meeting the Friday before the inaugural. Nothing was said about my resignation. I attended all the inaugural ceremonies, the services, the taking of the oath, and the luncheon. I talked to the Boss in a most friendly exchange after the luncheon. About four o'clock, my secretary told me Grace Tully had called and said the President would like to see me at twelve-thirty Sunday afternoon. At five-fifteen I received the letter from the White House asking me to get out.

"Jim, I must confess this shocked me. I proceeded to prepare a reply, but I decided it would be wiser if I were to sleep on it, which I did. The next morning I called the White House to ask if the President was still expecting me, in view of the letter I had received. I said I did not think the letter left much to be talked over. I was advised by the White House usher Charles Claunch that the President expected me.

"At the White House I was ushered into a side room, then I was moved into a larger room. After a half hour's wait, I was led to the President's study. I was with him about forty-five minutes and for the first time in a conference, I did the talking. I talked for forty of the forty-five minutes I was with him.

"I told him all the things I had wanted to say for a long time. I told him I had been sent insulting messages—directly and indirectly —down through the years, and had swallowed them, although many of them were not in good taste, because it was my desire to be helpful. I told him I knew he never liked me, but was willing to forget that in the interests of service. I told him I had been fighting in the trenches for twelve to thirteen hours a day, including Sundays, doing the best I could for the country. I told him I didn't think I deserved the treatment I got. I told him that, while I recognized that he had the right to fire me, he should have done it personally and not in the backhanded way he did do it. I told him what I thought of Wallace —not personally, that would have taken too long—but as Secretary of Commerce. I told him Wallace was just incompetent.

"Jim, I told him all that and a lot more. All he said was that he wanted me to remain in the government and suggested I have a talk with Stettinius (Secretary of State Edward R. Stettinius) about an ambassadorial post. I answered that I didn't want to stay in the government if he wanted me out of my present post. When I was through I got up to leave. The President didn't have much to say. He evaded my eyes. As I started out he said, 'Good-by, I'll be seeing you soon.' I looked at him and replied, 'No, Mr. President, this is good-by; I am not coming back.'

"If he had talked to me about it a month or so ago, Jim, I would have been glad to try and work it out so as to avoid any unpleasantness. As it was I returned to my office, revised my letter, and phoned the White House that I intended to give out his letter and my answer at eight o'clock. When no word came from the White House, I released the correspondence."

Ten weeks later, on April 12, I received news of the President's death from my daughter, Betty. I was in Baltimore to address the Maryland State Bankers' Association that evening. I was in my room at the Hotel Belvedere with Joe Kearns of the *Baltimore News-Post* and some representatives of the Press Association when Betty called.

"Have you heard the news?" she asked.

"What news?"

"The President is dead."

I was not as surprised as I was shocked by the passing of one whom I had known so well and with whom I had been associated so intimately. As memories of the past began crowding in on me, I was asked to give a statement, which I did as follows:

"The death of President Roosevelt is, of course, a shock to me, as it will be to all Americans and to millions throughout the world who have looked to him for leadership during these trying times. He has served as President of the United States during the most momentous years in the Nation's history.

"The fact that he was elected four times, breaking all precedents, is evidence of the confidence that had been reposed in him by so many millions of our citizens. It was that confidence that made it possible for him to give such inspiring leadership during this period.

"I shall always recall and cherish our close association during our years in New York State, and with his administration for seven and a half years in Washington. I am happy and proud to have had some small part in assisting his nomination and election as Governor of New York and as President of the United States."

That night, before addressing the bankers, I joined in a radio memorial program. I reviewed some of the triumphs in which we were associated, and closed with the prayer, *May his soul rest in peace.*

The following morning I informed the White House that I wished to attend the services in the White House and at the grave in Hyde Park. Saturday afternoon I went through the East Gate and was ushered into the Blue Room, where the heads of various governmental agencies were assembled, along with former Cabinet officers, like myself, and members of the President's personal staff. The air was heavy with the scent of flowers. Silence was broken by muffled sobs.

Promptly at four o'clock the services began with the singing of the hymn, *Eternal Father, Strong to Save.* Just before the close, Bishop Dun of Washington said:

"In his first inaugural the President bore testimony to his own deep faith: 'So first of all let me assert my firm belief that the only thing we have to fear is fear itself—nameless, unreasoning, unjustified terror which paralyzes needed efforts to convert retreat into advance.'

"As that was his first word to us, I am sure that he would wish it to be his last; that as we go forward to the tasks in which he has led us, we shall go forward without fear of the future, without fear of our allies or of our friends, and without fear of our own insufficiency."

After the services we were permitted into the East Room to file by the flag-draped coffin, which rested on a catafalque before an altar. Off to one side, I saw an empty wheel chair, a most symbolic vacant chair for the man whose body was fettered but whose courage ever placed him with the marchers.

The next day at the grave, I paid my final respects at simple, impressive services. Many scenes flashed through my mind during the religious and military rites, which no one present there will ever forget. The rose garden has since become a shrine.

I drove to Hyde Park to attend the services with John C. Farber, law partner of Basil O'Connor. Shortly after the burial, Colonel Harry Hooker came over to me and said that Mrs. Roosevelt would like to see me. I told Harry that she had had more than her share of trouble the past few days and I felt it would be intruding to even attempt to see her; but he insisted that I accompany him into the house, which I did. I talked with Mrs. Roosevelt briefly saying how sorry I was for her. She said she appreciated my presence at the White House and at the graveside that day.

The day of the White House services I drove out to the Naval Hospital at Bethesda, Maryland, to see Cordell Hull. I found the former Secretary of State greatly improved since I last saw him in November. His color was good and he had gained twelve pounds. He was still far from well but immeasurably improved. We talked, naturally enough, of the President's passing.

"I last saw him shortly before he went to Warm Springs, just a few days before his death," Cordell said. "When he came in to see me I was shocked by his appearance. He looked like death.

"He, himself, mentioned that he was not feeling well. I asked him, then, what was the matter and he said it was a sinus condition which caused him to have repeated nausea."

I asked Hull what they talked about.

"He told me about the Yalta conference," he said. "He was general and vague. Now and then he lost the thread of the conversation. He said that Churchill was a garrulous old man and talked about 90 per cent of the time, and that only ten per cent of the time was taken by Stalin and himself."

I asked whether Hull had seen the President before he left for Yalta.

"Yes," he said. "He called on me before leaving. I tried to convince him that the time had arrived to impress on Stalin and Churchill the position of the United States; that we should assert a definite position and not retreat an inch."

Hull spoke of his own resignation, saying:

"I went to see a certain party on a couple of occasions and told him I was no longer able to carry on. He urged me to stay. Once he sent McIntire (Admiral Ross T. McIntire, the White House physician) to see me. He pleaded with me to reconsider. But no one knew better than I that I was not myself and I made up my mind to accede to Mrs. Hull's wishes and my doctor's advice."

I asked about the Stettinius appointment.

"It was a personal appointment of the President," he said. "I did not object. I don't know anything about his ability. I assume Hopkins had much to do with the choice since he brought him into the government in the first place."

Hull told me that the afternoon of Pearl Harbor when the Cabinet met with the high command, General Marshall came up to him and said, "Everything you said would happen has happened." This, he said, was acknowledgment of his prediction in November that diplomacy had ended and the Japanese situation was in the hands of the Army and Navy.

In our evaluation of President Roosevelt, Cordell and I agreed that he was a sick man at Yalta and should not have been called upon to make decisions affecting this country and the world. Physical illness, we knew, taxed the mind and left him in no shape to bargain with such hard bargainers as the Russians and such astute diplomats as the British.

Since that day I have done much world traveling. Early in 1946 I went to Rome for the Consistory at which thirty-two churchmen, including four American prelates, were elevated to the rank of Cardinal, a religious pageant I shall never forget and for which I shall ever be grateful to Francis Cardinal Spellman, Archbishop of New York. I was back in Europe in March and April. In the fall of 1946, I went around the world. In these tours I saw many of the leading men of all nations, some of whom I had already met on visits here, others for the first time. May I note in passing, that of all the persons I have met in some degree of intimacy, I consider the greatest to be His Holiness, Pope Pius XII. His simple dignity, the breadth of his intellect, and devout humility have made him a beacon of enlightenment in a sorely troubled world. Winston Churchill, the embodiment of courageous statesmanship, and General Douglas MacArthur, perhaps our greatest soldier, are figures who live with us, yet stride in history.

Without exception the leading men of all nations expressed admiration for the courage of Franklin D. Roosevelt and the aid he had given in the fight against the common foe. Yet, on every side, I heard expressions of regret that he was not himself in the most critical days of world history. Had he not been physically and mentally tired at Teheran and Yalta, and at home, and had America had a more vigorous voice in international affairs, statesmen of the world are agreed almost without exception that many of the troubles vexing the world today would not have arisen.

Be that as it may, I am confident that the problems facing the world and the nation are not insurmountable. Each generation, like each individual, has its crises. These can be solved if met with patient understanding, wise industry, and faith in the right. In the case of America, I am certain that the difficulties confronting us will be resolved, as they have in the past, by the people themselves in the exercise of constitutional processes. I am confident that our example is one that will inspire the people of the world. Our heritage of freedom will be carried from our hearthstone like a precious torch to enkindle national hearthstones throughout the world. It will warm all peoples with the comforting fire of liberty.

INDEX